WAIS-IV CLINICAL USE AND INTERPRETATION

WAIS-IV CLINICAL USE AND INTERPRETATION

Edited by

LAWRENCE G. WEISS
Pearson Assessment, San Antonio, Texas, USA

DONALD H. SAKLOFSKE
*Division of Applied Psychology, University of Calgary,
Calgary, Alberta, Canada*

DIANE L. COALSON
Pearson Assessment, San Antonio, Texas, USA

SUSAN ENGI RAIFORD
Pearson Assessment, San Antonio, Texas, USA

Foreword by Alan S. Kaufman

ELSEVIER

AMSTERDAM • BOSTON • HEIDELBERG • LONDON
NEW YORK • OXFORD • PARIS • SAN DIEGO
SAN FRANCISCO • SINGAPORE • SYDNEY • TOKYO
Academic Press is an imprint of Elsevier

Academic Press is an imprint of Elsevier
32 Jamestown Road, London NW1 7BY, UK
30 Corporate Drive, Suite 400, Burlington, MA 01803, USA
525 B Street, Suite 1800, San Diego, CA 92101-4495, USA

First edition 2010

British Library Cataloguing-in-Publication Data
A catalogue record for this book is available from the British Library

Library of Congress Cataloging-in-Publication Data
A catalog record for this book is available from the Library of Congress

ISBN: 978-0-12-375035-8

For information on all Academic Press publications
visit our website at elsevierdirect.com

Typeset by TNQ Books and Journals Pvt Ltd.
www.tnq.co.in

Working together to grow
libraries in developing countries

www.elsevier.com | www.bookaid.org | www.sabre.org

ELSEVIER   BOOK AID
            International   Sabre Foundation

Transferred to Digital Printing in 2012

This book is dedicated to
My wife of 25 years, Judy Ann – LGW
Vicki, my beautiful wife – DHS
Jack Jones, my beloved grandfather – DLC
Robert Raiford, my husband, and Dennis
and Ann Engi, my parents – SER

Contents

PART I

THE WAIS-IV: DEVELOPMENT AND FOUNDATIONS

PART II

THE WAIS-IV: CLINICAL USE AND INTERPRETATION IN CONTEXT

5. The Flynn Effect and the Wechsler Scales
XIAOBIN ZHOU, JACQUES GRÉGOIRE, AND JIANJUN ZHU

6. WAIS-IV Use in Neuropsychological Assessment
C. MUNRO CULLUM AND GLENN J. LARRABEE

List of Contributors

Hsinyi Chen   Behavioral Science Corporation, Taipei, Taiwan

Diane L. Coalson   Pearson Assessment, San Antonio, Texas, USA

C. Munro Cullum   University of Texas, Southwestern Medical Center at Dallas, Dallas, Texas, USA

Lisa W. Drozdick   Pearson Assessment, San Antonio, Texas, USA

Gerald Goldstein   Mental Illness Research, Educational and Clinical Center (MIRECC) and Research Service, VA Pittsburgh Healthcare Center, Pittsburgh, Pennsylvania, USA

Jacques Grégoire   Université Catholique de Louvain, Louvain-la-Neuve, Belgium

Jossette G. Harris   University of Colorado School of Medicine, Denver, Colorado, USA

James A. Holdnack   Pearson Assessment, San Antonia, Texas, USA

Glenn J. Larrabee   Independent Practice, Sarasota, Florida, USA

Susan Engi Raiford   Pearson Assessment, San Antonio, Texas, USA

Donald H. Saklofske   Division of Applied Psychology, University of Calgary, Calgary, Alberta, Canada

Timothy A. Salthouse   University of Virginia, Gilmer Hall, Charlottesville, Virginia, USA

Lawrence G. Weiss   Pearson Assessment, San Antonio, Texas, USA

Xiaobin Zhou   Pearson Assessment, San Antonio, Texas, USA

Jianjun Zhu   Pearson Assessment, San Antonio, Texas, USA

Foreword

Alan S. Kaufman

Yale University School of Medicine, New Haven, Connecticut, USA

David Wechsler challenged the Stanford-Binet in the 1930s when no one else had either the courage or the inspiration. The original Stanford-Binet, published in 1916 by Lewis Terman, had many challengers (e.g., Goddard-Binet, Kuhlmann-Binet), all of whom were tied to Alfred Binet's ground-breaking age-based scale normed on Paris students. After Terman triumphed, largely because he had the insight to rearrange the Binet tasks assigned to each age level based on American data, and to actually obtain norms for children and adolescents living in the United States, his Binet test reigned as *the* measure of IQ.

That reign solidified in 1937 when Terman added a coauthor (Maud Merrill – like Terman, a professor at Stanford), an alternate form (the new Binet boasted Forms L and M), and a sophisticated statistical treatment of the data, thanks in large part to Dr Quinn McNemar. Noted educator Ellwood P. Cubberly (1937) wrote in the Editor's Introduction to the test manual, "after ten years of painstaking research, two new and equivalent scales, each more extensive than the original both in range and in number of tests, and each providing for greater objectivity in scoring, are at last ready for public use" (pp. vi–vii).

Dr Wechsler was not intimidated by the thoroughly revised and expanded Binet, touted in its own manual as the IQ test to end all IQ tests. He had vision. He insisted that a Performance Scale was just as necessary as a Verbal Scale to gain a full understanding of a person's mental functioning. Never mind the critics who asked unabashedly, "Why would anyone waste 3 minutes administering a single puzzle to an English-speaking person when a dozen or more Vocabulary words can be administered in the same time frame?" He offered the sophisticated standard score statistic to replace the antiquated and inadequate MA/CA X 100 formula. Terman and Merrill (1937) were well aware of standard scores; they provided a table that converted IQs to standard scores in the test manual, and praised the metric: "From the statistical point of view, every advantage is in favor of the standard score" (p. 27). Yet they continued to derive IQs by formula because "the majority of teachers, school administrators, social workers, physicians, and others who utilize mental test results have not learned to think in statistical terms. To such a person a rating expressed as '+2 sigma' is just so much Greek" (Terman & Merrill, 1937: 27–28).

Dr Wechsler, never condescending to test users, knew better. When he published the Wechsler-Bellevue for children and adults (Wechsler, 1939), a scant 2 years after the revised Binet became available, he included state-of-the-art Performance subtests as a featured IQ scale and he never doubted that clinicians were smart enough to "speak Greek." Those two departures from tradition moved the field of intellectual assessment a couple of light years forward. Yet if one wants to fully credit Dr Wechsler with innovation, one need look no farther than his norms group. Arguably, his most important innovation with the 1939 Wechsler-Bellevue was that *he actually tested representative samples of adults to include in the standardization sample.*

For the first Stanford-Binet, Terman's (1916) adult sample was small, haphazard, and unrepresentative: "Since our school children who were above 14 years and still in the grades were retarded left-overs, it was necessary to base the revision above this level on the tests of adults. These included 30 business men ..., 150 'migrating' unemployed men, ... 50 adolescent delinquents, ... and 50 high-school students tested by [Terman]" (p. 54). The Average Adult level was derived from "the mental ages for 62 adults, including the 30 business men and the 32 high-school pupils who were over 16 years of age" (Terman, 1916: 54–55).

Just as incredibly, Terman and Merrill (1937) tested *no one above age 18 years* for the standardization sample of Forms L and M of the Stanford-Binet. When testing adults, "It will be recalled that in the original Stanford-Binet, adult mental age was tentatively placed at sixteen years ... Unfortunately, the precise determination of this terminal age is complicated by the fact that it is extremely difficult to secure truly unselected test-populations above the age of fourteen or fifteen" (p. 29). For the revised Stanford-Binet, "A mental age of fifteen years represents the norm for all subjects who are sixteen years of age or older" (p. 30).

Dr Wechsler was not deterred by the difficulties in identifying representative samples of adults when he developed the Wechsler-Bellevue in the 1930s for ages 7 to 70 years. "With several of his psychologist friends, Wechsler tested nearly 2,000 children, adolescents, and adults in Coney Island, Brooklyn, New York. The sample didn't represent the whole country, and it was far too urban. But it was still quite good, because Wechsler knew from his own research that socioeconomic status was the key to getting a good 'norms' sample" (Kaufman, 2009: 30).

For all practical purposes, *Dr Wechsler developed the first real test of intelligence for adults in 1939*, even though the Binet had been used to assess the mental ability of the adult population for a generation. By the time the 1939 Wechsler-Bellevue was revised to become the WAIS in 1955, Wechsler's measurement of adult intelligence had reigned for years as *the* measure of adult IQ thanks to Wechsler's (1958) clinical approach to test interpretation, and to influential adult studies of brain damage (Reitan, 1955; Meyer & Jones, 1957), aging (Feingold, 1950; Jarvik *et al.*, 1962), and clinical pathology (Rapaport *et al.*, 1945–46).

More than 70 years after the original Wechsler-Bellevue was published, Wechsler's scales stand at the very top of the assessment dome for the assessment of children, adolescents, and adults. The WISC-IV is clearly the most popular IQ measure for children and adolescents, but it has some company on the assessment scene in schools, clinics, and private practices. Other acronyms are also tossed about when choosing a children's test for this or that type of referral, such as the CAS (Naglieri and Das, 1997), DAS-II (Elliott, 2007), KABC-II (Kaufman & Kaufman, 2004), SB-5 (Roid, 2003), and WJ III (Woodcock *et al.*, 2001).

By contrast, the WAIS-IV stands alone. For years, the WAIS has been synonymous with adult intelligence. The WAIS and its subsequent revisions have flicked aside would-be competitors like swatting flies. The KAIT (Kaufman & Kaufman, 1993) was developed from theory specifically to assess adolescents and adults. The SB-5 and WJ III are each normed through old age. None has made even a minor dent in the field of adult assessment. The WAIS-IV is King, having inherited the throne from the WAIS-III immediately on the latter's retirement from public office. And no one else is even in the Royal Court.

Dr Wechsler enjoyed his pre-eminence in the field, and was proud of the leading roles that the WISC-R and WAIS played on the assessment scene entering the decade of the 1980s. Yet he was not completely satisfied. He passed away in 1981, the same year that the WAIS-R, with its black carrying case and black manual, was published. Symbolically, the inadvertent choice of black provided a remembrance of the great man behind the Wechsler scales. To Dr Wechsler himself, the black might have denoted his remorse at not being able to demonstrate the integral link between cognitive and conative abilities (his name for the non-cognitive variables that affect test performance, such as motivation and perseverance). He was always impressed that factor analyses of his scales only accounted for about 60 percent of the variance. He was convinced that much of the remaining variance could be accounted for by conative variables, and he tried to support his point empirically by including the conative "level of aspiration" subtest in the standardization of the WAIS-R. Analyses of this experimental task did not solve the riddle of the unexplained variance, and the task was left on the cutting board. ("Level of Aspiration, which was studied as a possible means of broadening the coverage of the WAIS-R to include a measure of nonintellective ability … , had a number of interesting features, but seemed to require further research before it could be added as a regular member of the battery"; Wechsler, 1981: 10.)

To the publisher, the decision to eliminate the conative task was undoubtedly an objective, simple decision because of weak data. However, to Dr Wechsler the decision was deeply emotional. The main topic of my last conversation with Dr Wechsler, not long before he died, was his great disappointment at not being able to prove with data what he knew axiomatically to be true with every aspect of his being – that a person's Full Scale IQ and profile of test scores always reflect a dynamic integration of the person's intellectual and personality variables.

But how Dr Wechsler's legacy has lived on! Even without the data that he believed to be so critical to support his argument, he single-handedly changed the face of intellectual assessment from psychometric to clinical. The Binet tradition, as expounded by Terman and McNemar, was psychometric in orientation. Dr Wechsler changed that when he published the Wechsler-Bellevue in 1939 and wrote incisively about how to interpret his tests in clinical practice (Wechsler, 1939, 1950, 1958; see also Chapter 7 of this volume, by Gerald Goldstein and Don Saklofske, on psychopathology). The field of clinical assessment was born, and, except for some purists who insist that subtest profile interpretation and qualitative analysis of test scores are sacrilegious (for example, McDermott *et al.*, 1990), the practices of clinical assessment have thrived internationally and span the domains of clinical psychology, neuropsychology, and school psychology.

And what better proof is there of Wechsler's continued domination of the IQ scene than the WAIS-IV? This test has been crafted, refined, improved, and reconceptualized with such style and insight that the IQ test bar has been raised to new heights. The chapters in this book attest to the WAIS-IV's superior psychometric and practical features, and demonstrate the test's contextual role within the theoretical, clinical, and research domains of assessment, and, more broadly, within society. In Chapter 1, Diane Coalson, Susan Raiford, Don Saklofske, and Larry Weiss (the editors of this superb book) provide a compelling introduction to the historical and conceptual foundations of the WAIS-IV and outline Dr Wechsler's theoretical, practical, and clinical approach to assessment. Coalson and colleagues aptly refer to the development of the WAIS-IV as representing a product of "progressive innovation," and make the insightful observation that Wechsler's (1975) practical definition of intelligence "allowed the very flexibility needed for ongoing revisions to his intelligence scales in light of advances in the theory and measurement of intelligence."

Coalson *et al.* protest against "the myth that the Wechsler intelligence scales are outdated or atheoretical," a myth that has been perpetuated by several psychologists, including me. I have since reconsidered my stance on the lack of a theoretical framework for Wechsler's scales: "Though not specifically developed from CHC [Cattell-Horn-Carroll] theory, Wechsler's modern-day tests were specifically revised in the 1990s and 2000s to incorporate CHC theory and state-of-the-art research on working memory and other executive functions" (Kaufman, 2009: 101). Liz Lichtenberger and I stated that, "Unlike the earliest Wechsler tests, the WAIS-IV also was developed with specific theoretical foundations in mind. In fact, revisions were made purposely to reflect the latest knowledge from literature in the areas of intelligence theory, adult cognitive development, and cognitive neuroscience" (Lichtenberger & Kaufman, 2009: 20). Further, Liz and I incorporated the theory that underlies the WAIS-IV into our step-by-step interpretive system. That system grounds interpretation in CHC theory, neuropsychological processing theory, "and in the cognitive neuroscience research that forms the theoretical basis for the WAIS-IV" (Lichtenberger & Kaufman, 2009: 147).

Apart from the theoretical underpinnings that governed the development of the WISC-IV and WAIS-IV, these tests are certainly not outdated in terms of content. Starting with the third editions, they have been revitalized by including clever tests of working memory (Letter–Number Sequencing), fluid reasoning (Picture Concepts), and processing speed (Symbol Search). Regarding the innovations and important clinical features of the latest version of the WAIS:

- The WAIS-IV has put a new and innovative face on Wechsler's test batteries by including two novel, appealing, and theoretically-relevant measures of visual processing (*Gv*; Visual Puzzles) and fluid reasoning (*Gf*; Figure Weights). In all, the WAIS-IV comprises 15 subtests, 6 of which have no roots in the Wechsler-Bellevue or its earliest revisions. Raiford and colleagues' thorough Chapter 2, devoted to administration and scoring of the old and new subtests, has a strong research as well as clinical basis for the helpful tips to examiners. The sections on the subtests that are brand new to any Wechsler test (Figure Weights and Visual Puzzles) are especially valuable to all psychologists, and all of the information in this chapter will be valuable to graduate students who are learning the instrument.
- The Verbal and Performance IQs have been eliminated and replaced by four theory-driven Indexes. Picture Arrangement and Object Assembly are nowhere to be seen in the fourth editions of the WISC and WAIS, and the Perceptual Reasoning Index truly merits the inclusion of the word *Reasoning* (whereas its predecessor, the Perceptual *Organization* Index, did not). Chapter 3 (again by the four editors of this book) offers an exceptional theoretical and clinical foundation for interpreting the Index profile for any adult who is evaluated with the WAIS-IV. Indeed, these authors provide a rich historical perspective as well on the

passing of the interpretive torch: "In 2003 ...the WISC-IV broke the proverbial apron strings to VIQ and PIQ, eliminating them from the test, changing the name of the freedom from distractibility index to the working memory index to reflect the improved understanding of that construct, changing the name of the perceptual organization index to the perceptual reasoning index to reflect the increased focus on fluid reasoning among the newly created perceptual subtests, and elevating the four index scores to the primary role of clinical interpretation. The WAIS-IV followed suit in 2008." The Chapter 3 authors emphasize the need to understand the complexity of seemingly "pure" abilities like fluid reasoning, and they offer a broad-based research and theoretical framework for interpreting the Index profile that deals insightfully with executive functions, fluid reasoning, working memory, and processing speed. In Chapter 6, Munro Cullum and Glenn Larrabee extend the framework for interpreting the four Indexes by analyzing their implications for neuropsychological assessment. Similarly, in Chapter 7, Goldstein and Saklofske provide insights for interpreting the factors that underlie the WAIS-IV Indexes within the context of psychopathology, especially as the profile of scores pertains to schizophrenia, Autistic Spectrum Disorders, and traumatic brain injury.

- Continuing the important precedent established with the WAIS-III and WMS-III, the WAIS-IV was co-normed with the WMS-IV. In Chapter 9, Jim Holdnack and Lisa Drozdick tackle the daunting task of integrating these two new instruments in light of neuropsychological and clinical research and practice, and provide a wealth of key interpretive guidelines. They are especially effective in providing examiners with an in-depth understanding of the WMS-IV subtests and Indexes, and with a methodology for interpreting "contrast scores" both within the WMS-IV and across Wechsler's latest tests of IQ and memory.

- For the WISC-IV, Weiss and colleagues (2006) wrote a brilliant chapter on the societal and contextual factors that must be internalized by examiners if ethnic differences for children and adolescents on cognitive measures are to be understood and interpreted. As Dawn Flanagan and I wrote, Larry Weiss and his colleagues "reviewed the often-ignored body of literature on the roles of mental health status, physical health status, education, income, home environment, cognitive stimulation, and individual differences on intellectual development, and they discuss how these variables have a differential impact on different ethnic groups. ... We recommend reading this exceptional chapter in its entirety ... to be able to give 2-point responses to any questions you may be asked about SES, test bias, or ethnic differences on intelligence tests" (Flanagan & Kaufman, 2009: 49). In Chapter 4 of this book, Weiss and colleagues have struck gold again on these same issues, this time concerning ethnic differences for adolescents and adults on the WAIS-IV. As was done for the WISC-IV, the Chapter 4 authors have replaced the simple psychometric question, "How many IQ points does one ethnic group score higher than another?" with a complex society-driven and research-driven question: "How can we best interpret ethnic differences on the WAIS-IV in terms of opportunities for cognitive growth and development and with regard to a plethora of key SES and health variables?" The complexity of these issues is magnified when the Chapter 4 authors answer the "simple" psychometric question of the size of the ethnic differences. There is no easy answer because of a striking Age × Ethnicity interaction – that is to say, the White/African-American differences and the White/Hispanic differences are each about twice as large for adults ages 65–90 years as they are for adolescents aged 16–19 years. Thus, some type of developmental trend or unknown cohort effect is at work that conceivably pertains to the diverse health-related and SES factors summarized and integrated in Chapter 4, as well as to the Flynn effect (Chapter 5, by J. J. Zhu and colleagues) and the research on aging and IQ (Chapter 8 by Timothy Salthouse and Don Saklofske; see also Kaufman, 2009, Chapter 8; and Lichtenberger & Kaufman, 2009, Chapter 7). In particular, the analyses conducted by Salthouse and Saklofske in Chapter 8 are germane to understanding the age-related ethnic differences reported by Weiss and colleagues in Chapter 4. Salthouse and Saklofske investigated whether the constructs measured by the WAIS-IV Indexes were qualitatively different for ages 16–64 versus 65–90; their analyses suggested that the constructs were the same across the age range. A similar set of analyses that determines whether the constructs measured by the WAIS-IV are the same or different for whites, African Americans, and Hispanics – by age group – might shed light on the interesting results of the ethnic comparisons.

How would Dr Wechsler evaluate the WAIS-IV if he were transported to the twenty-first century? He would study the test manuals and the materials for hours, without saying a word or betraying an emotion. He would reread the manual to verify that Verbal IQ and Performance IQ were really gone. Then he would administer the new subtests and some of the new items (especially Comprehension) to a few random people, preferably clinical patients, testing the limits whenever he had a hunch about a hidden meaning in a verbal response or a subtle clinical behavior. Always the clinician, he would neither praise nor condemn any test, even his own, without getting its clinical feel.

Finally, he would speak. *"The new tests are brilliant! Figure Weights and Visual Puzzles are ingenious. And why not borrow Raven's matrices? I borrowed plenty from the Army Beta and the Army Individual Performance Scale."*

But then he would complain, *"Where is the V–P IQ discrepancy? The Indexes are fine, and I can see that they are embedded in theory and research, but that discrepancy is important – it will always be important. And I like the reduction in bonus points, that's good. I couldn't earn many when I reached 75 or 80. But where is Picture Arrangement? Those interpersonal situations are ideal clinical stimuli. And why is Block Design the only Perceptual Reasoning test that has you manipulate test materials? Why all the multiple choice and pointing?"*

Indeed, Dr Wechsler did prefer Performance tests to be manipulative. On more than one occasion he showed me the Army Beta inserts in his page-worn copy of *Army Mental Tests* (Yoakum & Yerkes, 1920). These inserts included all items on all Army Beta subtests, and he'd show me how the examinee had to draw in the missing part for each Picture Completion item. And we'd discuss why it was impractical to have children and adults draw in the missing part for WISC and WAIS items, but he never quite agreed with the practicality of naming or pointing to the missing part.

While he was complaining about the long-lost V–P IQ discrepancy and the lack of manipulatives and the elimination of Picture Arrangement, he would appear angry, but it would be a façade that would be betrayed by a wicked glint in his eyes. It was a familiar glint that meant that he was having fun with you, enjoying himself, feeling almost euphoric. He had that same glint in his eyes when he gave an invited APA address in 1974 that would later become the definitive framework of his theory of intelligence (Wechsler, 1975). In particular, I remember him enjoying the absurdity of reducing global intelligence to an array of "intelligences": "Thus as it has been found that a child's mental growth correlates with teething level, one might … speak of dental intelligence; by taking note of the age at which children begin spitting out unpleasant-tasting objects …, one could refer to this as an example of gustatory intelligence" (p. 137).

A moment after his eyes revealed that his complaints about the WAIS-IV were trivial, he would give a conspiratorial wink to his audience (which, in my imagination, includes me). He would then confide in a whisper that conveyed a touch of admiration and awe:

"Those PsychCorp psychologists did a first-rate job with the WAIS-IV, didn't they?"

Yes, they did. Aurelio, Larry, Diane, Susan, and their colleagues are special.

"What do you think – did they raise the bar? Is the gold standard now platinum?"

Indeed.

References

Cubberly, E. P. (1937). Editor's introduction. In L. M. Terman, & M. A. Merrill (Eds.), *Measuring Intelligence* (pp. v–vii). Boston, MA: Houghton Mifflin.

Elliott, C. (2007). *Differential Abilities Scale (2nd ed.). Technical Manual*. San Antonio, TX: Harcourt Assessment.

Feingold, A. (1950). A Psychometric Study of Senescent Twins. *Unpublished doctoral dissertation*. New York, NY: Columbia University.

Flanagan, D. P., & Kaufman, A. S. (2009). *Essentials of WISC-IV Assessment* (2nd ed.). New York, NY: Wiley.

Jarvik, L. F., Kallman, F. J., & Falek, A. (1962). Intellectual changes in aged twins. *Journal of Gerontology, 17*, 289–294.

Kaufman, A. S. (2009). *IQ testing 101*. New York, NY: Springer.

Kaufman, A. S., & Kaufman, N. L. (1993). *Kaufman Adolescent and Adult Intelligence Test (KAIT)*. Circle Pines, MN: American Guidance Service.

Kaufman, A. S., & Kaufman, N. L. (2004). *Kaufman Assessment Battery for Children* (2nd ed.). *(KABC-II)*. Circle Pines, MN: American Guidance Service.

Lichtenberger, E. O., & Kaufman, A. S. (2009). *Essentials of WAIS-IV Assessment*. New York, NY: Wiley.

McDermott, P. A., Fantuzzo, J. W., & Glutting, J. J. (1990). Just say no to subtest analysis: a critique on Wechsler theory and practice. *Journal of Psychoeducational Assessment, 8*, 290–302.

Meyer, V., & Jones, H. G. (1957). Patterns of cognitive test performance as functions of the lateral localization of cerebral abnormalities in the temporal lobe. *Journal of Mental Science, 103*, 758–772.

Naglieri, J. A., & Das, J. P. (1997). *Cognitive Assessment System Administration and Scoring Manual*. Chicago, IL: Riverside.

Rapaport, D., Gill, M., & Schafer, R. (1945–1946). *Diagnostic Psychological Testing, 2 volumes*. Chicago, IL: Year Book.

Reitan, R. M. (1955). Certain differential effects of left and right cerebral lesions in human adults. *Journal of Comparative and Physiological Psychology, 48*, 474–477.

Roid, G. (2003). *Stanford-Binet Intelligence Scales* (5th ed.). Itasca, IL: Riverside.

Terman, L. D. (1916). *The Measurement of Intelligence*. Boston, MA: Houghton Mifflin.

Terman, L. M., & Merrill, M. A. (1937). *Measuring Intelligence*. Boston, MA: Houghton Mifflin.

Wechsler, D. (1939). *Measurement of Adult Intelligence*. Baltimore, MD: Williams & Wilkins.

Wechsler, D. (1950). Cognitive, conative and non-intellective intelligence. *American Psychologist, 5*, 7–83.

Wechsler, D. (1955). *Manual for the Wechsler Adult Intelligence Scale (WAIS)*. San Antonio, TX: The Psychological Corporation.

Wechsler, D. (1958). *Measurement and Appraisal of Adult Intelligence* (4th ed.). Baltimore, MD: Williams & Wilkins.

Wechsler, D. (1975). Intelligence defined and undefined: a relativistic appraisal. *American Psychologist, 30*, 135–139.

Wechsler, D. (1981). *Manual for the Wechsler Adult Intelligence Scale – Revised (WAIS-R)*. San Antonio, TX: The Psychological Corporation.

Woodcock, R. W., McGrew, K. S., & Mather, N. (2001). *Woodcock-Johnson III*. Itasca, IL: Riverside.

Yoakum, C. S., & Yerkes, R. M. (1920). *Army Mental Tests*. New York, NY: Henry Holt.

Preface

The WAIS-IV represents the latest addition to David Wechsler's legacy of outstanding intelligence measures. Although the tests require periodic revision to meet the changing needs of the field, the foundations of the test remain prominent and steadfast. It is a great privilege both to be entrusted with a revision of a Wechsler scale, as was the case for Diane and Susie who served as WAIS-IV co-principal directors, and for the four of us to produce a book that will further inform researchers and clinicians on the use and interpretation of the WAIS-IV.

The strength of the Wechsler legacy allowed the development team to focus on the scale's future. The team's foremost thoughts were directed at better meeting the needs of scientists and practitioners today and in the next decade. The issues were numerous and complex, demanding close attention to such issues as reliability, validity, and clinical utility, as well as the more practical aspects of test development, including user-friendliness, component design, and the time-constraining realities of managed care.

Surpassing all of these concerns was a responsibility to the individual taking the test. Improvements to instructions and teaching ensure that all examinees begin each task with a similar and adequate understanding of the task demands. Additional attention to possible visual and auditory acuity problems of examinees resulted in modifications to test stimuli. A series of reviews by experts in cultural differences and international development teams targeted the goal of increased sensitivity to individual differences in test performance. Consideration of demographic shifts and the aging population was represented by an expert evaluation of common medications that may affect test performance, and ongoing evaluation of age differences in performance. The scale's development was characterized by the thoughtful consideration and extensive discussion of these and many other issues.

While it is a distinct privilege to be entrusted with a Wechsler revision, the responsibility it brings demands a constant remembrance of the impact that the scores can have on an individual's life. Diane and Susie were fortunate to have ready access to an outstanding array of colleagues and experts who embraced this welcomed responsibility. A panel of renowned experts from a variety of psychological fields was convened as an initial step in the development process. This panel provided ongoing advice and guidance throughout the WAIS-IV development, as well as for the simultaneous development of the WMS-IV. Many of these panel members continue their invaluable contributions as chapter authors for this book. The 4-year development program was most marked by the active engagement and dedication of all those involved: the development team, the advisory panel, numerous experts, hundreds of examiners, and thousands of examinees. We cannot express how grateful we are to all of those who touched the revision.

This text is designed to complement and extend the information contained within the manuals, allowing for a more clinically rich interpretation of an individual's WAIS-IV performance. The introductory chapter provides an overview of the scale's historical and contemporary foundations, and concludes with a description of the WAIS-IV content and structure. Chapter 2 includes practical administration and scoring information, from the unique perspective of the test's developers. Common administration and scoring errors are highlighted, as well as a reference for frequently asked questions. Additional chapters focus on important topics related to WAIS-IV interpretation that allow for a richer evaluation of test results. Two of these chapters describe interpretive challenges common to all measures of cognitive ability: cultural considerations and evaluation of the Flynn effect. An analysis of the WAIS-IV in relation to its use in neuropsychology and with individuals across the age span or who are affected by various psychopathology disorders are presented in chapters by leading experts in the field. Additional chapters cover topics that are more specific to WAIS-IV interpretation, including use of the WAIS-IV with the WMS-IV, and with special populations

The editors would like to thank Pearson for support of this project and permission to use the WAIS-IV standardization data and manual content for portions of this book. Nikki Levy, publisher at Academic Press, provided encouragement and direction to the editors throughout this project. As with our other Wechsler books, her efforts played an integral part in this volume's completion. Our sincere appreciation also goes to Senior Developmental Editor Barbara Makinster and Senior Project Manager Paul Gottehrer for their assistance in preparing the final manuscript for publication. Dr Alan Kaufman wrote a most informed foreword; it is his long relationship with Dr Wechsler that makes this preface even more relevant and personal. To all of our authors, many of whom served on the WAIS-IV and WMS-IV Advisory Panel, your valuable contributions to the understanding and assessment of intelligence continue even beyond the publication of the WAIS-IV.

Larry Weiss, Don Saklofske,
Diane Coalson, and Susan Raiford

PART I

THE WAIS-IV: DEVELOPMENT AND FOUNDATIONS

CHAPTER

1

WAIS-IV: Advances in the Assessment of Intelligence

Diane L. Coalson[1]*, Susan Engi Raiford*[1]*,*
Donald H. Saklofske[2]*, and Lawrence G. Weiss*[1]

[1] Pearson Assessment, San Antonio, Texas, USA
[2] Division of Applied Psychology, University of Calgary,
Calgary, Alberta, Canada

INTRODUCTION

The Wechsler Adult Intelligence Scale – Fourth Edition (WAIS-IV; Wechsler, 2008a) reflects the culmination of over 70 years of progressive revisions to the Wechsler line of adult intelligence measures. It is ironic that the very mention of historical foundations of the Wechsler scales contributes to the misperception that the scales are outdated. In fact, Wechsler's foresight in defining intelligence in practical terms has allowed the very flexibility needed for ongoing revisions to his intelligence scales in light of advances in theory, research, and the measurement of intelligence. The most recent editions of the Wechsler intelligence scales have involved dramatic changes based on burgeoning research advances in neuropsychology, cognitive neuroscience, and contemporary intelligence theory, as well as increasing sophistication in psychological measurement. Despite these substantial innovations, some critics perpetuate the myth that the Wechsler intelligence scales are outdated or atheoretical (Kamphaus, 1993; Shaw, Swerdlik, & Laurent, 1993; Flanagan & Kaufman, 2004). We respectfully disagree and, for this reason, elaborate somewhat on Wechsler's views about intelligence and the progressive adaptations to his intelligence scales in light of contemporary theory and research. We are hopeful that the historical references, often from Wechsler's own writings, will help to clarify the theoretical foundations of the Wechsler intelligence scales, in Wechsler's time and in ours.

WECHSLER'S THEORY OF INTELLIGENCE:
PAST AND PRESENT

Much has been written about the historical foundations of intelligence testing, and the reader is referred to these sources (for example, Thorndike, 1990; Sternberg, 2000; Goldstein & Beers, 2003; Tulsky, *et al.*, 2003) to gain a greater appreciation and understanding of the evolution of current assessment practices. The introductory chapters of the Tulsky *et al.* (2003) book provide an excellent overview of the history of intelligence and memory testing, including the origins of many subtests that continue to appear in the most recent editions of the Wechsler intelligence and memory scales. Appendix material in the Tulsky *et al.* (2003) book provides brief biographical sketches of pioneers in the field of intelligence testing, and the influence they had on Wechsler's ideas about intelligence test development.

David Wechsler entered the field of psychology at an incredibly exciting and innovative time. Preliminary attempts to measure intelligence by Galton and Cattell had spawned an interest in defining the construct of intelligence, most notably represented by the series of debates between Charles Spearman and Edward L. Thorndike on the structure of intelligence and their differing views regarding a general intelligence factor. Advances in psychometric theory and application, and particularly factor analysis, allowed for a closer evaluation of the content represented by the various intelligence measures.

At the time that Wechsler developed the Wechsler-Bellevue Intelligence Scale – Form I (WB-I; Wechsler, 1939) there were two primary theories of intelligence, represented by the views of Spearman and Thorndike. As clarified through their historical debates in the early part of the century, Spearman believed there was a general factor of intelligence, "g," that determined an individual's ability to perform any mental task. Based on evidence indicating low correlations among some intelligence measures, Spearman revised his original theory and added specific factors to the structure of intelligence (Spearman, 1904). Thus, Spearman's revised theory (1904) asserted that intelligence was composed of both a general and specific factors, with the general factor reflecting overall intelligence, and the various specific factors reflecting more specialized abilities that shared some variance with the general factor. In contrast, Thorndike did not support the position of a general factor in the structure of intelligence, instead asserting that there were different kinds of intelligence, such as abstract, social, and practical intelligences.

Although some may have assumed that Wechsler agreed with Spearman's view of "*g*" based on the inclusion of a summary score (i.e., the Full

Scale IQ) to represent general intelligence, he included aspects from both theoretical camps in his (1939) definition of intelligence as:

> the aggregate or global capacity of the individual to act purposefully, to think rationally, and to deal effectively with his [or her] environment. It is global because it characterizes the individual's behavior as a whole; it is an aggregate because it is composed of elements or abilities which, though not entirely independent, are qualitatively differentiable. **(Wechsler, 1939: 3)**

Thus, the definition clearly supports the existence of a general (or global) intelligence, but also asserts that general intelligence is composed of qualitatively different abilities. Wechsler further argued that these specific abilities included both cognitive abilities and other, non-intellective abilities such as drive, persistence, temperament, and curiosity, an interesting mix of other cognitive, personality, and conatative factors (Wechsler, 1950). Although he was not successful at incorporating measures of non-intellective factors into his intelligence scales during his lifetime, he was successful at selecting measures of cognitive ability (e.g., verbal comprehension, perceptual organization, working memory) for his scales that were later found to be important factors of intelligence (Carroll, 1993).

Perhaps it is the resilience of Wechsler's practical definition of intelligence that leads others to assert that his intelligence scales are outdated. Wechsler's original definition of intelligence remained unchanged throughout subsequent editions of his companion text for his adult intelligence scales, *The Measurement of Adult Intelligence* (Wechsler, 1939, 1941, 1944, 1958), as well as peer-reviewed journal articles (Wechsler, 1950, 1975). In fact, Wechsler's original definition continues to appear in the latest revisions of his intelligence scales (Wechsler, 2003, 2008a), as it is still relevant and practical in light of contemporary views on intelligence. Results of the most comprehensive factor-analytic investigations of intelligence measures to date suggest overwhelming evidence for a general intelligence factor at the apex of a hierarchical intelligence construct that is composed of a set of related, but distinguishable, abilities (Carroll, 1993, 1997). This finding has been replicated in cross-cultural studies of both the child and adult versions of the Wechsler intelligence tests (see, for example, Georgas, Weiss, van de Vijver, & Saklofske, 2003). Research on the predictive validity of general intelligence suggest that it is superior to more narrow cognitive domains in predicting such important life outcomes as academic and occupational performance (Deary, 2009; Gottfredson, 2009). Factor-analytic results also suggest that general intelligence is composed of 8–10 broad domains of intelligence that are, in turn, composed of more specific abilities (Carroll, 1993; Horn & Noll, 1997). In light of these cumulative findings, subsequent revisions of the Wechsler scales have expanded measures of additional cognitive domains (e.g., fluid reasoning, working memory, processing speed) while continuing to provide a reliable estimate of general intelligence, the Full Scale IQ (FSIQ).

Wechsler's foresight in distinguishing between intelligence and the cognitive abilities he used to measure it allowed him to avoid one of the major fallacies used to discredit intelligence testing: that is, that the lack of consensus in definitions of intelligence negates the construct validity of intelligence tests (Gottfredson, 2009). Disagreement about the definition of intelligence does not imply that intelligence scales do not measure intelligence. The most important Issue in evaluating what a scale measures is construct validation (Gottfredson, 2009; Gottfredson & Saklofske, 2009). With over 70 years of continued use and research, the Wechsler intelligence scales have an enormous literature base attesting to their validity as measures of intelligence.

Substantial changes have been made to the structure and content of more recent editions of the Wechsler scales, and the origins of many of these changes began during Wechsler's lifetime. As the methodology of factor analysis improved, Wechsler came to appreciate that a number of cognitive factors comprised intelligence. He embraced the use of alternate composite scores based on factor-analytic research (see Cohen, 1957a, 1959; Kaufman, 1975) and evidence from clinical studies indicating their utility in differential diagnosis (Wechsler, 1958). The impact of war and the resulting emergence of the field of neuropsychology were also evident in Wechsler's writings, with sections on brain damage and other neuro-psychological conditions receiving more attention as the years progressed. His later writings discuss the advent of computers, and the differences in computer- and human-based models of intelligence (Wechsler, 1958, 1963, 1975), as well as contemporary advances in physics and biochemistry that he hoped could shed light on memory function (Wechsler, 1963).

In addition to reacting to the psychometric and research trends of his time, Wechsler was keenly aware of practical and societal issues in intelligence testing. Despite his acknowledgment that additional cognitive factors comprised intelligence, he noted the impracticality of measuring numerous, narrow cognitive abilities, because their inclusion did not explain a sufficient amount of additional variance in intelligence to warrant their measurement (Wechsler, 1958). He instead focused on the measurement of broader domains of cognitive ability. He realized that the expanded use of intelligence testing in neuropsychological, academic, vocational, and legal settings warranted ongoing evidence of the scale's validity when used for different purposes, and he incorporated additional clinical studies and sections in his writings to address these new areas. In short, the scale revisions made during Wechsler's lifetime were based on psychometric and theoretical advances, as well as clinical research and practical need. They were not based on fundamental changes to his definition or theory of intelligence. These forces continue to be the primary impetus for more recent changes to the Wechsler intelligence scales, including the changes made to the Wechsler Adult Intelligence Scale – Third Edition (WAIS-III; Wechsler, 1997) as part of the latest revision, the WAIS-IV.

The following sections describe the structure and content of the WAIS-IV, including subtest descriptions and scores. Much of the information pertaining to the WAIS-IV structure is adapted from Chapter 2 in the *WAIS-IV Technical and Interpretive Manual*, which includes additional information regarding the scale's structure, as well as is information on the rationale for changes between the WAIS-III and WAIS-IV.

STRUCTURE AND CONTENT OF THE WAIS-IV

The basic structure of the WAIS-IV is depicted in Figure 1.1. The 15 subtests (12 subtests for adults over 69 years of age) are organized into 4 index scales representing different cognitive domains: Verbal Comprehension, Perceptual Reasoning, Working Memory, and Processing Speed. The index scales comprise the full scale. Core subtests are typically used to derive the composite scores (i.e., the index scores and FSIQ). Supplemental subtests (shown in parentheses) may be administered in addition to the core subtests to provide additional clinical information, or they may be administered in place of core subtests should one be spoiled or invalid.

Subtest descriptions

Verbal Comprehension subtests

The core Verbal Comprehension subtests are Similarities (SI), Vocabulary (VC), and Information (IN). Comprehension (CO) serves as

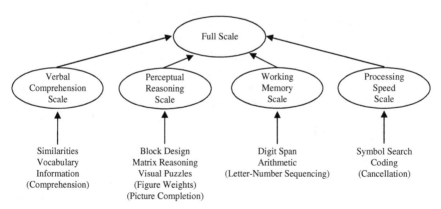

FIGURE 1.1   WAIS-IV structure.

a supplemental subtest. All of these subtests have appeared on previous versions of the Wechsler intelligence scales, and the items within the subtests are not timed.

Items on the Similarities subtest require that the individual describes how two common objects or concepts are similar. This subtest measures verbal concept formation, abstract verbal reasoning, categorical thinking, and the ability to distinguish between non-essential and essential features (Kaufman & Lichtenberger, 1999, 2006; Groth-Marnat, 2009; Lichtenberger & Kaufman, 2009; Sattler & Ryan, 2009).

The Vocabulary subtest is primarily composed of verbal items, but picture items are also included to extend the floor of the subtest. For picture items, the examinee names pictured objects; for verbal items, the individual defines words that are presented and read aloud by the examiner. This subtest measures verbal concept formation, language development, and word knowledge, and also requires long-term memory (Kaufman & Lichtenberger, 1999, 2006; Groth-Marnat, 2009; Lichtenberger & Kaufman, 2009; Sattler & Ryan, 2009).

Information items are posed as questions addressing a broad range of general knowledge. It measures fund of knowledge, long-term memory and retrieval, verbal comprehension, and crystallized intelligence (Kaufman & Lichtenberger, 1999, 2006; Groth-Marnat, 2009; Lichtenberger & Kaufman, 2009; Sattler & Ryan, 2009).

Similar to Information, items on the Comprehension subtest are posed as questions to the individual, but the content of the questions is based on an understanding of basic principles and social situations, rather than factual knowledge. This subtest measures verbal conceptualization, verbal expression, practical knowledge, social judgment, crystallized intelligence, and common sense (Kaufman & Lichtenberger, 1999, 2006; Groth-Marnat, 2009; Lichtenberger & Kaufman, 2009; Sattler & Ryan, 2009).

Perceptual Reasoning subtests

The core Perceptual Reasoning subtests are Block Design (BD), Matrix Reasoning (MR), and Visual Puzzles (VP). Figure Weights (FW) serves as a supplemental subtest for individuals aged 16–69 years, and Picture Completion (PCm) serves as a supplemental subtest for individuals aged 16–90 years. Block Design, Matrix Reasoning, and Picture Completion have appeared on previous versions of the Wechsler intelligence scales; Visual Puzzles and Figure Weights are new to the WAIS-IV.

Block Design items require that the individual reproduces pictured designs using specially designed blocks. The block faces vary, with some sides being red, some white, and others having a half-red and half-white pattern on the diagonal. The subtest items are timed. Block Design measures non-verbal reasoning; analysis and synthesis; visual perception and organization; and visual–motor coordination (Carroll, 1993; Kaufman & Lichtenberger, 1999, 2006; Groth-Marnat, 2009; Lichtenberger & Kaufman, 2009; Sattler & Ryan, 2009).

For items on Matrix Reasoning, the individual completes a matrix or serial reasoning problem by selecting the missing section from five response choices. Items are not timed. Matrix Reasoning measures fluid intelligence, visuospatial ability, simultaneous processing, and perceptual organization (Kaufman & Lichtenberger, 1999, 2006; Groth-Marnat, 2009; Lichtenberger & Kaufman, 2009; Sattler & Ryan, 2009).

To complete each Visual Puzzles item, the individual selects the three response options (from six) that could be combined to reproduce a geometric image. Items are timed. It was designed to be a non-motor task that would measure similar constructs to those measured by the WAIS-III Object Assembly subtest. It was devised to measure perceptual reasoning, visuospatial ability, analysis and synthesis, and simultaneous processing (Kaufman & Lichtenberger, 1999, 2006; Groth-Marnat, 2009; Lichtenberger & Kaufman, 2009; Sattler & Ryan, 2009).

For each Figure Weights item, the individual selects the response option (from five) that would keep a pictured scale in balance. The weights are represented by geometric shapes of different colors, and more difficult items require the individual to view more than one scale with established weight relationships to determine the response choice that keeps the scale balanced. Items are timed. It was designed to measure fluid reasoning; more specifically, quantitative and analogical reasoning (Wechsler, 2008a).

Picture Completion items consist of a pictured object or scene with a missing part. The individual must identify the missing part within 20 seconds. The subtest measures visual perception, perceptual organization, and attention to visual detail (Kaufman & Lichtenberger, 1999, 2006; Groth-Marnat, 2009; Lichtenberger & Kaufman, 2009; Sattler & Ryan, 2009).

Working Memory subtests

The core Working Memory subtests are Digit Span (DS) and Arithmetic (AR). Letter–Number Sequencing (LN) serves as a supplemental subtest for individuals aged 16–69 years.

Digit Span includes three tasks: Forward, Backward, and Sequencing. For the Forward task, the individual repeats numbers spoken by the examiner. The Backward task requires the individual to repeat numbers in the reverse order of that presented, and the Sequencing task requires the individual to sequence numbers from the lowest to highest number. Although there is no time limit for the individual to respond, the examiner reads each number out at the rate of one number per second. The working memory demands for the Backward and Sequencing tasks are greater than those of the Forward task, but all three tasks are designed to measure working memory. Digit Span also measures attention, auditory processing, and mental manipulation (Reynolds, 1997; Groth-Marnat, 2009; Sattler & Ryan, 2009). All three tasks are administered to each individual.

Arithmetic items require the individual to mentally solve arithmetical word problems within a time limit. The Arithmetic subtest measures working memory, mental manipulation, attention, concentration, sequential processing, and numerical reasoning (Kaufman & Lichtenberger, 1999, 2006; Groth-Marnat, 2009; Lichtenberger & Kaufman, 2009; Sattler & Ryan, 2009).

For Letter–Number Sequencing, the examiner reads a series of letters and numbers. The individual recalls the numbers first, in ascending order, and then the letters, in alphabetical order. Although there is no time limit for the individual to respond, the examiner reads each number or letter out at the rate of one number per second. Letter–Number Sequencing measures working memory, mental manipulation, attention, concentration, and short-term auditory memory (Kaufman & Lichtenberger, 1999, 2006; Groth-Marnat, 2009; Lichtenberger & Kaufman, 2009; Sattler & Ryan, 2009).

Processing Speed subtests

The core Processing Speed subtests include Symbol Search (SS) and Coding (CD). Cancellation (CA) serves as a supplemental subtest for individuals aged 16–69 years.

Symbol Search requires the individual to search for two target symbols within a row of symbols. Individuals use a pencil to mark either the matching symbol or a "no" box to indicate responses, and have 120 seconds to complete as many rows (items) as possible. Symbol Search measures visuomotor processing speed, short-term visual memory, visual discrimination, attention, and concentration (Kaufman & Lichtenberger, 1999, 2006; Groth-Marnat, 2009; Lichtenberger & Kaufman, 2009; Sattler & Ryan, 2009).

Coding requires that the individual copies simple symbols as quickly as possible, based on a key that pairs numbers with the symbols. Like Symbol Search, the individual is given 120 seconds to complete the subtest. Coding measures visuomotor processing speed, short-term visual memory, learning ability, cognitive flexibility, attention, concentration, and motivation (Kaufman & Lichtenberger, 1999, 2006; Groth-Marnat, 2009; Lichtenberger & Kaufman, 2009; Sattler & Ryan, 2009).

For Cancellation, the individual searches for specific colored shapes within a larger array of colored shapes, marking only the specified shapes. There are two items with different colors and shapes. Both items are administered to an individual, and each item has a time limit of 45 seconds. Although designed to measure the same construct as the Cancellation subtest of the Wechsler Intelligence Scale for Children – Fourth Edition (WISC-IV; Wechsler, 2003), the WAIS-IV Cancellation subtest uses abstract shapes rather than animals. Cancellation tasks are used to measure visuomotor processing speed, visual selective attention, and visual neglect (Geldmacher, Fritsch, & Riedel, 2000; Bate, Mathias, & Crawford, 2001; Wojciulik, Husain, Clarke, & Driver, 2001; Sattler & Ryan, 2009).

Score descriptions

A number of scores can be derived as part of a WAIS-IV administration, including scores at the subtest-, index-, and full-scale levels. Each subtest provides a score that is scaled to a metric with a mean of 10 and a standard deviation of 3. The sum of scaled scores for the subtests within a domain is used to derive the corresponding index score. For example, the sum of scaled scores for Similarities, Vocabulary, and Information is used in most situations to derive the VCI. Index scores include the Verbal Comprehension Index (VCI), the Perceptual Reasoning Index (PRI), the Working Memory Index (WMI), and the Processing Speed Index (PSI). A Full Scale IQ (FSIQ) is derived from the sum of subtest-scaled scores for all four domains. All of the composite scores, including the index scores and the FSIQ, are scaled to a metric with a mean of 100 and a standard deviation of 15.

In addition to the primary scores noted above, the WAIS-IV offers a number of optional scores. At the subtest level, the optional scores are designed to provide additional information related to the individual's performance on specific subtests. This process approach to assessment has its historical roots in the work of Edith Kaplan and her colleagues, who devised a number of process measures to further evaluate performance on the Wechsler intelligence scales. These measures provide a systematic and quantitative approach to the analysis of qualitative aspects of subtest performance. The WAIS-IV includes optional process scores for two subtests: Block Design and Digit Span. The Block Design No Time Bonus score (BDN) is based on the individual's Block Design performance without additional time-bonus points. Separate, optional scores are also available for the three Digit Span tasks: Forward, Backward, and Sequencing.

At the index level, the General Ability Index (GAI) is included as an optional index score. It is derived from the sum of scaled scores for the core Verbal Comprehension and Perceptual Reasoning subtests, thus resulting in a composite that is less influenced by the demands of working memory and processing speed than the FSIQ. The GAI was first introduced by Prifitera, Weiss, and Saklofske (1998) as an optional composite score for the Wechsler Intelligence Scale for Children – Third Edition (WISC-III; Wechsler, 1991). Tulsky, Saklofske, Wilkins, and Weiss (2001) developed a WAIS-III GAI subsequent to the scale's publication in 1997. Based on the increased clinical usage of this composite, information regarding the WAIS-IV GAI appears in the test manuals. Additional information regarding the history and interpretation of the GAI, as well as its counterpart, the Cognitive Proficiency Index (CPI), appears in Chapter 3 of this volume.

WAIS-III TO WAIS-IV: WHAT'S NEW?

Changes to structure and content

The most notable change between the WAIS-III and WAIS-IV structures involves the elimination of the traditional Verbal IQ (VIQ) and Performance IQ (PIQ) scores in favor of the four, factor-based index scores – a change that was foreshadowed by similar modifications to the structure of the WISC-IV. The third editions of the WISC and WAIS included a dual IQ/index score structure, in which the traditional FSIQ, VIQ, and PIQ scores remained the primary level of interpretation, and the index scores provided an alternative method for evaluating the individual's performance in more discrete domains of cognitive functioning. The dual IQ/index score structure served as a transition for those users who were accustomed to the traditional VIQ/PIQ split that had characterized the Wechsler intelligence scale since the publication of the Wechsler-Bellevue Intelligence Test – Form I (WB-I; Wechsler, 1939).

In part, the evolution of the index scores was based on an expanding base of factor-analytic evidence supporting the existence of additional factors within the Wechsler intelligence scales (Cohen, 1957a, 1957b, 1959; Kaufman, 1975, 1979). The emergence of the four-factor structure can be traced to the WISC-III. Prior to the WISC-III, both the adult and child versions of the Wechsler intelligence scales were commonly viewed as having three factors, based on numerous factor analytic investigations of the Wechsler scales (Cohen, 1957a, 1959; Kaufman, 1975). The first two factors represented verbal and performance abilities, and the third factor, termed the Freedom from Distractibility factor (FD), was composed of the Arithmetic, Digit Span, and Digit Symbol (now referred to as Coding) subtests. Interpretation of the FD factor varied, with some proposing it as a measure of attention and concentration (Kaufman, 1975), others describing it as a measure of memory (Cohen, 1957a), and still others contending that it measures sequencing ability (Bannatyne, 1974). Researchers working on the WISC-III revision developed the then-new Symbol Search subtest in an attempt to clarify the nature of the third factor, and the now familiar, four-factor structure emerged. The WAIS-III followed suit with the addition of a Symbol Search subtest, and the four-factor structure of the scale was again confirmed. The WISC-III Freedom from Distractibility Index was renamed as the Working Memory Index on the WAIS-III.

The primary impetus behind the rise of the index scores was borne from the clinical research literature suggesting that performance in more discrete domains of cognitive ability provided useful information for differential diagnosis (Wechsler, 1997). For example, individuals with Reading and Mathematics Disorder often have difficulties with tasks requiring working memory (Gathercole, Hitch, Service, & Martin, 1997; Wechsler, 2003), and individuals with traumatic brain injury (TBI) often have difficulty with tasks requiring processing speed (Mathias & Wheaton, 2007). Although diagnosis should never be based on a single score, the refined nature of the index scores enhances the interpretability of group and individual differences (see also Weiss, Saklofske, Prifitera, & Holdnack, 2006).

Although the structural changes between the WAIS-III and WAIS-IV are substantial, the scales measure very similar constructs, as indicated by the strength of the correlations between the WAIS-III and WAIS-IV composites provided in the manual (Wechsler, 2008a) and reproduced in Table 1.1.

Table 1.2 includes a comparison of subtests contributing to corresponding scores on the WAIS-III and WAIS-IV. The subtest comparisons are based on administration of core subtests in both measures.

As expected, the greatest difference in subtest contribution to composite scores is noted in the comparisons between corresponding IQ and Index scores. The WAIS-III VIQ included three subtests that do not appear in the WAIS-IV VCI: Comprehension, Arithmetic, and Digit Span. Inclusion of Arithmetic and Digit Span in the WAIS-III VIQ created a mixture of verbal and working memory tasks, making interpretation of the VIQ more difficult when performance across these domains varied. The WAIS-III PIQ included three subtests that do not appear in the WAIS-IV PRI: Picture Completion, Picture Arrangement (PA), and Coding. Unusual performance on the Coding subtest relative to the other PIQ subtests made interpretation of the PIQ problematic. The WAIS-IV VCI and PRI represent

TABLE 1.1   Correlations between WAIS-III and
WAIS-IV composites

Composite	Correlation
WAIS–III VIQ/WAIS-IV VCI	0.89
WAIS–III VCI/WAIS-IV VCI	0.91
WAIS–III PIQ/WAIS-IV PRI	0.83
WAIS–III POI/WAIS-IV PRI	0.84
WAIS–III WMI/WAIS-IV WMI	0.87
WAIS–III PSI/WAIS-IV PSI	0.86
WAIS–III FSIQ/WAIS-IV FSIQ	0.94

TABLE 1.2   Subtest contribution to composite scores on the WAIS-III and WAIS-IV

Composite	WAIS-III subtests	WAIS-IV subtests
VIQ/VCI	VC, SI, IN, CO, AR, DS	VC, SI, IN
PIQ/PRI	BD, MR, PCm, PA, CD	BD, MR, VP
VCI/VCI	VC, SI, IN	VC, SI, IN
POI/PRI	BD, MR, PCm	BD, MR, VP
WMI/WMI	AR, DS, LN	AR, DS
PSI/PSI	CD, SS	CD, SS
GAI/GAI	VC, SI, IN, BD, MR, PCm	VC, SI, IN, BD, MR, VP
FSIQ/FSIQ	VC, SI, IN, CO, BD, MR, PCm, PA, AR, DS, CD	VC, SI, IN, BD, MR, VP, AR, DS, CD, SS

purer measures of their corresponding cognitive domains than the WAIS-III VIQ and PIQ, thus improving interpretability when variable performance across cognitive domains is present.

The three subtests that contribute to the VCI are the same across the WAIS-III and the WAIS-IV, and include Vocabulary, Similarities, and Information. Two of the three subtests contributing to the WAIS-III POI are the same as those that contribute to the WAIS-IV PRI (Block Design and Matrix Reasoning). The third subtest on the WAIS-IV PRI is a new subtest, Visual Puzzles. It replaces Picture Completion as the third subtest comprising the WAIS-IV PRI. The WAIS-III WMI was composed of three subtests (Arithmetic, Digit Span, and Letter–Number Sequencing), whereas the WAIS-IV WMI is composed of only two subtests (Arithmetic and Digit Span). The subtests contributing to the WAIS-III and WAIS-IV PSI are the same, and include Coding and Symbol Search. Taken together, the subtest changes for the WAIS-IV Index scores are minimal, and should not result in major interpretive differences.

Table 1.3 includes the percentages of index-score contribution to the FSIQ in the WAIS-III and WAIS-IV. The proportions are similar across the two measures with the exception of the Processing Speed Index, which comprises 20 percent of the subtests in the WAIS-IV FSIQ versus only

TABLE 1.3   Index-score contribution to FSIQ for the WAIS-III and WAIS-IV

	VCI	PRI	WMI	PSI
WAIS-III	36.4%	36.4%	18.2%	9%
WAIS-IV	30%	30%	20%	20%

9 percent of subtests in the WAIS-III FSIQ. Thus, the contribution of the PSI to the FSIQ has more than doubled in the WAIS-IV relative to the WAIS-III.

Increased emphasis on the measurement of processing speed has been evident in recent revisions to both the child and adult versions of the Wechsler intelligence scales (e.g., WISC-III, WISC-IV, WAIS-III, and WAIS-IV). The addition of the Symbol Search subtest to the WISC-III and WAIS-III allowed the PSI factor to emerge. Subsequent research indicates that the PSI is sensitive to a variety of neuropsychological conditions, including traumatic brain injury (Kennedy, Clement, & Curtiss, 2003), epilepsy (Berg et al., 2008), multiple sclerosis (Forn, Belenguer, Parcet-Ibars, & Ávila, 2008) and Attention Deficit/Hyperactivity Disorder (Schwean & Saklofske, 2005). Research also indicates that processing speed may play a central role in age-related changes in intellectual ability (Salthouse, 2000).

The Cancellation subtest was added to the WISC-IV as a supplemental measure of processing speed that required less fine motor demands than Coding. The WAIS-IV includes a version of the Cancellation subtest for similar reasons. These measures have been extensively used in neuro-psychological settings as measures of visual neglect, response inhibition, and motor perseveration (Adair, Na, Schwartz, & Heilman, 1998; Geldmacher et al., 2000; Lezak, Howieson, Loring, Hannay, & Fischer, 2004).

Also evident in recent revisions is an increased emphasis on working memory content. The roots of working memory lie in the field of cognitive psychology, and date back to investigations by Baddeley and Hitch (1974). Although there is some disagreement as to the definition of working memory, it is generally considered to be an active form of memory, in which information is stored temporarily for further processing. Baddeley's (2003) model of working memory is the most comprehensive and accepted model at the current time. In this model, auditory (verbal) and visual information are stored and refreshed in separate systems, and a central executive controls the allocation of resources to these systems (see Chapter 3 for additional details of Baddeley's working memory model). Accordingly, the auditory and visual working memory tasks appear separately in the WAIS-IV and Wechsler Memory Scale – Fourth Edition (WMS-IV; Wechsler, 2009), respectively. Although the WAIS-III WMI was composed of only auditory tasks (Digit Span and Letter–Number Sequencing), the WMS-III WMI included one auditory (Letter–Number Sequencing) and one visual (Spatial Span) working memory task. Subsequent research indicates that the mixture of auditory and visual tasks on the WMS-III could lead to interpretive difficulties, especially when the WMIs of the two scales were discrepant (Wilde, Strauss, & Tulsky, 2004). The WAIS-IV WMI is derived from the scaled scores on the Digit Span and Arithmetic subtests, both of which are auditory measures. The supplemental subtest, Letter–Number Sequencing, is also an auditory measure. The WMS-IV Visual Working Memory Index (VWMI) is composed of new visual working memory tasks, including Spatial Addition and Symbol Span (see Chapter 9 for additional details about the WMS-IV VWMI).

Other content-related changes were made at the subtest level to enhance the measurement of working memory on Arithmetic and Digit Span. Arithmetic items were revised to decrease demands on verbal comprehension and mathematical knowledge, thus increasing demands on working memory. For example, excess verbiage was eliminated, and single-syllable names were chosen for the word problems. Increased item difficulty is obtained by increasing the number of sequential, simple calculations, rather than requiring the solution of more complex calculations. Based on research indicating that the Forward and Backward tasks of Digit Span had different cognitive demands (see, for example, Banken, 1985; Reynolds, 1997), Digit Span Sequencing was added as a third Digit Span task. Like the Backward task, the Sequencing task places greater demands on working memory than the Forward task, thus increasing the working memory load of the Digit Span subtest as a whole. Separate scaled scores are available for Digit Span Forward, Backward, and Sequencing, enabling the clinician to compare performance across the three tasks. It is interesting to note that the researchers working on the WAIS-IV revision considered eliminating the Forward task, but Pilot data indicated its elimination resulted in lower scores on the Backward task, perhaps resulting from a loss of progressive instruction. In addition, retention of the Forward task ensured that the floor of the subtest was sufficient for individuals with suspected or confirmed intellectual disability (Wechsler, 2008a).

Fluid reasoning has been noted as a key aspect of cognitive functioning in many contemporary models of cognitive ability (Cattell & Horn, 1978; Carroll, 1997; Sternberg, 2000). According to Carroll (1993: 583), tasks that require fluid reasoning involve "manipulating abstractions, rules, generalizations, and logical relationships." The addition of the Matrix Reasoning subtest to the WAIS-III, Wechsler Preschool and Primary Scale of Intelligence – Third Edition (WPPSI-III; Wechsler, 2002), and WISC-IV was aimed at increasing the direct measurement of fluid reasoning. The increased emphasis on fluid reasoning was also represented by renaming of the WISC-III Perceptual Organization Index as the Perceptual Reasoning Index in the WISC-IV. The WAIS-IV follows this lead in nomenclature change, and also introduces a new subtest to measure fluid reasoning: Figure Weights.

The Figure Weights subtest was developed to measure a specific aspect of fluid reasoning, quantitative reasoning. Quantitative reasoning tasks involve reasoning processes that can be expressed mathematically, emphasizing inductive or deductive logic (Carroll, 1993). The subtest does not use traditional mathematical content, but instead uses the concept of balancing weights on two sides of a scale. The Figure Weights subtest also involves working memory, as indicated by results of factor analyses (Wechsler, 2008a). The involvement of working memory increases with item difficulty, as more difficult items require that a greater number of shape–weight relationships be retained and evaluated to find the correct solution. This relationship between reasoning and working memory is not surprising, based on related research suggesting a dynamic interplay between fluid reasoning, working memory, and processing speed (Kyllonen & Christal, 1990; de Ribaupierre & Lecerf, 2006; Unsworth & Engle, 2007; Salthouse & Pink, 2008). The dynamic relationship between fluid reasoning, working memory, and processing speed, as well as its importance in learning and memory, is discussed in more detail in Chapter 3.

Other structural and content-related changes in the WAIS-IV include the addition of the Visual Puzzles subtest, and the deletion of several WAIS-III subtests and optional procedures. The Visual Puzzles subtest was created to measure constructs similar to those assessed by the Object Assembly subtest, including perceptual organization, spatial reasoning, and analysis and synthesis of part–whole relationships. This development was planned due to several limitations of Object Assembly. Although the Object Assembly subtest provided a good measure of perceptual organization (Larrabee, 2004), limitations impacting its use included age-appropriateness, ease of administration, testing time, reliability, and motor demands. Thus, development efforts were aimed at finding a replacement or new measure that tapped similar constructs. Psychometric results support the improved reliability of Visual Puzzles relative to Object Assembly, as well as the relationship of this subtest to other measures on the Perceptual Reasoning scale. Future research is needed with this new subtest to determine if it shows evidence of the same clinical utility as the Object Assembly subtest.

In addition to Object Assembly, the Picture Arrangement subtest was dropped from the WAIS-IV. Elimination of these subtests aided in accomplishing several research goals, including the reduction of overall administration time and the need for time-bonus points on perceptual reasoning measures. Both of these subtests had relatively poorer psychometric properties than other subtests (e.g., reliability), and the Picture Arrangement subtest was frequently "overinterpreted" as a measure of social judgment or sequencing ability.

A more difficult decision involved the removal of optional procedures for the Coding subtest. The Coding subtest, called Digit Symbol–Coding on the WAIS-III, included two optional procedures, Digit Symbol–Incidental Learning and Digit Symbol–Copy. These tasks were designed to further evaluate an individual's performance of the Digit Symbol–Coding subtest, by teasing apart the possible effects of incidental learning and graphomotor speed on subtest performance. One of the primary goals of WAIS-IV revision was to add new measures of fluid reasoning, working

memory, and processing speed, while reducing or maintaining administration time. Extensive market research with WAIS-IIII users indicated that
the incidence of usage for these subtests was low, so the decision was made
to eliminate them from the standardization edition. The WAIS-III Digit
Symbol–Copy procedure can still be used as a measure of graphomotor
speed, but comparisons between this score and scores from the WAIS-IV
Coding subtest are not supported. For those who are interested in
obtaining additional information about the incidental learning and
graphomotor speed aspects of the Coding subtest, Sattler and Ryan (2009)
have included recall and copy tasks for use with the WAIS-IV in their text,
Assessment with the WAIS-IV.

Twelve WAIS-III subtests were retained on the WAIS-IV, but the item
content, administration procedures, or scoring has changed. Chapter 2 (see
Appendix) includes a detailed description of the administration and
scoring changes made to retained subtests on the WAIS-IV. This information should be especially helpful to those practitioners who are making the
transition from the WAIS-III to the WAIS-IV. The *WAIS-IV Technical and
Interpretive Manual* (Wechsler, 2008b) includes an item-level analysis of
changes between the WAIS-III and WAIS-IV (e.g., how many items were
dropped, retained, or modified), and the reader is referred to those sections
for additional information.

Other changes

Other improvements were made on the WAIS-IV that are not necessarily related to changes in structure or content. A number of changes were
based on increasing the developmental appropriateness of the scale for
older adults, based on sensory and psychomotor changes related to normal
aging (Storandt, 1994; Kaufman & Lichtenberger, 1999, 2006; Lezak *et al.*,
2004). Although these changes were based primarily on the needs of older
adults, they should also make the WAIS-IV a more appropriate measure for
individuals of all ages with similar difficulties. Based on the decline of
processing speed with increasing age (see, for example, Lee, Gorsuch,
Saklofske, & Patterson, 2008), the use of time-bonus points on the
perceptual reasoning subtests has been drastically reduced. Time-bonus
points were eliminated entirely on Arithmetic, and limited to six ceiling
items on Block Design. Based on possible issues with auditory discrimination, the occurrence of rhyming letters and numbers within a trial was
virtually eliminated on Digit Span and Letter–Number Sequencing. Similarly, concerns with possible deficits in visual acuity prompted enlarge-
ment of all visual stimuli. As mentioned previously, a reduction in motor
demands was also desired. Cancellation provides an alternative processing
speed measure with reduced fine motor demands compared to Coding,

and the addition of Visual Puzzles similarly reduces the motor demands of subtests in the perceptual reasoning domain relative to the WAIS-III.

Although not specifically intended for older adults, the WAIS-IV instructions emphasize teaching to a greater degree than the WAIS-III, with all examinees receiving instruction regarding the demands of the subtest task. This differs from previous versions, in which corrective feedback was provided only when the examinee provided an incorrect response. By teaching all examinees in the same manner, the possible effects of differential teaching are minimized while further ensuring that low scores are not due to an examinee misunderstanding the task at hand. This is especially important for older individuals who may be unfamiliar with the types of items included on a subtest (e.g., matrix problems), or individuals with less educational opportunity. Taken together with the reduced number of core subtests, the average testing time of 80 minutes for the WAIS-III has been reduced to 67 minutes on the WAIS-IV – a time saving of over 15 percent. The reduced testing time should result in benefits in terms of further limiting fatigue, as well as providing the practitioner with additional time to evaluate other aspects of cognitive functioning, such as adaptive behavior, memory, and executive function.

CONCLUSION

The WAIS-IV is the latest revision of Wechsler's adult intelligence scales, the most widely used tests of intelligence for adults. It represents a continuing tradition of change and innovation that has been most evident in recent revisions of the scale. The increasing rate of change mirrors a similar increase in productivity in related areas of research, including neuropsychology, cognitive psychology, cognitive neuroscience, and intelligence theory. It is likely that continuing advances in related fields will contribute to the revision goals of future editions.

One of the most promising areas for future research is functional brain imaging (Dingfelder, 2009). The use of intelligence measures in brain imaging studies is becoming more common, with evidence suggesting more localized activation of brain regions for specific cognitive abilities (e.g., spatial ability), and more diffuse activation of brain areas for general intellectual ability (Colom et al., 2009; Haier et al., 2009). Other studies indicate a positive correlation between cortical thickness and general intelligence (Karama et al., 2009). Even more relevant is a recent study employing lesion-mapping techniques for an evaluation of WAIS-III index scores, with results indicating more localized regions for the VCI, POI, and WMI than the PSI, which appears to be more diffuse in nature (Gläscher et al., 2009). Based on the rate of progress in the field of brain imaging, psychologists and educators alike should re-examine their current knowledge about intelligence to include relevant literature on the neural basis of intelligence (Haier & Jung, 2008).

The WAIS-IV is the product of progressive innovations over the last 70 years. The authors would like to express their respect and appreciation to Dr Wechsler for his remarkable contributions to the field of intelligence assessment, and for modeling a method of test development that strives for psychometric, clinical, and practical excellence on the basis of research from a wide variety of disciplines. It is this foundation that has allowed the Wechsler scales to stand the test of time, as they adapt to the ever-changing world around them.

References

Adair, J. C., Na, D. L., Schwartz, R. L., & Heilman, K. M. (1998). Analysis of primary and secondary influences on spatial neglect. *Brain and Cognition, 37*, 351–367.

Baddeley, A. D. (2003). Working memory: looking back and looking forward. *Nature Reviews Neuroscience, 4*(10), 829–839.

Baddeley, A. D., & Hitch, G. (1974). Working memory. In G. H. Bower (Ed.), *The Psychology of Learning and Motivation, Vol. 8, Advances in Research and Theory* (pp. 47–89). New York, NY: Academic Press.

Banken, J. A. (1985). Clinical utility of considering Digits Forward and Digits Backward as separate components of the Wechsler Adult Intelligence Scale – Revised. *Journal of Clinical Psychology, 41*(5), 686–691.

Bannatyne, A. (1974). Diagnosis: A note on recategorization of the WISC scaled scores. *Journal of Learning Disabilities, 7*, 272–274.

Bate, A. J., Mathias, J. L., & Crawford, J. R. (2001). Performance on the Test of Everyday Attention and standard tests of attention following severe traumatic brain injury. *Clinical Neuropsychologist, 15*(3), 405–422.

Berg, A. T., Langfitt, J. T., Testa, F. M., DiMario, F., Kulas, J., Westerveld, M., & Levy, S. R. (2008). Residual cognitive effects of uncomplicated idiopathic and cryptogenic epilepsy. *Epilepsy and Behavior, 13*(4), 614–619.

Carroll, J. B. (1993). *Human Cognitive Abilities: A Survey of Factor-analytic Studies*. Cambridge: Cambridge University Press.

Carroll, J. B. (1997). The three-stratum theory of cognitive abilities. Contemporary intellectual assessment: theories, tests, and issues. In D. P. Flanagan, J. L. Genshaft, & P. L. Harrison (Eds.), *Contemporary Intellectual Assessment: Theories, Tests, and Issues* (pp. 122–130). New York, NY: Guilford Press.

Cattell, R. B., & Horn, J. L. (1978). A check on the theory of fluid and crystallized intelligence with description of new subtest designs. *Journal of Educational Measurement, 15*, 139–164.

Cohen, J. (1957a). The factorial structure of the WAIS between early adulthood and old age. *Journal of Consulting Psychology, 21*(4), 283–290.

Cohen, J. (1957b). A factor-analytically based rationale for the Wechsler Adult Intelligence Scale. *Journal of Consulting Psychology, 21*(6), 451–457.

Cohen, J. (1959). The factorial structure of the WISC at ages 7–6, 10–6, and 13–6. *Journal of Consulting Psychology, 23*(4), 285–299.

Colom, R., Haier, R. J., Head, K., Álvarez-Linera, J., Quiroga, M. Á., Shih, P. C., & Jung, R. E. (2009). Gray matter correlates of fluid, crystallized, and spatial intelligence: Testing the P-FIT model. *Intelligence, 37*, 124–135.

Deary, I. J. (2009). Introduction to the special issue on cognitive epidemiology. *Intelligence, 37*(6), 517–519.

de Ribaupierre, A., & Lecerf, T. (2006). Relationships between working memory and intelligence from a developmental perspective: Convergent evidence from a neo-Piagetian and a psychometric approach. *European Journal of Cognitive Psychology, 18*, 109–137.

Dingfelder, S. F. (2009). From the research lab to the operating room. *Monitor on Psychology, 40*, 4043.

Flanagan, D. P., & Kaufman, A. S. (2004). *Essentials of WISC-IV Assessment.* Hoboken, NJ: Wiley.

Flanagan, D. P., & Kaufman, A. S. (2009). *Essentials of WISC-IV Assessment* (2nd ed.). Hoboken, NJ: Wiley.

Forn, C., Belenguer, A., Parcet-Ibars, M. A., & Ávila, C. (2008). Information-processing speed is the primary deficit underlying the poor performance of multiple sclerosis patients in the Paced Auditory Serial Addition Test (PASAT). *Journal of Clinical and Experimental Neuropsychology, 30*(7), 789–796.

Gathercole, S. E., Hitch, G. J., Service, E., & Martin, A. J. (1997). Phonological short-term memory and new word learning in children. *Developmental Psychology, 33*(6), 966–979.

Geldmacher, D. S., Fritsch, T., & Riedel, T. M. (2000). Effects of stimulus properties and age on random-array letter cancellation tasks. *Aging, Neuropsychology, and Cognition, 7*(3), 194–204.

Georgas, J., Weiss, L. G., van de Vijver, F. J. R., & Saklofske, D. H. (Eds.). (2003). *Culture and Children's Intelligence: Cross-cultural Analysis of the WISC-III.* San Diego, CA: Academic Press.

Gläscher, J., Tranel, D., Paul, L. K., Rudrauf, D., Rorden, C., Hornaday, A., Grabowski, T., Damasio, H., & Adolphs, R. (2009). Lesion mapping of cognitive abilities linked to intelligence. *Neuron, 61*, 681–691.

Goldstein, G., & Beers, S. R. (Eds.). (2003). *Comprehensive Handbook of Psychological Assessment, Vol. 1, Intellectual and Neuropsychological Assessment.* Hoboken, NJ: Wiley.

Gottfredson, L. S. (2009). Logical fallacies used to dismiss the evidence on intelligence testing. In R. P. Phelps (Ed.), *Correcting Fallacies about Educational and Psychological Testing* (pp. 11–65). Washington, DC: American Psychological Association.

Gottfredson, L., & Saklofske, D. H. (2009). Intelligence: Foundations and issues in assessment. *Canadian Psychology, 50*, 183–195.

Groth-Marnat, G. (2009). *Handbook of psychological assessment* (5th ed.). Hoboken, NJ: Wiley.

Haier, R. J., Colom, R., Schroeder, D. H., Condon, C. A., Tang, C., Eaves, E., & Head, K. (2009). Gray matter and intelligence factors: is there a neuro-g? *Intelligence, 37*, 136–144.

Haier, R. J., & Jung, R. E. (2008). Brain imaging studies of intelligence and creativity: What is the picture for education? *Roeper Review, 30*, 171–180.

Horn, J. L., & Noll, J. (1997). Human cognitive capabilities: Gf–Gc theory. In D. P. Flanagan, J. L. Genshaft, & P. L. Harrison (Eds.), *Contemporary Intellectual Assessment: Theories, Tests, and Issues* (pp. 53–91). New York, NY: Guilford Press.

Kamphaus, R. W. (1993). *Clinical Assessment of Children's Intelligence: A Handbook for Professional Practice.* Needham Heights, MA: Allyn and Bacon.

Karama, S., Ad-Dab'bagh, Y., Haier, R. J., Deary, I. J., Lyttelton, O. C., Lepage, C., Evans, A. C., & The Brain Development Cooperative Group. (2009). Positive association between cognitive ability and cortical thickness in a representative US sample of healthy 6- to 18-year-olds. *Intelligence, 37*, 145–155.

Kaufman, A. S. (1975). Factor analysis of the WISC-R at 11 age levels between 6½ to 16½ years. *Journal of Consulting and Clinical Psychology, 43*(2), 135–147.

Kaufman, A. S. (1979). WISC-R research: Implications for interpretation. *School Psychology Review, 8*(1), 5–27.

Kaufman, A. S., & Lichtenberger, E. O. (1999). *Essentials of WAIS-III Assessment*. New York, NY: Wiley.

Kaufman, A. S., & Lichtenberger, E. O. (2006). *Assessing Adolescent and Adult Intelligence* (3rd ed.). Hoboken, NJ: Wiley.

Kennedy, J. E., Clement, P. F., & Curtiss, G. (2003). WAIS-III Processing Speed Index scores after TBI: The influence of working memory, psychomotor speed and perceptual processing. *Clinical Neuropsychologist, 17*(3), 303–307.

Kyllonen, P. C., & Christal, R. E. (1990). Reasoning ability is (little more than) working memory capacity? *Intelligence, 14*(4), 389–433.

Larrabee, G. (2004). A review of clinical interpretation of the WAIS-III and WMS-III: Where do we go from here and what should we do with the WAIS-IV and WMS-IV? *Journal of Clinical and Experimental Psychology, 26*(5), 706–717.

Lee, H. F., Gorsuch, R., Saklofske, D. H., & Patterson, C. (2008). Cognitive differences for ages 16 to 89 (Canadian WAIS-III): Curvilinear with Flynn and Processing Speed Corrections. *Journal of Psychoeducational Assessment, 26*(4), 382–394.

Lezak, M. D., Howieson, D. B., Loring, D. W., Hannay, H. J., & Fischer, J. S. (2004). *Neuropsychological Assessment* (4th ed.). New York, NY: Oxford University Press.

Lichtenberger, E. O., & Kaufman, A. S. (2009). *Essentials of WAIS-IV Assessment*. New York, NY: Wiley.

Mathias, J. L., & Wheaton, P. (2007). Changes in attention and information-processing speed following severe traumatic brain injury: A meta-analytic review. *Neuropsychology, 21*(2), 212–223.

Prifitera, A., & Saklofske, D. H. (Eds.). (1998). *WISC-III Clinical Use and Interpretation: Scientist–Practitioner Perspectives*. San Diego, CA: Academic Press.

Prifitera, A., Weiss, L. G., & Saklofske, D. H. (1998). The WISC-III in context. In A. Prifitera, & D. H. Saklofske (Eds.), *WISC-III Clinical Use and Interpretation: Scientist–Practitioner Perspectives* (pp. 1–38). San Diego, CA: Academic Press.

Reynolds, C. R. (1997). Forward and backward memory span should not be combined for clinical analysis. *Archives of Clinical Neuropsychology, 12*(1), 29–40.

Salthouse, T. A. (2000). Aging and measures of processing speed. *Biological Psychology, 54*, 35–54.

Salthouse, T. A., & Pink, J. E. (2008). Why is working memory related to intelligence? *Psychonomic Bulletin and Review, 15*(2), 364–371.

Sattler, J. M., & Ryan, J. J. (2009). *Assessment with the WAIS-IV*. San Diego, CA: Author.

Schwean, V., & Saklofske, D. H. (2005). Assessment of attention deficit hyperactivity disorder with the WISC-IV. In A. Prifitera, D. Saklofske, & L. G. Weiss (Eds.), *WISC-IV Clinical Use and Interpretation: Scientist–Practitioner Perspectives* (pp. 235–280). San Diego, CA: Elsevier Academic Press.

Shaw, S.R., Swerdlik, M.E., & Laurent, J. (1993). Review of the *WISC-III Intelligence Scale for Children* (3rd ed.). *Journal of Psychoeducational Assessment*, 151–160.

Spearman, C. (1904). "General Intelligence," objectively determined and measured. *American Journal of Psychology, 15*, 201–293.

Sternberg, R. J. (2000). *Handbook of Intelligence*. New York, NY: Cambridge University Press.

Storandt, M. (1994). General principles of assessment of older adults. In M. Storandt, & G. R. VandenBos (Eds.), *Neuropsychological Assessment of Dementia and Depression in Older Adults: A Clinician's Guide* (pp. 7–32). Washington, DC: American Psychological Association.

Thorndike, R. M. (1990). Origins of intelligence and its measurement. *Journal of Psychoeducational Assessment, 8*(3), 223–230.

Tulsky, D. S., Saklofske, D. H., Chelune, G. J., Heaton, R. K., Ivnik, R. J., Bornstein, R., Prifitera, A., & Ledbetter, M. F. (Eds.). (2003). *Clinical Interpretation of the WAIS-III and WMS-III*. San Diego, CA: Academic Press.

Tulsky, D. S., Saklofske, D. H., Wilkins, C., & Weiss, L. G. (2001). Development of a General Ability Index for the Wechsler Adult Intelligence Scale (3rd ed.). *Psychological Assessment, 13*(4), 566–571.

Unsworth, N., & Engle, R. W. (2007). On the division of short-term and working memory: An examination of simple and complex span and their relation to higher order abilities. *Psychological Bulletin, 133*(6), 1038–1066.

Wechsler, D. (1939). *The Measurement of Adult Intelligence*. Baltimore, MD: Williams & Wilkins.

Wechsler, D. (1941). *The Measurement of Adult Intelligence* (2nd ed.). Baltimore, MD: Williams & Wilkins.

Wechsler, D. (1944). *The Measurement of Adult Intelligence* (3rd ed.). Baltimore, MD: Williams & Wilkins.

Wechsler, D. (1950). Cognitive, conative, and non-intellective intelligence. *American Psychologist, 5*, 78–83.

Wechsler, D. (1958). *The Measurement and Appraisal of Adult Intelligence* (4th ed.). Oxford: Williams & Wilkins.

Wechsler, D. (1963). Engrams, memory storage, and mnemonic coding. *American Psychologist, 18*(3), 149–153.

Wechsler, D. (1975). Intelligence defined and undefined: a relativistic appraisal. *American Psychologist, 30*(2), 135–139.

Wechsler, D. (1991). *Wechsler Intelligence Scale for Children* (3rd ed.). San Antonio, TX: Psychological Corporation.

Wechsler, D. (1997). *Wechsler Adult Intelligence Scale* (3rd ed.). San Antonio, TX: Psychological Corporation.

Wechsler, D. (2002). *Wechsler Preschool and Primary Scale of Intelligence* (3rd ed.). San Antonio, TX: Psychological Corporation.

Wechsler, D. (2003). *Wechsler Intelligence Scale for Children* (4th ed.). San Antonio, TX: Psychological Corporation.

Wechsler, D. (2008a). *Wechsler Adult Intelligence Scale* (4th ed.). San Antonio, TX: Pearson.

Wechsler, D. (2008b). *WAIS-IV Technical and Interpretive Manual*. San Antonio, TX: Pearson.

Wechsler, D. (2009). *Wechsler Memory Scale* (4th ed.). San Antonio, TX: Pearson.

Weiss, L. G., Saklofske, D. H., Prifitera, A., & Holdnack, J. (2006). *WISC-IV Advanced Clinical Interpretation*. San Diego, CA: Elsevier.

Wilde, N. J., Strauss, E., & Tulsky, D. S. (2004). Memory span on the Wechsler scales. *Journal of Clinical and Experimental Neuropsychology, 26*(4), 539–549.

Wojciulik, E., Husain, M., Clarke, K., & Driver, J. (2001). Spatial working memory deficit in unilateral neglect. *Neuropsychologia, 39*(4), 390–396.

Practical Issues in WAIS-IV Administration and Scoring

Susan Engi Raiford[1], *Diane L. Coalson*[1],
Donald H. Saklofske[2], *and Lawrence G. Weiss*[1]

[1] Pearson Assessment, San Antonio, Texas, USA
[2] Division of Applied Psychology, University of Calgary,
Calgary, Alberta, Canada

INTRODUCTION

This chapter presents practical issues to consider when administering and scoring the Wechsler Adult Intelligence Scale – Fourth Edition (WAIS-IV; Wechsler, 2008). Clinical training programs may use this chapter with new trainees to provide an overview of administration and scoring issues that are both common to the Wechsler intelligence scales and specific to the WAIS-IV. The chapter also provides responses to frequently asked questions encountered in technical support requests.

The organization of the first section of this chapter, "Administration and scoring considerations," corresponds to the four scales that comprise the instrument – namely, Verbal Comprehension, Perceptual Reasoning, Working Memory, and Processing Speed. This section reviews general administration and scoring issues relevant to most or all subtests comprising each respective scale, and subtest administration and scoring issues. The second section of the chapter, "Key prompts," provides a table organized by subtest (in administration order) that contains all commonly used verbatim prompts. Examiners may wish to lay it on the testing surface behind the freestanding Administration and Scoring Manual during the first several WAIS–IV administrations (before prompts have been committed to memory) to eliminate the need to turn manual pages back to the general directions during item administration. The chapter concludes with a section that addresses common administration and scoring questions. An Appendix addressed to WAIS–III users provides an overview of changes to retained subtests; administration and scoring.

ADMINISTRATION AND SCORING CONSIDERATIONS

Verbal Comprehension scale

General administration and scoring tips

Administering only three Verbal Comprehension subtests (i.e., Similarities, Vocabulary, and Information) permits derivation of the Verbal Comprehension Index (VCI) and provides all Verbal Comprehension subtest scores necessary to calculate the Full Scale IQ (FSIQ). Comprehension need not be administered unless subtest substitution is planned, one of the core subtests is invalidated, or additional clinical information provided by the subtest is desired.

It is important to become familiar with the sample response sets for each item. Sets are organized in such a way that they facilitate the most precise and quick scoring possible (as suggested in Slate, Jones, Murray, & Coulter, 1993). The groups of responses that appear together on single lines are similar in nature. Higher-level responses and more common responses are located at the upper left of the sets wherever possible. Queried responses also appear at the upper left of the set of responses for each point value. Queries should involve a neutral inquiry, as suggested in the Administration and Scoring Manual, to decrease the possibility that the examinee will feel defensive or discouraged (Lacritz & Cullum, 2003).

Neglecting to record the examinee's response verbatim is one of the most common recording errors committed on the Wechsler intelligence scales (Alfonso, Johnson, Patinella, & Rader, 1998; Loe, Kadlubek, & Marks, 2007; Slate *et al.*, 1993). To facilitate accurate scoring, it is particularly critical to record the entire response verbatim on Verbal Comprehension subtests. The space to record verbatim responses on the Verbal Comprehension subtests is maximized to encourage and facilitate this practice.

The most common administration error committed on the Wechsler intelligence scales is neglecting to query responses that should be queried (Alfonso *et al.*, 1998; Loe *et al.*, 2007; Slate *et al.*, 1993). Querying when the manual indicates that the response should not be queried is somewhat less frequently observed, but still common (Slate *et al.*, 1993). It is therefore critical to focus on learning to query when (and only when) it is appropriate.

One of the most prevalent scoring errors is assigning inaccurate point values to responses on the Verbal Comprehension subtests. In our experience, familiarity with the general scoring principles (Similarities and

Vocabulary) and general concepts (Comprehension) decreases scoring errors. When scoring a verbatim response, first try to match it to the sample responses for that item. The sample responses contain the most frequent responses received from the standardization samples. If the response cannot be matched, refer to the general scoring principles and general concepts to score the response.

The items on Verbal Comprehension subtests do not have strict time limits. In most cases, 30 seconds should be sufficient for most examinees to respond. This is a guideline, however, and should not be used rigidly. If an examinee has been performing poorly and considers responses for long periods of time without any perceived benefit, the examinee can be encouraged to respond by saying **"Do you have an answer?"** as stated on page 40 of the Administration and Scoring Manual. If he or she does not respond, you may move to the next item. This guideline ensures smooth administration, and is designed to maximize examinee engagement.

In some cases on some subtests, a discontinue criterion can take effect within the reversal items (i.e., prior to the start point). Do not award credit for any items that were administered but fall after the discontinue point in the item sequence.

Subtest-specific information

Similarities A number of administration and scoring points bear mentioning. The sample item should be administered to all examinees to allow practice completing an item. Some of the most difficult items involve the use of "opposites." The highest-level responses for these express that the two words describe opposite ends of a unifying continuum, and specify the unifying continuum. At times, an examinee may respond to these (or other) items by stating how the two words are different. After all subtests have been administered, it is appropriate to return to the item(s) to test the limits, as suggested by Lacritz and Cullum (2003). At that time, point out to the examinee that his or her response specified how the two words are different, and ask the examinee to explain how they are alike. The impact of the additional support and explanation then can be described in the psychological report. The discontinue criterion necessitates close monitoring of item scores to prevent unnecessary item administration. The examinee can meet the discontinue criterion within the reversal items.

Vocabulary Vocabulary is comprised of both picture items and verbally presented items. All items require use of the Stimulus Book. Picture items are scored 0 or 1 point. All verbal items, however, are scored 0, 1, or 2 points to provide differentiation among examinees of varying ability levels. It is important to note differences between 1- and 2-point responses for these items to permit accurate scoring.

Vocabulary has a longer administration time than most subtests. Efficient scoring and recording helps to preserve rapport and interest. It is important, however, that queries be administered as indicated. It is also critical to monitor item scores closely to discontinue appropriately to ensure administration time is not excessive. As with Similarities, examinees may meet the discontinue criterion within the reversal items.

Information   Information has very few administration or scoring challenges. The most difficult items to score are those that involve describing famous historical figures. All items contain 0-point sample responses to clarify the scoring rules. Examiners should become familiar with those 0-point responses that should be queried to provide examinees with opportunities to improve their responses. In addition, specific prompts are provided to clarify vague responses on some items. Memorizing these prompts facilitates smoother administration. Examinees can meet the discontinue criterion upon reversal if they score 0 points on the first item and each of the two reversal items.

Comprehension   As previously stated, Comprehension need not be administered to obtain any composite scores. It can provide rich clinical information, however, and can inform an assessment of social concept formation and verbal reasoning. The average administration time for Comprehension is typically longer than that of any other subtest. Recording and scoring efficiently to maintain a steady administration pace is therefore paramount. The best strategy to facilitate this goal is to become very familiar with the scoring criteria for items and monitor item scores closely to discontinue when appropriate. Note that the discontinue criterion can be met by scoring 0 points on the first item and each of the two reversal items.

It is important to become familiar with the item content on Comprehension. A few items involve proverb interpretation: These proverbs are antiquities translated from Eastern and South-American cultures. They are relatively easy to score, and appear midway through the subtest to introduce examinees to the item type before the items become more difficult.

Items that require expression of multiple general concepts require strong familiarity with those concepts. Do not query a second time if a post-query response falls within the same general concept. Strong familiarity with the general concepts also helps to reduce neglected queries where only one concept was expressed in a response. During an early research phase in the WAIS-IV project, the research directors attempted to reduce or eliminate multiple general concept scoring to improve ease of administration and scoring and reduce the need to query. Multiple general concept items, at that stage, were experimentally converted to items with simpler 2-, 1-, or 0-point scoring. Following these conversions, the medium-ability and high-ability examinees were more poorly differentiated, the reliability of the entire subtest declined substantially, and the items became far easier when the requirement to consider the item from multiple angles was eliminated. It was concluded that despite the increased ease of administration and scoring with the other item type, the multiple general concept items tap an important component of the abilities measured by this subtest. The more complex scoring structures were therefore retained.

Perceptual Reasoning scale

General administration and scoring tips

Administering only three Perceptual Reasoning subtests (i.e., Block Design, Matrix Reasoning, and Visual Puzzles) permits derivation of the Perceptual Reasoning Index (PRI) and provides all Perceptual Reasoning subtest scores necessary to calculate the FSIQ. Figure Weights and Picture Completion need not be administered unless subtest substitution is planned, one of the core subtests is invalidated, or additional clinical information provided by the subtest is desired.

Prior to the first administration, become familiar with the Perceptual Reasoning subtests to ensure proper administration. Smooth and coordinated use of the materials (e.g., Administration and Scoring Manual, Stimulus Books, Record Form, and stopwatch) maximizes examinee engagement, whereas fumbling and awkwardness can distract the examinee. Distraction due to examiner inexperience is particularly problematic on many of these subtests because most (excluding Matrix Reasoning) measure performance in the context of strict time limits. Any attention lapses due to examiner error may therefore impact examinee performance.

It is important to understand the contrast between the strict item time limits on Block Design, Visual Puzzles, Figure Weights, and Picture Completion, and the 30-second item guideline on Matrix Reasoning. Strict time limits involve using a stopwatch and moving to the next item after the time limit expires. No credit is awarded for correct responses or self-corrections after the time limit expires. For these subtests, examiners *must* record item completion times correctly to permit accurate scoring.

In contrast, Matrix Reasoning does not require the use of a stopwatch, but the non-obtrusive use of a stopwatch is not prohibited if clinicians wish to inform comparisons with performance on other subtests that are timed. For Matrix Reasoning, the examinee should be permitted to continue working after 30 seconds if he or she is benefiting from additional time, as items become more difficult. In addition, examinees can self-correct responses even after being administered subsequent items.

On the subtests noted in the following section, a discontinue criterion can be met within the reversal items. In this case, do not award credit for any items that were administered but fall after the discontinue point in the item sequence.

Subtest-specific information

Block Design   Block Design has the longest administration time of any Perceptual Reasoning subtest, and one of the longest of all subtests in the scale. Efficient administration, recording, and scoring are therefore critical to maintaining examinee effort and rapport. Monitor item scores closely to discontinue when appropriate and avoid excessive administration time, as the discontinue criterion is two consecutive scores of 0 and can be met within the reversal items. Smooth and coordinated use of the Administration and Scoring Manual, the Stimulus Book, the Record Form, the blocks, and the stopwatch requires several practice administrations, but will also help to reduce administration time.

A coordinated Block Design administration also requires proper and informed use of the materials. This issue is particularly relevant to Block Design because it is the first subtest in the sequence when the scale is administered in standard order. Use the "crackback" feature of the Administration and Scoring Manual. The manual becomes free-standing, so that verbatim instructions and correct responses are not visible to the examinee, and the Record Form can be shielded behind the manual. To use the crackback feature, open the manual and push the bottom half of the cover backward to create the base. Position the Stimulus Book as instructed in the Administration and Scoring Manual. The Stimulus Book sections are opened and pages are turned toward the examinee. This orientation places the pages to be turned in easy reach. The Stimulus Book's front cover should be oriented so that it can be read by the examiner, and the coil-bound edge should be oriented toward the examinee. Then, grasp the subtest tab and open it toward the examinee.

During practice administrations, simulate a variety of scenarios. Administer both trials of the Sample Item, proceed to Item 5, then reverse to administer both trials of Items 4, 3, 2, then 1. Request that your practice examinee discontinues within the reversal items to permit use of the scoring guidelines.

Practice presenting the blocks appropriately. Examiners frequently neglect to present the top surfaces of the blocks in the manner specified in the Administration and Scoring Manual (Moon, Blakey, Gorsuch, & Fantuzzo, 1991), but there is a paucity of studies examining the impact of this common practice on clinical groups. Remember to present only the blocks needed for the particular item. Four blocks are used for the sample item and Items 1–2 (i.e., for each item, two blocks for the model built by the examiner, and two blocks for the examinee to construct the design). Eight blocks are used for Items 3–4 (i.e., for each item, four for the model, and four for the design). The examinee uses four blocks for Items 5–10, and nine blocks for Items 11–14.

Do not give cues to examinees about rotation of blocks. It is important to avoid correcting rotation errors more than permitted. Correct only the first rotation error (i.e., any rotation of the design that is 30 degrees or more). Note that *only the first rotation error on the subtest is corrected*. Subsequent rotation errors are *not* corrected. Two four-block diamond items appear between the four-block square items and nine-block square items to ease the transition between four and nine blocks: Do *not* offer the examinee cues to rotate the blocks, either in response to examinee questions or spontaneously.

Accurate timing is important when administering Block Design. Remind the examinee to tell you when he or she finishes an item, because a difference of a few seconds could impact the score due to time-bonus points and strict time limits. If unclear, it is acceptable to ask the examinee if he or she is finished. Time limits for nine-block items are always 2 minutes. It is common to forget to record completion time in seconds for items with time limits greater than 60 seconds. Common scoring errors on items 9–14 occur in this situation. For example, 1 minute 20 seconds can be mistaken for 120 seconds. The response, in these situations, could receive less credit than actually earned. Be sure to record completion times in seconds, and to circle the score corresponding to the appropriate completion time.

Some items are administered using only the Stimulus Book picture, and others are administered using both a model and the Stimulus Book picture. The sample item is administered to all examinees to introduce the task, and requires use of both a model and the Stimulus Book picture. All items prior to the start point are presented with both a model and a Stimulus Book picture to simplify the easiest items, and prepare low-ability examinees for the transition to picture-only items. For these easier items, the proper placement of the model and Stimulus Book together should be noted (see Figure 3.1 in the Administration and Scoring Manual) as the arrangement varies for a right- versus a left-handed examinee. Start point and subsequent items are presented using only a Stimulus Book picture.

The Block Design No Time Bonus (BDN) process score is calculated by awarding only four points for correctly completed items for which time-bonus points are possible. Calculate this score carefully, not awarding more than 4 points for any item. A discrepancy comparison may be calculated with the Block Design subtest scaled score to facilitate an examination of time-bonus points; impact on examinee scores, if this question is of interest.

Matrix Reasoning   Matrix Reasoning is relatively simple to administer and score. An explicit prompt is available to reduce awkwardness of transitions from one item to the next. Practice appropriate timing for administration of this prompt, "**Do you have an answer?**" The timing of the prompt is adjusted accordingly if the examinee appears to benefit from additional time to respond. The most common Matrix Reasoning administration error is to apply the 30-second guideline as a strict time limit. Give the examinee increasing time if he or she is still working at 30 seconds. Continue this practice if the examinee benefits from the additional time. Monitor item scores closely, and discontinue when appropriate. Note that the discontinue criterion can be met within the reversal items.

Visual Puzzles   Visual Puzzles, a new subtest, is relatively easy to administer and score, but some points bear mentioning. Administer both the demonstration item and the sample item, as each provides important information about the task to the examinee. The demonstration item models how to complete an item, teaches that pieces cannot be stacked to complete the puzzle, and that exactly three pieces must be selected for the response. The sample item teaches that pieces may need to be rotated to complete the puzzle, and allows practice completing an item.

An efficient administration is more readily achieved with attention to the following. Practice use of the stopwatch and appropriate timing for administration of the prompt "**Do you have an answer?**" Note that time limits are longer on items later in the item sequence, and that the timing of this prompt is adjusted accordingly (i.e., 10 seconds before the item time limit expires). Rehearse the prompt to choose three responses, which is given if the examinee responds with more or less than required. Note that the discontinue criterion can be met within the reversal items; monitor the discontinue criterion appropriately to prevent excessive administration time.

If an examinee asks if pieces can be "flipped" ("turned over" so that the underside that cannot be seen is facing up) to obtain the answer, in the interest of rapport, clarify that they cannot be flipped. This question makes the assumption that pieces are the same design on the underside as on the top. A response that requires flipping a piece, therefore, does not represent the best response.

Figure Weights   Whereas administration of Figure Weights is not required to derive composite scores, it can provide rich clinical information in a number of situations as a measure of non-verbal quantitative reasoning. Be aware that you should not administer this subtest to individuals aged 70–90, as no norms are available for these ages.

It is relatively simple to administer and score with awareness of a few key points. Be sure to administer both of the demonstration items as well as the sample item, as each provides important information to the examinee. Demonstration Item A familiarizes the examinee with operation of a scale. It additionally is used to teach the examinee that color, shape, and quantity are relevant to responses. Demonstration Item B models how to complete an item. The sample item allows the examinee to practice completing an item. Remember to provide the verbatim instruction before Item 16, at the transition between items with two and three scales. This instruction teaches examinees that, for three-scale items, all three scales should be considered in the response.

Figure Weights administration requires awareness of timing concerns. Practice use of the stopwatch and appropriate timing for administration of the prompt "**Do you have an answer?**" Note that, similar to Visual Puzzles, time limits are longer on items later in the item sequence, and the timing of the prompt is adjusted accordingly (i.e., 10 seconds before the time limit expires). To avoid excessive administration time, monitor item scores closely, because the discontinue criterion can be met within the reversal items.

Picture Completion Administration of Picture Completion is more challenging than any of the other Perceptual Reasoning subtests apart from Block Design. Familiarity with the following aspects of administration can help to ensure scores are valid and administration time is not excessive. Administer the sample item to all examinees, to allow practice completing an item prior to test item administration. Remember to ask the examinee to point to the missing part to supplement ambiguous verbal responses. Become familiar with the verbal responses that require the examinee to supplement with a correct pointing response to receive credit. Awareness of these responses reduces scanning time to determine if a pointing response is required, and more readily facilitates the examinee's timely response. Monitor item scores closely to discontinue when appropriate. The discontinue criterion can be met if the examinee scores 0 points on the first item and each of the three reversal items.

Examiners must be familiar with use of the three prompts that are given one time only during administration of Picture Completion. If the examiner has not committed these prompts to memory, time can expire before the prompt is given and the examinee has a chance to respond. These prompts appear on the Record Form, and can therefore be provided quickly and accurately without turning back to the manual page where the prompts appear. This is beneficial because the examinee is operating within a time limit. Examiners may wish to check off each prompt if and when it is provided as a reminder not to repeat it, as this is one of the most common administration errors on this subtest (Kaufman & Lichtenberger, 1999). Multiple provisions of any of these prompts violates standard administration and can result in artificially inflated scores.

Working Memory scale

General administration and scoring tips

Administering only two subtests (Digit Span and Arithmetic) permits derivation of the Working Memory Index (WMI) and provides all Working Memory subtest scores necessary to calculate the FSIQ. Letter–Number Sequencing need not be administered unless substitution of that subtest is planned, one of the core subtests is invalidated, or additional clinical information provided by that subtest is desired.

Care must be taken with respect to enunciation, rate, and voice inflection when presenting Working Memory subtest items. Speaking clearly during administration of the Working Memory subtests is essential. Presentation of stimuli on Digit Span and Letter–Number Sequencing should occur at the rate of approximately one digit or letter per second. Varying from this presentation rate can impact performance (Baddeley & Lewis, 1984; Engle & Marshall, 1983). Remember to hold the pitch of your voice steady on all characters, then to drop the pitch of your voice on the last character (digit or letter) of Digit Span and Letter–Number Sequencing trials. Practicing the presentation rate and checking proper voice inflection with an experienced examiner is helpful.

Repetition is treated differently on Working Memory subtests than on subtests from other scales. Repetition is not permitted on any trial of Digit Span or Letter–Number Sequencing. *Only* one repetition per item is permitted on Arithmetic. It is therefore crucial to ensure assistive listening devices (if applicable) are functioning properly prior to administration. If it is suspected that an assistive listening device is not functioning properly, it is appropriate to ask the examinee to repeat single words, digits, or letters before commencing.

Lacritz and Cullum (2003) observe that occasionally examinees chunk digits or letters when structuring Digit Span or Letter–Number Sequencing responses. For example, in response to 1 – 2 – 3 – 4, the examinee might say "twelve, thirty-four." In this situation, it is appropriate to explain to examinees that they should repeat the digits (or letters) one at a time.

Subtest-specific information

Digit Span   Digit Span presentation rate and pitch should be consistent with standard procedures. One of the most common administration errors is to present digits faster than one per second. It is critical to practice the proper presentation rate. You may wish to tap your foot lightly under the table to ensure a standard presentation rate. Another common error is to vary voice pitch when pronouncing each digit in a sequence. Consistent pitch should be used to enunciate all except the final digit, for which voice pitch should drop slightly to indicate presentation is complete and the examinee may begin to respond. Varying voice pitch may facilitate use of a chunking strategy, which may result in an overestimate of ability.

Administer all trials as instructed. *Never* present only a single trial of a given length and subsequently award credit for subsequent trials of that length to shorten administration time. This practice is problematic because trials vary in terms of difficulty. In some cases, smaller numbers are used to make the first trial of a given span length easier than the second trial. Bypassing the second trial may therefore result in awarding credit for trials more difficult than the first.

Administer all three parts of the subtest. Digit Span Forward, Digit Span Backward, and Digit Span Sequencing all are necessary to derive the Digit Span subtest scaled score. Forgoing administration of any part of Digit Span results in a lower raw score, and therefore an artificially low subtest scaled score. The Digit Span Forward and Digit Span Backward scores *cannot* be averaged to obtain an estimate of the Digit Span Sequencing score. This practice will result in inaccurate scaled scores. During an early research phase in the WAIS-IV project, the research directors investigated if Digit Span Forward could be eliminated (i.e., if the scaled score for Digit Span could be obtained by administering Digit Span Backward and Digit Span Sequencing *only*). The result was that Digit Span Backward scores dropped, even among high-ability examinees, and the floor of the subtest became much weaker for low-ability examinees. Digit Span Forward appears to fill an essential role as a "warm-up" task for higher-ability examinees prior to Digit Span Backward and Digit Span Sequencing. Its inclusion additionally offers a stronger floor for lower-ability examinees that cannot be achieved with Digit Span Backward and Digit Span Sequencing, even with the simplest of items.

It is important to accurately record the examinee's response verbatim. If recording the digits is challenging because the examinee speaks too quickly, examiners occasionally place checkmarks above the digits on the Record Form. This practice can result in some loss of data, however, because incorrect digits were not recorded. For example, if the examinee consistently misheard or inaccurately recalled "5" as "9," a qualitative observation is not possible if those data are not present. Note that rhyming digits within a single trial are minimized to ensure these observations are meaningful and possible.

Digit Span Backward contains multiple trials with two digits, all of which should be administered as directed. There are a total of six trials that are two digits in length (i.e., a sample item with two trials and two test items with two trials each). These trials provide a floor for Digit Span Backward, and the difficulty of each trial varies.

Digit Span Sequencing is the last part of the subtest, and must be administered after Digit Span Forward and Digit Span Backward. Remember to administer both trials of the Digit Span Sequencing sample item. The first trial is used to teach the examinee to sequence the digits in ascending order. The second trial is used to make the examinee aware that any digits may be included more than once in a given trial, and that digits should be repeated in a trial as many times as they are presented. Digits must be repeated in some of the longer sequences, because the longest sequences are nine digits long: Sequencing the digits without repetitions, therefore, would become easier as trials increased in length. Examinees more frequently respond incorrectly to trials involving repeated digits.

Discontinue a given part of Digit Span after an examinee obtains scores of 0 on *both trials* of an item. Do not discontinue if the examinee scores 0 on two consecutive trials *across* two items (i.e., the last trial of an item, and the first trial of the subsequent item). This practice can result in an underestimate of the examinee's ability. Discontinue administration *only* when the examinee scores 0 on *both* trials of an item.

A number of optional process scores can be derived to inform Digit Span interpretation. The Digit Span Forward (DSF), Digit Span Backward (DSB), and Digit Span Sequencing (DSS) process scores permit examination of performance separately on the three parts, as well as discrepancy comparisons among the three parts. The Longest Digit Span Forward (LDSF), Longest Digit Span Backward (LDSB), and Longest Digit Span Sequencing (LDSS) process scores permit examination of maximum performance on each task relative to the normative sample.

Arithmetic The most frequent Arithmetic administration questions center on repetitions. All examinees are told explicitly in the subtest introduction that one repetition request is permitted per item. Provide *only* one repetition of any single item upon request: Respond to requests for subsequent repetitions of the item with the verbatim prompt in the manual that explains items can only be repeated once. If a repetition is requested, do *not* stop timing while repeating or while the examinee responds. Do not award credit for responses after time expires, even if still in the process of repeating when time expires. Although at first blush this may seem to unfairly penalize an examinee, all examinees in the standardization samples were subject to these same constraints. The norms, therefore, reflect this guideline. Finally, do *not* answer any of the examinee's specific questions about an item by repeating only the relevant information from the item. The entire item must be repeated. Extracting and repeating only a portion of the information in response to a specific question is an unfair advantage, because it reduces the working memory demands of the item.

A few more points about administration should be noted. Administer the sample item to all examinees to provide practice in completing an item before test items begin. Pictures are used as stimuli for the easiest items, so the Stimulus Book is sometimes necessary for administration. Monitor item scores closely to discontinue when appropriate. The examinee can meet the discontinue criterion within the reversal items.

A few users have commented that the use of names from other cultures that appear on two of the Arithmetic items may be distracting. Names for all items were selected based on their length (all names are a single syllable to minimize construct-irrelevant information), as well as consistency and ease of pronunciation in common use. Diversity was also a consideration. The research directors selected these names from among those of our own work colleagues (one of whom works as a statistical analyst for the Wechsler scales and other projects, and was born in China), family members, or friends (including a number of psychologists). If it is thought that the use of one of these names has caused the examinee to respond incorrectly, it is acceptable to re-administer the item following administration of all subtests using an alternate name to test the limits. The differences can be described in the psychological report. Because all names are monosyllabic, it is best to select a name that adheres to this specification.

Letter–Number Sequencing Administration of Letter–Number Sequencing is not required to derive composite scores. It may serve as an acceptable substitute for Digit Span or Arithmetic in situations where administration was spoiled. Do not administer Letter–Number Sequencing to individuals aged 70–90, as norms are not available for that age range.

Letter–Number Sequencing has few administration challenges. Similar to Digit Span, the most frequent Letter–Number Sequencing administration error is to present numbers and letters faster than the standard rate of one per second. It is particularly important to practice this subtest, as it can be more challenging to keep pace consistent with both numbers and letters than with numbers alone. Also similar to Digit Span, another common Letter–Number Sequencing administration error is to vary voice pitch used when pronouncing each number or letter in the sequence. The same pitch should be used for all characters (i.e., numbers and letters) in a sequence, except for the final character, for which voice pitch should drop slightly to indicate presentation is complete and the examinee may begin to respond.

All items, even those with trials that use few letters and numbers, must be administered as directed. This ensures an adequate range of scores, and minimizes the difficulty of easy items. *Never* present only a single trial of a given length and award credit for subsequent trials of that length to shorten administration time. Trials that include the same number of characters have different levels of difficulty, based on the selection of numbers and letters from an earlier position in the number series or alphabet (e.g., the numbers 1–5 and the letters A–D). Bypassing subsequent trials may therefore result in awarding credit for trials more difficult than the first. The use of additional short trials also permits teaching the task before moving to trials with additional numbers and letters. Do not discontinue if the examinee scores 0 on three consecutive trials *across two items*. Discontinue administration *only* when the examinee scores 0 on *all three trials of a single item*.

It is critical to accurately record the verbatim response. Examiners sometimes choose to place checkmarks above numbers and letters on the Record Form if the examinee speaks quickly. As previously noted, however, this practice can result in some loss of data if all information was not recorded. These data may be even more informative on Letter–Number Sequencing than on Digit Span, as so many letters rhyme with one another and with the number "3". Wherever possible, letters and numbers that rhyme were not included in a single trial to ensure that process observations about misperceived stimuli can be more readily interpreted.

Teaching the task occurs in stages. Sample Item A is used to teach the examinee to repeat numbers before letters, and is followed by test items based only on this portion of the directions. Sample Item B is used to teach examinees to sequence numbers in ascending order and letters alphabetically. This staged approach to teaching minimized the occurrence of examinees repeating the letters before the numbers. Examinees who do so receive full credit for their responses, because it was determined during research phases that examinees that provided the responses using the two different methods did not differ with respect to working memory ability: Order of the classes (numbers and letters) was irrelevant, and either order places demands on working memory. In addition, examinees that repeated the letters before the numbers were rare enough that the occurrence rate, even among clinical groups, did not warrant complicating the scoring procedure.

An optional process score can be derived to inform Letter–Number Sequencing interpretation. The Longest Letter–Number Sequence (LLNS) process score permits examination of maximum performance on the task relative to the normative sample. It can be particularly informative in cases where performance is variable (e.g., the examinee misses one or two trials on each item or span length).

Processing Speed scale

General administration and scoring tips

Administering only two subtests (Symbol Search and Coding) permits derivation of the Processing Speed Index (PSI) and provides all Processing Speed subtest scores necessary to calculate the FSIQ. Cancellation need not be administered unless substitution of that subtest is planned, one of the core subtests is invalidated, or additional clinical information provided by that subtest is desired.

Smooth administration and close attention to time limits of Processing Speed subtests is critical. Practice using the Response Booklets, administering the demonstration and sample items, and using the stopwatch, prior to the first administration. Allow only the appropriate amount of time for examinees to complete the subtests. Ensure discontinues do not occur too early due to misreading the stopwatch. This is a particular issue on Symbol Search and Coding, which have time limits of 120 seconds: When the stopwatch reads 1:20 (i.e., 1 minute 20 seconds) it can be mistaken for 120 seconds, which results in substantial reduction of the potential score. Become well-familiar with the stopwatch to be used prior to administration, to determine if time is given in minutes and seconds or in seconds only.

Subtest-specific information

Symbol Search   Symbol Search is relatively easy to administer and score. The symbols are bold and large to minimize visual acuity concerns. Examinees mark the matching shape in the search group or the "NO" box to permit qualitative observation of errors.

Give appropriate attention to learning how to teach the task. Study the demonstration items and memorize the answers to the sample items prior to administering the subtest. It is common to fumble necessary feedback when administering this subtest for the first time. Corrective and reinforcing feedback is most effective immediately after responses to sample items. Memorizing the answers to the sample items will facilitate this practice. The Administration and Scoring Manual states that if the examinee has a question not already accounted for in the provided verbatim prompts prior to administration of test items, explain further if necessary. If the examinee seems confused in response to feedback on the sample items, it is acceptable to provide more details, including the information that the symbols must be exactly alike (Lacritz & Cullum, 2003). If an examinee asks if both of the target symbols might be in the search group, explain further.

Do not teach or permit the examinee to use anything other than a slash mark to respond. This occurs rarely, and usually is seen first on the sample items. Provide corrective feedback immediately when this is first observed. At times examiners incorrectly complete demonstration items with an "X," and thereby prime examinees to make the same error. This slows performance, and can result in an artificially low estimate of processing speed ability.

Close attention to examinee responses is critical. Self-corrections on Symbol Search item responses are permitted, as long as they occur within the time limit. Do not permit the examinee to use or search for an eraser. Encourage him or her to keep going, and merely to indicate the correct response. If items are skipped the examinee should be prompted immediately, and as often as necessary, to complete the item. Do not score a skipped item as incorrect; skipped items are ignored in calculation of the raw score. Count the items completed correctly, and subtract the items completed incorrectly, when calculating the final score.

The Scoring Key facilitates accurate, efficient scoring. It reproduces the test items in miniature, with the correct responses appearing in bold. When the Response Booklet is open, the key is placed covering the page on the right to score the page on the left, and is aligned with the item rows. The key should be slid over to cover the page on the left when scoring the page on the right.

Coding Coding is relatively easy to administer and score, but attention to a few details will ensure smooth administration. Practice the new verbatim instructions and completing the demonstration items prior to the first administration. It is desirable to memorize answers to the sample items prior to administering the subtest, to facilitate smooth feedback (corrective or reinforcing) to the examinee. Responses to the sample items are relatively quickly checked with the key at the top of the page. Providing timely feedback is therefore less challenging than with Symbol Search sample items.

A number of other design features bear mentioning, as they are relevant to administration. The large vertical space between the key at the top of the page and the items minimizes the chance that left-handed individuals will block the key from their view while completing the subtest, although this can occur. An accommodation should be made in this case, as outlined in the Administration and Scoring Manual: A second, unobstructed copy of the key is made available. It is therefore important to ensure two copies of the Response Booklet are at hand during test administration. The bold numbers and symbols minimize concerns with visual acuity during administration.

The WAIS-III Digit Symbol–Copy procedure can be used with the WAIS-III norms if a measure of simple graphomotor speed is desired. Sattler and Ryan's *Assessment with the WAIS-IV* (Sattler & Ryan, 2009) provides versions of recall and copy procedures that can be used to obtain clinical data for qualitative observations of incidental learning and graphomotor speed.

Cancellation Administration of Cancellation is not required to derive composite scores. It may serve as an acceptable substitute for Coding in situations where fine motor ability is a concern, or for either Symbol Search or Coding in the event that one of the two subtests is spoiled. It can also provide insight about attentiveness and impulsivity through process observation of omission and commission errors, and is reminiscent of some inhibition control tasks for this reason. However, do not administer Cancellation to individuals aged 70–90, as norms are not available for these ages.

Similar to Symbol Search, do not permit the examinee to use anything other than a slash mark to respond. When this occurs, it usually is first seen on the sample items, and should be corrected immediately when first observed. Immediately correct an examinee who is using "Xs" rather than slash marks to respond. At times examiners complete demonstration items with "Xs," which models this practice and primes the examinee to respond in this manner. This can slow performance, and result in an underestimate of the examinee's ability.

Ensure that the examinee completes the rows all the way across the 17 × 11 page, rather than stopping midway across the page. Open the Response Booklet to *expose the full two-page spread* for each item. Practice the prompt that instructs the examinee to complete the row across the entire two-page spread. This is critical, as administration time for each item is only 45 seconds.

Examinees are not permitted to mark all occurrences of the first target shape in a row (or on the page), then return to the beginning of the same row (or to the beginning of the page) to mark all occurrences of the second target shape. Under these conditions, provide the verbatim prompt that the examinee cannot go back to mark any shapes that are missed.

Ensure both items are administered: Do not omit Item 2. Both Item 1 and Item 2 are necessary to calculate the subtest scaled score. Close the Response Booklet after administration of Item 1. Expose Demonstration Item B and Sample Item B (corresponding to Item 2), and repeat the same procedures used to administer Item 1.

Examinees may ask if mistakes can be corrected. Self-corrections on Cancellation item responses are permitted, as long as they occur within the time limit and no subsequent target shapes have been marked. Do not permit examinees to search for an eraser; encourage them to mark or scratch out the correction and go on.

Attention to the examinee's responses is critical during this subtest. If the examinee attempts to skip a row, prompt immediately that this is not permitted. Do not use the administration time to prepare for the next item or subtest, for this reason.

Occasionally, examinees write too faintly to be seen through the Cancellation Scoring Template. While helpful, the Scoring Template is not necessary to score the subtest. If marks are too faint to see through the Scoring Template, remove it and simply count each correct shape with a mark through it and each incorrect shape with a mark through it. Double-check your work under these conditions, however.

KEY PROMPTS

This section provides a table organized by subtest (in administration order) that contains all commonly used verbatim prompts (Table 2.1). Examiners may wish to lay this table on the testing surface behind the freestanding Administration and Scoring Manual during the first several WAIS-IV administrations (before the prompts have been committed to memory). This will eliminate the need to flip backward to the general directions during item administration.

FREQUENTLY ASKED ADMINISTRATION AND SCORING QUESTIONS

This section addresses a number of questions most frequently asked about the WAIS-IV in workshops and trainings, and via email and telephone. This section is not intended to provide exhaustive answers to all relevant questions about administration and scoring. It is critical to obtain relevant training and experience prior to administration. Students should refer to more comprehensive texts (e.g., Lichtenberger & Kaufman, 2009; Sattler & Ryan, 2009) that are designed for those new to the Wechsler scales.

Why are some 0-point or 1-point responses on the verbal subtests not queried?

Queries are used to elicit additional information when a response is incomplete, vague, or unclear. Queries should not be given to improve clearly wrong responses, but just to allow clarification or elaboration. During standardization, it was determined that querying certain responses did not result in any additional information. Therefore, these responses are not followed by **(Q)** in the sample responses. Query these responses if, based on your clinical judgment, performance on surrounding items, and other test behavior observations, you believe the examinee may be able to improve upon the initial response. The responses marked with a **(Q)** in the manual must be queried.

If I query a response, and the examinee then gives another answer that is listed in the sample responses as a response that should be queried, I'm not sure what to do. Should I query more than once on verbal items if necessary?

Data on querying was extensively examined for the WAIS-IV. In general, if a **(Q)** appears next to a sample response, it indicates that examinees of varying ability levels gave that response, and additional

TABLE 2.1   Commonly used WAIS-IV prompts by subtest, in administration order

Situation	Prompt
Block Design	
On the sample item or Items 1–4, examinee attempts to replicate the model (including the side faces of the blocks) exactly	Point to the top faces of the blocks and say, **Only the tops of the blocks need to be the same.**
Examinee constructs his or her first rotated design	Rotate the blocks to the correct position and say, **See, it goes this way.**
Similarities	
Response is not clear, too vague to be easily scored, or is a sample response followed by a **(Q)**	Say, **What do you mean?** or **Tell me more about it** (or some other neutral inquiry).
Digit Span	
Examinee starts to respond before you've finished reading a trial	Present the rest of the trial and allow the examinee to respond. Award appropriate credit for the response and then say, **Remember to wait until I'm finished before you start.**
Examinee asks for you to repeat a trial	Say, **I cannot repeat the sequence. Just take your best guess.**
Examinee provides multiple responses or self-corrects after initial response, and it is unclear which response was intended	Say, **You said** [*insert examinee's response*] **and you said** [*insert examinee's response*]. **Which one did you mean?**
Examinee asks if response to a Digit Sequencing item should include repeated numbers	Say, **You may have to say the same number more than one time.**
Matrix Reasoning	
Examinee responds with any verbalization other than number of response option to indicate response	Say, **Show me.**
Examinee selects multiple response options for an item or self-corrects after initial response, and it is unclear which response was intended	Say, **You (said, pointed to)** [*insert examinee's response*] **and you (said, pointed to)** [*insert examinee's response*]. **Which one did you mean?**
Examinee has not responded in approximately 30 seconds (or an appropriately adjusted time period if items are getting more difficult and examinee is benefiting from additional time)	Say, **Do you have an answer?**

(*Continued*)

TABLE 2.1 Commonly used WAIS-IV prompts by subtest, in administration order—Cont'd

Situation	Prompt
Discontinue criterion has not been met, examinee has not responded after prompted, and reasonable amount of time has passed	Say, **Let's try another one.**

Vocabulary

Situation	Prompt
Picture Item: Examinee provides a marginal but appropriate response	Say, **Yes, but what else is it called?**
Picture Item: Examinee provides an appropriate response that is too general	Say, **Yes, but what kind of** [*insert examinee's response*] **is it?**
Picture Item: Examinee provides a functional description or uses hand gestures that are consistent with the picture	Say, **Yes, but what is it called?**
Verbal Item: Examinee mistakenly hears a different word and responds incorrectly	Say, **Listen carefully, what does** [*insert stimulus word*] **mean?**
Verbal Item: Response is not clear, too vague to be easily scored, or is a sample response followed by a **(Q)**	Say, **What do you mean?** or **Tell me more about it** (or some other neutral inquiry).
Verbal Item: Examinee does not respond orally or points to an object in the room	Say, **Tell me in words what that is.**

Arithmetic

Situation	Prompt
Examinee requests a second repetition of an item	Say, **I cannot repeat the item again.**
Examinee provides multiple responses or self-corrects after initial response, and it is unclear which response was intended	Say, **You said** [*insert examinee's response*] **and you said** [*insert examinee's response*]. **Which one did you mean?**

Symbol Search

Situation	Prompt
Examinee asks for an eraser, or what to do about an error	Say, **That's OK. Just keep working as fast as you can.**
Examinee marks target symbol as response	Say, **You should make your marks over here** (point across search group and NO box).
Examinee responds with anything other than slash mark	Point to error and say, **Draw one line through the symbols or NO boxes that you mark.**
Examinee omits item or starts completing page in reverse order	Say, **Do them in order. Don't skip any.** Point to first omitted item and say, **Do this one next.**
Examinee reaches end of page before time limit and forgets to turn to next page	Turn page for examinee and say, **Keep working as fast as you can.**

TABLE 2.1 Commonly used WAIS-IV prompts by subtest, in administration order—Cont'd

Situation	Prompt
Visual Puzzles	
Examinee says one or more pieces are turned relative to completed puzzle	Say, **You may have to turn a piece in your mind to make it fit the puzzle.**
Examinee responds with any verbalization other than numbers of response options to indicate responses	Say, **Show me.**
Examinee asks if responses must be provided in numerical order that corresponds to position in puzzle	Say, **The pieces you choose do not have to be in order.**
Examinee selects fewer than three response options	Say, **You need to choose three pieces to make the puzzle.**
Examinee selects greater than three response options	Say, **Which three pieces did you mean?**
Examinee has not responded when 10 seconds remain before item time limit expires	Say, **Do you have an answer?**
Examinee indicates not knowing the answer, or time limit has expired, and discontinue criterion has not been met	Say, **Let's try another one.**
Information	
Response is not clear, too vague to be easily scored, or is a sample response followed by a **(Q)**	Say, **What do you mean?** or **Tell me more about it** (or some other neutral inquiry).
Examinee gives contradictory verbal and non-verbal responses	Say, **Which one do you mean?**
Coding	
Examinee asks for an eraser, or what to do about an error	Say, **That's OK. Just keep working as fast as you can.**
Examinee omits item or starts completing row in reverse order	Say, **Do them in order. Don't skip any.** Point to first omitted item and say, **Do this one next.**
Letter–Number Sequencing	
Examinee starts to respond before you've finished reading a trial	Present the rest of the trial and allow the examinee to respond. Award appropriate credit for the response and then say, **Remember to wait until I'm finished before you start.**
Examinee asks for you to repeat a trial	Say, **I cannot repeat the sequence. Just take your best guess.**

(Continued)

TABLE 2.1 Commonly used WAIS-IV prompts by subtest, in administration order—Cont'd

Situation	Prompt
Examinee provides multiple responses to a trial or self-corrects after initial response, and it is unclear which response was intended	Say, **You said** [*insert examinee's response*] **and you said** [*insert examinee's response*]. **Which one did you mean?**

Figure Weights

Situation	Prompt
Examinee responds with any verbalization other than number of response option to indicate response	Say, **Show me.**
Examinee selects multiple response options or self-corrects after initial response, and it is unclear which response was intended	Say, **You (said, pointed to)** [*insert examinee's response*] **and you (said, pointed to)** [*insert examinee's response*]. **Which one did you mean?**
Examinee has not responded when 10 seconds remain before item time limit expires	Say, **Do you have an answer?**
Examinee indicates not knowing the answer, or time limit has expired, and discontinue criterion has not been met	Say, **Let's try another one.**

Comprehension

Situation	Prompt
Response is not clear, too vague to be easily scored, or is a sample response followed by a **(Q)**	Say, **What do you mean?** or **Tell me more about it** (or some other neutral inquiry).

Cancellation

Situation	Prompt
Examinee asks for an eraser, or what to do about an error	Say, **That's OK. Just keep working as fast as you can.**
Examinee responds with anything other than slash mark	Point to error and say, **Draw one line through the shapes that you mark.**
Examinee attempts to omit row or complete row in reverse order	Say, **Don't skip any rows and do them in order.** Point to first shape in row to be completed and say, **Start the row here.**
Examinee tries to reverse direction to mark missed target	Say, **You cannot go back to mark any shapes that you miss. Just keep working as fast as you can.**
Examinee attempts to complete half of 17 × 11 spread for test item (i.e., scans a row to the midline and then starts next row)	Say, **Work all the way across each row, starting here** (point to the first shape in the row to be completed) **and ending here** (point to the last shape in the row to be completed).
Examinee is unsure which was last shape scanned	Say, **Just take your best guess.**

TABLE 2.1   Commonly used WAIS-IV prompts by subtest, in administration order—Cont'd

Situation	Prompt
Picture Completion	
Examinee does not spontaneously point when providing verbal response that requires correct pointing response for clarification, or gives ambiguous or incomplete verbal response	Say, **Show me where you mean.**
Examinee names pictured object instead of naming or pointing to missing part	Say, **Yes, but what is missing?**
Examinee refers to or points to part that is off the page	Say, **A part is missing in the picture. What is it that is missing?**
Examinee refers to or points to unessential missing part	Say, **Yes, but what is the most important part missing?**

query may provide discriminating information. Thus, it may be best to query any response that has a **(Q)**, regardless of the number of times a query has been provided, if there is a sufficient level of rapport and engagement. Multiple queries are rare, but occur more often on the Comprehension subtest, which has items with multiple general concepts required for a 2-point response. Single queries occur more frequently. The number of times that queries can be given in general is not specified in the Administration and Scoring Manual. For Comprehension, the special guidelines for querying multiple general concept items should be reviewed carefully.

What should I do if the response my examinee gave doesn't match any of the sample responses?

To keep the sample responses user-friendly, not every response can be represented in the Administration and Scoring Manual. The sample responses include common responses or responses that serve to clarify scoring. To score a response that doesn't match any of the sample responses, first look for a sample response that is similar in nature to the examinee's response. Then, refer to the General Scoring Principles in the Administration and Scoring Manual. Consult with a colleague or supervisor if the scoring still seems unclear.

My examinee is color blind. Is that a factor in administration?

Individuals with color blindness were not excluded from the standardization samples. Every effort was made to ensure that items are free of bias against these individuals. Item color combinations were reviewed by experts in color blindness. Items were additionally administered to individuals with color blindness during the early stages of the test development process. Acetate overlays have been utilized so that test developers can understand the appearance of colors to these individuals. All items were printed in grayscale to simulate their appearance to those with monochromatic color perception. All items were additionally subjected to a computer program that simulates every type of color blindness, to ensure that the intensity and saturation of colors are not confused or contributing to ambiguity.

When should I administer a supplemental subtest?

Under certain conditions, a supplemental subtest can be substituted for a core subtest when deriving composite scores. At times, a core subtest can be spoiled or invalidated, which necessitates substitution. Clinical reasons may sometimes underlie the decision to substitute. This decision should be made prior to subtest administration, and not after scaled scores are derived. For example, an individual with motor impairment may be administered Figure Weights as a substitute for Block Design. After the subtests are given, generally the decisions about which subtests will be used to derive composite scores should not be changed. Do not give all the core and supplemental subtests and choose to use the highest subtest scaled scores when computing composite scores.

Supplemental subtests may sometimes be administered to provide additional clinical information on cognitive abilities, or related to referral questions. Figure Weights might be administered to provide additional information about non-verbal quantitative reasoning in a referral to assess for Mathematics Disorder. Administering supplemental subtests may also be informative when the scores within an index are widely discrepant. Additional information from the supplemental subtest can help tease out factors contributing to disparate results.

What are the limitations on substitution when deriving composite scores?

One supplemental subtest may be substituted per index score. However, a maximum of two supplemental subtests may be substituted for two out of the set of ten core subtests to retain the validity of the FSIQ. Refer to page 29 of the Administration and Scoring Manual for more information about supplemental subtest substitution.

Are there norms for individuals with certain clinical conditions, such as depression and Attention-Deficit/Hyperactivity Disorder (ADHD)?

Norms are scores that permit the user to evaluate examinee performance in relation to others of his or her same age. Norms are not provided for specific clinical conditions. They are developed using the normative sample. However, various special group studies were conducted to validate clinical utility. The results of the following studies are reported with a comparison of mean special group scores to the mean scores of demographically matched controls in Chapter 5 of the *WAIS-IV Technical and Interpretive Manual*: Intellectually Gifted, Intellectual Disability–Mild Severity, Intellectual Disability–Moderate Severity, Borderline Intellectual Functioning, Reading Disorder, Mathematics Disorder, ADHD, Traumatic Brain Injury, Autistic Disorder, Asperger's Disorder, Major Depressive Disorder, Mild Cognitive Impairment, and Probable Dementia of the Alzheimer's Type–Mild Severity.

What is the General Ability Index (GAI)? How do I derive it? Should I derive it?

What is the GAI? The GAI is a composite score based on the three Verbal Comprehension subtests and the three Perceptual Reasoning subtests that contribute to the VCI and the PRI. The GAI excludes contribution of Working Memory and Processing Speed subtests.

How do I derive the GAI? The GAI is the only score in the WAIS-IV that cannot be derived using the Administration and Scoring Manual. It does not appear on the Record Form or in the Administration and Scoring Manual because it is an optional score with limited applications. The GAI norms table and information about interpretation of the GAI appears in Appendix C of the Technical and Interpretive Manual. The norms table is similar in appearance and function to other composite norms tables.

Should I derive the GAI? Discussion of conditions for appropriate use of the WAIS-IV GAI appears in Appendix C of the Technical and Interpretive Manual, and in Chapters 1 and 3 of this book.

Do I need the Technical and Interpretive Manual to administer and score the WAIS-IV?

The Technical and Interpretive Manual is unnecessary for administration and scoring, unless the GAI will be derived. However, read the Technical and Interpretive Manual in its entirety. Chapter 2 is informative when attempting to understand the changes relevant to WAIS-IV administration and scoring.

I was able to locate the Qualitative Descriptors (i.e., Superior, High Average, Average, Low Average, etc.) for the composite scores in Chapter 6 of the Technical and Interpretive Manual, but where are the corresponding descriptors for individual subtest scaled scores?

Qualitative descriptors for the subtest scores do not appear in the manuals. It is not recommended to use the composite descriptors for the subtests, because the score ranges differ. Other references provide qualitative descriptors for subtests that are based on the standard deviations. Sattler (2008: 367–368) provides three- and five-category systems to describe subtest scaled scores. For three categories, a scaled score from 1 to 7 is described as a "weakness or poorly developed or below-average ability," with a corresponding percentile rank of 1–16; a scaled score from 8 to 12 is described as average, with a corresponding percentile rank of 25–75; and a scaled score of 13 to 19 is described as a "strength or well-developed or above average ability," with a corresponding percentile rank of 84–99. For five categories, a scaled score from 1 to 4 is described as "exceptional weakness, very poorly developed, or far below average ability," with a corresponding percentile rank of 1–2; a scaled score from 5 to 7 is described as "weakness, poorly developed, or below average," with a corresponding percentile rank of 5–16; a scaled score from 8 to 12 is described as "average ability," with a corresponding percentile rank of 25–75; a scaled score from 13 to 15 is described as "strength, well developed, or above average," with a corresponding percentile rank of 84–95; and a scaled score from 16 to 19 is described as "exceptional strength, very well developed, or superior" with a corresponding percentile rank of 98–99.

Why are the reference group scaled scores I obtained for a 20-year-old individual almost exactly the same as the regular scaled scores?

This occurs because the reference group scaled scores are based on individuals aged 20–34; therefore, the examinee's age group is included in the reference group.

CONCLUSION

Awareness of the practical aspects of WAIS-IV administration and scoring facilitates standard administration and efficient use of examiners; time. Ensuring that the practical aspects of WAIS-IV administration and scoring occur in a standard manner facilitates efficient and accurate assessment. To the extent that standard administration is followed, users can have more confidence that results, interpretation, and clinical impressions reflect an accurate estimate of the examinee's ability.

Appendix
What WAIS-III users should know about WAIS-IV

This Appendix provides an overview of changes to WAIS-IV subtests; administration and scoring. When evaluating the applicability of prior versions; accumulated validity evidence to the new edition, it is helpful to consider the changes to the instrument (Sattler, 2008), such as administration and scoring changes to retained subtests and revisions to test structure (see Chapter 1). Awareness of changes facilitates an efficient transition between the WAIS-III and the WAIS-IV.

VERBAL COMPREHENSION SCALE

General information

Unlike the Wechsler Adult Intelligence Scale – Third Edition (WAIS-III; Wechsler, 1997), no Verbal IQ is available on the WAIS-IV, for reasons discussed in Chapter 1 of this book. Administering only three Verbal Comprehension subtests (i.e., Similarities, Vocabulary, and Information) permits derivation of the Verbal Comprehension Index (VCI) and provides all Verbal Comprehension subtest scores necessary to calculate the Full Scale IQ (FSIQ). Comprehension need not be administered unless subtest substitution is planned, one of the core subtests is invalidated, or additional clinical information provided by the subtest is desired.

Sample responses for retained items have been changed; WAIS-III users therefore may wish to practice using the new sample responses prior to the first administration. The sets of sample responses have been expanded and reorganized to facilitate more precise and quick scoring (as suggested in Slate et al., 1993). They have been moved and regrouped to increase user-friendliness, and more logic governs the groups of responses that appear together on single lines. Higher-level responses and more common responses have been relocated to the upper left-hand portion of the sets wherever possible. Queried responses also appear at the upper left of the set of responses for each point value. Responses have also changed point values in a few cases, due to the overall changes in the set of responses received from the WAIS-IV samples.

Discontinue rules for all Verbal Comprehension subtests on the WAIS-IV involve fewer consecutive scores of 0 than on the WAIS-III. These changes were made to minimize examinee frustration and fatigue and maximize efficiency in the test session.

Subtest-specific information

Similarities

Similarities administration is similar to the prior edition, with some changes and exceptions. A sample item has been added to provide practice completing an item; it should be administered to all examinees. There are several new items with which to become familiar. Sample responses for many of the retained items have changed, so WAIS-III users may find it is helpful to practice using the sample responses a few times prior to their first administration of the WAIS-IV. The discontinue criterion has been decreased from four to three consecutive scores of 0. The examinee can now, as a result of the shorter discontinue rule, meet the discontinue criterion within the reversal items.

Vocabulary

Vocabulary administration is similar to that of the prior edition, with some changes to note. There are a number of new items with which to become familiar. The point values awarded to some sample responses for retained items have changed. Unlike the WAIS-III, for which some verbally-presented items were also scored using a 0- or 1-point rubric, all verbal items are now scored 0, 1, or 2 points to provide increased differentiation. Item numbers have been moved from the examinee stimulus pages to the pages that face the examiner in the Stimulus Book. This change was designed to decrease the likelihood that examinees will detect a reversal if it occurs: The examinee receives fewer potential cues about performance, and effort and rapport is more readily preserved. The most noticeable change is that made to the discontinue criterion: It has been reduced from six to three consecutive scores of 0. As with Similarities, examinees may meet the discontinue criterion within the reversal items.

Information

Some changes to the Information subtest bear mentioning. All items now contain 0-point sample responses to clarify the scoring rules. Become familiar with those 0-point responses that should be queried to provide examinees with opportunities to improve their responses. There is a slight increase in the number of specific prompts to clarify vague responses on some items. The discontinue criterion has been decreased from six to three consecutive scores of 0. Examinees can now meet the discontinue criterion upon reversal if they score 0 points on the first item and each of the two reversal items.

Comprehension

Comprehension administration remains largely unchanged, but item content and scoring is noticeably different. All retained items were revised. In some cases, revisions were made to the item wording to improve clarity. The sample responses were reorganized and expanded, and in some cases the general concepts have changed noticeably. Some new items appear throughout the subtest. A few more items involving proverb interpretation were added. These proverbs are antiquities translated from Eastern and South-American cultures. They are relatively easy to score, and appear earlier in the item sequence than on the WAIS-III to introduce examinees to the item type before the items become more difficult. The discontinue criterion has been reduced from four to three consecutive scores of 0. The examinee can now meet the discontinue criterion by scoring 0 points on the first item and each of the two reversal items.

PERCEPTUAL REASONING SCALE

General information

Similar to the Verbal IQ, the Performance IQ is not available on the WAIS-IV, for reasons discussed in Chapters 1 and 3 of this book. Administering only three Perceptual Reasoning subtests (i.e., Block Design, Matrix Reasoning, and Visual Puzzles) permits derivation of the Perceptual Reasoning Index (PRI) and provides all Perceptual Reasoning subtest scores necessary to calculate the FSIQ. Figure Weights and Picture Completion need not be administered unless subtest substitution is planned, one of the core subtests is invalidated, or additional clinical information provided by the subtest is desired.

Examiners experienced with the WAIS-III will note that the elimination of the manipulatives associated with Picture Arrangement (cards) and Object Assembly (puzzle pieces) results in reduced opportunities for item set-up and administration errors, as well as decreased kit weight. These subtests also involved greater potential for scoring errors (e.g., clerical errors in recording time-bonus points, incorrectly recording responses). Visual Puzzles and Figure Weights still require the use of a stopwatch and a Stimulus Book, but are quicker and simpler to administer and score.

Similar to the WAIS-IV Verbal Comprehension subtest discontinue rules, WAIS-IV Perceptual Reasoning subtest discontinue rules also involve fewer consecutive scores of 0 than on WAIS-III. On the subtests noted in the following section, a discontinue criterion now can be met within the reversal items (those prior to the start point).

Subtest-specific information

Block Design

WAIS-III users will note several changes to this subtest. Because Block Design is the first subtest in administration order, changes to the materials should be noted prior to administration. The Stimulus Book has been modified for the WAIS-IV, so that sections are opened and pages are turned toward the examinee. This modification places the pages to be turned in easier reach. The Stimulus Book is positioned differently as a result: Ensure that the coil-bound edge is oriented toward the examinee. Then, grasp the subtest tab and open it toward the examinee.

There are changes to item content and administration procedures as well. A sample item administered to all examinees has been added to introduce the task. All items prior to the start point, including the sample item, are now presented with both a model and a Stimulus Book picture to simplify administration, reduce the difficulty of the easiest items, and prepare the examinee for picture-only items. The proper placement of the model and Stimulus Book together should be reviewed (see Figure 3.1 in the Administration and Scoring Manual), as the combination is used on more items relative to the WAIS-III and varies for a right- versus a left-handed examinee. Start point and subsequent items are presented using only a Stimulus Book picture. Two four-block diamond items have been added between the four-block square items and nine-block square items, to ease the transition between four and nine blocks. Become familiar with these new designs to permit quick scoring. The number of items with time-bonus points has been reduced from eight to six, which simplifies scoring. The discontinue criterion has been reduced from three to two consecutive scores of 0. Monitor item scores closely to discontinue when appropriate. Also note that the discontinue criterion now can be met within the reversal items.

WAIS-III users will also notice a new process score, Block Design No Time Bonus (BDN), appears on the WAIS-IV. This process score is calculated by awarding only four points for correctly completed items for which time-bonus points are possible. A discrepancy comparison with the Block Design subtest scaled score may be calculated, if examination of time-bonus points; impact on examinee scores is of interest.

Matrix Reasoning

WAIS-III users will notice some changes to this subtest. The number of item types was reduced from four to two, and more explicit teaching is provided for the two item types. A new prompt, **"Do you have an answer?"** can be provided to ensure administration progresses at a steady pace. The timing of the prompt is adjusted accordingly if the examinee benefits from additional time. The discontinue criterion has been reduced from four to three consecutive scores of 0. Note that the discontinue criterion now can be met within the reversal items.

Visual Puzzles and Figure Weights

Visual Puzzles and Figure Weights, both new Perceptual Reasoning subtests, are relatively easy to administer and score. Read the section in the main body of the chapter to become familiar with these subtests. Do *not* administer Figure Weights to individuals aged 70–90. Norms are not available for these ages.

Picture Completion

There are some key changes to this subtest to note. A sample item was added to allow practice in completing an item prior to test item administration. There are three prompts that are given one time only during administration of Picture Completion. These now appear on the Record Form, and can therefore be provided more quickly and accurately, and without turning back to the manual page where the prompts appear. The discontinue criterion has been reduced from five to four consecutive scores of 0, and now can be met if the examinee scores 0 points on the first item and each of the three reversal items.

WORKING MEMORY SCALE

General information

Administering only two subtests (Digit Span and Arithmetic) permits derivation of the Working Memory Index (WMI) and provides all Working Memory subtest scores necessary to calculate the FSIQ. Unlike the WAIS-III, Letter–Number Sequencing need not be administered unless substitution of that subtest is planned, one of the core subtests is invalidated, or additional clinical information provided by that subtest is desired.

Subtest-specific information

Digit Span

WAIS-III users will note a number of changes to this subtest. Rhyming digits within a single trial were eliminated wherever possible, so these observations may be more useful than on prior editions. Digit Span Backward no longer has a three-digit sample trial: all sample trials are two digits in length. This change eliminates the awkwardness of moving from the three-digit sample trial to two-digit test item trials. Digit Span Backward now contains a total of six trials that are two digits in length (i.e., a sample item with two trials, and two test items with two trials each). This change provides a better floor for Digit Span Backward. All of these trials should be administered, as the difficulty of each trial varies. Digit Span Sequencing is new for the WAIS-IV. Read the section corresponding to Digit Span in the main body of the chapter to become familiar with this part of the subtest.

WAIS-III users will also notice six process scores for Digit Span appear on the WAIS-IV. Digit Span Forward (DSF), Digit Span Backward (DSB), Digit Span Sequencing (DSS) permit examination of performance separately on the three parts, as well as discrepancy comparisons among the three parts. Longest Digit Span Forward (LDSF), Longest Digit Span Backward (LDSB), and Longest Digit Span Sequencing (LDSS) permit examination of maximum performance on each task relative to the normative sample.

Arithmetic

A number of modifications have been made to this subtest. A sample item that should be administered to all examinees has been added to provide practice in completing an item. Pictures, rather than blocks, are now used as stimuli for the easiest items. The time limit has been made uniform for all items, and time-bonus points were eliminated. All examinees now are instructed explicitly in the subtest introduction that one repetition request is permitted per item. This change was made in response to concerns that personality traits could unfairly advantage some examinees, as explicit instruction about requesting repetitions was not previously provided. The discontinue criterion has been reduced from four to three consecutive scores of 0, and the examinee now can meet the discontinue criterion within the reversal items.

Items involving currency or the English system of measurement were modified to improve the likelihood that they would remain contemporary. References to currency or measurement systems were changed to other units, although the mental arithmetic required for many items remains consistent with the prior edition. The rising price of gasoline and other changes related to the consumer price index are therefore no longer an issue. Furthermore, this change makes the subtest more internationally portable, and less likely to unfairly advantage examinees raised in the United States of America.

Names from other cultures used in two of the Arithmetic items were selected based on their length (all names are a single syllable), as well as consistency and ease of pronunciation in common use. Diversity was also a consideration. If it is thought that the use of one of these names has caused the examinee to respond incorrectly, it is acceptable to re-administer the item following administration of all subtests using an alternate name to test the limits. Because all names are monosyllabic, it is best to select a name that adheres to this specification. The differences can be described in the psychological report; however, do not award credit for the item.

Letter–Number Sequencing

Be aware of the following changes before administering Letter–Number Sequencing. Norms are not available for ages 70–90, so do not administer to examinees in this age range. Teaching the task now occurs in stages. Previously, examinees were simultaneously taught to repeat numbers before letters, and to sequence the numbers in ascending order and letters alphabetically. This approach may have confused some examinees, as the first two sample trials were two characters long (one letter and one number) and no numerical or alphabetical sequencing was necessary. Sample Item A now is used to teach the examinee to repeat numbers before letters, and is followed by test items based only on this portion of the directions. Sample Item B now is used to teach examinees to sequence numbers in ascending order and letters alphabetically. This staged approach to teaching decreased the occurrence of examinees repeating the letters before the numbers.

Relative to the WAIS-III version of this subtest, there are more trials with fewer letters and numbers, but all must be administered. This change ensured an adequate range of scores, and reduced the difficulty of easy items. Trials that include the same number of characters have different levels of difficulty, based on the selection of numbers and letters from an earlier position in the number series or alphabet (e.g., the numbers 1–5 and the letters A–D). WAIS-III users will note that rhyming numbers and letters within a single trial were eliminated wherever possible, to permit more accurate observations of misheard stimuli.

An new optional process score can be derived to inform Letter–Number Sequencing interpretation. The Longest Letter–Number Sequence (LLNS) process score permits examination of maximum performance on the task relative to the normative sample. It can be particularly informative in cases where performance is variable (e.g., the examinee misses one or two trials on each item or span length).

PROCESSING SPEED SCALE

General information

Administering only two subtests (Symbol Search and Coding) permits derivation of the Processing Speed Index (PSI) and provides all Processing Speed subtest scores necessary to calculate the FSIQ. Cancellation need not be administered unless substitution of that subtest is planned, one of the core subtests is invalidated, or additional clinical information provided by that subtest is desired.

Subtest-specific information

Symbol Search

The most noticeable change to Symbol Search is that the symbols are bolder and enlarged to reduce visual acuity concerns. Another obvious change is that the "YES" box that appeared on the WAIS-III version of this subtest does not appear on the WAIS-IV version. Examinees now mark either the matching shape in the search group, or the "NO" box. This change permits qualitative observation of errors, and prompted some modifications to the verbatim instructions to examinees.

The verbatim instructions have been altered substantially due to these changes. Study the demonstration items and memorize the answers to the sample items prior to administering the subtest to prevent fumbling necessary feedback when administering the new version for the first time.

A change in scoring procedure was also made due to the change from dichotomous scoring to multiple-choice scoring. The Scoring Key utilizes a different format to accommodate the new administration format. It reproduces the test items in miniature, with the correct responses appearing in bold. Unlike the WAIS-III version, the key is no longer placed over each page to score. When the Response Booklet is open, the Scoring Key is placed covering the page on the right to score the page on the left, and is aligned with the item rows. The key is slid over to cover the page on the left when scoring the page on the right.

Coding (formerly Digit Symbol–Coding)

WAIS-III users will note a few changes to this subtest. The larger vertical space between the key at the top of the page and the items will decrease the chance that left-handed individuals will block the key from their view while completing the subtest, although this still can occur. The numbers have been randomized, and now appear an equal number of times across each row. Process observations regarding increasing speed of completion across the subtest are therefore more meaningful than on prior editions, as examinees are exposed to each paired associate an equal number of times as the subtest progresses. The bolder numbers and symbols reduce concerns with visual acuity during administration.

The optional Incidental Learning and Copy procedures from the WAIS-III do not appear on the WAIS-IV. The WAIS-III Digit Symbol–Copy procedure can still be used with the WAIS-III norms if a measure of simple graphomotor speed is desired. Furthermore, Sattler and Ryan's *Assessment with the WAIS-IV* (2009) provides versions of the Recall and Copy procedures that can be used to obtain clinical data for qualitative observations of incidental learning and graphomotor speed.

Cancellation

Cancellation is a new subtest for the WAIS-IV. Read the section on Cancellation in the main body of the chapter to become familiar with this subtest. Do not administer Cancellation to individuals aged 70–90. Norms are not available for these ages.

References

Alfonso, V. C., Johnson, A., Patinella, L., & Rader, D. E. (1998). Common WISC-III examiner errors: evidence from graduate students in training. *Psychology in the Schools, 35*, 119–125.

Baddeley, A., & Lewis, V. (1984). When does rapid presentation enhance digit span? *Bulletin of the Psychonomic Society, 22*, 403–405.

Engle, R. W., & Marshall, K. (1983). Do developmental changes in digit span result from acquisition strategies? *Journal of Experimental Child Psychology, 36*, 429–436.

Kaufman, A. S., & Lichtenberger, E. O. (1999). *Essentials of WAIS-III Assessment*. New York, NY: Wiley.

Lacritz, L. H., & Cullum, C. M. (2003). The WAIS-III and WMS-III: Practical issues and frequently asked questions. In D. S. Tulsky, D. H. Saklofske, G. J. Chelune & R. K. Heaton et al. (Eds.), *Clinical Interpretation of the WAIS-III and WMS-III* (pp. 491–532). New York, NY: Academic Press.

Lichtenberger, E. O., & Kaufman, A. S. (2009). *Essentials of WAIS-IV Assessment*. New York, NY: Wiley.

Loe, S. A., Kadlubek, R. M., & Marks, W. J. (2007). Administration and scoring errors on the WISC-IV among graduate student examiners. *Journal of Psychoeducational Assessment, 25*, 237–247.

Moon, G. W., Blakey, W. A., Gorsuch, R. L., & Fantuzzo, J. W. (1991). Frequent WAIS-R administration errors: An ignored source of inaccurate measurement. *Professional Psychology: Research and Practice, 22*, 256–258.

Sattler, J. M. (2008). *Assessment of Children: Cognitive Foundations* (5th ed.). San Diego, CA: Author.

Sattler, J. M., & Ryan, J. J. (2009). *Assessment with the WAIS-IV*. San Diego, CA: Jerome M. Sattler.

Slate, J. R., Jones, C. H., Murray, R. A., & Coulter, C. (1993). Evidence that practitioners err in administering and scoring the WAIS-R. *Measurement and Evaluation in Counseling and Development, 25*, 156–166.

Wechsler, D. (1997). *Wechsler Adult Intelligence Scale* (3rd ed.). San Antonio, TX: Psychological Corporation.

Wechsler, D. (2008). *Wechsler Adult Intelligence Scale* (4th ed.). San Antonio, TX: Pearson.

Theoretical, Empirical and Clinical Foundations of the WAIS-IV Index Scores

Lawrence G. Weiss[1], *Donald H. Saklofske*[2],
Diane L. Coalson[1]*, and Susan Engi Raiford*[1]

[1] Pearson Assessment, San Antonio, Texas, USA
[2] Division of Applied Psychology, University of Calgary,
Calgary, Alberta, Canada

INTRODUCTION

In a major theoretical shift from the original Wechsler model, the WAIS-IV index scores have become the primary level of clinical interpretation. Some readers may recall that the original Wechsler model of intelligence was based on a two-part structure comprising the Verbal IQ (VIQ) and Performance IQ (PIQ). As described in Chapter 1, the Wechsler theoretical model now includes verbal conceptualization, perceptual reasoning, working memory, and processing speed. This shift began in 1991, when the WISC-III became the first of the Wechsler scales to offer these four factor-based index scores as an optional alternative to the traditional VIQ/PIQ structure. The WAIS-III followed suit in 1997, with the same dual model in which the four index scores were offered but considered supplemental to main VIQ and PIQ scores. At that time, working memory was referred to as "freedom from distractibility" – an older term that reflected the incomplete understanding of the construct at that time. In 2003, however, the WISC-IV cut the proverbial apron strings to VIQ and PIQ, eliminating them from the test, changing the name of the Freedom from Distractibility Index to the Working Memory Index to reflect the improved understanding of that construct, changing the name of the Perceptual Organization Index to the Perceptual Reasoning Index to reflect the increased focus on fluid reasoning among the newly created perceptual subtests, and elevating the four index scores to the primary role of clinical interpretation. The WAIS-IV followed suit in 2008, thereby completing the long planned theoretical transformation of the Wechsler series of tests by their scientific caretakers at PsychCorp/Pearson.

To be fair to Dr Wechsler's legacy, however, his model has always included subtests which researchers now understand as measures of working memory and processing speed. These were buried inside the VIQ and PIQ, depending on whether the stimuli and response processes were verbal or visual-perceptual, respectively. Still, Dr Wechsler knew that mental manipulation of numbers was importantly related to intelligence, and that is why he included the Arithmetic and Digit Span subtests in the VIQ. Similarly, he knew that quick visual scanning played an important role in cognition, and so he included the Digit Symbol–Coding subtests as part of the PIQ.

Contemporary researchers have developed well-articulated modern theories about the underlying neurocognitive processes taped by these tasks and how they are related to intelligence. Arithmetic and Digit Span are now understood as tapping working memory. Coding, or Digit Symbol as it was originally named, is now understood as a measure of cognitive processing speed. As more has been learned about these areas, the Wechsler tests have changed over time such that these constructs have been disentangled from VIQ and PIQ, and stand alone. Furthermore, new tasks, such as Letter Number Sequencing and Cancellation, were added to elaborate the assessment of working memory and processing speed respectively. Also, Digit Span was significantly revised by adding the digit sequencing items to make it a better measure of working memory based on our current understanding of that construct.

Similarly, although the term "fluid reasoning" was not used in Dr Wechsler's time, several of the Wechsler subtests are believed to be related to it (i.e., Similarities, Block Design). As fluid reasoning has been further researched, new subtests have been developed that measure this construct more directly, such as Matrix Reasoning (which first appeared in WISC-III and was then added to WISC-IV, WAIS-III and WAIS-IV), Picture Concepts (which first appeared in WISC-IV and was then added to WPPSI-III), and Figure Weights and Visual Puzzles (which appear for the first time in WAIS-IV).

Without Dr Wechsler's far-reaching clinical insights, the field of intellectual assessment would not be as it is today. However, the WAIS-IV is a very different test than the one that Dr Wechsler left us – one that builds upon multiple modern theories of cognitive neuroscience informed by ongoing clinical and neuropsychological research.

THE WAIS-IV INDEX SCORES

Verbal Comprehension Index

The VCI reflects an individual's ability to comprehend verbal stimuli, reason with semantic material, and communicate thoughts and ideas with words. Such abilities are imperative for intelligent functioning in modern society.

Although the VCI includes tasks that require prior knowledge of certain words and information, it would be a mistake to consider this index only as a measure of words and facts taught in school. Clearly, some base knowledge of words must be assumed in order to measure verbal reasoning – after all, one could not measure verbal reasoning without using words. Barring an unusually limiting environment, however, performance on these tasks reflects individual's; ability to grasp verbally presented facts typically available in the world around them, reason with semantic constructs, and to express their reasoning with words. Crystallized knowledge is the background within which these abilities are assessed. It is defined as the breadth and depth of a person's acquired knowledge of a culture, and the effective application of this knowledge. This store of primarily verbal or language-based knowledge may represent those abilities that have been developed largely through the investment of other abilities during educational and general life experience (McGrew & Flanagan, 1998: 20).

The Vocabulary (VC) and Information (IN) subtests require that a fact or the meaning of a word was learned, can be recalled, and expressed coherently. There is no apparent demand for reason in this subtest; it is essentially the case that one "knows" the word. However, VC is one of the highest "g" loaded subtests, and one of the best predictors of overall intelligence. We believe this is for two reasons: first, higher-order thinking requires analysis of increasingly differentiated verbal constructs; and second, more pieces of related information can be chunked into a coherent whole for quicker processing. Individuals with larger vocabularies have words to describe increasingly differentiated views of the world. Second, they can chunk larger concepts into a single word for more efficient reasoning. While they may have enjoyed a more enriched learning environment, they must also be able to apply their knowledge appropriately. Knowledge of advanced vocabulary words requires the individual to accurately comprehend nuances of situations – which requires a higher level of intelligence. For example, do we say that the AIDS vaccine was "discovered" or "invented" – what is the difference? As another example, consider that to use the word "obviate" appropriately in conversation, one must first perceive that some action will make another action unnecessary. Finally, how intelligent does one need to be to tell the difference between "placating" and "appeasing" another person? Thus, crystallized knowledge is not a simple matter of reciting learned facts or definitions of words, but the ability to acquire higher levels of crystallized knowledge reflects the intelligence necessary to comprehend that knowledge and, furthermore, appropriate application of the stored information requires advanced comprehension of the situation.

The Similarities (SI) and Comprehension (CO) subtests also require a base knowledge of information; however, they are considered more fluid tasks because they involve some direct reasoning with crystallized words and facts. For example, CO items typically assume certain facts are known (e.g., cars must have license plates), but the reasons for these facts are typically not taught directly in school. The patient must engage in reasoning to answer the question (e.g., Why must cars have license plates?). The Similarities (SI) subtest asks how two words representing objects or concepts are alike. The two words are expected to be known, but their relationship is not usually taught directly in most educational settings and must be reasoned. Consider, for example, the patient's response process when the examiner asks how "war" and "peace" are alike. A correct response requires that both concepts have been acquired and stored in long-term memory, and that the patient be able to access that knowledge from semantic memory upon demand. Once these words are recalled, the patient can begin the reasoning process to determine how they are similar. This reasoning process appears to take place within a temporary working memory space. The ability to reason in this way may be related to a certain type of working memory capacity and the efficiency with which ideas are worked in this transient memory space before the trace fades – as will be elaborated further in subsequent sections of this chapter. Similar issues are in play with Comprehension (CO).

The SI and CO subtests require a higher level of reasoning for successful performance than do the VC and IN subtests. Patients with deficits in crystallized knowledge and/or retrieval from long-term memory of previously acquired information may score higher on SM and CO than on VC and IN if they have adequate verbal reasoning ability. Conversely, patients with an age-appropriate knowledge base that is readily accessible but who have deficits in higher-order categorization of abstract verbal concepts may show the reverse score pattern.

Recall that a low score on an intelligence test such as the WAIS-IV may reflect low ability, a lack of opportunity to develop particular abilities, or some kind of "interference" that compromises the acquisition or expression of particular abilities (e.g., traumatic brain injury, mild cognitive impairment, aphasia, epilepsy, etc.). Prior to making an interpretation of low verbal ability, the psychologist should also ask: was the knowledge encoded but cannot now be recalled (for several possible reasons), or was it never acquired in the first place? One useful methodology for addressing this issue is the "recognition paradigm." All of the WAIS-IV VC subtests involve free recall, which is a much more difficult cognitive task than cued recall or recognition. Some patients who answered incorrectly because they could not retrieve the information from long-term storage may more readily recall the information if given a clue, or may recognize the correct information from a set of possible answers. We can see this in our everyday lives when someone tries to recall the name of a colleague by using clues such as which university she is from, or the letter-sound her name begins with, but once a possible name is suggested it is instantly recognized as correct or incorrect. In these situations, it may be instructive to consider the patient's responses to the California Verbal Learning Test – Second Edition (Delis, Kramer, Kaplan & Ober, 2000), which requires the patient to learn a list of words over five trials with immediate and delayed recall followed by cued recall and recognition. In this way, the examiner can explore if the incorrect responses were a function of lack of knowledge or of lack of access to knowledge previously learned and stored in the semantic lexicon. Clearly, this makes a critical difference in interpretation, and is one reason we describe intelligence test scores in terms of current functioning rather than immutable capacity.

Perceptual Reasoning Index

The construct measured by the PRI has changed from primarily perceptual organization with some fluid reasoning in WAIS-III to primarily fluid reasoning with some perceptual organization in WAIS-IV (Wechsler, 2008). As described in Chapter 1, in order to make room for newly created fluid reasoning subtests, the traditional Picture Arrangement and Object Assembly subtests were removed from the current edition and Picture Completion was made supplemental. Block Design and Matrix Reasoning remain in the core PRI, and Visual Puzzles (VP) was created as a new core subtest. In addition, Figure Weights (FW) was created as a new supplemental subtest.

Figure Weights was designed to measure quantitative and analogical reasoning. Quantitative reasoning tasks involve reasoning processes that can be expressed mathematically, emphasizing either inductive or deductive logic. While the solution to each FW item can be expressed with algebraic equations, there is no task requirement to do so – thus eliminating the demand for acquired knowledge of advanced mathematical equations. Although Figure Weights involves working memory, it reduces this involvement relative to typical quantitative tasks (e.g., mental arithmetic) through the visual presentation of items in a stimulus book which allows the patient to continually refresh stimuli held in working memory while solving the problem.

Visual Puzzles was designed to measure non-verbal fluid reasoning and the ability to analyze and synthesize abstract visual material. Successful performance requires the ability to maintain a visual image in mind temporarily while mentally rotating, inverting and otherwise manipulating that image and matching the resulting percept to a visual target. Like many tasks on the Wechsler series of tests, VP requires the integration of multiple related cognitive processes, including visual perception, simultaneous processing, working memory, spatial visualization, and spatial manipulation.

While it would seem ideal to assess fluid reasoning alone without tapping other domains of cognition, this is patently impossible. Reasoning must take place on some subject. Just like verbal reasoning can not be assessed without invoking verbal stimuli and therefore some base of crystallized knowledge, non-verbal fluid reasoning cannot occur in a sterile vacuum. Once any type of stimulus is presented, other factors come into play. Some may view matrix analogies tasks as pure measures of fluid reasoning; however, even the presentation of an abstract visual image that has no known meaning and cannot be verbally encoded will invoke multiple cognitive domains as described above in the discussion of VP. Even though factor-analytic studies show that each task loads primarily on one factor, there are often minor loadings on other factors. Indeed, it may be that the successful integration of multiple cognitive processes to solve a novel problem is the essence of fluid reasoning.

This is an opportune spot to briefly mention the relationship of other cognitive functions with WAIS-IV scores. Organization, planning, and other executive functions can impact performance on various WAIS-IV subtests. However, if we move away from the focus on test performance and consider intelligence in the broader ecology of society, we can at least say that executive functions influence the expression of intelligent behavior at work and in life. Clearly, we all know bright, well-educated colleagues whose disorganization and poor planning interfere with their ability to achieve otherwise obtainable career goals. Similarly, many of us can think of friends and relatives whose diligence at work has begot considerable success even though they seem no smarter than the rest of us. But are executive functions really something apart from intelligence – simply mediators of how well a person utilizes his or her intelligence in the larger world outside the testing room? To what extent might executive functions be an integral part of an ecological view of intelligence? To what extent might executive functions even influence the growth of other intellectual abilities during the developmental years? More to the point, what are the theoretical, clinical, and empirical relationships of intelligence and executive function?

Although the term *executive function* (EF) was not coined at the time, Dr Wechsler knew that such abilities were importantly related to intelligence because his original tests included tasks that we would call executive functioning today. The WISC-R and WISC-III included a Mazes subtest that was widely believed to measure planning and organization. It was an optional subtest, however, and rarely used by practitioners because of the long administration time. For this and other reasons, Mazes was dropped from the WISC-III, but the assessment of organization and planning abilities was never replaced by another subtest in the Wechsler model.

Executive functions, as currently conceptualized, involve more than planning and organization. Although there is no formally agreed-upon definition, executive functioning may be tentatively defined as the effective integration of multiple cognitive processes relevant to goal-directed behavior (Salthouse, 2009). A list of specific cognitive processes included under this umbrella term was offered by Cheung, Mitsis, and Halperin (2004) as planning, decision-making, judgment, working memory, set-shifting, and cognitive flexibility that enables one to orient toward the future and self-regulate toward a goal. Chan, Shum, Toulopoulou, and Chen (2008) similarly offered a wide range of cognitive processes and behavioral competencies, including verbal reasoning, problem-solving, planning, sequencing, the ability to sustain attention, resistance to inter-ference, utilization of feedback, multi-tasking, cognitive flexibility, and the ability to deal with novelty.

Salthouse (2009) directly addressed the theoretically important question of the relationship of EF and IQ by studying the pattern of convergent and divergent validity between fluid reasoning tasks and three key measures of executive functions: inhibition control, switching, and updating in non-clinical samples. Inhibition control involves the ability to focus attention on relevant information and processes while inhibiting irrelevant ones. Switching is described as scheduling processes in complex tasks which require switching of focused attention between tasks. Updating involves checking the contents of working memory to determine the next step in a sequential task and then updating the contents. Salthouse reported that convergent validity among these measures was not significantly higher than the typical correlations among all cognitive abilities – reflecting a lack of homogeneity of the EF construct. More importantly, he showed evidence of divergent validity for inhibition control and fluid reasoning measures, but not for measures of switching or updating with fluid reasoning. Salt-house concluded that the EF construct needs better specification before it can finally be determined whether it is a useful construct distinct from fluid reasoning.

It is unknown if evidence of divergent validity between EF and fluid reasoning would emerge in specific clinically disordered samples, or if there is divergent validity between EF and measures of crystallized intel-ligence. Also, the Salthouse study did not address the emotion-regulation aspects of EF. However, his controversial study is important, because it raises a key theoretical question about the construct overlap between fluid intelligence and executive functions. Are executive functions really something different and apart from fluid intelligence? What would a structural model of general cognitive ability look like that included both EF and the four major domains in the contemporary Wechsler model of intelligence as expressed in WISC-IV and WAIS-IV? Perhaps more precisely, which facets of EF have substantial construct overlap with which domains of intelligence, and which EF functions serve as moderators or mediators of these domains of intelligence or the dynamic interactions among them? As may become clearer in subsequent sections of this chapter, several aspects of EF are part and parcel of working memory, and working memory is closely related to fluid reasoning.

Taking all this into account, practitioners should consider the effect of a patient's executive processes on intellectual performance by including a measure of executive functioning as part of any comprehensive evaluation of cognitive abilities. The *WAIS-IV Technical and Interpretative Manual* provides a correlation study with the Delis–Kaplan Executive Function System (Delis, Kaplan, & Kramer, 2001) which includes nine well-known measures of various executive functions.

Working Memory Index

The WMI measures attention, concentration, and working memory. Working memory is the ability to hold information in mind temporarily while performing some operation or manipulation with that information, or engaging in an interfering task, and then accurately reproducing the updated information or correctly acting on it. Working memory can be thought of as mental control (an executive process) involving reasonably higher-order tasks (rather than rote tasks), and it presumes attention and concentration. As described by Jonides, Lacey, and Nee (2005: 2):

> Working memory is a system that can store a small amount of information briefly, keeping that information quickly accessible and available for transformation by rules and strategies, while updating it frequently.

Baddeley (2003) has developed the seminal model of the working memory system. He proposes a phonological loop and a visual–spatial sketch pad in which verbal and visual stimuli respectively are stored and refreshed, and a central executive that controls attention directed toward these sources. A fourth component, known as the *episodic buffer*, was subsequently included in this model. This buffer is assumed to be attentionally controlled by the central executive, and to be accessible to conscious awareness. Baddeley regards the episodic buffer as a crucial feature of the capacity of working memory to act as a global workspace that is accessed by conscious awareness. When working memory requires information from long-term storage, it may be "downloaded" into the episodic buffer rather then simply activated within long-term memory (Baddeley, 2003).

Models of working memory and their neural underpinnings are still being actively researched and refined, and the associated terminology will continue to evolve for some time. The term *registration* is used herein to convey the process by which stimuli are taken in and maintained in immediate memory. Capacity for registering information in immediate memory can be measured by the length of the person's immediate forward span. *Mental manipulation* implies updating or transforming information active in immediate memory. This can be as simple as rehearsal and chunking of information to keep it active, continuously refreshing the contents of the storage buffer based on new input, or involve abstract manipulation of the stored content. The precise point in this process at which working memory resources are invoked is debatable. For example, although attending to, storing and repeating a license-plate number may appear only to involve short-term memory, the role of working memory may enter the picture when there is interference from other sources, or a mnemonic is employed to assist in remembering the alphanumeric characters, or the observer is also asked to recall the type of car. Thus, these processes may be more of a continuum, as the point at which one moves from passive registration of auditory stimuli to active strategies for maintenance is not always clear.

The WMI composite consists of two primary subtests, Digit Span (DS) and Arithmetic (AR), and the supplemental Letter–Number Sequencing (LN). The DS subtest has changed substantially from previous Wechsler tests in order to reflect advances in the understanding of working memory. In WAIS-IV, Digit Span Sequencing (DSS) was added to the traditional Digit Span Forward (DSF) and Digit Span Backward (DSB) tasks. This was done because of concern that DSF was a measure of short-term and not working memory, based on research which indicated different cognitive demands for DSF and DFB (Reynolds, 1997). Digit Span Forward (DSF) requires initial registration of the verbal stimuli – a prerequisite for mental manipulation of the stimuli. In some cases, DSF also requires auditory rehearsal to maintain the memory trace until the item presentation is concluded. To the extent that longer spans of digits require the application of a method for maintaining the trace, such as rehearsal or chunking, then some degree of mental manipulation of the stimuli is also involved. The point in the DSF item set at which this is required will vary as a function of age and ability level, and the response processes utilized by the examinee. In Digit Span Backward (DSB), the patient must hold a string of numbers in short-term memory store while reversing the given sequence, and then correctly reproduce the numbers in the new order. This is a clear example of mental manipulation. As with DSF, the developmental level and other cognitive factors such as general mental ability and processing speed (see section below) may vary the role played by working memory in the DSB item set – for example, short spans of digits backward may tax working memory resources only marginally in older or brighter patients. Again, the point at which these patients substantially invoke working memory resources on DSB will vary by age and ability. In DSS, the patient hears a string of numbers presented out of order and must repeat them in numerical order. The task is more difficult than it sounds because the numbers presented are not continuous, creating gaps in the rearranged number line, and some numbers are repeated. Thus, the working memory demands of DSB and DSS are similar. DSF was retained as part of the subtest to reflect the role of registration in short-term memory as a precursor skill to working memory, and to maintain a set of easier items for evaluation of low-functioning patients.

Inclusion of Arithmetic as a core working memory measure has been an issue in previous editions of the Wechsler scales because the word problem format resulted in the subtest having a substantial cross-loading with the verbal factor in factor analyses, and it was dependent on learning advanced mathematical skills and speeded performance. WISC-IV removed AR from the core for these reasons, and because children and adolescents are still learning mathematics. The current reformulation of the AR subtest is substantially transformed from previous editions, and is a much improved measure of working memory. Compared to its predecessors, the WAIS-IV AR subtest contains reduced verbiage in the word problems, fewer items with time bonuses, and simpler numerical calculations with more steps – which reduces the pull of mathematical skill and increases the activation of working memory. For these reasons, combined with results of the clinical studies (mentioned below), AR was placed back in the core of the test for WAIS-IV. Further considerations included the ecological nature of mental arithmetic tasks for adults. We are frequently called upon to mentally calculate arithmetic problems in real-life situations – a few obvious examples include estimating driving time, halving a recipe in the kitchen, determining the value of a 30 percent off coupon at a clothing store, estimating if $40 of gas is enough to fill the car's gas tank, determining the value of a 20 percent tip on a restaurant bill, making change, and exchanging currencies between US or Canadian Dollars, Euros or Pesos.

Employed adults with serious deficits in working memory may have considerable difficulties at work. A weakness in working memory may make the processing of complex information more time consuming and tax the patient's mental energies more quickly compared to co-workers, perhaps contributing to more frequent errors on a variety of job-related tasks that require sustained attention and concentration. Working memory deficits may not be restricted to issues with numbers, as reflected in these WAIS-IV subtests. Adults with auditory working memory disorders may experience difficulty jotting down notes of key points in a business meeting while continuing to attend to the meeting, keeping in mind the next point they want to make in a business negotiation or sales-call while listening to the other party, shifting attention to return a phone call after being interrupted by the boss, or sustaining concentration to complete a monthly budget report without being distracted by routine emails – as well as the good judgment to shift tasks when an email arrives with a red flag signifying urgent. Executive function system deficits in planning, organization and the ability to shift cognitive sets should be evaluated with these individuals. In addition, examiners should be alert to the social and behavioral consequences of mental fatigue and work stress that can ensue from these disorders, and carefully assess the level of social support and emotional resiliency possessed by the patient. Such issues might be considered in vocational evaluations of job fit.

For young adults in school who have not learned grade-level skills related to arithmetic calculation and mathematical operations, or any adults with a history of primary mathematical disability, the Arithmetic subtest may not be an accurate indication of working memory. The Arithmetic subtest assesses a complex set of cognitive skills and abilities, and a low score may have several appropriate interpretations depending on the clinical context. For example, a patient with low scores on all three (DS, LN, AR) subtests is more likely to have a problem with WM than is the patient who earns average or above scores on DS and LN but below-average scores on AR. In the latter instance the issue may be more one of not having learned the arithmetic skills called for, or of having a specific learning difficulty related to arithmetic and mathematics. Alternatively, a patient who earns a higher score on AR than DS or LN may be one for whom arithmetic is well grounded in work life (e.g., an accountant, math teacher, actuary, etc.). For this reason, we encourage psychologists to administer the three WM subtests whenever there is a question about either WM or arithmetic skills.

A serious deficit in working memory can not only create difficulties at work and in daily life functioning, but may also have major implications for the academic lives of young adults in school or vocational training programs. The role of WM has been implicated in learning and attention disorders. Students diagnosed with LD or AD/HD may be more likely to experience problems with working memory, as suggested by significantly lower scores on this index. Schwean and Saklofske (2005) summarized the results of several studies of children and adolescents with AD/HD suggesting that they tended to earn their lowest scores on the WM composite. This finding was also replicated in the clinical group studies reported in the

WISC-III and WISC-IV Technical Manuals (Wechsler, 1991, 2003) and the Canadian WISC-IV standardization project, with WM producing the largest effect size of the four index scores between the LD and match control groups. For the WAIS-IV, the effect size of differences between specific clinical groups and matched controls was examined and reported in the Technical Manual. The WMI showed the largest effect sizes of the four index scores in the reading and mathematics disorder groups, and the second largest (after PSI) for the AD/HD group.

As always, caution must always be applied when using group data to make diagnostic inferences about individuals. The WAIS-IV was never intended to be diagnostic of AD/HD or LD, and nor can it be, given the complexity of these disorders. Such nomethetic descriptions should rather be used as another "indicator" supporting or not the eventual diagnosis of any condition in which cognition is implicated. Thus we are clearly advocating that diagnosis is of an individual, and the test score findings from the WAIS-IV or any other assessment battery be demonstrated to be relevant to each individual rather than being assumed to apply to all patients with a particular diagnosis, or being used as a diagnostic "marker" (see Kaufman, 1994).

Finally, it should be remembered that all three of the WM subtests described above tap only verbal stimuli assumed to activate auditory working memory structures, and not spatial or visual working memory. The WMS-IV includes visual working memory tasks – that is, a working memory task using visual not verbal stimuli and assumed to activate Baddeley's visual–spatial sketch pad as opposed to the phonological loop. Score differences between these tasks may reflect individual differences in visual versus auditory working memory abilities.

Processing Speed Index (PSI)

The PSI measures the speed of mental processing, using visual stimuli and graphomotor skills, and is importantly related to the efficient use of other cognitive abilities. A weakness in simple visual scanning and tracking may leave a patient less time and mental energy for the complex task of understanding new material.

The PSI is composed of the Coding (CD), Symbol Search (SS), and Cancellation (CA) subtests. These tasks utilize an apparently simple visual scanning and tracking format. A direct test of speed and accuracy, the CD subtest assesses the patient's ability to quickly and correctly scan and sequence simple visual information. Performance on this subtest also may be influenced by short-term visual memory, attention, or visual–motor coordination. Thus, while a low score does raise the question of processing speed, it may also be influenced by graphomotor problems, so practitioners should be alert to alternative reasons for low scores. Patients may complete fewer items on this task if they present with fine motor difficulties due to stroke, chronic alcoholism, medication side effects, etc., but this does not necessarily imply a problem with processing speed. An obsessive-compulsive patient may also earn lower scores on CD, again not due to a processing speed deficit but rather because of a personality disposition.

The SS subtest requires the patient to inspect several sets of symbols and indicate if special target symbols appeared in each set. It is also a direct test of speed and accuracy, and assesses scanning speed and sequential tracking of simple visual information. Performance on this subtest may be influenced by visual discrimination and visual–motor coordination. Here again we alert psychologists to use their observation skills and also ensure that the findings from the WAIS-IV corroborate or are supported by other "clinically relevant" findings. For example, a manic patient who rushes through this task will likely make sufficient errors that will lower the SS score. Again, this is not necessarily due to an underlying processing speed deficit, but may rather be a behavioral correlate (i.e., impulsivity) of a psychiatric disorder.

Cancellation is a supplemental processing speed subtest for ages 16–69 only. This task first appeared on WISC-IV, and a variation of that task for adults was developed for inclusion in WAIS-IV. Working within a specified time limit, the examinee scans a structured arrangement of shapes and marks targets shapes. It is similar to previously developed cancellation tasks designed to measure processing speed, visual selective attention, vigilance, perceptual speed, and visual–motor ability (Geldmacher, Fritsch, & Riedel, 2000; Bate, Mathias, & Crawford, 2001; Wojciulik, Husain, Clarke, & Driver, 2001; Sattler, 2008a, 2008b). Cancellation tasks have been used extensively in neuropsychological settings as measures of visual neglect, response inhibition, and motor perseveration (Adair, Na, Schwartz, & Heilman, 1998; Na, Adair, Kang, Chung, Lee, & Heilman, 1999; Geldmacher *et al.*, 2000; Lezak, Howieson, & Loring, 2004). Relative to the WISC-IV version of CA, the decision-making component of the WAIS-IV CA subtest was designed to place more complex cognitive demands on patients: The decision-making component requires patients to simultaneously discriminate both the color and shape of the stimuli, and inhibit responding when only one of these two features is present.

From a neurodevelopmental perspective, there are large and obvious age-related trends in processing speed that are accompanied by age-related changes in the number of transient connections to the central nervous system and increases in myelination. Several investigators have found that measures of infant processing-speed predict later IQ scores (see, for example, Dougherty and Haith, 1997), and WISC-IV PSI scores have been shown to be potentially sensitive to neurological disorders such as epilepsy (Wechsler, 1991).

Thus, speed of mental processing is more than simply doing a task at a faster or slower rate, but in itself is a key cognitive and individual differences variable. There is consistent evidence that both simple and choice reaction time correlate about 0.20 or slightly higher with scores from intelligence tests, while inspection time (hypothesized by some to be a measure of the rate that information is processed) correlates about 0.40 with intelligence test scores (see Deary, 2001; Deary & Stough, 1996). The significant role of mental speed has been implicated in studies of cognition and aging. Salthouse (1996a, 1996b, 2000a, 2000b) has argued that the decline observed in general mental ability with age is, in the main, due to a slowing of mental processing speed. In fact, removing the effects of mental speed on intelligence test scores also removes the largest effects that have been linked to age.

In contrast to reaction-time measures, the PSI subtests included in tests such as the WAIS-IV are relatively simple visual scanning tasks for most patients. However, it would be a mistake to think of the PSI as a measure of simple clerical functions that are not relevant or related to intellectual functioning. While PSI is listed last in representations of Wechsler factor structures as a matter of convention, it frequently emerges third in most factor analyses, and accounts for greater variance in intelligence then does the working memory factor. In matched controlled clinical group studies with the WAIS-IV, the PSI was observed to have the largest effect sizes among the four index scores in the traumatic brain injury, Alzheimer's, autism, Asperger's, ADHD, and depression groups – although the effect size for the depression group was small. In most cases, one or more other index scores came a close second in terms of effect sizes: the PRI had the next highest effect size for the TBI group, the VCI had the next highest effect size for the autism group, and the WMI had the next highest effect size for the ADHD group. While these studies are instructive with regard to the possible interplay among cognitive functions in specific disorders, we once again discourage practitioners from considering these profiles as diagnostic markers, and encourage complete clinical evaluations based on test results combined with history and background factors.

As operationally defined in WASI-IV, the PSI indicates the rapidity with which a patient processes simple or routine information without making errors of either omission or commission. Many novel learning tasks involve information processing that is both routine (such as reading a policy memo at work) and complex (such as determining the impact of the memo on one's job function). When speed of processing information is at least in the average range, or a relative strength for a patient, this may facilitate both reasoning and the acquisition of new information. Slowness in the speed of processing routine information may make the task of comprehending and integrating novel information more time consuming and, consequently, more difficult. It may be hypothesized that working adults with processing-speed deficits learn less material in the same amount of time, or take longer to learn the same amount of material compared to co-workers without processing speed deficits. These individuals mentally tire more easily at work because of the additional cognitive effort required to perform routine tasks at desk jobs, perhaps leading to more frequent paperwork errors, job stress, poor job evaluations, and possible job failures. As the years pass, these individuals are likely to spend less time on mentally demanding tasks involving new learning, thus leading to smaller stores of crystallized knowledge over time relative to colleagues, and possibly stalled or derailed career paths. As described, slow PS taxes the entire cognitive network and has wide-ranging effects on other cognitive processes that are observable outside the testing room, thus having important consequences in the lives of such individuals. In summary, processing speed interacts in a critical way with other higher-order cognitive functions, and may impact general cognitive functioning, new learning, and everyday performance (Weiss, Saklofske, & Prifitera, 2005).

Toward a dynamic model of intellectual abilities

The evidence in support of working memory and processing speed in a description of intelligence is increasingly convincing. Kail (2000) concluded that processing speed is not simply one of many different independent factors that contribute to intelligence; instead, processing speed is thought to be linked causally to other elements of intelligence. More to the point, Jonides and colleagues (2005: 2) stated that "without working memory, people would not be able to reason, solve problems, speak and understand language, and engage in other activities associated with intelligent life."

The relationship between these constructs is beginning to be better understood. Fry and Hale (1996) administered measures of processing speed, working memory, and fluid intelligence to patients and adolescents between 7 and 19 years of age. Age-related increases in speed of processing were associated with increases in working memory capacity, which in turn were associated with higher scores on measures of fluid reasoning. This study suggests that, as children and adolescents develop normally, more rapid processing of information results in more effective use of working memory space, which enhances performance on many reasoning tasks.

The interrelationship between WM and PS was also described by Kyllonen and Christal (1990). High correlations were reported between these working memory research tasks and traditional measures of intelligence believed to tap reasoning ability. High scores on the reasoning tasks were differentially sensitive to the extent of a person's previous knowledge, whereas successful performance on working memory tasks was more dependent on the person's ability to process information rapidly. The interrelatedness between working memory, reasoning, prior knowledge, and processing speed led Kyllonen and Christal (1990) to conclude that reasoning ability is little more than working memory capacity. In this regard, Baddeley's (2003) proposal for an episodic buffer in which crystallized knowledge is downloaded from long-term storage by a central executive for further manipulation is rather intriguing for the study of the relationship between working memory, crystallized knowledge, and fluid reasoning ability. More recently, Salthouse (2009) challenged the commonly held view that executive functions are distinct from measures of reasoning.

Potentially relevant to young adults in school, a number of child and adolescent studies have indicated that WMI contributes the second largest amount of variance, after VCI, to the prediction of reading, writing, and mathematics scores on the WIAT and other measures of achievement (Konold, 1999; Hale, Fiorello, Kavanagh, Hoeppner, & Gaither, 2001). High correlations between working memory and reading comprehension have been replicated numerous times (see Daneman & Merikle, 1996). Similar findings have been observed for a range of other academic tasks, including spelling (Ormrod & Cochran, 1988), the acquisition of logic (Kyllonen & Stephens, 1990), note-taking (Kiewra & Benton, 1988), and following directions (Engle, Carullo, & Collins, 1991). Generally, the magnitude of these correlations is near 0.50 (Baddeley, 2003), suggesting a moderate relationship between working memory and various academic outcomes.

The precise mechanisms by which working memory is related to fluid reasoning are complex, and likely multiply determined. The original resource-sharing model (Daneman & Carpenter, 1980) emphasizes a trade off between storage and processing demands such that working memory span is a function of the amount of resources one has available for storage after the processing demands of the task are met. However, other researchers postulate that working memory space itself may not be limited, but its use is limited by the efficiency of various processes that control it. For example, the efficiency with which one can perform the processing component of a particular span task affects the duration for which the target items need to be retained in memory (Hitch, Towse, & Hutton, 2001). Thus, working memory capacity will appear larger when processing proceeds efficiently, regardless of the size of the working memory space. Processing can proceed efficiently when the task invokes a crystallized base of knowledge that is readily retrieved from long-term storage, quickly activated in short-term storage, and easily chunked into large and meaningful units based on the individual's prior experience and expertise with the material. Thus, there are few pure working memory tasks, and any pure task that could be created would artificially separate the various reciprocal processes that operate together to form the working memory system. Good working memory tasks bring all of these influences together in the same way as the natural world.

The role of the central executive is critical to the relationship between working memory and fluid reasoning. The central executive controls attention to the target task in the face of interfering or distracting stimuli (Kane, Bleckley, Conway, & Engle, 2001). The more efficiently attention is focused, the more effectively working memory is utilized, regardless of working memory capacity. Similarly, the ability to inhibit irrelevant information, or the degree to which working memory is "clutter free," also may influence efficient cognitive performance regardless of the size of the working memory space (Lustig, May, & Hasher, 2001). Thus, individual differences in performance on working memory tasks may reflect primarily differences in various executive functions such as the ability to sustain focused attention and inhibit competing responses, rather than the size of one's working memory space – particularly in real-life situations, outside of the research laboratory, where interference and distraction are commonplace. Current research suggests that it may be the central executive component of WM that accounts for the strong relationship between WM and fluid reasoning tasks, through the mechanism of controlled attention (Engle, Tuholski, Laughlin, & Conway, 1999).

Together with the central executive, the episodic buffer plays a role in the efficient processing of information in working memory. As the source of controlled attention, the central executive activates long-term memory traces through controlled retrieval, and maintains them in buffer storage systems for use by the visual–spatial sketch pad and phonological loop. For any given individual there are obvious differences in the long-term traces that can be activated in the buffer, based on prior knowledge and familiarity with the task at hand. The more prior knowledge the person brings to a WM problem, the less fluid reasoning is required to respond correctly.

Perceptual processing speed is another important cognitive ability that influences the efficiency of working memory functions. Fry and Hale (1996: 237) stated that as patients age and mature, the changes that occur in processing speed lead to changes in working memory and "in turn, lead to changes in performance on tests of fluid intelligence." Although moderately correlated with each other, working memory and perceptual processing speed are differentially related to fluid reasoning. Working memory correlates moderately, while perceptual processing speed correlates weakly, with fluid reasoning ability as measured by Ravens Progressive Matrices (Ackerman, Geier, & Boyle, 2002). It appears that processing speed exerts its effect on fluid reasoning indirectly through its facilitation of working memory. While working memory ability may be primarily related to one's capacity for controlled attention, the relationship between working memory and fluid reasoning also appears to be mediated by processing speed.

There is almost no meaningful activity in life that can be successfully performed by one narrow-band cognitive ability in isolation. Research in this area is still unfolding. However, practitioners should keep in mind that scores on factor-based indexes are not necessarily orthogonal; multiple reciprocal interactions are expected among the underlying neurological pathways. Understanding the clinical and behavioral correlates of these reciprocally interacting cognitive abilities – including the executive functions – is critical to ecologically meaningful theories regarding the development, expression, and maintenance of intelligence over the course of a lifetime.

Individuals who process routine information quickly conserve working memory space for higher-order reasoning. In effect, they have more time to manipulate information in working memory before the memory trace fades or has to be refreshed through rehearsal or other means. With apologies to Albert Einstein, there indeed may be a relationship between time and space such that processing cognitive information in less time effectively expands working memory space. And if working memory is the space in which fluid reasoning happens, then there is more opportunity for problem-solving to occur through manipulation and transformation of the material held in working memory.

Crystallized knowledge also may expand working memory space. As new facts and ideas are integrated with previously learned knowledge structures, increasingly larger chunks of information can be held in working memory and manipulated or combined with other chunks in novel ways. If an advanced vocabulary word, for example, can be accessed from LTM through the episodic buffer and held in the phonological loop to represent a broader set of facts, then there is still time and space for other material to be integrated into the thinking process. Thus, the effective integration of these and other specific cognitive functions through the central executive may lie at the heart of intelligence.

A dynamic model of cognitive information processing suggests that impairments – whether developmental or acquired – which interfere with the rapid processing of information may burden the working memory structures and reduce the patient's capacity for comprehension and new learning. For example, traumatic brain injury reduces processing speed, which reduces effective working memory and thereby makes problem-solving and the acquisition of new learning more effortful and difficult.

The relevance of an interactive and dynamic view of intelligence has considerable implications for the practicing psychologist engaged in the process of differential diagnosis. While the steps for analyzing the

Wechsler scales presented in many textbooks suggest a simple sequential approach, each subtest, as well as the index scores, assesses cognitively complex traits. It is impossible to think of a patient's performance on, say, the Similarities subtest without also thinking of the role of working memory and speed of processing in the acquisition of these vocabulary words, in their retrieval from long-term storage, and in the service of engaging in the task of abstract fluid reasoning.

It is worth remembering, however, that the VC and PR subtests still have the highest "g" loadings on the WAIS-IV and on all of the Wechsler intelligence tests. While the "g" loadings for the WM and PS subtests are lower, however, they represent abilities that play a critical role in overall intellectual functioning, including the acquisition of new learning and the ability to utilize encoded (crystallized) knowledge to solve new problems.

Analyzing differences among index scores

Practitioners often have reason to formulate *a priori* hypotheses about a pattern of strengths and weaknesses among the index scores based on the referral question, medical history, previous test data, or other information. In these situations, it is best to consult Appendix B of the WAIS-IV Administration and Scoring Manual (Wechsler, 2008), which shows critical differences necessary to obtain statistically significant differences with any pair of index scores, and the base rate of differences of various sizes by ability level.

When no *a priori* hypothesis is formulated, use of these tables may be slightly misleading if they are used to evaluate all possible comparisons. In this case it is better practice to examine the difference of each index score from the mean of all four index scores using the critical values and base rate tables provided in Table 3.1 of this chapter, because these incorporate corrections for multiple comparisons. Table 3.1 shows the base rates of various differences between each index score and the average index score for the overall sample. As a general rule of thumb, 12 or more point differences are likely to be clinically meaningful for all comparisons except PSI, which may require 14 point differences. Research is ongoing to determine if these critical differences vary by ability level.

THE WAIS-IV COMPOSITE SCORES

In this section, we present two relatively new composites – the General Ability and Cognitive Proficiency Indexes – and address issues related to fractured profiles and interpretation of the Full Scale IQ score.

TABLE 3.1   Cumulative percentages of the absolute differences between each index score and the Average Index (AI) score

Cumulative percentage	Absolute difference			
	|VCI − AI|	|PRI − AI|	|WMI − AI|	|PSI − AI|
50	5.75	5.50	5.25	6.50
45	6.25	6.00	6.00	7.39
40	7.00	6.75	6.50	8.25
35	8.00	7.75	7.50	9.25
30	8.75	8.50	8.25	10.18
25	9.75	9.25	9.25	11.00
20	11.00	10.50	10.25	12.50
15	12.00	11.75	11.50	14.25
10	14.25	13.25	13.00	16.25
5	17.00	15.75	15.75	19.75
2	20.50	19.25	19.00	23.50
1	22.00	21.00	21.50	26.25

General Ability Index (GAI)

The GAI is a "composite" index score that summarizes performance on the VCI and PRI into a single number. These two indexes contain the most highly "*g*" loaded subtests within WAIS-IV. The WAIS-IV GAI excludes the contributions of the WMI and PSI to intelligence. Thus, the GAI and FSIQ can lead to different impressions of a patient's overall ability when there is variability across the four indexes.

GAI norms tables for use with WAIS-IV may be found in Appendix C of the *WAIS-IV Technical and Interpretive Manual* (Wechsler, 2008). This Appendix also contains tables useful for comparing GAI and FSIQ scores through examining differences required for statistical significance by age, and base rates of differences of various sizes.

The GAI was first developed for use with WISC-III in ability–achievement discrepancy analyses (Prifitera, Weiss, & Saklofske, 1998) because many learning-disabled students exhibit cognitive processing deficits in working memory and processing speed concomitant with their learning disabilities. Depressed performance on WM and PS tasks lowers the FSIQ for many learning-disabled students, which decreases the magnitude of the discrepancy between ability and achievement, and may result in denial of needed special education services. In this situation, the

GAI may be used in the ability–achievement discrepancy analysis in order to aid in the determination of eligibility for special education.

Other uses for the GAI have since been identified. For example, the GAI may be an appropriate estimate of overall ability when physical or sensory disorders invalidate performance on the working memory or processing speed tasks, or both. Another possible use is in approximating the pre-injury cognitive status and memory abilities of patients with traumatic brain injury. This is because TBI is known to impair processing speed and short-term memory more than verbal knowledge and some perceptual abilities. However, better methodologies for estimating pre-injury ability presently exist based on pseudo-word reading tasks combined with demographic variables to estimate pre-injury ability, and these have been made available for use with WAIS-IV (Wechsler, 2009).

In our first WISC-IV book, we suggested that some practitioners may prefer the GAI as an alternative way of summarizing overall ability (Prifitera, Saklofske, & Weiss, 2005). This suggestion has led to an increasing number of psychological evaluations in which the GAI is described as a better estimate of overall ability than FSIQ whenever the WMI or PSI score are significantly lower than the VCI or PRI scores. As we subsequently stated, this is not what we intended, and can be a very problematic practice (Prifitera *et al.*, 2005). We intended GAI to be used only when there are sound clinical reasons to exclude WMI and PSI, such as invalid administration due to lack of effort; sensory or physical impairments; disturbance of the testing session; etc. In some of these situations it may be possible to prorate a single subtest, which would be a better practice.

Ultimately, we believe that working memory and processing speed are essential components of a comprehensive assessment of intelligence, and excluding them from the estimate of overall intelligence simply because the patient's abilities in those areas are relative weaknesses is poor practice. Such practice will result in unrealistically high estimates of intelligence for these patients, possibly excluding them from needed services and creating employment expectations that they can not live up to. To be clear, the problem is not with reporting the GAI, but with describing it as the best estimate of overall intelligence.

Cognitive Proficiency Index (CPI)

The Cognitive Proficiency Index (CPI) summarizes performance on the Working Memory and Processing Speed Indexes of the WAIS-IV into a single score. Creating a new composite by combining WMI and PSI was first suggested in relation to WISC-III by Dumont and Willis (2001), and subsequently extended to WISC-IV by Weiss, Saklofske, Prifitera, and Holdnack (2006). In the present book, we extend our work on CPI to WAIS-IV.

The CPI represents a set of functions whose common element is the proficiency with which one processes certain types of cognitive information. Proficient processing – through quick visual speed and good mental control – facilitates fluid reasoning and the acquisition of new material by reducing the cognitive demands of novel or higher-order tasks (Weiss *et al.*, 2006). More simply, efficient cognitive processing facilitates learning and problem-solving by "freeing up" cognitive resources for more advanced, higher-level skills.

The WAIS-IV CPI excludes the contributions of verbal comprehension and perceptual reasoning to intelligence. Thus, CPI and GAI can provide different views into patient's cognitive abilities when there is significant variability across the relevant index scores. Both views are sometimes necessary to form a complete picture of an individual's strengths and weaknesses that is not distorted by combining a set of diverse abilities into a single overall score. Rather than reporting GAI as the best estimate of overall ability when the profile of abilities is diverse, it is sometimes better practice to describe both the GAI and CPI in the psychological evaluation. Work is ongoing to examine the factor structure and clinical validity of this proposed model.

Norms tables for CPI are provided in Table 3.2. To use this table, add the subtest scaled scores for the four subtests that enter the WMI and PSI to obtain the CPI sum of scaled scores. Locate this sum of scaled scores in the table, and read across the row to obtain the CPI score. Table 3.3 shows the differences between GAI and CPI scores required for statistical significance (critical values). Table 3.4 shows the base rates of GAI–CPI differences by direction and ability level. For the overall sample, 15 point differences may be an adequate rule of thumb for interpretable findings. However, the base rate of GAI–CPI difference scores varies considerably by ability level. Below FSIQ 110, GAI < CPI profiles are more likely than GAI > CPI profiles. The reverse pattern is observed at higher ability levels, where GAI > CPI profiles are more common. In general, differences scores that occur in 10 percent or less of the sample for a particular ability level should be considered rare and interpretable, unless there are specific *a priori* reasons to expect a particular discrepancy. For example, a GAI > CPI difference score that occurs in 15–20 percent of the sample may still be interpretable in the context of certain brain insults or injuries. Before interpreting GAI, CPI, or the difference between them, however, practitioners should ensure that there are not large differences between VCI and PRI, or between WMI and PSI. In such instances, the four index scores should be interpreted individually.

Inherent in the discussion of GAI and CPI above is the early possibility of a modification to the current Wechsler model of intelligence. In the current Wechsler model (since 1990), the FSIQ is comprised of four factors that each contribute directly and independently to the FSIQ.

TABLE 3.2 WAIS-IV CPI equivalents of sums of scaled scores

Sum of scaled scores	CPI	90% Confidence interval	95% Confidence interval	Percentile rank
4	40	38–48	37–49	< 0.1
5	41	39–49	38–50	< 0.1
6	43	41–51	40–52	< 0.1
7	45	43–53	42–54	< 0.1
8	47	44–55	43–56	< 0.1
9	49	46–57	45–58	< 0.1
10	51	48–59	47–60	0.1
11	53	50–61	49–62	0.1
12	55	52–62	51–63	0.1
13	57	54–64	53–65	0.2
14	58	55–65	54–66	0.3
15	60	57–67	56–68	0.4
16	62	59–69	58–70	1
17	64	61–71	60–72	1
18	66	62–73	61–74	1
19	68	64–75	63–76	2
20	70	66–77	65–78	2
21	71	67–78	66–79	3
22	72	68–79	67–80	3
23	74	70–81	69–82	4
24	75	71–81	70–82	5
25	77	73–83	72–84	6
26	78	74–84	73–85	7
27	79	75–85	74–86	8
28	80	76–86	75–87	9
29	82	78–88	77–89	12
30	83	79–89	78–90	13
31	85	81–91	80–92	16
32	87	82–93	81–94	19
33	89	84–95	83–96	23
34	91	86–97	85–98	27
35	93	88–99	87–100	32
36	94	89–100	88–101	34
37	96	91–101	90–102	39
38	98	93–103	92–104	45
39	99	94–104	93–105	47
40	100	95–105	94–106	50

(*Continued*)

TABLE 3.2 WAIS-IV CPI equivalents of sums of scaled scores—Cont'd

Sum of scaled scores	CPI	90% Confidence interval	95% Confidence interval	Percentile rank
41	101	96–106	95–107	53
42	102	97–107	96–108	55
43	103	98–108	97–109	58
44	105	100–110	99–111	63
45	106	100–111	99–112	66
46	108	102–113	101–114	70
47	110	104–115	103–116	75
48	112	106–117	105–118	79
49	114	108–119	107–120	82
50	116	110–120	109–121	86
51	118	112–122	111–123	88
52	120	114–124	113–125	91
53	121	115–125	114–126	92
54	123	117–127	116–128	94
55	125	119–129	118–130	95
56	126	119–130	118–131	96
57	128	121–132	120–133	97
58	129	122–133	121–134	97
59	131	124–135	123–136	98
60	133	126–137	125–138	99
61	135	128–138	127–139	99
62	137	130–140	129–141	99
63	139	132–142	131–143	99.5
64	141	134–144	133–145	99.7
65	143	136–146	135–147	99.8
66	146	138–149	137–150	99.9
67	148	140–151	139–152	99.9
68	150	142–153	141–154	> 99.9
69	152	144–155	143–156	> 99.9
70	155	147–157	146–158	> 99.9
71	157	149–159	148–160	> 99.9
72	160	152–162	151–163	> 99.9
73	160	152–162	151–163	> 99.9
74	160	152–162	151–163	> 99.9
75	160	152–162	151–163	> 99.9
76	160	152–162	151–163	> 99.9

TABLE 3.3   Critical values of WAIS-IV CPI–GAI differences required for statistical significance

Age group	Level of significance	CPI−GAI
16–17	0.15	7.17
	0.05	9.75
18–19	0.15	6.48
	0.05	8.82
20–24	0.15	6.48
	0.05	8.82
25–29	0.15	6.11
	0.05	8.31
30–34	0.15	6.48
	0.05	8.82
35–44	0.15	6.48
	0.05	8.82
45–54	0.15	6.1
	0.05	8.31
55–64	0.15	6.11
	0.05	8.31
65–69	0.15	5.71
	0.05	7.77
70–74	0.15	6.11
	0.05	8.31
75–79	0.15	5.72
	0.05	7.78
80–84	0.15	6.11
	0.05	8.31
85–90	0.15	6.11
	0.05	8.31
All age	0.15	6.25
	0.05	8.51

In this modified model, the FSIQ is comprised of general reasoning abilities (both verbal perceptual) and cognitive processing functions (consisting of working memory and processing speed). Here, the GAI and CPI lie intermediate between the FSIQ and the four factors.

TABLE 3.4   Base rates of WAIS-IV GAI–CPI discrepancy scores by direction for the total sample and selected levels of FSIQ

Discrepancy	Total sample GAI<CPI	Total sample GAI>CPI	FSIQ <80 GAI<CPI	FSIQ <80 GAI>CPI	FSIQ 80–89 GAI<CPI	FSIQ 80–89 GAI>CPI	FSIQ 90–109 GAI<CPI	FSIQ 90–109 GAI>CPI	FSIQ 110–119 GAI<CPI	FSIQ 110–119 GAI>CPI	FSIQ >119 GAI<CPI	FSIQ >119 GAI>CPI
25	1.6	1.6	0.5	0.0	1.5	0.6	1.5	1.6	1.6	2.7	3.0	3.0
24	1.9	2.3	1.1	0.0	2.1	1.2	1.6	2.1	2.1	4.0	3.0	4.0
23	2.2	3.0	1.1	0.5	2.4	1.8	2.0	2.9	2.1	5.1	4.0	4.5
22	2.8	3.6	1.1	1.1	3.3	2.1	2.6	3.3	2.9	6.1	4.0	5.5
21	3.5	5.0	1.6	1.1	4.9	3.0	3.2	4.2	3.7	9.0	4.0	8.5
20	4.0	5.6	1.6	2.1	5.8	3.3	3.3	4.6	4.8	10.4	5.0	9.0
19	5.0	6.5	2.1	2.1	7.0	4.0	4.2	5.2	5.3	12.2	8.0	11.5
18	6.2	7.3	2.1	2.6	9.1	4.0	5.2	6.1	6.9	12.8	9.0	13.0
17	7.1	8.4	2.6	3.7	10.0	4.3	6.2	6.8	8.5	15.2	9.0	16.0
16	8.3	9.9	4.8	4.2	12.5	5.5	7.1	8.0	8.8	16.8	10.5	20.0
15	10.2	11.6	6.3	4.8	15.5	6.1	8.6	9.3	12.0	20.5	10.5	23.0
14	12.1	12.9	8.5	4.8	17.0	7.6	11.0	10.8	13.0	21.8	12.0	24.5
13	14.4	14.8	9.0	7.9	20.7	8.5	13.6	12.6	14.4	23.9	13.5	27.0

12	16.0	17.2	9.5	10.6	23.4	10.9	15.2	14.5	15.7	27.9	15.0	29.0
11	18.7	19.2	11.6	12.7	25.5	13.1	18.2	16.2	16.8	30.6	21.0	31.0
10	20.9	21.6	13.8	15.9	28.0	15.2	20.0	18.7	19.1	32.2	24.0	34.0
9	23.6	24.2	15.9	20.1	32.5	16.7	23.1	21.2	21.0	35.1	24.0	37.0
8	26.2	26.5	19.0	22.2	34.0	20.1	25.9	23.3	23.4	36.7	26.5	39.5
7	28.8	29.3	21.2	26.5	37.4	21.6	29.3	26.1	24.5	39.6	27.5	42.5
6	31.5	31.9	22.2	28.6	42.6	25.5	32.0	28.5	26.3	42.0	29.5	45.5
5	34.7	34.3	25.4	30.7	45.0	28.3	36.2	30.7	28.2	44.7	31.0	48.0
4	38.0	36.9	30.7	33.9	47.1	31.3	39.7	33.0	31.1	47.9	33.0	50.0
3	42.0	40.2	36.0	38.1	51.7	33.7	43.3	36.9	34.6	50.5	38.0	52.0
2	45.7	44.0	42.3	42.3	54.1	35.9	47.5	41.5	38.6	53.2	39.0	55.5
1	50.4	46.6	48.1	47.1	59.6	37.7	52.6	44.6	41.8	54.5	41.5	57.0
Mean	9.2	10.1	7.1	7.7	10.1	9.1	8.7	9.4	9.9	12.2	11.1	12.4
SD	6.8	7.1	6	5.3	6.9	6	6.5	7	7.3	7.5	7.9	7.5
Median	8	9	5	7	9	8	7	8	9	12	11	12

Preliminary factor-analytic work on the modified model suggests that there is little difference in how it fits the data as compared to the model in which the four factors contribute directly to the FSIQ (Saklofske, Zhu, Coalson, & Raiford, 2010). In this case, the law of parsimony would rule such that the simpler model would be considered superior if it were to fit the data equally well. One caveat could trump this law, however: if the more complex model were found to have superior clinical validity. What we know about the clinical validity of this model is limited to date. Such analyses are ongoing with existing WAIS-IV data from adult clinical subjects collected during the standardization project, and may generate new studies as well.

For adolescents, comparing WISC-IV GAI and CPI to each other and to school achievement was found to be potentially useful in the identification of psychological processing deficits in patients with certain learning disabilities. Weiss and colleagues (2006) examined the prevalence of large CPI < GAI profiles occurring simultaneously with large Achievement < GAI profiles, and 2 percent of the non-clinical sample met both criteria. The percentage of students receiving LD services that met both criteria ranged between 45 and 50 percent in the various reading- and writing-disorder samples.

Psychometric cautions about profile analysis notwithstanding (McDermott, Fantuzzo, & Glutting, 1990), results of these analyses are consistent with recent research which supports the practice of going beyond the FSIQ to examine a pattern of cognitive strengths and weaknesses among the four WAIS-IV index scores in psychoeducational evaluations. When the four index scores were entered simultaneously into a regression equation predicting academic achievement, the resulting variance explained was larger than that for the FSIQ in all academic areas examined (Konold, 1999; Mayes & Calhoun, 2007). Taken together, these data provide empirical support for an approach to evaluating LD which involves a pattern of cognitive strengths and weaknesses among the WAIS-IV index scores. Readers interested in professional issues surrounding use of neurocognitive assessment in LD evaluations are referred to Hale and Fiorello (2004).

Issues in estimating overall ability

Unlike every other Wechsler interpretative system that has been written, we discuss FSIQ last, rather than first. This is not to devalue the explanatory and predictive power of the FSIQ, but rather to emphasize the descriptive clinical power of the WAIS-IV indexes and to place the FSIQ in its proper role as a summary statement at the end of the psychological evaluation. The FSIQ has strong explanatory power at the group and individual levels. Still, the use of an overall summary score sometimes may mask individual differences among the broad domains of general ability.

This is why we suggest that the first line of clinical interpretation rests with the index scores.

Some authors have argued that a large amount of subtest scatter invalidates the FSIQ (see, for example, Fiorello, Hale, Holdnack, Kavanagh, Terrell, & Long, 2007). Consequently, some practitioners refuse to report a FSIQ when there is significant scatter among the index scores. They label the FSIQ as invalid, and even appear disappointed in the test. However, our view is that fractured profiles are rich with clinically meaningful information that provides skilled practitioners with an opportunity to understand the cognitive drivers of the patient's behavior and make more targeted recommendations for assisting them. Thus, scatter can be useful both diagnostically and prescriptively. In fact, when all four index scores "hang together" within a few points of each other and the FSIQ is "valid," there is little to say in the report about a patient's unique set of abilities and how those individual differences serve to shape his or her perceptions of and relationship with the occupational and social worlds in which they live.

The patient's overall level of cognitive ability provides a critical backdrop to interpretation of individual differences among the various domains of ability as assessed by the index scores. The calculation of a Full Scale IQ (FSIQ) continues to be important for this and several other reasons. From a purely psychometric perspective, a general factor tends to emerge in studies of intelligence (Carroll, 1993). This fact, combined with the integrity of the four-factor structure and the magnitude of the correlations between the index scores, makes a psychometrically compelling case for the interpretation of the FSIQ.

Further, recent WISC-IV studies suggest that FSIQ may be an equally valid measure of general ability for individuals or groups having highly variable index scores as for those having consistent index scores (Daniel, 2007), and that there may be no difference in the predictive validity of FSIQ for low-scatter and high-scatter groups (Watkins, Glutting, & Lei, 2007).

FSIQ is an especially strong predictor of occupational success, memory functioning, and school achievement. FSIQ and achievement correlate more strongly than any other two variables known to the behavioral sciences, typically around .70. This means that FSIQ explains about half the variance in achievement. There is no known variable or collection of variables that comes close to fully accounting for the other half. Beyond the relationship with achievement, there is considerable ecological and criterion validity for the use of an overall estimate of general intelligence in a variety of areas related to success in life including pre-employment testing and predicting job performance (Gottfredson, 1997, 1998; Kuncel, Hezlett, and Ones, 2004).

SUMMARY AND COMMENT

Each revision of the various Wechsler intelligence scales has both added to and modified the Wechsler model of intelligence based on the extant literature of the time. Following the lead of the WISC-IV (Wechsler, 2003), the WAIS-IV (Wechsler, 2008) has taken bold new steps to bring modern clinical research on working memory and processing speed to the forefront of the Wechsler model. A number of significant improvements and modifications have been made to the Wechsler family of tests, driven by the demands of clinical practice, but also reflecting advances in theory, research, and measurement sophistication. In Wechsler's original model, verbal intelligence (VIQ) and performance intelligence (PIQ) combined to form full-scale intelligence (FSIQ). His original model included, as part of the VIQ, two subtests designed to measure what we now call working memory (i.e., Arithmetic and Digit Span). Similarly, the original model included, as part of the PIQ, one subtest designed to measure what we now call processing speed (i.e., Coding). Ongoing neuropsychological research and psychometric advances have highlighted the clinical import of these constructs, and subsequent editions of the test have systematically added more subtests in these areas. Over the years, the Wechsler model has systematically expanded the domain coverage of the FSIQ to more fully represent these clinically important constructs. Other advances include revision of the verbal subtests to include more verbal reasoning than crystallized knowledge, and the revision of the performance subtests to include more fluid reasoning than visual spatial skills.

In a major departure from the original Wechsler tests, the focus of interpreting the WAIS-IV now rests solidly on a four-factor structure that is grounded in a wide body of research in clinical neuropsychology. Basic interpretation of the WAIS-IV requires understanding of the clinical and behavioral correlates of these four domains of intelligence. Advanced interpretation further requires appreciation of the dynamic and reciprocal interactions between crystallized knowledge, fluid reasoning, working memory, processing speed, and executive functions. There are few activities of value in life that can be accomplished through only one of these domains, and an ecologically valid theory of intelligence requires an integrated model of how these abilities work together as described in this chapter.

While the psychometric fit of the WISC-III, WAIS-III, WISC-IV and WAIS-IV to a four-factor model has been beyond question for decades, the evolution of the Wechsler scales has been guided less by factor analysis, as in the Carroll-Horn-Cattell model of intelligence (Carroll, 1993), and more by ongoing clinical and neurocognitive research. Nevertheless, there is a fair amount of overlap between these theories, and this congruence among independent research groups is ultimately confirming the progress our science continues to make in building increasingly advanced models of intelligence.

References

Ackerman, P. L., Geier, M. E., & Boyle, M. O. (2002). Individual differences in working memory within a nomological network of cognitive and perceptual speed abilities. *Journal of Experimental Psychology: General, 131*(4), 567–589.

Adair, J. C., Na, D. L., Schwartz, R. L., & Heilman, K. M. (1998). Analysis of primary and secondary influences on spatial neglect. *Brain and Cognition, 37,* 351–367.

Baddeley, A. (2003). Working memory: looking back and looking forward. *Nature Reviews/ Neuroscience, 4,* 829–839.

Bate, A. J., Mathias, J. L., & Crawford, J. R. (2001). Performance on the test of everyday attention and standard tests of attention following sever traumatic brain injury. *The Clinical Neuropsychologist, 15,* 405–422.

Carroll, J. B. (1993). Human Cognitive Abilities: A Survey of Factor-analytic Studies. New York, NY: Cambridge University Press.

Chan, R. C. K., Shum, D., Toulopoulou, T., & Chen, E. Y. H. (2008). Assessment of executive functions: Review of instruments and identification of critical issues. *Archives of Clinical Neuropsychology, 23,* 201–216.

Cheung, A. M., Mitsis, E. M., & Halperin, J. M. (2004). The relationship of behavioral inhibition to executive functions in young adults. *Journal of Clinical and Experimental Neuropsychology, 26,* 393–403.

Daneman, M., & Carpenter, P. A. (1980). Individual differences in working memory and reading. *Journal of Verbal Learning and Verbal Behavior, 19,* 450–466.

Daneman, M., & Merikle, M. (1996). Working memory and language comprehension: A meta-analysis. *Psychonomic Bulletin Review, 3,* 422–433.

Daniel, M. H. (2007). "Scatter" and the construct validity of FSIQ: Comment on Fiorello *et al. Applied Neuropsychology, 14*(4), 291–295.

Deary, I. J. (2001). *Intelligence: A Very Short Introduction.* Oxford: Oxford University Press.

Deary, I. J., & Stough, C. (1996). Intelligence and inspection time: Achievements, prospects, and problems. *American Psychologist, 51,* 599–608.

Delis, D., Kramer, J., Kaplan, E., & Ober, B. (2000). *Manual for the California Verbal Learning Test – Second Edition.* San Antonio, TX: Pearson.

Delis, D., Kaplan, E., & Kramer, J. (2001). *Manual for the Delis–Kaplan Executive Function System.* San Antonio, TX: Pearson.

Dougherty, T. M., & Haith, M. M. (1997). Infant expectations and reaction times as predictors of childhood speed of processing and IQ. *Developmental Psychology, 33*(1), 146–155.

Dumont, R. & Willis, J. (2001). Use of the Tellegen and Briggs formula to determine the Dumont–Willis Indexes (DWI-1 and DWI-2) for the WISC-III. Online. Available: http://alpha.fdu.edu/psychology/.

Engle, R. W., Carullo, J. J., & Collins, K. W. (1991). Individual differences in working memory for comprehension and following directions. *Journal of Educational Research, 84,* 253–262.

Engle, R. W., Tuholski, S. W., Laughlin, J. E., & Conway, A. R. A. (1999). Working memory, short term memory, and general fluid intelligence: a latent variable approach. *Journal of Experimental Psychology: General, 128*(3), 309–331.

Fiorello, C. A., Hale, J. B., Holdnack, J. A., Kavanagh, J. A., Terrell, J., & Long, L. (2007). Interpreting intelligence test results for children with disabilities: Is global intelligence relevant? *Applied Neuropsychology, 14*, 2–12.

Fry, A. F., & Hale, S. (1996). Processing speed, working memory, and fluid intelligence: Evidence for a developmental cascade. *Psychological Science, 7*(4), 237–241.

Geldmacher, D. S., Fritsch, T., & Riedel, T. M. (2000). Effects of stimulus properties and age on random-array letter cancellation tasks. *Aging, Neuropsychology, and Cognition, 7*(3), 194–204.

Gottfredson, L. S. (1997). Why g matters: the complexity of everyday life. *Intelligence, 24*, 79–132.

Gottfredson, L. S. (1998). The general intelligence factor. *Scientific American Presents, 9*, 24–29.

Hale, J. B., & Fiorello, C. A. (2004). *School Neuropsychology: A Practitioner's Handbook*. New York, NY: Guilford.

Hale, J. B., Fiorello, C. A., Kavanagh, J. A., Hoeppner, J. B., & Gaither, R. A. (2001). WISC-III predictors of academic achievement for children with learning disabilities: are global and factor scores comparable? *School Psychology Quarterly Special Issue, 16*(1), 31–55.

Hitch, G. J., Towse, J. N., & Hutton, U. M. Z. (2001). What limits children's working memory span? Theoretical accounts and applications for scholastic development. *Journal of Experimental Psychology: General, 130*, 184–198.

Jonides, J., Lacey, S. C., & Nee, D. E. (2005). Process of working memory in mind and brain. *Current Directions in Psychological Science, 14*, 2–5.

Kail, R. (2000). Speed of information processing: developmental change and links to intelligence. *Journal of Psychology Special Issue: Developmental Perspectives in Intelligence, 38*(1), 51–61.

Kane, M. J., Bleckley, M. K., Conway, A. R. A., & Engle, R. W. (2001). A controlled attention view of working memory capacity. *Journal of Experimental Psychology: General, 130*, 169–183.

Kaufman, A. S. (1994). *Intelligent Testing with the WISC-III*. New York, NY: Wiley.

Kiewra, K. A., & Benton, S. L. (1988). The relationship between information processing ability and note taking. *Contemporary Educational Psychology, 13*, 3–44.

Konold, T. R. (1999). Evaluating discrepancy analysis with the WISC-III and WIAT. *Journal of Psychoeducational Assessment, 17*, 24–35.

Kuncel, N. R., Hezlett, S. A., & Ones, D. S. (2004). Academic performance, career potential, creativity, and job performance: Can one construct predict them all? *Journal of Personality and Social Psychology, 86*, 148–161.

Kyllonen, P. C., & Christal, R. E. (1990). Reasoning ability is (little more than) working memory capacity. *Intelligence, 14*, 389–433.

Kyllonen, P. C., & Stephens, D. L. (1990). Cognitive abilities as the determinant of success in acquiring logic skills. *Learning and Individual Differences, 2*, 129–160.

Lezak, M. D., Howieson, D. B., Loring, D. W., Hannay, H. J., & Fischer, J. S. (2004). *Neuropsychological Assessment* (4th ed.). New York, NY: Oxford University Press.

Lustig, C., May, C. P., & Hasher, L. (2001). Working memory span and the role of proactive interference. *Journal of Experimental Psychology: General, 130*, 199–207.

Mayes, S. D., & Calhoun, S. L. (2007). Wechsler Intelligence Scale for Children – Third and Fourth Edition predictors of academic achievement in children with attention-deficit hyperactivity disorder. *School Psychology Quarterly, 22*(2), 234–249.

McDermott, P. A., Fantuzzo, J. W., & Glutting, J. J. (1990). Just say no to subtest analysis: A critique on Wechsler theory and practice. *Journal of Psychoeducational Assessment, 8*, 290–302.

McGrew, K., & Flanagan, D. P. (1998). *The Intelligence Test Desk Reference (ITDR) Gf–Gc Cross-Battery Assessment*. Boston, MA: Allyn and Bacon.

Na, D. L., Adair, J. C., Kang, Y., Chung, C. S., Lee, K. H., & Heilman, K. M. (1999). Motor perseverative behavior on a line cancellation task. *Neurology, 52*(8), 1569–1576.

Ormrod, J. E., & Cochran, K. F. (1988). Relationship of verbal ability and working memory to spelling achievement and learning to spell. *Reading Research Instruction, 28*, 33–43.

Prifitera, A., Weiss, L. G., & Saklofske, D. H. (1998). The WISC-III in context. In A. Prifitera, & D. H. Saklofske (Eds.), *WISC-III Clinical Use and Interpretation: Scientist–Practitioner Perspectives* (pp. 1–38). San Diego, CA: Academic Press.

Prifitera, A., Saklofske, D. H., & Weiss, L. G. (2005). *WISC-IV Clinical Use and Interpretation: Scientist–Practitioner Perspectives.* San Diego, CA: Academic Press.

Prifitera, A., Saklofske, D. H., & Weiss, L. G. (2008). *Clinical Assessment and Intervention* (2nd ed.). San Diego: Academic Press.

Reynolds, C. R. (1997). Forward and backward memory span should not be combined for clinical analysis. *Archives of Clinical Neuropsychology, 12*, 29–40.

Saklofske, D.H., Zhu, J., Coalson, D.L., & Raiford, S.E. (2010). Factor structure of the WAIS-IV GAI and CPI indexes. Unpublished paper.

Salthouse, T. A. (1996a). Constraints on theories of cognitive aging. *Psychonomic Bulletin and Review, 3*, 287–299.

Salthouse, T. A. (1996b). The processing speed theory of adult age differences in cognition. *Psychological Review, 103*, 403–428.

Salthouse, T. A. (2000a). Pressing issues in cognitive aging. In D. C. Park, & N. Schwarz (Eds.), *Cognitive Aging: A Primer* (pp. 43–54). Philadelphia, PA: Psychology Press.

Salthouse, T. A. (2000b). Steps toward the explanation of adult age differences in cognition. In T. J. Perfect, & E. A. Maylor (Eds.), *Models of Cognitive Aging* (pp. 19–49). New York, NY: Oxford University Press.

Salthouse, T.A. (2009). Operationalization and Validity of the Construct of Executive Functioning. Continuing Education Workshop presented at the Annual Meeting of the International Neuropsychological Society, Athens, GA.

Sattler, J. M. (2008a). *Assessment of Children: Cognitive Foundations* (5th ed.). San Diego, CA: Author.

Sattler, J. M. (2008b). *Resource Guide to Accompany Assessment of Children: Cognitive Foundations* (5th ed.). San Diego, CA: Author.

Schwean, V. L., & Saklofske, D. H. (2005). Assessment of attention deficit hyperactivity disorder with the WISC-IV. In A. Prifitera, D. H. Saklofske, & L. G. Weiss (Eds.), *WISC-IV Clinical Use and Interpretation: Scientist–Practitioner Perspectives* (pp. 235–280). San Diego, CA: Elsevier.

Watkins, M. W., Glutting, J. J., & Lei, P. W. (2007). Validity of the full-scale IQ when there is significant variability among WISC-III and WISC-IV factor scores. *Applied Neuropsychology, 14*, 13–20.

Wechsler, D. (1991). *Wechsler Intelligence Scale for Children – (3rd ed.).* San Antonio, TX: Psychological Corporation.

Wechsler, D. (2003). *Manual for the Wechsler Intelligence Scale for Children – (4th ed.).* San Antonio, TX: Psychological Corporation.

Wechsler, D. (2008). *Manual for the Wechsler Adult Intelligence Scale – (4th ed.).* San Antonio, TX: Pearson.

Wechsler, D. (2009). *Advanced Clinical Solutions for Use with WAIS-IV and WMS-IV.* San Antonio, TX: Pearson.

Weiss, L. G., Saklofske, D. H., & Prifitera, A. (2003). Clinical interpretation of the WISC-III factor scores. In C. R. Reynolds, & R. W. Kamphaus (Eds.), *Handbook of Psychological and Educational Assessment of Children: Intelligence and Achievement* (2nd ed.). New York, NY: Guilford Press.

Weiss, L. G., Saklofske, D. H., & Prifitera, A. (2005). Interpreting the WISC-IV index scores. In A. Prifitera, D. H. Saklofske, & L. G. Weiss (Eds.), *WISC-IV Clinical Use and Interpretation: Scientist–Practitioner Perspectives* (pp. 71–100). San Diego, CA: Academic Press.

Weiss, L. G., Saklofske, D. H., Prifitera, A., & Holdnack, J. A. (2006). *WISC-IV: Advanced Clinical Interpretation*. San Diego, CA: Academic Press.

Wojciulik, E., Husain, M., Clarke, K., & Driver, J. (2001). Spatial working memory deficit in unilateral neglect. *Neuropsychologia, 39*, 390–396.

THE WAIS-IV: CLINICAL USE AND INTERPRETATION IN CONTEXT

4

WAIS-IV Use in Societal Context

Lawrence G. Weiss [1], Hsinyi Chen [2], Josette G. Harris [3], James A. Holdnack [1], and Donald H. Saklofske [4]

[1] Pearson Assessment, San Antonio, Texas, USA
[2] Behavioral Science Corporation, Taipei, Taiwan
[3] University of Colorado School of Medicine, Denver, Colorado, USA
[4] Division of Applied Psychology, University of Calgary, Calgary, Alberta, Canada

INTRODUCTION

An individual's intelligence is traditionally measured relative to a sample of people the same age that is representative of a national population. This helps psychologists answer the question of how a particular person compares to other people across the nation in which that individual lives and competes. This is important because intelligence has been repeatedly shown to be predictive of a wide variety of important life outcomes (Gottfredson, 1998). However, even though we may live in the United States or Australia or China, no person lives in the country "as a whole." Rather, people live in neighborhoods or communities that can vary along simple dimensions such as size (San Antonio, the Bronx, Ontario), and along more complex dimensions such that communities may reflect unique characteristics that can impact the development and maintenance of cognitive abilities in novel ways. Those who measure intelligence also want to know how the person being tested compares to other people in the same community or culture. This is the essence of *contextual interpretation*. It is contextually informed interpretation of population-based cognitive ability scores in concert with salient demographic and environmental variables.

Most chapters written on intelligence test interpretation conclude with a statement such as: "The examiner should also take into account other factors such as the client's educational, medical, cultural, and family history – as well as other test scores." This advice has been repeated so frequently that it is often taken for granted, and while most psychologists acknowledge its veracity, not all implement it in practice. With experience, however, many psychologists come to understand that each profile of test scores has a range of meanings depending on the person's history and the context of the evaluation. In fact, one defining characteristic of an expert assessment psychologist may well be the ability to refine standard, cook-book interpretations of test profiles based on environmental, medical, and other relevant contextual issues.

In *WISC-IV Advanced Clinical Interpretation*, we devoted the first chapter to an exploration of the enriching and inhibiting influences of environment on cognitive development of children and adolescents (Weiss, Saklofske, Prifitera, & Holdnack, 2006a). Some of that ground is revisited in the present chapter because the WAIS-IV also is utilized with adolescents. Further, the adults we assess with the WAIS-IV were once developing children and adolescents, and those early experiences played a critical role in shaping their cognitive abilities as adults. Just as important, the environmental contexts surrounding adults of all ages also may impact cognitive functioning. For example, the range of physical and psychological stressors on individuals living in war-torn countries, suffering from malnutrition due to famine, or affected by environmental pollutants (e.g., mercury, lead) impacts all humans of all ages, albeit in potentially different ways. In applying these discussions to adults, we provide information that may facilitate the integration of salient cultural and home environmental considerations into routine practice with adults. In doing so, we continue to challenge the belief that the intellectual growth and development of individuals represents the unfolding of a predominantly fixed trait only marginally influenced by the nature and quality of environmental opportunities and experiences. As we discuss these issues, we cross-reference studies of other Wechsler intelligence test versions (i.e., WISC-IV, WPPSI-III). This is because the Wechsler series of intelligence tests is based on the same underlying model of intelligence that includes verbal conceptualization, perceptual reasoning, working memory and processing speed (see Chapter 3 in this volume).

BIAS ISSUES IN INTELLECTUAL ASSESSMENT

Prior to beginning our discussion of contextually informed interpretation of cognitive test scores, we must devote several pages to the widely held conception that cultural demographic differences in IQ test scores are due to biases built into the test. Our intent in this section of the chapter is to put aside these concerns so that we can focus on contextual mediators of cognitive performance, skill acquisition and maintenance. We discuss advances in item and method bias research, and show that disproportionate representation of individuals in specific categories or groups is not limited to cognitive and achievement test scores but is present in many areas of life. We acknowledge a legacy of controversy in these areas, and must address it so that we can move forward.

Item bias has been studied extensively, and all reputable test developers take special precautions to avoid it. Best practice in test development first entails systematic reviews of all items for potential bias by panels of cultural experts, and such methodology is well documented and practiced (see Georgas, Weiss, van de Vijver, & Saklofske, 2003). Test developers typically determine representation of ethnic minority examinees in acquiring test cases based upon census percentages, but purposely exceed the percentages so that advanced statistical techniques may be undertaken to detect and replace items that perform differently across ethnic groups. Conceptually, these techniques seek to identify items on which subjects from different demographic groups score differently despite possessing the same overall ability on the particular construct being assessed.

When items are identified as operating differently by examinee group, the reason for any identified differences cannot be determined by these analyses alone. Expert panels commonly predict that certain items will be biased because some groups have less direct experience with the subject of those items than other groups, but then find that various statistical procedures designed to detect bias do not identify the same items as the panel. Perhaps this is because the cultural expert panel is not typically required to provide an evidence-based theory to explain how culture, as they conceive it, interacts with item content. At the same time, statistical techniques sometimes point to a particular item as problematic when the expert panel can find no contextual reason. This may be due to the very large number of statistical comparisons undertaken (e.g., every test item is evaluated across multiple racial and ethnic group comparisons, and also by gender, region of the country, and educational level), and so even with a $p < 0.01$ criteria there may be some items that randomly test positive for differential functioning when more than a thousand comparisons are made.

For these and other reasons this line of research is no longer referred to as item bias research but as an analysis of differential item functioning (DIF), because the underlying reasons that items perform differently across groups are not always known. In light of the care taken in the development of items for most modern intelligence tests, it seems unlikely that item bias accounts for the bulk of the variance in demographic differences in IQ test scores. However, differential item performance statistics are not very suitable to detect factors that influence entire tests as opposed to single items (van de Vijver & Bleichrodt, 2001). This is because most DIF studies match respondents from different racial/ethnic groups by using total test scores as the indication of ability or intelligence. If one presumes that some aspect of the dominant culture is inherent in the construct being evaluated by the test, and not just in isolated items, then by matching on test scores researchers may be matching on adherence to some unknown aspect of the majority culture. This larger issue can be framed as one of possible construct or method bias in which the construct being tested, or the method used to measure the construct, functions differently across groups.

This type of bias is more general than item bias, and more difficult to study empirically. According to this view, the formats and frameworks of most major intelligence tests are literacy dependent and middle-class oriented. Further, the testing paradigm itself is a stimulus response set that could be considered a social-communication style specific to Western European cultures (Kayser, 1989). The testing paradigm assumes that the test-takers will perform to the best of their ability, try to provide relevant answers, respond even when the task does not make sense to them, and feel comfortable answering questions from people who are strangers to them. In some cultures, individuals are expected to greet unfamiliar events with silence, or to be silent in the presence of a stranger. Guessing is not encouraged in other cultures, and learning takes place through practice rather than explanation. Unfortunately, there are methodological difficulties in determining the amount of variance that may be explained by each of these factors. No studies have attempted to parse out the extent to which these influences may be ameliorated by the examinees' experiences within the US educational system, where western paradigms are pervasive. At the same time, evidence from studies of adults suggests that amount of US educational experience may explain significant variance in WAIS-III scores of immigrants (Harris, Tulsky, & Schultheis, 2003).

So, an important question is whether a test measures the same constructs across groups. One common way to examine this question is through factor analysis, and more sophisticated approaches include measurement invariance techniques. Basically, if it can be shown that the various facets (i.e., subtests) of a test correlate with each other in similar ways across groups, then such findings are typically taken as evidence in support of the hypothesis that the test is measuring the same constructs across those cultures. A series of studies has shown invariance of the four-factor WAIS-III measurement model between large and representative samples of subjects in the US, Australia, and Canada, as well as across education levels and age bands (Bowden, Lissner, McCarthy, Weiss, & Holdnack, 2003; Bowden, Lloyd, Weiss, & Holdnack, 2006; Bowden, Lange, Weiss, & Saklofske, 2008). While these studies are important, it must be noted that they are limited to comparisons between

English-speaking nations that are westernized, industrialized, and share common historical roots.

In a large international study of 16 North American, European and Asian nations, Georgas and colleagues (2003) found reasonable consistency of the factor structure of WISC-III, with each nation studied reporting either three or four factors. In all cases, the difference between the three- and four-factor solutions was due to a single subtest (Arithmetic) cross-loading on two factors (i.e., verbal and working memory). Importantly, these analyses included not only nations from 3 continents and 16 countries which speak 11 different languages, but also both westernized and non-westernized societies (i.e., South Korea, Japan, and Taiwan). Another important finding from this study is that the mean FSIQ scores for the countries were found to vary systematically with the level of affluence and education of the countries as indicated by key economic indicators such as gross national product (GNP), percent of the GNP spent on education, and percent of the countries' workforce in agriculture. Encompassing as this study is, we also should note that there were no pre-industrialized nations included.

Still, examining differences in mean scores across groups is a relatively simple but flawed procedure for assessing cultural bias in tests (see Gottfredson & Saklofske, 2009). A more sophisticated approach is to examine how the relationship of intelligence test scores to important criterion variables differs across groups. This begs the question, however, of what is an appropriate criterion variable for validating an intelligence test. In many (though not all) cultures educational success is considered an important behavioral outcome of intelligence, and thus the prediction of academic achievement from IQ has been studied extensively. Studies have shown a general absence of differential prediction of standardized achievement test scores from IQ scores across racial/ethnic groups for WISC-R (Reschly & Reschly, 1979; Reschly & Sabers, 1979; Reynolds & Hartlage, 1979; Reynolds & Gutkin, 1980; Poteat, Wuensch, & Gregg, 1988), and this finding has been replicated with WISC-III for nationally standardized achievement test scores in reading, writing, and math (Weiss, Prifitera, & Roid, 1993; Weiss & Prifitera, 1995). Typically, these regression-based studies show differences in the intercept but not the slope, and this lack of difference in the slopes is taken as evidence in support of a lack of differential prediction. In other words, IQ scores predict scores on standardized achievement tests equally well for all demographic groups studied. Yet the possibility exists that this finding is attributable to bias being equally present in both the predictor (i.e., the standardized intelligence test) and the criterion (i.e., the standardized achievement test). This question was partially addressed by Weiss and colleagues (1993), who used teacher-assigned classroom grades as the criterion rather then standardized achievement test scores; again, no differential prediction was observed. A general lack of differential prediction to achievement was also recently demonstrated with WSIC-IV (Konold & Canivez, 2010).

It is unknown whether the construct of intelligence as we currently conceptualize it, albeit reliably measured with replicable factor structure across many cultures, predicts behaviors and outcomes that would be uniquely defined as intelligent by each culture, and particularly by non-industrialized cultures. Many researchers weight as important studies which show a relationship between intelligence and academic achievement, because the societies in which they live tend to value education as an important outcome of intelligence. In cultures of pre-industrialized nations, or perhaps some subcultures of industrialized nations where success in school is not necessarily central to success in life, however, such studies may not be as relevant. Other valued outcomes of intelligence may vary considerably across cultures, and might include such behaviors as the ability to resolve conflict among peers, influence one's elders, build useful machines without instructions, survive in a dangerous neighborhood, grow nutritious crops in poor soil, etc. The point is that while tests of intelligence have stable factor structures across groups and predict academic achievement very well, this does not necessarily mean that they predict things which every culture would consider intelligent. Demonstrating the stability of the factor structure across cultures is an important yet insufficient step in demonstrating cross-cultural validity. Further, if we were to design a new test to predict culturally-specific outcomes of intelligence, we would begin by seeking to understand what constitutes intelligent behaviors as defined by that population, and then create tasks designed to predict those behavioral outcomes. If the important outcomes (i.e., the criterion) of intelligence differ across cultures, then we might not end up with the same constructs that comprise most modern tests of intelligence – but we don't know that.

DEMOGRAPHIC DIFFERENCES IN VARIOUS AREAS OF LIFE

Although the literature on test bias acknowledges the role of socioeconomic status on intelligence test scores, it has largely ignored the known effects of poverty on the development and maintenance of cognitive abilities. This is a serious oversight, because poverty is known to be disproportionately represented across racial/ethnic groups.

This section explores racial/ethnic differences in several important areas of life. We confine this discussion to areas that are theoretically and conceptually related to the development and maintenance of cognitive abilities, intellectual performance, and skill acquisition. Compared with non-minority populations in the US, overrepresentation of racial and ethnic groups has been documented for physical and mental illness, educational underachievement and high school drop-out rate, single- as opposed to dual-parent family homes, unemployment rates, reduced median family income, diminished school funding, lower mean scores on state-mandated high school exit exams, substandard schools, and more. Data reported in this section are from a supplemental report of the Surgeon General (US Department of Health and Human Services, 2001), except where otherwise noted.

Prior to beginning this section, however, we wish to make clear that this discussion is not merely about race or ethnicity. Rather, it is about indirect factors that circumscribe what people can accomplish regardless of race or ethnicity. There has been confusion on this point; because racial/ethnic groups tend to fall into diverse SES categories, people mistakenly believe that they are seeing racial differences when SES-related differences are examined. More importantly, people mistakenly attribute cause and effect to these data in only one direction: that differences in intelligence cause differences in SES. To the contrary, we intend to make the case that differences in SES cause differences in intelligence by limiting opportunities for individuals to achieve their full intellectual potential as they grow and develop cognitively from childhood and adolescence through young and middle adulthood. We focus our discussion on African Americans and Hispanics living in the United States because these are the data we have available through our work on the WAIS-IV standardization project, but we consider that the concepts presented may have wider utility.

Racial/ethnic group disparities in education

We discuss group differences in education because it is widely known that IQ test scores vary sharply and systematically with years of educational attainment. This may be because more intelligent people pursue higher levels of education where their particular abilities are more likely to be rewarded. Perhaps more to the point, however, education is significantly correlated with IQ test scores. Furthermore, this relationship between education and IQ is maintained through childhood, adolescence, and adulthood. For children and adolescents, researchers typically examine the parents' level of education, and it has been shown repeatedly that parental level of education is a good predictor of intelligence for those under 20 years of age. Overall, the correlation of parental level of education with WISC-IV FSIQ scores is as follows: 0.43 for ages 6–16 years (Weiss et al., 2006b), and 0.42 for ages 16–19 years. For ages 20–90 years, the educational attainment of adults – herein referred to as self education – correlates 0.53 with WAIS-IV FSIQ. Thus, the association between intelligence and education is slightly higher in adults than in children or adolescents. Perhaps this is because self education is used for adults while parent education is used for children and adolescents. Self educational attainment reflects both socio-economic and personal factors directly related to educational attainment (e.g., achievement orientation, individual ability), while parent education reflects background factors that influence the educational attainment of children indirectly.

Table 4.1 shows the mean WAIS-IV FSIQ score at different levels of educational attainment for adolescents ages 16–19 and adults ages 20–90. Mean FSIQ scores increase substantially with each subsequent level of education obtained. From the lowest to highest education levels, mean FSIQ scores increased by approximately 23 and 28 points for adolescents and adults, respectively.

Table 4.2 shows the the percentages of each racial/ethnic group that obtained various levels of education based on adults ages 20–90 (US Bureau of the Census, 2005). College entrance rates are highest for Asians (62.5 percent) and Whites (51.2 percent), and smaller for African Americans (40.1 percent) and Hispanics (29.1 percent). High school drop-out rates are largest for Hispanics (43.8 percent) and African Americans (25.7 percent), and smaller for Asians (16 percent) and Whites (14.7 percent). Thus, large differences in completion of secondary education and college entry are observed by racial and ethnic group.

As dramatic as it is, the 43.8 percent high school drop-out rate for Hispanics does not tell the whole story. There is a large disparity in graduation rates between Hispanics who were born in the US as compared to those born in other countries. In fact, the drop-out rate for foreign-born Hispanics is more than twice the drop-out rate for US-born Hispanics in the same age range (Kaufman, Kwon, Klein, & Chapman, 1999). This may in part reflect language competency issues for foreign-born Hispanics, who perhaps experience greater difficulties with language mastery, depending upon the age of immigration and classroom placement. In addition, economic factors may force some older children into the workforce at an

TABLE 4.1   Mean WAIS-IV FSIQ scores by education level and age band

Education level	Ages 16–19	Ages 20–90
8th grade or less	84.12	82.99
9th–11th grades	91.44	88.77
High school graduate or GED (12th grade)	96.18	97.28
Some college (13–15 years of education)	100.26	102.28
College graduate or above (16+ years of education)	106.97	110.77

Note: Ages 16–19 based on parent education; ages 20–90 based on self education.

TABLE 4.2 Percentage of each racial/ethnic group that completed high school and entered college

	High school drop-out rate	College entrance rate
White	14.7	51.2
African American	25.7	40.1
Hispanic	43.8	29.1
Asian	16.0	62.5

Note: Based on US Bureau of the Census (2005) for ages 20–90.

earlier age, particularly those already struggling with language and academic mastery.

Racial/ethnic group disparities in mental health status

Group disparities in mental health status show that group differences are not limited to educational status. Goldstein and Saklofske (see Chapter 7 of this volume) show how cognitive profiles of individuals with major psychiatric disorders differ from those of non-clinical subjects, especially with respect to level of performance. An appreciation of mental health disparities among groups is also relevant to a discussion of factors that moderate cognitive growth, because people preoccupied with significant mental health problems may have fewer cognitive resources available to apply to learning, be it through formal educational pursuits or solving mentally challenging problems in everyday life. Further, we propose that parents with significant mental health problems may have fewer personal resources available to fully attend to the cognitive enrichment and academic growth of their developing children.

Although rates of psychological disorders among African Americans and Whites appear to be similar after controlling for differences in socio-economic status, experts generally consider such conclusions to be uncertain because of the disproportionate representation of African Americans in high-risk populations that are not readily accessible by researchers (e.g., homeless, incarcerated). Similarly, there is little basis for firm conclusions about the rate of mental health disorders among African American children – although when present, their mental health needs are less likely to receive treatment than in White youths. The proportion of individuals with mental illness is much higher among those who are homeless, incarcerated, or in foster care, and African Americans are disproportionately represented in these settings. The proportion of the homeless population that is African American is at least 40 percent, and possibly higher. About 45 percent of children in foster care are African American, and many of these are victims of abuse or neglect. Although

Whites are nearly twice as likely as African Americans to commit suicide, this may be due to the very high rate of suicide among older White males.

Availability of mental health services depends on where one lives, and the presence or absence of health insurance. A large percentage of African Americans live in areas with limited access to both physical and mental health care services, and nearly 25 percent of African Americans have no health insurance, as compared to approximately 10 percent of Whites. Medicaid, which subsidizes the poor and uninsured, covers nearly 21 percent of African Americans. The proportion of African Americans that do not access mental health services due to the perceived stigma is 2.5 times greater than in Whites. Thus, attitudes about mental health disorders among African Americans may reduce utilization of existing services.

With respect to Hispanics, most studies support the lack of difference in rates of mental illness as compared to Whites; however, sample size issues have restricted the generalizability of this finding beyond the Mexican American population. Further, this summary statement masks important differences between US and foreign-born Mexican Americans. The lifetime prevalence of mental disorders is 25 percent for Mexican immigrants in the US, but 48 percent for US-born Mexican Americans. Also, length of stay in the US is positively correlated with increased incidence of mental illness for immigrants. Mexican immigrants with less than 13 years of US residence have better mental health than their US-born counterparts and the overall US sample. The picture is different for children, with most studies reporting higher rates of anxiety and depression among Hispanic versus White children and adolescents. Most of these studies are limited, however, by methodological issues with self-reported symptoms. Although the overall rate of suicide among Hispanics (6 percent) is lower than among Whites (13 percent), Hispanic adolescents in high school report proportionately more suicidal ideation and specific attempts than both Whites and African Americans. Similarly, although the overall rate of alcohol use is similar between Hispanics and Whites, there are differences in the rates of alcohol abuse among Mexican American men (31 percent) as compared to non-Hispanic White men (21 percent). The rate of substance abuse is much higher among US-born Mexican Americans than among Mexican immigrants (7 : 1 for women, and 2 : 1 for men). Relatively few Hispanics are homeless or in foster care. Hispanic youth are over-represented (18 percent) in residential placement facilities for juvenile offenders compared to African American and White juveniles.

In general, Hispanics underutilize and in many cases receive insufficient mental health care services relative to Whites. Approximately 11 percent of Mexican Americans with mental disorders access services as compared to 22 percent of Whites. The rate is even lower among those born in Mexico (5 percent) as compared to those born in the US (12 percent).

Although the overall picture is complicated, the general trend appears to be that recently arrived Mexican immigrants have relatively good mental health, and maintain this advantage for at least a decade. However, mental health problems are much more prevalent among those that have been in the US longer, those born in the US, and for children and adolescents. More studies of Hispanics from other countries of origin are clearly needed. For example, many Hispanics from Central America have historically emigrated to escape civil wars in Nicaragua, El Salvador, and Guatemala, and refugees who have experienced trauma are at high risk for depression and post-traumatic stress disorder. But the strengths observed in the Mexican immigrant population are noteworthy. One factor may be a tendency of new immigrants to compare their lives in the US to those of their families in Mexico (typically a positive comparison), whereas those residing in the US longer, or born in the US, tend to compare their situations to a US standard (more often a negative comparison). Another area of strength involves cultural attitudes toward mental health disorders. Among Mexicans at least, views on causes of mental illness appear to be more external than internal, and this may predispose families to respond supportively to relatives with mental disorders. There appears to be a cultural norm to care for illness within the family, regardless of whether it is physical or mental. This may be reflected in underutilization of mental health services, at least for some illnesses and disorders. Availability of treatment providers who speak Spanish may be an additional factor in treatment access.

Racial/ethnic group disparities in physical health status

Next, we point out that group disparities are not restricted to educational attainment, rates of mental health disorders, or access to healthcare services, but exist for physical health as well. The relevance of group disparities in physical health to a discussion of intelligence rests on the proposition that there are indirect relationships between physical, mental, and cognitive status that operate through multiple mechanisms. As discussed above with regard to mental illness, seriously or chronically physically ill people may have less time and energy to invest in activities related to their own intellectual growth or that of their children. Further, some physical illnesses, or their treatments, have direct effects on cognitive functioning.

African Americans have substantially more physical health problems than individuals from other racial and ethnic groups. One of the more sensitive indicators of a population's health status is infant mortality, and the rate of infant mortality for African Americans is twice that for Whites. In most population studies, infant mortality tends to decrease with maternal education, yet the rate of infant mortality for even the most educated African American women is higher than that for the least educated White women. As compared to Whites, African American adults present rates of diabetes more than three times higher, heart disease more than 40 percent higher, prostate cancer more than double, and HIV/AIDS more than seven times higher. HIV/AIDS is now one of the five top causes of death among African Americans.

The high rate of HIV/AIDS is of particular interest in our discussion of cognitive functioning because HIV infection can lead to various mental syndromes, from mild cognitive impairment to clinical dementia, as well as precipitate the onset of mood disorders or psychosis. Overall mental functioning can be gravely compromised in individuals who are HIV positive, by the combination of opportunistic infections, substance abuse, and the negative effects of treatment (McDaniel, Purcell, & Farber, 1997). The secondary, environmental effects of parents with HIV-related cognitive impairments on the cognitive development of their children are unknown, and this is becoming increasingly important with improved survival rates of the disease.

Another health risk in the African American population is sickle cell disease. Steen, Fineberg-Buchner, Hankins, Weiss, Prifitera, and Mulhern (2005) demonstrated that children with hemoglobin sickle cell, the most serious form of sickle cell disease, show evidence of substantial cognitive impairment even when there is no evidence of structural brain abnormality on magnetic resonance imaging. The effect, approximately 12 FSIQ points on WISC-III, was found as compared to a control group matched for age, race, and gender. Although no SES information was collected on the patient group, we also compared the patient sample to controls whose parents did not finish high school. The effect was reduced by about half, but still substantial. In both cases, the effect was evenly distributed across verbal and performance scores, and there was a significant effect for age such that the cognitive effects of the disease appear to worsen over time. Also of interest is the even larger differences observed between controls and the portion of the patient sample that showed abnormalities on magnetic resonance imaging. In interpreting these finding, one should keep in mind that children with active diseases tend to miss considerable numbers of days in school, and the impact of the reduced instruction on cognitive development may be important as a secondary cause of the low test scores observed. While the neurological mechanism responsible for the observed cognitive deficits in children with sickle cell disease is being debated (i.e., stroke, "silent" infarction, or disease-related diffuse brain injury), there is growing evidence for the effect of the disease on cognition. Although generally thought of as a genetic disorder specific to African or African American populations, sickle cell disease is actually associated with cultures that historically have lived in high malarial environments, and has been observed in White populations of Mediterranean descent in the US. In addition, regions of Mexico such as the Yucatan peninsula are presently considered high malarial areas, and many hospitals in the US do not currently accept blood donations from individuals who have visited that region within the previous year. Based on the studies cited above, we suggest that psychologists consider inquiring about family history of sickle cell disease when evaluating African Americans with cognitive delays, or any person whose family descends from a high malarial area.

The infant mortality rate among Hispanics is less than half that among African Americans, and lower than the rate among Whites. Cuban and Puerto Rican Americans show the expected pattern of lower infant mortality rates with higher levels of maternal education, but the pattern is not so prominent among Mexican Americans or immigrants from Central America. Compared to Whites, Hispanics have higher rates of diabetes, tuberculosis, high blood pressure, and obesity. Health indicators for Puerto Rican Americans are worse than for Hispanics from other countries of origin.

Racial/ethnic group disparities in income

Group differences in income directly impact the socio-economic status of individuals and their spouses, and relate to IQ test scores of offspring through various social and psychological mechanisms that will be discussed throughout this chapter. Group differences in income is a particularly sensitive topic, because there is considerable evidence that African Americans and Hispanics experience discrimination in hiring – which, of course, contributes to lower incomes on average for them relative to Whites. Further, the income statistics neither distinguish newly arrived Hispanic immigrants from Americans of Hispanic decent, nor differentiate US-born African Americans from recent Black immigrants from Africa, Haiti, or Jamaica. As observed above, this latter issue is a problem that is endemic to most research on racial/ethnic group differences. Finally, higher-paying occupations often require higher levels of education, which may be less accessible to lower-income families unable to afford college tuition. Thus, there are large differences in income between racial/ethnic groups, which may be partially related to a legacy of unfair hiring, promotion, and pay practices in some industries and regions of the country, and partially related to differences in occupational opportunity as mediated by educational attainment and, in some cases, English language competencies. As noted above, educational attainment is substantially different across racial/ethnic groups, which is partly due to accessibility and availability of resources. With these caveats, the following information about income disparities is reviewed here from a 2001 report of the US Surgeon General.

In 1999, 22 percent of all African American families had incomes below the poverty line as compared to 10 percent of all US families. For children, the gap is larger. Approximately 37 percent of African American children live in poverty, as compared to 20 percent of all US children. The gap is still larger for those living in severe poverty. Severe poverty is defined as family income more than 50 percent below the poverty line. The percentage of African American children living in severe poverty is more than three times larger than for White children.

On the other hand, household income rose 31 percent for African Americans between 1967 and 1997 – much faster than the 18 percent increase for Whites during the same time period. Further, nearly a quarter of African Americans now have annual family incomes greater than $50,000. Thus, the African American community may have become somewhat more diverse in terms of socio-economic status during the last generation. Still, the proportion of Whites with incomes above $50,000 is vastly higher, and most millionaires are White.

With respect to Hispanics, median family income and educational level varies substantially with country of origin. Median family incomes range from a high of $39,530 for Cubans to a low of $27,883 for Mexicans, with Puerto Ricans at $28,953. The percentage of Hispanics living below the poverty line ranges from 14 percent of Cubans to 31 percent of Puerto Ricans, with Mexican Americans at 27 percent. These discrepancies reflect real differences in the patterns of immigration from the various Spanish-speaking countries. For example, Mexicans with little education and few job skills tend to immigrate to the US in search of employment opportunities, whereas political and social issues have motivated many economically successful and more highly-educated Cubans to leave their country. Thus, the socio-economic level of Hispanics living in the US systematically varies with country of origin based on differing, historical patterns of immigration.

The proportion of Hispanic children living in poverty is higher than the national average. While 17.1 percent of all children live below the poverty level in the US, 30.4 percent of all Hispanic children living in the US are below the poverty level (US Bureau of the Census, 2003).

Implications of demographic differences in various areas of life

Some reviewers will undoubtedly critique our overview of racial/ethnic group disparities in various areas of life as too limited to do the topic justice, while other readers may wonder why we spent so much time on the topic, and how these issues are relevant to intellectual assessment. In many cases the magnitude of the gaps described above are shocking, and have serious political, legal, and economic implications for our country. Our intention in including this discussion in the current chapter is more modest. First, we wish to make the basic point that disparities between racial/ethnic groups have been observed in many important areas of life, and are not limited to IQ test scores. We do not imply cause and effect in either direction, but simply note that racial/ethnic group discrepancies are not unique to IQ tests.

Second, and much more importantly for our purposes in this chapter, the differences described above suggest, for the most part, that people of different racial ethnic backgrounds have differing levels of opportunity for cognitive growth and development. The effects of these differences on the development of cognitive abilities are critical during childhood, but also continue well into middle adulthood, depending on level of education, income, mental and physical health, and the resources available in the communities in which people live.

Americans are fond of saying that all children are born with equal opportunity, and that any child can grow up to be President of the United States. The election of Barack Obama as the first African American US President demonstrates that this is true – although not for immigrant children. Still, while opportunity under the law may be equal, implementation of the law can sometimes vary by jurisdiction for racial/ethnic groups, as suggested by differential rates of incarceration. However, this is not the kind of opportunity we are talking about in this chapter. We are talking about opportunity in terms of the development of a person's cognitive abilities; the opportunity for a child's mind to grow and expand to its fullest potential through late adolescence and into early and middle adulthood. Further, we are talking about the kind of opportunity that allows people to maintain good cognitive functioning in late adulthood – barring any disease processes – by living intellectually stimulating lives through mentally active work, community service, and challenging hobbies. Our central tenant is that IQ is not an immutable trait, but a basic ability that can be influenced – to some reasonable extent – positively or negatively during the long course of cognitive development beginning in childhood and continuing through adolescence and into early or middle adulthood. Cognitive development can be influenced by the environment in multiple, interactive, and reciprocal ways. We know, for example, that parental education level correlates with children's IQ test scores. While this may be partly due to the inherited level of cognitive ability passed from parent to child, we also know that the level of education obtained by the parents is highly correlated with the parents' occupational status and household income. This in turn is related to the quality of schools and libraries available in the neighborhoods that are affordable to the parents, the role models present in those neighborhoods, the culturally defined expectations for educational attainment in that context, the expectations for the child's occupational future that surround him or her in the family and community, and the extent to which a young adult can pursue academic or other cognitively enriching activities free from concerns about economic survival or fears of personal safety that may interfere with vocational education and career development.

In many ways, education is only a proxy for a host of variables related to the quantity and quality of cognitively enriching activities available to a person, and that parents can provide for their children. Therefore, education is only a gross indicator replete with numerous exceptions. Certainly, there are many individuals with little formal education who are quite successful in business and society, and their success affords critical opportunities to their offspring that belie expectations based on their own education. Similarly, many readers of this chapter will likely know that even advanced academic credentials do not always equate with success in life. What is amazing is that, with all of its imperfections, one variable – education – relates so much to cognitive ability.

THE ROLE OF COGNITIVE STIMULATION IN INTELLECTUAL DEVELOPMENT

At this point in the discussion, we elaborate upon our central thesis: Enriching, cognitively stimulating environments enhance intellectual development and maintenance of cognitive abilities, whereas impoverishing environments inhibit that growth. Further, the factors that inhibit cognitive enrichment interact with each other such that the presence of one factor makes the occurrence of other inhibitory factors more probable. The net result is even worse than the sum of its parts – akin to geometric rather than arithmetic increases. Finally, the negative effects of cognitively impoverished environments accumulate over the course of a lifetime, and the impact further worsens with age. As we have pointed out previously, the IQ gap between African American and White children is substantially larger for teenagers than for pre-adolescent children, and this finding has been consistent across the 12 years that we have studied the phenomenon in WISC-III (Prifitera, Weiss, & Saklofske, 1998) and WISC-IV (Prifitera, Weiss, Saklofske, & Rolfhus, 2005). The terms "enrichment" and "impoverishment," as used here, are not considered synonymous with the financial status of rich and poor; these terms refer to cognitively enriching versus impoverishing environments – specifically, environments that encourage growth, exploration, learning, creativity, self-esteem, etc.

Ceci (1996) has proposed a bio-ecological model of intellectual development which involves (1) the existence of multiple cognitive abilities that develop independently of each other, (2) the interactive and synergistic effect of gene–environment developments, (3) the role of specific types of environmental resources (e.g., proximal behavioral processes and distal family resources) that influence how much of a genotype gets actualized in what type of environment, and (4) the role of motivation in determining how much a person's environmental resources aid in the actualization of his or her potential. According to this model, certain epochs in development can be thought of as sensitive periods during which a unique disposition exists for a specific cognitive ability – called a "cognitive muscle" in Ceci's model – to crystallize in response to its interaction with the environment. Not all cognitive abilities are under maturational control, however, as new synaptic structures may be formed in response to learning that may vary widely among people at different developmental periods. Yet the sensitive period for many abilities appears to be neurologically determined such that the proper type of environmental stimulation must be present during the critical developmental period, and providing that same stimulation at another time may not have the same impact. In this model, the relative contributions of environment and genetic endowment to intellectual outcome change with developmental stage. For example, general intelligence at age 7 relates to key aspects of home environment at ages 1 and 2, but not at ages 3 or 4 (Rice, Fulker, Defries, & Plomin, 1988). This suggests that it may not be possible to fully compensate for an impoverished early environment by enhancing the child's later environment. Where we need more research is in the elucidation of the key paths and the critical developmental timing.

Interestingly, this model does not separate intelligence from achievement because schooling is assumed to elicit certain cognitive potentials that underlie both. Further, problem-solving as operationalized in most intelligence tests relies on some combination of past knowledge and novel insights. We would add that the act of academic learning enhances formation of new synaptic connections and neural networks, and therefore increases intellectual ability directly, in addition to the indirect effect of accumulated knowledge on problem-solving. Thus, schooling and the quality of education play a powerful role in intellectual development. This is part of the reason why achievement and crystallized knowledge exhibit substantial overlap with reasoning ability in psychometric studies of intelligence tests. Although theoretically distinct, these constructs are reciprocally interactive in real life.

Distal resources are background factors such as SES that affect cognitive development indirectly through the opportunities afforded or denied. Proximal processes are behaviors that directly impact cognitive development. Proximal processes occur within the context of distal resources, and interact to influence the extent to which cognitive potentials will be actualized. For maximum benefit, the process must be enduring and lead to progressively more complex forms of behavior. Parental monitoring is an example of an important proximal process. This refers to parents who keep track of their children, know if they are doing their homework, who they associate with after school, where they are when they are out with friends, and so forth. Parents who engage in this form of monitoring tend to have children who obtain higher grades in school (Bronfenbrenner & Ceci, 1994). In the bio-ecological model, proximal processes are referred to as the engines that drive intellectual development, with higher levels of proximal processes associated with increasing levels of intellectual competence.

The distal environment includes the larger context in which the proximal, parent–child behaviors occur. Perhaps the most important distal resource is SES, because it relates to many other distal resources such as neighborhood safety, school quality, library access, as well as the education, knowledge and experience that the parent brings with him or her into the proximal processes. For example, helping the developing child with homework, an effective proximal process, requires that someone in the home possesses enough background knowledge about the content of the child's lessons, a distal environmental resource, to help the child when he or she studies.

Ceci argues that distal resources can place limits on the efficiency of proximal processes because the distal environment contains the resources that need to be imported into the proximal processes in order for them to work to full advantage, and because an adequate distal environment provides the stability necessary for the developing child to receive maximum benefit from the proximal processes over time. While an educated parent may be able to help a child with algebra homework, a valuable distal resource, a parent with little education can still provide a valuable proximal process of quiet space and a regular time for homework and ensure that the assigned work is completed. This monitoring and support can be very beneficial.

At the same time, it is unlikely that there is a universal environment whose presence facilitates performance for all children, or even for all children in the same culture. The likelihood of person by environment interactions suggests that there are different developmental pathways to achievement. School and home environments may be benevolent, malevolent, or null with respect to a variety of dimensions. Practitioners conducting clinical assessments with adults might include an evaluation of distal environmental resources within the family and community, and consider how these factors facilitate or inhibit their clients' expectations for themselves and their children.

HOME ENVIRONMENT INFLUENCES ON COGNITIVE DEVELOPMENT

We now touch on the role of home environment – not in terms of fixed demographic characteristics such as education or income, but in terms of specific in-home behaviors that facilitate or inhibit cognitive development of children regardless of educational level or demographic group. Some readers will wonder why we discuss child development at all in a book about adult intelligence. Our answer is simple: all adults were once children. The childhood experiences of adults we test today account for substantial variance in their own level of cognitive functioning, which in turn has significant impact on the next generation. Further, there is considerable variability in home environment both within and between racial ethnic groups. Readers interested in a more complete discussion of this topic are referred to Weiss and colleagues (2006b).

Several studies correlated home environment and SES ratings with children's measured intelligence and/or academic achievement (Bradley, Caldwell, & Elardo, 1977; Trotman, 1977; Ramey, Farran, & Campbell, 1979; Bradley & Caldwell, 1981, 1982; Bradley *et al.*, 1989; Johnson, Swank, Howie, Baldwin, Owen, & Luttman, 1993; Brooks-Gunn, Klebanov, & Duncan, 1996). Although SES was variably defined across studies, this collection of papers generally shows that for African American children the relationship between SES and IQ test scores was neither as strong as the relation between home environment and IQ test scores, nor as strong as the relationship between SES and IQ test scores among White children. This may reflect the likely truncated upper limit of SES within the African American groups. Some writers speculate that historical limitations in educational and employment opportunities unique to African American parents lead to more within-SES-group variability in parental behavior germane to children's intellectual development. In the studies cited above, home environment ratings typically added significant information to the prediction of IQ scores from SES for African American children, and this increment in variance explained was often larger than that for White children. What this means is that SES, however it is measured, may not be as powerful a predictor of IQ test scores for African American as compared to White children and adolescents. It also means that home environment factors may play a more powerful role in the prediction of IQ test scores for African American than for White children.

Several studies have examined the relation of home environment and cognitive ability in Mexican American children (Henderson & Merritt, 1968; Henderson, 1972; Henderson, Bergan, & Hurt, 1972; Johnson, Breckenridge, & McGowan, 1984; Valencia, Henderson, & Rankin, 1985; Bradley *et al.*, 1989). In general, the results of these studies support the view that parents' in-home behavior is important to cognitive development and academic performance. Mexican American parents who demonstrate higher degrees of valuing language (e.g., reading to the child), valuing school-related behavior (e.g., reinforcing good work), and providing a supportive environment for school learning (e.g., helping the child recognize words or letters during the preschool stage) have children who tend to score higher on tests of basic concepts and early achievement (Henderson *et al.*, 1972), and neither SES nor family size made a significant unique contribution to predicting cognitive ability scores beyond that accounted for by home environment (Valencia *et al.*, 1985).

The association of home environment with academic achievement has also been studied. Higher levels of parent involvement in their children's educational experiences at home have been associated with children's higher achievement scores in reading and writing, as well as higher report card grades (Epstein, 1991; Griffith, 1996; Sui-Chu & Williams, 1996; Keith, Keith, Quirk, Sperduto, Santillo, & Killings, 1998). Studies have shown that parental beliefs and expectations about their children's learning are strongly related to children's beliefs about their own competencies, as well as their actual achievement (Galper, Wigfield, & Seefeldt, 1997). Improving the home learning environment has been shown to increase children's motivation and self-efficacy (Mantzicopoulos, 1997; Dickinson & DeTemple, 1998; Parker, Boak, Griffin, Ripple, & Peay, 1999).

Fantuzzo, McWayne, Perry, and Childs (2004) extended the above finding using a longitudinal study of very low SES African American children in an urban Head Start program. Specific in-home behaviors on the part of parents significantly predicted children's receptive vocabulary skills at the end of the school year, as well as motivation, attention/ persistence, and lower levels of classroom behavior problems. Homes with high levels of parent involvement in their children's education were characterized by specific behaviors reflecting active promotion of a learning environment at home. These environmental behaviors included creating space for learning activities at home, providing learning oppor- tunities for the child in the community, supervision and monitoring of class assignments and projects, daily conversations about school, and reading to young children at home.

One concern about this line of research is that it may be viewed as a deprivation model in which low-SES homes are considered deficient in certain characteristics that lead to high scores on IQ and achievement tests. Such homes may also be abundant in characteristics not necessarily valued by the researcher. Still, there is growing evidence that home environment is an important predictor of cognitive development both within and between cultures. There is a hopeful message in these findings in that as home environment changes on these key dimensions, IQ and achievement test scores will also increase. At the same time, however, these children exist in a world where institutional racism is still present to some degree, and limits opportunities for cognitive enrichment through access to high- quality schools or, as adults, through mentally challenging work, etc.

THE ROLE OF THE PERSON IN THE DEVELOPMENT AND MAINTENANCE OF COGNITIVE ABILITIES

Without detracting from the critical role that familial and societal forces play in the cognitive development of individuals, we believe that it is also important to examine the role of individual differences in each person's approach to the environment. Assuming that proper cognitive stimulation is present at the right time, there are non-cognitive characteristics of each individual that mediate the actualization and maintenance of cognitive potential. The list of possible non-cognitive factors is long, and encompasses basic temperament and personality factors. Some people actively engage with the world around them, drawing inspiration and energy from others, and proactively seeking positive reinforcement from their environment. This approach to one's environment enhances cognitive abilities. Others turn inward for energy and insight, passively accommodate to the world around them, and seek only to avoid negative stimulation from the environment. This stance seeks to preserve current status, and if extreme, may inhibit cognitive potential. This *enhancing* versus *preserving* trait is one of the three basic dimensions of Millon's theory of normal personology (Weiss, 1997, 2002). People that seek out versus shut off stimulation will have different experiences even in the same environment, and their opportunities for sustaining cognitive growth into early and middle adulthood will likewise differ. Some people are receptive to new information, continuously revising and refining concepts based on an open exchange of information with the world around them. This curious, open, perceiving stance may facilitate cognitive growth. Others prefer to systematize new information into known categories as soon as possible, and reject or ignore additional information as soon as an acceptable classification can be made. While a strong organizational framework can be a positive influence on cognitive development, a closed, judging stance can inhibit intellectual growth through middle adulthood if extreme.

Also relevant to cognitive development, learning and the life-long expression of intelligent behavior are general conative (i.e., non-cognitive) characteristics such as focus, motivation, and volition. Focus involves directionality of goal. Volition involves intensity toward the goal, or will. Motivation can be proximal or distal. A proximal motivation would be a specific near-term goal. A distal motivation might be a desired state (e.g., to be respected by one's peers) or a core trait (e.g., need for achievement). The list of positive characteristics is long, but includes self-efficacy and self-concept. Self-efficacy is driven by positive self-concept in combination with learned skill sets. Self-efficacy is task-specific, whereas self-concept is general. People who have high self-efficacy with respect to intellectual tasks may have experienced initial successes with similar tasks. They also are likely to gain more from new intellectual activities then others of similar intelligence, especially if they are intellectually engaged in the task and highly motivated to master it. Intellectual engagement and mastery motivation are critical elements of cognitive growth, along with the ability to self-regulate one's actions toward a goal. Presence of these personal characteristics may enhance cognitive development and the likelihood of success at a variety of life endeavors. However, different factors may be related to success versus failure at intellectual endeavors. After controlling for intellectual level, it may not be simply the absence of positive factors but the presence of specific negative personal factors that are associated with failure to thrive intellectually. Negative predictors may include severe procrastination, motivation to avoid failure, extreme perfectionism, excessive rumination, distractibility from goals, rigid categorical thinking (i.e., functional fixedness), cognitive interference due to social-emotional disorders, or diagnosed psychopathology Lacking from the psychologist's tool kit is a practical and reliable way to measure these conative factors. Still, practitioners conducting psychological and neuropsychological evaluations may find it useful to broaden the scope of their assessment and inquire about these non-cognitive traits as potential moderators of cognitive development, prophylactics of normal age-related decline, or catalysts for cognitive rehabilitation.

PATTERNS OF IQ AND INDEX SCORE DIFFERENCES ACROSS RACIAL/ETHNIC GROUPS

With the above discussion on test bias, fairness, and demographic differences in various areas of life as background, we now present mean WAIS-IV IQ and index scores by racial/ethnic group in Table 4.3. Although we have taken care to elaborate the psychometric, environmental, and individual difference variables that must be considered when interpreting these data, we are nonetheless concerned that some will take this information out of context and interpret it either as evidence of genetically determined differences in intelligence among the races, or as proof of test bias. We are convinced that such interpretations would be scientifically unsound, divisive to society, and harmful to patients.

TABLE 4.3   Mean and standard deviation (SD) of WAIS-IV index and FSIQ scores for each racial/ethnic group ($n = 2200$)

	White ($n = 1540$)	African American ($n = 260$)	Hispanic ($n = 289$)	Asian ($n = 71$)	Other ($n = 40$)
VCI	102.92 (13.87)	91.15 (14.25)	91.41 (15.25)	103.77 (15.31)	100.63 (13.87)
PRI	102.87 (14.35)	88.33 (12.90)	94.1 (13.43)	104.34 (14.66)	98.15 (14.56)
WMI	102.68 (14.10)	92.12 (14.07)	91.76 (15.16)	104.41 (14.45)	99.65 (13.75)
PSI	101.86 (14.33)	91.89 (14.94)	95.75 (14.51)	107.59 (16.14)	98.03 (16.16)
FSIQ	103.21 (13.77)	88.67 (13.68)	91.63 (14.29)	106.07 (15.01)	98.93 (13.99)

As we have shown above, education levels vary substantially and systematically by racial/ethnic group. This fact has critical implications for the collection of standardization samples when developing intelligence, and neuropsychological tests. The first step in defining an appropriate standardization sample is to identify the variables that account for substantial variance in the construct of interest, and stratify the sample to represent the population on those variables. For intelligence tests, these variables have traditionally been socio-economic status, race/ethnicity, age, gender, and region of the country. These variables may act singly, or in complex interactions such that race/ethnicity may be masking other underlying causal variables. Most test authors select education level as the single indicator of socio-economic status (SES) because of its high correlation with direct indicators of SES, such as household income and occupation, and because it is more reliably reported than income. Given the truncated range of education in the non-White and Hispanic groups resulting from the differential drop-out rates and other factors reported above, however, education may work as a better indicator of indirect SES effects on test scores for Whites than for African Americans and Hispanics.

Current practice in test development is to fully cross all stratification variables with each other, and most major intelligence test publishers follow this practice. Thus, for example, the percentage of Hispanics or African Americans with college degrees in the standardization sample will be much less than that of college-educated Whites in the sample. While this sampling methodology accurately reflects each population as it exists in society, it exaggerates the difference between the mean IQ test scores of these groups because the SES levels of the various racial/ethnic subsamples are not equal in the test's standardization sample. If test publishers were to use the same national SES percentages for all racial/ethnic groups, the IQ score gap between groups would be smaller – although not eliminated for all groups, as we will demonstrate later in this chapter. At the same time, however, this alternate sampling procedure would obscure the magnitude of societal differences in the cognitive milieu of people from diverse cultural and linguistic groups.

As shown in Table 4.3, the highest mean FSIQ score was obtained by the Asian sample (106.1), followed by the White (103.2), Hispanic (91.6), and African American (88.7) samples. The largest difference is observed between the Asian and African American groups – more than a full standard deviation (17.4 points). The White/African American difference is 14.5 FSIQ points, and the Hispanic/White difference is 11.6 points. Recall that these data are based on samples matched to the US Census for education and region of the country within racial/ethnic group. Thus, these racial/ethnic samples reflect all the educational and social inequities that exist between these groups in the population, as elaborated above. Also noteworthy is that the "Other" group (consisting of Native American

Indians, Alaskan Natives and Pacific Islanders) obtained a mean WISC-IV FSIQ score of 98.9 – which is very near the population mean of 100.

As noted above, it is sometimes assumed that African Americans and Hispanics score lower than Whites because the test assesses middle-class White socio-cultural values not fully shared by culturally and linguistically diverse groups. It is noteworthy, therefore, that the Asian sample scores highest, because the Asian sample is very culturally and linguistically diverse as compared to Whites in the US, and is arguably the most culturally distant of the groups assessed in this chapter.

Several additional points are notable concerning differences in the profile of mean index scores within and across groups. While the White group presents mean scores across the four indexes that are all within 1 point of each other, the African American group shows VCI scores 2.8 points higher than PRI. This is important in terms of interpreting VCI/PRI discrepancies in a culturally sensitive manner. It is commonly assumed that the verbal subtests are the most biased for African Americans due to this group's distance from the dominant culture and use of African-American English, but the currently available data do not support this view. However, no studies to date have examined the linguistic diversity within the group classified as African American, which includes Black immigrants from multiple countries and cultures. While the African American group is traditionally considered monolingual, this assumption may not be valid. Researchers tend to limit discussion of African American linguistic diversity to dialects. Within the group classified as African American, however, there is the indigenous African American language (Gullah), as well as French, Spanish, Portuguese, many continental African languages (e.g., Amharic), and Caribbean languages (e.g., Haitian Creole). Because researchers traditionally have assumed that the African American group is monolingual, the influence of language on acculturation and cognitive or achievement test performance has not been adequately investigated.

For the African American group, the PSI score is 3.5 points higher than PRI. For the Hispanic group, the highest index score is the PSI. These observations are of particular interest, because it is sometimes assumed that Hispanics and African Americans score lower on IQ measures like the WAIS-IV because of the speeded nature of some of the tasks. The reasoning behind this is that speed and time are valued differently by culturally diverse groups, so on tasks requiring quick performance, African Americans and Hispanics are likely to score lower. These data suggest that common assumptions about the cultural effects of speed and timed performance among African American and Hispanic test-takers may not be supported by the currently available data.

It is also worth pointing out that the racial ethnic gaps in FSIQ scores are generally larger for adults than for children and adolescents. For example, the mean FSIQ score for African Americans is 3 points higher on WISC-IV (91.7) than on WAIS-IV (88.7), while the White mean remained constant across the tests (approximately 103). Thus, the 14.5 point African American/White gap found for adults is 11.5 points for children and adolescents. For Hispanics, this comparison revealed similar but smaller trends.

Furthermore, the racial ethnic gaps are even smaller for children than adolescents. Using matched samples, we previously showed that the African American/White gap in WISC-IV FSIQ is 11.8 points for adolescents and 6 points for children. Similarly, we showed that the Hispanic/White gap was 8 points for adolescents and 1.3 points for children (Prifitera et al., 2005).

Taken together, these findings raise the question of possible generational changes in societal conditions that improve opportunities for cognitive growth and development. Clearly, increases in mean IQ scores have been well documented over many generations – with younger generations obtaining higher scores – and while the reasons for these changes are unknown, they are typically attributed to societal improvements in health, nutrition, and education (Flynn, 1984, 1987; Flynn & Weiss, 2007).

Following this line of reasoning, we examined WAIS-IV mean scores in five birth cohorts for each racial ethnic group, and clear generational increases emerged for the African American and Hispanic groups as shown in Table 4.4. This pattern of scores across generations showed little change between birth cohorts 2 and 3 for Hispanics, and between cohorts 3 and 4 for African Americans. Also, cohort 5 showed a significant reversal among Hispanics. Still, the general trend toward increasing scores with younger subjects is striking. For those born between 1917 and 1942 the mean FSIQ score was 83.6 and 85.1 for the African American and Hispanic groups, respectively. For those born between 1988 and 1991 the mean FSIQ score was 92.2 and 92.9 for African American and Hispanic groups,

TABLE 4.4   WAIS-IV mean FSIQ scores for African Americans and Hispanics by birth cohort

	Birth cohort				
	1	**2**	**3**	**4**	**5**
	1917–1942 (ages 65–90)	**1943–1962 (ages 45–64)**	**1963–1977 (ages 30–44)**	**1978–1987 (ages 20–29)**	**1988–1991 (ages 16–19)**
AA	83.6 ($n = 57$)	86.3 ($n = 42$)	90.7 ($n = 53$)	90.4 ($n = 55$)	92.2 ($n = 53$)
Hispanic	85.1 ($n = 39$)	89.9 ($n = 42$)	89.6 ($n = 65$)	96.5 ($n = 79$)	92.9 ($n = 64$)

respectively. These FSIQ score increases are 8.6 and 7.8 points for the African American and Hispanic groups, respectively, which is more than half a standard deviation.

We considered that higher IQ scores for later birth cohorts may be related to the trend toward more years of education among the younger age groups. If this were the case we would anticipate the largest effects on the VCI, which is sometimes believed to be more related to crystallized knowledge as taught in schools than are the other index scores. We examined the trend for each index score, however, and found that the trend was present for all index scores, and VCI did not demonstrate the largest increase. To further test the hypothesis that FSIQ increases for younger cohorts are attributable to increased levels of education, analyses of covariance (ANCOVA) were computed separately for the African American and Hispanic samples treating FSIQ as the dependent variable, birth cohort as the independent variable (using the bands shown in Table 4.4), and years of education as a covariate. These analyses revealed that there are significant age effects for FSIQ after controlling for amount of education across birth cohorts for both the African American (F = 2.94, $p < 0.05$, df = 3, $\eta^2 = 0.0202$) and Hispanic (F = 5.72, $p < 0.05$, df = 3, $\eta^2 = 0.0377$) samples. At the same time these effect sizes are small, which indicates that while there are large differences between education groups, the variability in FSIQ scores within education groups is also large for both African Americans and Hispanics. It is also noteworthy that the effect sizes were very similar with and without controlling for education. This finding is consistent with research with other data sets that has also found relatively small attenuation of the cross-sectional age differences in cognitive functioning after adjusting for amount of education (Salthouse, 2010).

Of course, these analyses only control for the amount of education, and can yield no information about possible changes in the quality of educational experiences available to African American and Hispanic groups across generations. Still, the results suggest that the higher scores obtained by younger generations are not likely due to having more years of education.

The White mean varied by less than 1 point across age bands, as expected, because the test's score distribution is normed by age and the sample is in the majority White. Thus, the racial ethnic gaps are narrowing with each succeeding generation. Table 4.5 shows the mean FSIQ scores differences for the African American/White and Hispanic/White comparisons by birth cohort. These gaps clearly decrease for younger ages. While the WAIS-IV FSIQ mean difference for African American/White comparison is 14.5 points across all ages, it is 19.3 points for those over age 65, and 10 points for adolescents. Thus, the African American/White IQ score gap has decreased by 9.3 points between the oldest and youngest subjects. Similarly, while the Hispanic/White mean difference is

TABLE 4.5   WAIS-IV mean difference scores between racial/ethnic groups
by birth cohort

	Birth cohort				
	1917–1942 (ages 65–90)	1943–1962 (ages 45–64)	1963–1977 (ages 30–44)	1978–1987 (ages 20–29)	1988–1991 (ages 16–19)
African American/White	19.3	17.2	13.1	13.4	10.0
Hispanic/White	17.9	13.62	14.2	7.3	9.3

Note: Ages shown are at time of standardization testing in 2007.

11.5 points in the total sample, it is 17.9 points for those over age 65, but 7.3 points for those in their twenties, and then reverses to 9.3 points for adolescents. Caution is warranted in interpretation, however, as these data are cross-sectional, not longitudinal, and so it is not known if the younger birth cohorts will maintain their somewhat higher IQ scores as they age. However, cohort-substitution studies have produced results that agree remarkably well with cross-sectional cognitive data (Kaufman, 2009: 276).

In the early part of the last century, Spearman (1927, cited in Vroon, 1980) hypothesized that group differences in IQ test scores could be explained by innate differences in "*g*" between the races, and this position continues to rear its controversial head 70 years later (Jensen, 1998; Murray, 2005). Some will likely follow this antiquated line of reasoning and argue that the AA FSIQ was increased in WAIS-IV by increasing the contribution of subtests with lower "*g*" loadings (e.g., Digit Span and Symbol Search) in the FSIQ, and they could be correct in so far as psychometric studies of "*g*" are concerned. However, we would point out that many of the subtests which are purported to be stronger measures of "*g*" are also those that are more readily influenced by environmental opportunity, such as Vocabulary. Further, the more "*g*"-saturated abstract and fluid reasoning tasks found in the perceptual scale have also been shown to be susceptible to the effects of changes in environment over time (Flynn, 1984, 1987; Neisser, 1998). Finally, the WM and PS subtests tap neurocognitive abilities, which may be less influenced by environment.

At this point in our discussion, it may be worth stating the obvious: studies showing between-group differences in IQ test scores say nothing about the source of those differences. As Sternberg, Grigorenko, and Kidd (2005) concluded, the statement that racial differences in IQ or academic achievement are of genetic origin is a "leap of imagination." We have repeatedly noted that race/ethnicity is likely to be a proxy variable for a set of active mechanisms that have only been partially identified. In fact, the reason why between-group differences appear to exist may be because the variables that they are substituting for have not been fully identified. Thus, we are not in agreement with Spearman's hypothesis that differences in IQ scores across racial/ethnic groups reflect differences in genotypic ability. We seek to reframe the question in terms of differential opportunity for development of cognitive abilities. Alternatively, cognitively enriched environments may be a synonym for acculturative experiences. Thus, Spearman's hypothesis for IQ score differences across racial/ethnic groups could be reframed in terms of either differential opportunity for cognitive development, or differential acculturation experiences. In the next section, we report the results of a series of analyses designed to evaluate the extent to which differences in socio-economic status account for FSIQ differences between racial and ethnic groups.

SES MEDIATORS OF FSIQ DIFFERENCES BETWEEN CULTURALLY DIVERSE GROUPS

In this section, we explore how SES mediates the gap between racial and ethnic groups in intelligence test scores using the WAIS-IV standardization over-sample. This discussion is not about nature/nurture, or about race and IQ. It is about helping people understand why test scores may vary based on contextual factors, and using that information to help clients.

We applied a regression-based methodology recommended by Helms, Jernigan, and Mascher (2005) to examine how much of the variance in FSIQ test scores attributed to racial/ethnic group is reduced when relevant mediator variables are introduced. Table 4.6 shows these analyses for the African American/White and Hispanic/White comparisons for ages 20–90. In Model 1 of the African American/White analysis, we regress FSIQ on race. As shown in the table, race accounts for 14.98 percent of the variance in FSIQ score, and the mean African American/White difference is 14.88 points. (Note: The results in these analyses may differ slightly from the mean FSIQ difference reported above based on use of the standardization over-sample, which is slightly larger then the standardization sample.) In Model 2, we regress FSIQ on education. As shown in the table, education alone accounts for almost twice as much variance (29 percent) in FSIQ as does race alone. In Model 3, we introduce occupation, income, region, and gender to the education model. Occupation is self reported in 17 categories, ranging from unemployed not seeking work to executive. Subjects were asked to indicate their current and highest job categories, and the latter was used. For income, we used the median income of the subject's zip code. Region of residence indicates the four regions of the country (Northeast, Midwest, South, and West) used to stratify the standardization sample. Model 3 accounts for 35.1 percent of the variance, which is 6.1 percent more than the education alone model. Finally, in

TABLE 4.6 Ages 20–90: Hierarchical regression analyses of mediators of mean racial and ethnic differences in WAIS-IV FSIQ scores

Analyses of African American (n = 297) and White (n = 1219) samples ages 20–90

		R^2	R^2 DIFF	% of African American/White effect mediated	Mean African American/White difference after mediation
Model 1	Race	0.1498			14.88
Model 2	Education	0.2902			
Model 3	Education, occupation, income, region, gender	0.3514	0.0612		
Model 4	Education, occupation, income, region, gender, race	0.4437	0.0923	38.4%	11.23

Analyses of Hispanic (n = 344) and White (n = 1219) samples ages 20–90

		R^2	R^2 DIFF	% of Hispanic/White effect mediated	Mean Hispanic/White difference after mediation
Model 1	Ethnicity	0.1112			11.95
Model 2	Education	0.3113			
Model 3	Education, occupation, income, region, gender	0.3713	0.0600		
Model 4	Education, occupation, income, region, gender, ethnicity	0.4090	0.0377	66.1%	6.56

Note: Mediators are the adult's level of education in 5 bands, occupation in 17 bands, income as estimated by zip code, 4 regions of the country, gender, and racial/ethnic group.
Copyright © 2009 by Pearson, Inc. Reproduced with permission. All rights reserved.

Model 4, we add race to all previously entered variables. Model 4 shows that the amount of variance in FSIQ scores remaining for race to explain was 9.23 percent after controlling for education, occupation, income, region, and gender. Combined, these variables mediated 38.4 percent of the African American/White effect. Controlling for these variables reduced the mean difference score to 11.23 points.

In Model 1 of the Hispanic/White analysis, we regress FSIQ on ethnicity. As shown in the table, ethnicity accounts for 11.12 percent of the variance in FSIQ scores, and the mean Hispanic/White difference is 11.95 points. (Note: The results in these analyses may differ slightly from the mean FSIQ difference reported above based on use of the standardization over-sample, which is slightly larger then the standardization sample.) In Model 2, we regress FSIQ on education. As shown in the table, education alone accounts for almost three times as much variance (31.13 percent) in FSIQ as does ethnicity alone. In Model 3, we again introduce occupation, income, region, and gender to the education model. Model 3 accounts for 37.13 percent of the variance, which is 6.0 percent more than the education alone model. Finally, in Model 4, we add ethnicity to all previously entered variables. Model 4 shows that the amount of variance in FSIQ scores remaining for ethnicity to explain was 3.77 percent after controlling for education, occupation, income, region, and gender. Combined, these variables mediated 66.1 percent of the Hispanic/White effect. Controlling for these variables reduced the mean difference score to 6.56 points.

Table 4.7 shows the same analyses for ages 16–19. In Model 1 of the African American/White analysis, we regress FSIQ on race. As shown in the table, race accounts for 5.37 percent of the variance in FSIQ score, and the mean African American/White difference is 7.89 points. (Note: The results in these analyses may differ slightly from the mean FSIQ difference reported above based on use of the standardization over-sample, which is slightly larger then the standardization sample.) In Model 2, we regress FSIQ on parent education. As shown in the table, parent education alone accounts for three times as much variance (15.26 percent) in FSIQ as does race alone. In Model 3, we introduce parent occupation, parent income, region, and the subject's gender to the parent education model. Model 3 accounts for 22.49 percent of the variance, which is 7.23 percent more than the parent education alone model. Finally, in Model 4, we add race to all previously entered variables. Model 4 shows that the amount of variance in FSIQ scores remaining for race to explain was 1.46 percent after controlling for parental education, occupation, income, region, and subject gender. Combined, these variables mediated 72.8 percent of the African American/White effect for adolescents. Controlling for these variables reduced the mean difference score to 3.87 points.

In Model 1 of the Hispanic/White analysis for ages 16–19, we regress FSIQ on ethnicity. As shown in the table, ethnicity accounts for

TABLE 4.7 Ages 16–19: Hierarchical regression analyses of parental mediators of mean racial/ethnic differences in WAIS-IV FSIQ

Analyses of African American ($n = 25$) and White ($n = 106$) samples ages 16–19

	R^2	R^2 DIFF	% of African American/White effect mediated	Mean African American/White difference after mediation
Model 1 Race	0.0537			7.89
Model 2 Education	0.1526			
Model 3 Education, occupation, income, region, gender	0.2249	0.0723		
Model 4 Education, occupation, income, region, gender, race	0.2395	0.0146	72.8%	3.87

Analyses of Hispanic ($n = 24$) and White ($n = 106$) samples ages 16–19

	R^2	R^2 DIFF	% of Hispanic/White effect mediated	Mean Hispanic/White difference after mediation
Model 1 Ethnicity	0.1201			11.96
Model 2 Education	0.2532			
Model 3 Education, occupation, income, region, gender	0.2931	0.0399		
Model 4 Education, occupation, income, region, gender, ethnicity	0.3119	0.0188	84.3%	3.95

12.01 percent of the variance in FSIQ scores, and the mean Hispanic/White difference is 11.96 points. (Note: The results in these analyses may differ slightly from the mean FSIQ difference reported above based on use of the standardization over-sample, which is slightly larger then the standardization sample.) In Model 2, we regress FSIQ on parent education. As shown in the table, parent education alone accounts for slightly more than twice as much variance (25.32 percent) in FSIQ as does ethnicity alone. In Model 3, we again introduce parental occupation, parent income, region, and the subject's gender to the parent education model. Model 3 accounts for 29.31 percent of the variance, which is 3.9 percent more than the parent education alone model. Finally, in Model 4, we add ethnicity to all previously entered variables. Model 4 shows that the amount of variance in FSIQ scores remaining for ethnicity to explain was 1.88 percent after controlling for parent education, occupation, income, region, and subject gender. Combined, these variables mediated 84.3 percent of the Hispanic/White effect for adolescents. Controlling for these variables reduced the mean difference score to 3.95 points.

Several key themes are obvious from careful inspection of these results. First, education accounts for far greater variance in IQ test scores than racial ethnic status – twice as much or more. Second, education explains more variance in IQ scores for adults than adolescents. In part, this may be because parental rather than self education is used with adolescents, so the effect is indirect. Third, parent education explains considerably less variance in IQ for African American than Hispanic adolescents. Fourth, after controlling for all SES mediators available in this data set, the amount of variance remaining for racial ethnic status is higher for adults than adolescents, and clearly highest for African American adults. Further, the percent of the IQ gap mediated in the full models is lower for adults than adolescents, and lowest for African American adults. Taken together, these observations suggest that the mediators used in this study are less strongly related to cognitive ability for African American adults as compared to either African American adolescents or Hispanics of any age.

Theoretically, if SES fully explains differential opportunities in cognitive development, then controlling for SES should eliminate IQ test score differences between groups. Why do most studies show score differences between the African American and White groups after controlling for key SES variables such as education, income, region, etc.? Part of the answer is that these variables exert their effects indirectly, and are therefore called *distal* rather than *proximal*. Indirect effects are typically less precise than direct effects. Another part of the answer is that unmeasured inequities in societal forces – as described above – may dampen the positive effects of increased education on growth opportunities for African Americans. For example, the quality of education available to culturally diverse groups has not historically been equal. Degrees from high schools in different regions may not have the same value, depending in part on the amount of educational funding in the local district. Historical inequities in employment practices may have limited the earning opportunities for otherwise well-educated African Americans, which in turn may restrict the neighborhoods that are affordable to them, and thus the quality of schools available to their children. And historical inequities in banking and housing practices have likely contributed to the overall problem. These and other social inequities may have been more powerful factors for older generations of African Americans and Hispanics, but are still present to some degree in younger generations.

The indirect nature of the distal variables, as discussed above, means that the relationship is not perfect. These are "proxy" variables – that is, they serve as convenient indicators of other variables that are difficult to measure directly. The level of education attained is a powerful demographic variable influencing cognitive ability scores. Although not perfectly correlated with the financial situation of the family, this variable serves as a reasonable proxy for overall socio-economic status. Education is in turn related to a host of important variables, including the employment opportunities, income level, housing, neighborhood, access to prenatal and postnatal care for offspring, adequacy of nutrition during infancy and early development, and quality of educational experience available to the next generation. Much of this may have to do with enriched early stimulation and opportunity to learn and grow in a safe and secure environment. Researchers assume that people with more education have better access to good jobs, pediatric care, quality schools, and safe neighborhoods – but this is not always the case. Because of the historical inequities noted above, education, income, and other SES-related variables may operate differently in different groups. The typically strong associations between intelligence, education, employment, and income may have been muted by historical patterns of discrimination that continue to some degree today, but were clearly stronger among the older birth cohorts. To date, no matched studies have been accomplished that directly control for all medical, societal, legal, environmental, financial, and educational factors known to account for variance in cognitive development.

Similarly, medical researchers have found that controlling for SES eliminates race disparities in health outcomes for some, but not all, medical disorders, and that psychosocial factors have been found to mitigate the relationship between SES and health outcomes. Such factors have been shown to include perceptions of unfair treatment (race, gender), cynical hostility, anger expression, coping style, and locus of control (Whitfield, Weidner, Clark, & Anderson, 2002).

More generally, results gleaned from research studies (such as those reviewed in this chapter) provide invaluable information that informs psychologists, sociologists, political scientists, and others about group characteristics. However, psychology is unique in its commitment to understanding an individual's differences. Although research studies may provide helpful insights as to qualities that enhance or attenuate cognitive development and maintenance for groups, psychologists must not assume that the group data characterize every individual being assessed. When we uncritically apply group-level research findings in our clinical practices, we may inadvertently stereotype the very individuals who were referred to us for help.

It is for all of these reasons that we wish to leave behind the study of racial/ethnic differences in cognitive ability test scores and turn the reader's attention to proximal mediators of the development, expression, and maintenance of cognitive abilities for all people. Our direction is influenced by Helms and colleagues (2005), who called upon the field to cease the use of race as an independent variable in psychological research. This direction is also consistent with recent advances in the study of the humane genome that have led writers from diverse academic disciplines to argue that race is a socially constructed and biologically meaningless concept (Cavalli-Sforza, 2001; Schwartz, 2001; Marks, 2002), while others suggest that the division lines between racial/ethnic groups are highly fluid and that most genetic variation exists within genetic groups, not between them (Foster & Sharp, 2002: 848). Further, despite the lightning pace of recent advances in genetics, attempts to establish genes for intelligence have so far found only weak effects, been inconclusive, or failed to replicate (Plomin *et al.*, 1995; Chorney *et al.*, 1998; Hill *et al.*, 1999; Hill, Chorney, & Plomin, 2002).

At some point in the future psychological researchers will most certainly cease using racial/ethnic status groupings, because of the increasing fluidity of racial and ethnic boundaries as well as the wide variability of culture and language within racial and ethnic groups. Future researchers may wish to study how socially constructed concepts of culture other than race mediate development of particular cognitive abilities.

At this point, we leave behind the study of racial/ethnic differences in intelligence, as others are already doing. We now turn the proverbial corner and begin a preliminary discussion of personal and developmental variables that influence cognitive skill acquisition and maintenance of cognitive abilities for adults within and across cultural groups – that is, regardless of one's race or ethnicity.

ARE THERE INDIVIDUAL MEDIATORS OF INTELLIGENCE THAT ARE UNIVERSAL?

Several supplemental survey questions were asked of all subjects who participated in the standardization of the WAIS-IV. From this group of questions we selected a subset that were found useful in the preparation of formulas for the purpose of estimating premorbid IQ and index scores of patients who had been tested following a brain injury or the onset of a brain disorder which had presumably reduced their scores from some pre-injury level (see *Advanced Clinical Solutions*; Wechsler, 2009). The first set of items is shown in Table 4.8, and has been tentatively labeled personal factors. One of the questions asks for the individual's subjective impression of the SES level of the neighborhood in which he or she lives. Subjective experiences of SES are important when they are different from objective ratings such as neighborhood income. For example, as noted earlier, some immigrants compare themselves to the status of relatives in their country of origin, and may not feel poor even though they would be considered poor by US standards. On the other side of the SES continuum, although the first author of this chapter lives in an upper middle-class professional neighborhood, he sometimes feels stress because all three of his first cousins are highly successful stockbrokers who live in mansions! The point is that stress induced by perceived SES disparities is quite real to the individual, and can be a driver of risk behaviors for physical and mental health. Further, such stress also can be a driver of behaviors associated with intellectual stimulation and growth, or environmental stagnation and cognitive decline. Partly for this reason, a second question from the

TABLE 4.8   Personal Items

1. The neighborhood I currently live in is

   a. Wealthy
   b. Well-off
   c. Average
   d. Somewhat poor
   e. Poor
2. When I change jobs, it is a step up for me
   a. Strongly agree
   b. Agree
   c. Neither agree nor disagree
   d. Disagree
   e. Strongly disagree
3. How many times per month do you participate in social gatherings or activities?
4. How many times per month do you participate in aerobic activities (e.g., jogging, walking, running, stair climbing)?
5. How many times per month do you participate in weightlifting?
6. How many hours sleep did you have last night?
   a. Open response

Note: For items 3–5, the response options were as follows: Never, 1–2 times per month, 3–4 times per month, 5+ times per month. Item 6 utilized an open ended response format.

supplemental survey asks whether job changes are typically steps upward. Further questions ask about the number of times per month the person participates in social activities, aerobics, or weightlifting. Finally, one question asks how much sleep the person had the night before testing. These questions assume that staying social active and physically healthy are related to maintenance of cognitive abilities.

Another set of items recorded the educational level of the subject's mother and father, and then asked for the subject's subjective rating of the quality of the elementary school he or she attended on a five=point scale ranging from superior to poor. These three items are tentatively called developmental background factors. They are used only in the analyses of adults ages 20–90. This is because parent education is already accounted for in our prediction models for adolescents.

Table 4.9 shows a series of prediction models designed to examine the impact of these personal and developmental factors on FSIQ for adults ages 20–90. Model 1 shows that the adult's education level accounts for 28.7 percent of the variance in FSIQ. As expected, education accounts for a large amount of variance in intelligence. Model 2 shows that developmental factors account for 22.9 percent of the variance in FSIQ. Model 3 shows that personal factors account for 9.5 percent of the variance. Model 4 shows that developmental and personal factors together account for 25.6 percent of the variance. This means that personal factors account for 2.6 percent incremental variance after controlling for developmental factors. Model 5 shows that the combined contributions of education, occupation, income, region, and gender account for 35.6 percent of the variance. In Model 6, we enter developmental and personal factors first and then add education, occupation, income, region, and gender. This full model explains 40.4 percent of the variance in FSIQ scores of adults ages 20–90. Model 6 also shows that the combined contribution of education, occupation, income, region, and gender reduces from 35.6 percent to

TABLE 4.9   Ages 20–90: Hierarchical regression analyses of personal and developmental factors as mediators of WAIS-IV FSIQ

		R^2	R^2 DIFF
Model 1	EDL	0.2871	
Model 2	Developmental factor	0.2296	
Model 3	Personal factor	0.0950	
Model 4	Developmental + Personal	0.2558	
Model 5	EDL + Occupation + Income + Region + Sex	0.3564	
Model 6	Developmental + Personal + EDL + Occupation + Income + Region + Sex	0.4042	0.1484 (compared to Model 4)

14.8 percent after controlling for developmental and personal factors. We elected to enter developmental and personal factors first in the full model, because these variables precede most of the others in time and may be drivers of future educational attainment, occupation, and income for adults.

In Table 4.10, we examine these same issues for adolescents ages 16–19, except we eliminate the developmental factor, as this is substantially the same as the parent education variable which is already in the model. In this age group, parent education alone accounts for 16.1 percent variance in Model 1. Personal factors alone account for 19.8 percent of the variance in Model 2. Personal factors and parent education combine to explain 26.6 percent of the variance in Model 3, which also demonstrates that the effect of parent education decreases from 16.1 percent alone to 6.7 percent after controlling for personal factors. Parent education, occupation, income, region, and gender of subject combine to account for 20.1 percent variance in Model 4. This means that parent occupation, income, region, and subject gender combined account for approximately 4 percent incremental variance after controlling for parent education. In Model 5, personal factors are added to Model 4 and entered last. This full model explains 28.8 percent of the variance in WAIS-IV FSIQ scores for adolescents between the ages of 16 and 19. Model 5 also shows that the effect of personal factors decreases from 19.8 percent alone to 8.7 percent after controlling for parent education, occupation, income, region, and subject gender. We elected to enter personal factors last in the full model for adolescents because we suspect that these variables generally exert their effect within the context of the family-related variables (e.g., parent education, occupation and income).

Several interpretations can be stated based on these analyses. For adolescents, personal factors account for more variance (approximately 20 percent) in WAIS-IV FSIQ than does parent education (approximately

TABLE 4.10   Ages 16–19: Hierarchical regression analyses of personal and developmental factors as mediators of WAIS-IV FSIQ

		R^2	R^2 DIFF
Model 1	EDL	0.1614	
Model 2	Personal factors	0.1986	
Model 3	Personal factors + EDL	0.2657	
Model 4	EDL + Occupation + Income + Region + Sex	0.2013	
Model 5	EDL + Occupation + Income + Region + Sex + Personal factors	0.2885	0.0872 (compared to Model 4)

Note: EDL is parent education for ages 16–19, and self education for ages 20–90.

16 percent). The effect of parent education reduces by more than half after controlling for personal factors. Further, the explanatory power of the personal factor remains substantial (approximately 9 percent) even after controlling for parent education, occupation, income, region, and subject gender.

Personal factors accounted for more variance among adolescents than adults. For adults ages 20–90, the developmental factor (including mother and father's education and perceived elementary school quality) accounted for a surprisingly large amount of variance (approximately 23 percent), although not as much as self education (approximately 29 percent). All factors combined explained more variance for adults (approximately 40 percent) than adolescents (approximately 29 percent). One hypothesis for this finding is that the predictive power of IQ for major life outcomes may increase with age. Alternatively, these factors may mediate opportunities for cognitive stimulation, which has a cumulative effect on cognitive functioning over time.

This is the second study we are aware of which shows another variable to be more powerful than parent education in predicting the FSIQ score of children or adolescents. We previously showed that parental expectations for children's academic success accounted for substantially more variance than parent education and income combined in WISC-IV FSIQ of children and adolescents ages 6–16. We concluded that when it comes to cognitive development of children, what parents do in the home with their children is more important than what they are in the world outside the home (Weiss *et al.*, 2006b).

Implicit assumptions are often made about how more educated mothers interact with their children in different ways from mothers with less formal education. More educated mothers are assumed to provide increased language stimulation to infants and toddlers, read more often to preschool age children, assist elementary school children more with homework, and generally provide more intellectually stimulating activities throughout childhood and adolescence. This is a broadly sweeping assumption that deserves to be examined in more detail. It is quite possible that there is considerable variability in parenting practices within SES groups, and that this variability influences the cognitive development of children.

Research with the WPPSI-III suggests that three home environment variables play an important role in the development of verbal abilities among young children. These variables are the numbers of hours per week that the parents spend reading to the child, that the child spends on the computer, and the child spends watching television. Mean WPPSI-III Verbal IQ (VIQ) scores increased with number of hours spent reading and on the computer, and decreased with number of hours watching television. There is also a clear relationship between these variables and parent education. At the same time, however, there was substantial variability in the frequency of these behaviors within levels of parent education. Thus, even among young children whose parents have similar levels of education, spending more time reading and using the computer, and less time watching television, is associated with higher verbal ability test scores (Sichi, 2003).

We would be the last to suggest that education is not important. To the contrary, our point is that individual differences in behavior and perceptions matter, too. Intelligence test scores are not isomorphic with parent education, self education, occupation, income, race, or ethnicity. Intelligence is not predetermined by these socio-demographic factors, although these factors seem to account for increasing variance with age.

In interpreting these results, it is also important to keep in mind the rather limited set of personal and developmental factors included. What is perhaps most intriguing is that meaningful effects can be demonstrated with such a small and incomplete survey of all the personal and developmental factors that research has shown to be related to intellectual growth and maintenance of intellectual abilities.

SUMMARY

We have endeavored in this chapter to make the case that contextual interpretation entails more than the historical regurgitation of racial and ethnic differences in performance on cognitive ability tests. These differences are neither due to item or test bias, nor are they unique with respect to many other important areas of life, such as educational attainment, mental and physical health, occupation and income. There is both an intersection and an overlap of factors that impact the development of intellectual abilities and processes, and one's capability to demonstrate those abilities, including both proximal and distal resources and social norms. We have offered a view that intelligence is malleable, within limits, by environmental factors that mediate opportunities for cognitive growth and maintenance of cognitive abilities, and that the effects of these mediators may be cumulative across the lifespan. We have presented evidence to suggest that racial ethnic differences in test scores may be decreasing with successive generations, and suggest that this may be because the cumulative effects of institutional racism were more pronounced on older generations, although it must be conceded that such factors are still present to some degree today. Further, racial/ethnic differences are likely to be proxies for a multitude of other variables that we are just beginning to identify and study. We have shown that personal factors account for significant variance in intelligence. We suggest that future researchers go beyond these easily collected proxy variables (i.e., race/ethnicity, and SES) and directly study the factors that are related to the development and maintenance of cognitive abilities both within and across culturally and linguistically diverse groups.

References

Bowden, S.C., Lissner, D., McCarthy, K.A., Weiss, L.G., & Holdnack, J.A. (2003). Equivalence of WAIS-III standardization data collected in Australia when compared to data collected in the US. Presentation at the CNN Satellite Symposium of the Australian Psychological Society Conference, Perth.

Bowden, S. C., Lloyd, D., Weiss, L. G., & Holdnack, J. A. (2006). Age related invariance of abilities measured with the Wechsler Adult Intelligence Scale – III. *Psychological Assessment, 18*(3), 334–339.

Bowden, S. C., Lange, R. T., Weiss, L. G., & Saklofske, D. (2008). Equivalence of the measurement model underlying the Wechsler Adult Intelligence Scale – III in the United States and Canada. *Educational and Psychological Measurement, 68*(6), 1024–1040.

Bradley, R. H., & Caldwell, B. M. (1981). The HOME inventory: A validation of the preschool for Black children. *Child Development, 53*, 708–710.

Bradley, R. H., & Caldwell, B. M. (1982). The consistency of the home environment and its relation to child development. *International Journal of Behavioral Development, 5*, 445–465.

Bradley, R. H., Caldwell, B. M., & Elardo, R. (1977). Home environment, social status, and mental test performance. *Journal of Educational Psychology, 69*, 697–701.

Bradley, R. H., Caldwell, B. M., Rock, S., Barnard, K., Gray, C., Hammond, M., Mitchell, S., Siegel, L., Ramey, C., Gottfried, A. W., & Johnson, D. L. (1989). Home environment and cognitive development in the first three years of life: A collaborative study involving six sites and three ethnic groups in North America. *Developmental Psychology, 28*, 217–235.

Bronfenbrenner, U., & Ceci, S. J. (1994). Nature–nurture reconceptualized in developmental perspective: A bio-ecological model. *Psychological Review, 101*, 568–586.

Brooks-Gunn, J., Klebanov, P. K., & Duncan, G. J. (1996). Ethnic differences in children's intelligence test scores: Role of economic deprivation, home environment, and maternal characteristics. *Child Development, 67*, 396–408.

Cavalli-Sforza, L. L. (2001). *Genes, Peoples, and Languages*. Berkeley, CA: University of California Press.

Ceci, S. J. (1996). *On Intelligence: A Bioecological Treatise on Intellectual Development* (expanded ed.). Cambridge, MA: Harvard University Press.

Chorney, M. J., Chorney, K., Seese, N., Owen, M. J., Daniels, J., McGuffin, P., et al. (1998). A quantitative trait locus associated with cognitive ability in children. *Psychological Science, 9*, 159–166.

Dickinson, D. K., & DeTemple, J. (1998). Putting parents in the picture: Maternal reports of preschoolers' literacy as a predictor of early reading. *Early Childhood Research Quarterly, 13*, 241–261.

Epstein, J. L. (1991). Effects on student achievement of teachers' practices of parent involvement. In S. B. Silvern (Ed.), *Advances in Reading/Language Research, Vol. 5, Literacy through Family, Community, and School Interaction* (pp. 61–276). Greenwich, CT: JAI Press.

Fantuzzo, J., McWayne, C., Perry, M. A., & Childs, S. (2004). Multiple dimensions of family involvement and their relations to behavioral and learning competencies for urban, low-income children. *School Psychology Review, 33*, 467–480.

Flynn, J. R. (1984). The mean IQ of Americans: massive gains 1932 to 1978. *Psychological Bulletin, 95*, 29–51.

Flynn, J.R. (1987). Massive IQ gains in 14 nations. *Psychological Bulletin, 101*, 171–191.

Flynn, J. R., & Weiss, L. (2007). American IQ gains from 1932 to 2002: The WISC subtests and educational progress. *International Journal of Testing, 7*, 1–16.

Foster, M. W., & Sharp, R. R. (2002). Race, ethnicity, and genomics: social classifications as proxies of biological heterogeneity. *Genome Research, 12*, 844–850.

Galper, A., Wigfield, A., & Seefeldt, C. (1997). Head Start parents' beliefs about their children's abilities, task values, and performances on different activities. *Child Development, 68*, 897–907.

Georgas, J., Weiss, L. G., van de Vijver, F. J. R., & Saklofske, D. H. (2003). *Culture and Children's Intelligence: Cross-cultural Analysis of the WISC–III*. San Diego, CA: Academic Press.

Gottfredson, L.S. (1998).The general intelligence factor. Scientific American, November, 1–10. Online. Available: http://www.scientificamerican.com/specialissues/1198intelligence/1198gottfred.html (accessed February 5, 2002).

Gottfredson, L. S., & Saklofske, D. H. (2009). Intelligence: Foundations and issues in assessment. *Canadian Psychology, 50*(3), 183–195.

Griffith, J. (1996). Relation of parental involvement, empowerment, and school traits to student academic performance. *Journal of Educational Research, 90*, 33–41.

Harris, J. G., Tulsky, D. S., & Schultheis, M. T. (2003). Assessment of the non-native English speaker: assimilating history and research findings to guide practice. In S. S. Tulsky, D. H. Saklofske, & G. J. Chelune et al. (Eds.), *Clinical Interpretation of the WAIS-III and WMS-III*. San Diego, CA: Elsevier, Inc.

Helms, J. E., Jernigan, M., & Mascher, J. (2005). The meaning of race in psychology and how to change it: A methodological perspective. *American Psychologist, 60*, 27–36.

Henderson, R. W. (1972). Environmental predictors of academic performance of disadvantaged Mexican-American children. *Journal of Consulting and Clinical Psychology, 38*, 297.

Henderson, R. W., & Merritt, C. B. (1968). Environmental background of Mexican-American children with different potentials for school success. *Journal of Social Psychology, 75*, 101–106.

Henderson, R. W., Bergan, J. R., & Hurt, M., Jr. (1972). Development and validation of the Henderson Environmental Learning Process Scale. *Journal of Social Psychology, 88*, 185–196.

Hill, L., Craig, I. W., Asherson, P., Ball, D., Eley, T., Ninomiya, T., et al. (1999). DNA pooling and dense marker maps: a systematic search for genes for cognitive ability. *NeuroReport, 10*, 843–848.

Hill, L., Chorney, M. C., & Plomin, R. (2002). A quantitative trait locus (not) associated with cognitive ability? *Psychological Science, 13*, 561–562.

Jensen, A. R. (1998). *The g Factor: The Science of Mental Ability*. Westport, CT: Praeger.

Johnson, D. L., Breckenridge, J., & McGowan, R. (1984). Home environment and early cognitive development in Mexican-American children. In A. W. Gottfried (Ed.), *Home Environment and Early Cognitive Development: Longitudinal Research* (pp. 151–195). Orlando, FL: Academic Press.

Johnson, D. L., Swank, P., Howie, V. M., Baldwin, C. D., Owen, M., & Luttman, D. (1993). Does HOME add to the prediction of child intelligence over and above SES? *Journal of Genetic Psychology, 154*, 33–40.

Kaufman, A. S. (2009). Clinical applications II: Age and intelligence across the adult life span. In E. O. Lichtenberger, & A. S. Kaufman (Eds.), *Essentials of WAIS-IV Assessment*. Hoboken, NJ: John Wiley and Sons.

Kaufman, P., Kwon, J.Y., Klein, S., & Chapman, C.D. (1999). Dropout rates in the United States: 1998. Statistical Analysis Report (NCES Report No. 2000-022. Online. Available: http://nces.ed.gov/pubs2000/2000022.pdf (accessed July 25, 2001).

Kayser, H. (1989). Speech and language assessment of Spanish-English speaking children. *Language, Speech, and Hearing Services in Schools, 20*, 226–244.

Keith, T. Z., Keith, P. B., Quirk, K. J., Sperduto, J., Santillo, S., & Killings, S. (1998). Longitudinal effects of parent involvement on high school grades: Similarities and differences across gender and ethnic groups. *Journal of School Psychology, 36*, 335–363.

Konold, T. R., & Canivez, G. L. (2010). Differential relationships among WISC-IV and WIAT-II scales: An evaluation of potentially moderating child demographics. *Educational and Psychological Measurement*, in press.

Mantzicopoulos, P. Y. (1997). The relationship of family variables to Head Start's children's pre-academic competence. *Early Education and Development, 8*, 357–375.

Marks, J. (2002). Folk heredity. In J. M. Fish (Ed.), *Race and Intelligence: Separating Science from Myth* (pp. 95–112). Mahwah, NJ: Erlbaum.

McDaniel, J. S., Purcell, D. W., & Farber, E. W. (1997). Severe mental illness and HIV-related medical and neuropsychiatric sequelae. *Clinical Psychology Review, 17*, 311–325.

Murray, C. (2005). The inequality taboo. *Commentary*, 13–22, September.

Neisser, U. (1998). Introduction: rising test scores and what they mean. In U. Neisser (Ed.), *The rising Curve: Long Term Gains in IQ and Related Measures* (pp. 3–22). Washington, DC: American Psychological Association.

Parker, F. L., Boak, A. Y., Griffin, K. W., Ripple, C., & Peay, L. (1999). Parent–child relationship, home learning environment, and school readiness. *School Psychology Review, 28*, 413–425.

Plomin, R., Mclearn, G. E., Smith, D. L., Skuder, P., Vignetti, S., Chorney, M. J., et al. (1995). Allelic associations between 100 DNA markers and high versus low IQ. *Intelligence, 21*, 31–48.

Poteat, G. M., Wuensch, K. L., & Gregg, N. B. (1988). An investigation of differential prediction with the WISC-R. *Journal of School Psychology, 26*, 59–68.

Prifitera, A., Weiss, L. G., & Saklofske, D. H. (1998). WISC-III in context. In A. Prifitera, & D. H. Saklofske (Eds.), *WISC-III Clinical Use and Interpretation: Scientist–Practitioner Perspectives*. San Diego, CA: Academic Press.

Prifitera, A., Weiss, L. G., Saklofske, D. H., & Rolfhus, E. (2005). The WISC-IV in the clinical assessment context. In A. Prifitera, D. H. Saklofske, & L. G. Weiss (Eds.), *WISC-IV Clinical Use and Interpretation: Scientist–Practitioner Perspectives*. San Diego, CA: Elsevier Academic Press.

Ramey, C., Farran, D. C., & Campbell, F. A. (1979). Predicting IQ from mother–child interactions. *Child Development, 50*, 804–814.

Reschly, D. J., & Reschly, J. E. (1979). Validity of WISC-R factor scores in predicting achievement and attention for four sociocultural groups. *Journal of School Psychology, 17*, 355–361.

Reschly, D. J., & Sabers, D. L. (1979). Analysis of test bias in four groups with the regression definition. *Journal of Educational Measurement, 16*, 1–9.

Reynolds, C. R., & Gutkin, T. B. (1980). Stability of the WISC-R factor structure across sex at two age levels. *Journal of Clinical Psychology, 36*, 775–777.

Reynolds, C. R., & Hartlage, L. C. (1979). Comparison of WISC and WISC-R regression lines for academic prediction with Black and White referred children. *Journal of Consulting and Clinical Psychology, 47*, 589–591.

Rice, T., Fulker, D. W., Defries, J. C., & Plomin, R. (1988). Path analysis of IQ during infancy and early childhood and the Index of the Home Environment in the Colorado Adoption Project. *Behavior Genetics, 16*, 107–125.

Salthouse, T. A. (2010). *Major Issues in Cognitive Aging*. New York, NY: Oxford University Press.

Schaefer, B. (2004). A demographic survey of learning behaviors among American students. *School Psychology Review, 33*, 481–497.

Schwartz, R. S. (2001). Racial profiling in medical research. *New England Journal of Medicine, 344*, 1392–1393.

Sichi, M. (2003). *Influence of Free-time Activities on Children's Verbal IQ: A look at how the hours a child spends reading, using the computer, and watching TV may affect verbal skills*. Poster session presented at the Texas Psychological Association conference, San Antonio, Texas, November.

Spearman, C. (1927). *The Abilities of Man.* New York, NY: Macmillan.

Steele, C. M. (1992). Race and the schooling of black Americans. *The Atlantic, 269,* 68–72.

Steen, R. G., Fineberg-Buchner, C., Hankins, G., Weiss, L., Prifitera, A., & Mulhern, R. K. (2005). Cognitive deficits in children with sickle cell disease. *Journal of Child Neurology, 20*(2), 102–107.

Sternberg, R. J., Grigorenko, E. L., & Kidd, K. (2005). Intelligence, race, and genetics. *American Psychologist, 60,* 46–57.

Sui-Chu, E., & Williams, J. D. (1996). Effects of parental involvement on eighth-grade achievement. *Sociology of Education, 69,* 126–141.

Trotman, F. K. (1977). Race, IQ, and the middle class. *Journal of Educational Psychology, 69,* 266–273.

US Bureau of the Census. (2003). *Current population survey, October 2003: School enrollment supplement file [CD-ROM].* Washington, DC: Author.

US Bureau of the Census. (2005). *Current population survey, October 2005: School enrollment supplement file [CD-ROM].* Washington, DC: Author.

US Department of Health and Human Services. (2001). *Head Start FACES: Longitudinal Findings on Program Performance. Third Progress Report.* Washington, DC: Author.

Valencia, R. R., Henderson, R. W., & Rankin, R. J. (1985). Family status, family constellation, and home environmental variables as predictors of cognitive performance of Mexican-American children. *Journal of Educational Psychology, 77,* 323–331.

van de Vijver, F. J. R., & Bleichrodt, N. (2001). Conclusies [Conclusions]. In N Bleichrodt, & F. J. R. van de Vijver (Eds.), *Diagnosteik bij allochtonen: Mogelijkheden en heperkingen van psychologische tests [Diagnosing Immigrants: Possibilities and Limitations of Psychological Tests]* (pp. 237–243). Lisse, The Netherlands: Swets.

Vroon, P. A. (1980). Intelligence on Myths and Measurement. In G. E. Stelmach (Ed.), *Advances in Psychology 3* (pp. 27–44). New York, NY: North Holland.

Wechsler, D. (2009). *Advanced Clinical Solutions for Use with WAIS-IV and WMS-IV.* San Antonio, TX: Pearson.

Weiss, L. G. (1997). The MIPS: gauging the dimensions of normality. In T. Millon (Ed.), *The Millon Inventories: Clinical and Personality Assessment.* New York, NY: Guilford Press.

Weiss, L. G. (2002). Essentials of MIPS Assessment. In S. Strack (Ed.), *Essentials of Millon Inventories Assessment* (2nd ed.). New York, NY: John Wiley & Sons, Inc.

Weiss, L. G., & Prifitera, A. (1995). An evaluation of differential prediction of WIAT achievement scores from WISC-III FSIQ across ethnic and gender groups. *Journal of School Psychology, 33*(4), 297–304.

Weiss, L. G., Prifitera, A., & Roid, G. (1993). The WISC-III and the fairness of predicting achievement across ethnic and gender groups. *Journal of Psychoeducational Assessment,* 35–42, (monograph series, Advances in Psychological Assessment, Wechsler Intelligence Scale for Children – 3rd ed.).

Weiss, L. G., Saklofske, D. H., Prifitera, A., & Holdnack, J. A. (2006a). *WISC-IV Advanced Clinical Assessment.* San Diego, CA: Elsevier, Inc.

Weiss, L. G., Harris, J. G., Prifitera, A., Courville, T., Rolfhus, E., Saklofske, D. H., & Holdnack, J. A. (2006b). WISC-IV interpretation in societal context. In L. G. Weiss, D. H. Saklofske, A. Prifitera, & J. A. Holdnack (Eds.), *WISC-IV Advanced Clinical Interpretation.* San Diego, CA: Elsevier Science.

Whitfield, K. E., Weidner, G., Clark, R., & Anderson, N. B. (2002). Sociodemographic diversity and behavioral medicine. *Journal of Consulting and Clinical Psychology, 70*(3), 463–481.

CHAPTER

5

The Flynn Effect and the Wechsler Scales

Xiaobin Zhou [1], Jacques Grégoire [2], and Jianjun Zhu [1]

[1] Pearson Assessment, San Antonio, Texas, USA
[2] Université Catholique de Louvain, Louvain-la-Neuve, Belgium

INTRODUCTION

In a seminal article, published in 1984, Flynn presented a meta-analysis of 73 American studies comparing the IQ obtained from two versions of an intelligence test for the same individuals. He observed a generally higher IQ on the older version of the test than on the newer version. As an IQ corresponds to a percentile on the score distribution of the standardization sample of the test, Flynn concluded that the mean IQ of the standardization samples was rising over time. Analyzing this evolution across every edition of the Standford-Binet and the Wechsler scales from 1932 to 1978, Flynn observed an average IQ increase of 13.8 points in the American population – an increase of 0.30 IQ points per year. As the raw scores of the tests are always normalized while the mean IQ is arbitrarily fixed at 100, this change in IQ across generations had, until then, been unnoticed except by a few researchers (see, for example, Tuddenham, 1948).

Flynn's first study was based on comparisons between IQ tests that were modified over time. For example, in each revision of the Wechsler scales, items could be modified, and subtests could be dropped or added. Therefore, it was impossible to distinguish whether the rising IQ was due to the population getting smarter or to the test modifications. To solve this problem, Flynn (1987) analyzed the change of the IQ using a test that stayed unchanged over time – the Raven's Progressive Matrices. In several European countries, most 18-year-old men had been tested with the Raven when beginning military national service. These samples of the population were almost exhaustive, eliminating possible sampling bias. In countries such as the Netherlands, Belgium, and Norway, data were collected each year over a period of 20 years or more. Analysis of these data confirmed Flynn's initial finding of an increase in IQ. For example, in the Netherlands the mean IQ measured with the Raven increased from 100 in 1952 to 112.43 in 1972, and in Norway the average IQ rose from 100 in 1954 to 110 in 1974. Similar IQ increases were observed in several other countries, and became known as the "Flynn effect."

In this chapter, we investigate the Flynn effect observed in the family of the Wechsler intelligence tests, including the recent WAIS-IV. We examine the Flynn effect in multiple subgroups of the population. We also compare the magnitude of the Flynn effect observed across domains and under multiple test constructs. In the end, we provide one explanation for the cause of the Flynn effect.

Variability of the Flynn effect

The phenomenon of IQ increase in Western populations has received cumulative support (Daley, Whaley, Sigman, Espinosa, & Neumann, 2003; Nettelbeck & Wilson, 2003; Rodgers & Wanstrom, 2007). However, the Flynn effect has not been found to be a general increase in intellectual ability; rather, it varies by the domain of intelligence measured or the instrument used (see, for example, Truscott & Frank, 2001; Wicherts *et al.*, 2004; Kaufman & Lichtenberger, 2006; Yang, Zhu, Pinon, & Wilkins, 2006). It is most significant with tasks measuring fluid intelligence, such as the Raven's Progressive Matrices (Flynn, 1998a: 26–27; Lynn, 2009). These tasks are usually considered as being little influenced by education and culture because they do not rely on previous knowledge and learned solutions, but require an inductive reasoning based on the analysis of the stimuli. In contrast, the Flynn effect is very small in most of the intellectual verbal tasks, and is moderate in the intellectual visuospatial tasks.

Flynn considered that the IQ gain in Western populations was a linear function. He first estimated the annual gain as 0.33 of an IQ point (Flynn, 1984). He later reduced this estimate and suggested adjusting the IQ test norms by 0.25 per year (Flynn, 1998b). However, such a systematic adjustment is speculative, postulating that the IQ gain observed in the past would indefinitely continue at the same pace. Increasing evidence has suggested that there are large variations in IQ change over time. For example, the magnitude of IQ change was found to vary in different nations (see, for example, Must, Must, & Raudik, 2003) and at different points in history (see, for example, Colom, Lluis-Font, & Andres-Pueyo, 2005), or perhaps the Flynn effect may have even ceased or reversed in recent years. For instance, Sundet, Barlaug, and Torjussen (2004) examined the evolution of Norwegian conscripts' scores in a Raven-like test from 1957 to 2002, and observed the expected Flynn effect from the mid-1950s to the beginning of the 1990s. However, no significant increase was found between 1993 and 2002. Moreover, they observed the Flynn effect on a crystallized intelligence test (word similarities) until the mid-1970s, but a flat trend during the following 30 years. The authors concluded that the Flynn effect might have come to an end in Norway. Teasdale and Owen (2008) made a similar observation in Denmark. The performances of young adults in several intelligence subtests increased at a lower pace than previously between 1988 and 1998, and then slightly decreased. Between 1998 and 2003, the mean IQ of young Danish males fell significantly, by about 1.5 points.

Few studies have analyzed the Flynn effect according to gender. Flynn (1998c) presented strong data from the Israeli army. Male and female performance results in an adaptation of the Raven's Progressive Matrices were collected every year at the beginning of military national service, when conscripts were aged 17. Over a period of 13 years, the gain was identical in males and females.

The variability of IQ change across ability range has been demonstrated in a number of studies. In his initial research, Flynn (1984: 9) cautioned researchers that applying the allowance calculated based on the Flynn effect when estimating IQs may be "reliable only for scores in the normal range of 90 to 110." This word of caution was supported by later studies. For example, based on Dutch draftees' IQ scores obtained from a group intelligence test composed of four subtests (letter matrices, verbal analogies, number sequences, and geometric figures), Teasdale and Owen (1989) identified that the magnitude of IQ change varies across the distribution of intelligence level, observing an important IQ gain in the lower and median categories of intelligence, but a non-significant increase in the upper intelligence category. In another study, Spitz (1989) collected studies that compared WAIS and WAIS-R Full Scale IQ change across the IQ range of 50–130. The researcher showed that larger IQ differences and reversed IQ changes are evident at IQ levels below and above average, respectively.

What causes the Flynn effect?

The variability of the Flynn effect suggests that either the population IQ change is not a simple phenomenon that can be explained by a single factor, or, if it is the result of a single factor, the influence of this factor is different in different subgroups of the population or in different domains of ability. Researchers have studied some factors (for example, is it a real IQ gain due to social, population, or genetic factors, or is it simply a psychometric artifact?) that may have played a role inside the "black box" behind the Flynn effect. As significant genetic modifications of a population only occur over very extended periods, the IQ gain observed during a 50-year period cannot be explained by modification of the genetic characteristics of Western populations. Several other hypotheses have been proposed to explain this effect, but, considered separately, none of them provided a sufficient explanation. The Flynn effect seems rather to be a consequence of several interrelated factors.

Educational progress during the twentieth century seems to be a strong factor underlying the Flynn effect. Several studies have shown the impact of schooling on intelligence (Ceci & Williams, 1997). During the last century, in industrialized countries, schooling became compulsory. The percentage of children attending secondary and higher education programs strongly increased. In the same period, the percentage of illiterate people dropped sharply. Moreover, a growing number of children attended nursery school regularly, with a clear impact on their intellectual development (Fernandez-Ballesteros & Juan-Espinosa, 2001). Barber (2005) analyzed the relationship between schooling and IQ using data collected in 81 countries. He observed that the intellectual differences between countries were mainly related to literacy rate, attendance at secondary school, and agricultural population percentage. In more agricultural societies working procedures are often traditional, changing slowly. Individuals can therefore rely on what they learn in their younger years for their whole occupational life. On the other hand, in industrialized countries lifelong learning is necessary. Because of the growing impact of technology in everyday life, people continually have to learn how to use new appliances and procedures. In industrialized countries, working requires fewer and fewer physical aptitudes, but more and more intellectual ones (Fernandez-Ballesteros & Juan-Espinosa, 2001).

In the past 50 years, education has also changed within families. Increase in family incomes, elevation of parents' educational level, and diminution of the average number of children per family have profoundly modified children's education. Parents now have more time and money to spend on their children's education. They also have more information about the normal development of a child and how to stimulate it. Espy, Molfese, and DiLalla (2001) conducted a longitudinal study on 105 children aged from 3 to 6. They confirmed that positive educational conditions within the family support the development of the components of intelligence.

Although, overall, education levels have improved over time, the rate of this development is not equal in all countries. Some developing countries, such as China, are catching up with developed countries at a fast pace. At the same time, in developed countries a high percentage of the population has already reached a high degree of educational attainment, and thus the rate of educational development is slowing down. Thus, if education is a key underlying factor in the Flynn effect, we would expect the IQ increase to be more prominent in developing countries than in developed countries. In fact, this pattern is supported by a comparison of the recent standardization data for the WISC-IV in the US, mainland China, and Hong Kong. Among these three samples, the US population has the highest education level (i.e., about 85 percent of the 6- to 16-year-olds have parents with at least a high school education), and the Flynn effect is 0.25 points per year. In mainland China, only 54 percent of parents of children within this age band have a high school education, and the Flynn effect using the WISC (China) is 0.59 per year (Wechsler, 2008a). The parental education level in Hong Kong is between that in the US and that in China, but is more similar to that in the US (that is, about 85 percent have a high school education, although a smaller percentage attended college compared to the US). The Flynn effect there is 0.30 per year (Wechsler, 2010). Thus, not only may the improvement in education have caused an increase in the population's intelligence, but the changing pace of this improvement may also have caused variations in the magnitude of the Flynn effect in different countries and at different periods in a country's development.

Another important factor underlying the Flynn effect is the considerable improvement in bioenvironmental conditions of life since the end of World War II. Bioenvironmental conditions refer to the interactions between the environment and individual biophysical characteristics. For more than half a century, in developed countries, improvements in health and nutrition had a considerable impact on physical development. In these countries, infant mortality was falling rapidly, while the average individual height was growing regularly. Schmidt, Jorgensen, and Michaelsen (1995) observed such an increase in average height, between 1960 and 1990, among conscripts in 11 European countries. During this period, the average height of Dutch conscripts increased from 1.72 m to 1.77 m (i.e., from 5'6" to 5'8"). They also observed a close relationship between this increase in height and the reduction in infant mortality during the first month of life. This reduction in mortality is itself related to nutritional improvement and a decrease in infectious diseases. It is plausible that factors related to height increase also had an impact on intellectual development. Tuvemo, Jonsson, and Persson (1999) conducted a study on 32,887 conscripts, and observed a significant relationship between their height and their intellectual performances. Several studies regarding children's malnutrition have clearly shown the impact of insufficient nutrition on both physical and intellectual development (Pollit, 2000). When nutrition and health care improve, an increase in intellectual abilities is also observed in the population (Daley *et al.*, 2003). However, the importance of nutrition and health on intelligence is still under debate (Flynn, 2009), and the relationship between these variables is probably not linear.

Based on Bronfenbrenner's bioecological model, Dickens and Flynn (2001) proposed an integrative interpretation of the Flynn effect. Innate cognitive abilities would benefit from positive environmental conditions, which could stimulate their development. Individuals could then look for the most favorable environment that could be positive for their intellectual development. According to this process, small modifications in biological and social environments could have important multiplier effects. During the twentieth century, in industrialized countries, several positive bio-environmental factors appeared, providing an opportunity for genetic intellectual potential to develop. But will this intellectual potential continue to develop? According to Bronfenbrenner and Ceci (1994), the proportion of the genetic potential not already actualized is unknown, and even unknowable. As trees do not grow to the sky, human intelligence has likely some developmental limits that will be reached sooner or later. Regarding height potential, a ceiling seems to have been reached in some countries where positive bioenvironmental conditions appeared earlier – in Norway and Sweden, for example, the height of conscripts is no longer increasing (Schmidt *et al.*, 1995). At the same time, in countries where positive bioenvironmental conditions appeared later (for example, Southern European countries), height is continuing to increase. A similar phenomenon is now being observed for intelligence. In Norway and Denmark the Flynn effect has not been observed since the 1990s, and intelligence seems to have reached a plateau.

Current research

Whatever the evolution of the Flynn effect, a lot is still to be discovered about this phenomenon. It has mainly been identified through standard-ized intelligence tests, with its impact varying across the tasks. The extent to which the Flynn effect generalizes across cognitive ability domains is still an unresolved issue. Recently, researchers started studying the Flynn effect with more focused cognitive tasks, designed to measure specific components of the cognition (Rönnlund & Nilsson, 2009). These studies could be useful in understanding the variability of the Flynn effect according to the intelligence subtests. Another unresolved issue is to what extend the Flynn effect is homogeneous within the same population, as Teasdale and Owen (1989) showed that the Flynn effect could vary according to the IQ level. In a recent study, Zhou, Zhu, and Weiss (2010) explored the performance IQ (PIQ) change across ability levels on a series of Wechsler scales. Their results showed evidence of the variation of the PIQ change at different verbal levels, although the direction of the varia-tion was not conclusive. More studies should be conducted to analyze the evolution of the IQ performance curves across time in the same population. If the variability of IQ change within the same group is too large, even if an IQ change trend is found to be robust on average, the usability of this average change rate in field assessment is questionable.

Research reported in this chapter is devoted to comparisons and modeling of the Full Scale IQ (FSIQ) changes among subsamples of examinees categorized by demographics and by ability levels. Changes in the FSIQ between recent editions of three Wechsler intelligence scales – the Wechsler Adult Intelligence Scale (i.e., WAIS-R, WAIS-III, and WAIS-IV; Wechsler, 1981, 1997, 2008b), the Wechsler Preschool and Primary Scale of Intelligence (i.e., WPPSI-R and WPPSI-III; Wechsler, 1989, 2002), and the Wechsler Intelligence Scale for Children (i.e., WISC-III and WISC-IV; Wechsler, 1991, 2003) – were investigated. The inclusion of the WPPSI and the WISC extends the discussion of findings to the full age range covered by the family of Wechsler scales. Additionally, in order to provide a broader perspective on the different measures of cognitive abilities, the change in Cognitive Proficiency Index (CPI) in the WAIS and the WISC, and scores on two non-Wechsler scales – the General Conceptual Ability (GCA) in the Differential Ability Scales (i.e., DAS and DAS-II; Elliott, 1990, 2007), and the cognitive/mental composite scores in the Bayley Scales of Infant and Toddler Development (i.e., BSID-II and Bayley-III; Bayley, 1993, 2006) – were also studied. We expect that, with the data from the latest member of the Wechsler scales, the WAIS-IV, our analysis will provide more insights into the nature and causes of the Flynn effect.

RESEARCH METHOD

Samples

The validity samples collected for the newer edition of the aforementioned scales were used. All samples were collected to represent the percentages of key national demographics (i.e., age-groups, gender, ethnicity, and self or parent education level). The test administration was counterbalanced, such that approximately half of the sample was tested on the earlier edition first and the other half was tested on the newer edition first. For the Wechsler scales, the testing interval between the two administrations ranged from 5 days to 84 days with a mean testing interval of 28–35 days. For the DAS, the testing interval ranged from 6 to 68 days with a mean interval of 21 days. For the Bayley, the testing interval ranged from 1 to 27 days, with a mean interval of 6 days.

The total sample sizes were 174, 231, 191, and 238 for the WPPSI-R and WPPSI-III, WISC-III and WISC-IV, WAIS-R and WAIS-III, and WAIS-III and WAIS-IV, respectively. The sample size for the DAS and DAS-II was 310, and the sample size for the BSID-II and Bayley-III was 94. Within each sample, the demographic compositions of the two testing orders were balanced on most categories. Detailed demographic information for each sample is presented in Table 5.1.

TABLE 5.1A   Percentages of demographic categories in the samples

	WPPSI-III and WPPSI-R			WISC-IV and WISC-III			WAIS-III and WAIS-R			WAIS-IV and WAIS-III		
	WPPSI-III First	WPPSI-R First	Total	WISC-IV First	WISC-III First	Total	WAIS-III First	WAIS-R First	Total	WAIS-IV First	WAIS-III First	Total
Age (in years)												
Mean	4.9	5.0	4.9	11.3	11.4	11.4	47.4	47.2	47.3	54.2	51.2	52.7
Std	1.1	1.2	1.1	3.0	2.9	3.0	21.0	20.4	20.6	24.8	24.2	24.5
Gender												
Female	45.5	50.0	47.7	53.6	53.8	53.7	52.6	51.0	51.8	61.7	62.7	62.2
Male	54.5	50.0	52.3	46.4	46.2	46.3	47.4	49.0	48.2	38.3	37.3	37.8
Race/ethnicity												
White	56.8	52.3	54.6	76.8	81.1	78.8	82.1	76.0	79.1	65.8	67.8	66.8
African American	15.9	26.7	21.3	2.4	1.9	2.2	8.4	14.6	11.5	17.5	17.8	17.6
Hispanic	23.9	18.6	21.3	16.8	10.4	13.9	6.3	7.3	6.8	10.0	7.6	8.8
Other	3.4	2.3	2.9	4.0	6.6	5.2	3.2	2.1	2.6	6.6	6.8	6.7
Education[1]												
≤8 years	5.7	3.5	4.6	0.8	4.7	2.6	8.4	3.1	5.8	7.5	4.2	5.9
9–11 years	13.6	8.1	10.9	11.2	6.6	9.1	9.5	9.4	9.4	13.4	5.9	9.7
12 years	31.8	32.6	32.2	29.6	28.3	29.0	43.2	24.0	33.5	27.5	35.6	31.5
13–15 years	37.5	31.4	34.5	39.2	34.9	37.2	20	30.2	25.1	26.7	29.7	28.2
≥16 years	11.4	24.4	17.8	19.2	25.5	22.1	18.9	33.3	26.2	25.0	24.6	24.8
N	88	86	174	125	106	231	95	96	191	120	118	238

[1] Parent education was used for examinees aged 19 and under; self education was used for examinees aged 20 and older.

TABLE 5.1B Percentages of demographic categories in the samples—Cont'd

	Bayley-III and BSID-II			DAS-II and DAS		
	Bayley-III First	BSID-II First	Total	DAS-II First	DAS First	Total
Age (in years)						
Mean	1.3	1.3	1.3	8.0	8.0	8.0
Std	1.0	1.0	1.0	4.2	4.1	4.2
Gender						
Female	41.3	54.2	47.9	51.6	49.0	50.3
Male	58.7	45.8	52.1	48.4	51.0	49.7
Race/ethnicity						
White	60.9	54.2	57.4	48.4	54.8	51.6
African American	8.7	20.8	14.9	14.4	15.9	15.2
Hispanic	17.4	18.8	18.1	22.9	21.7	22.3
Other	13.0	6.3	9.6	14.4	7.6	11.0
Education[1]						
≤8 years	2.2	2.1	2.1	4.6	3.2	3.9
9-11 years	8.7	16.7	12.8	9.2	9.6	9.4
12 years	23.9	12.5	18.1	24.8	25.5	25.2
13-15 years	32.6	31.3	31.9	30.1	33.8	31.9
≥ 16 years	32.6	37.5	35.1	31.4	28.0	29.7
N	*46*	*48*	*94*	*153*	*157*	*310*

[1]Parent education was used for examinees aged 19 and under; self education was used for examinees aged 20 and older.

Analysis

For ease of discussion and consistency of terms used in the remainder of this chapter, score change in all the instruments compared is calculated using the score obtained on the older version of the test minus the comparable score obtained on the newer version; and is presented as the difference per decade. Thus, a positive change indicates a gain, while a negative value indicates a score decrease (i.e., the reversed Flynn effect). The year of publication for each instrument was used to estimate the time gap between the two versions of the test. Table 5.2 shows the publication gaps for all the instruments.

TABLE 5.2   Publication gaps and average score change per decade

Scales	Publication gap	Mean (std) early version	Mean (std) later version	Score change[1] per decade
WPPSI-R and WPPSI-III[2] (ages 3–7)	13	100.59 (13.38)	99.40 (14.35)	0.9
WISC-III and WISC-IV[2] (ages 6–16)	12	107.52 (14.63)	104.48 (13.85)	2.5
WAIS-R and WAIS-III[2] (ages 16–89)	16	105.76 (14.35)	102.98 (15.18)	1.7
WAIS-III and WAIS-IV[2] (ages 16–90)	11	102.95 (14.91)	100.01 (15.20)	2.7
DAS and DAS-II[3]	17	105.40 (15.07)	102.71 (12.69)	1.6
Early years (ages 2–6, n = 151)		*104.53 (14.75)*	*102.54 (12.89)*	*1.2*
School age (ages 7–18, n = 159)		*106.23 (15.38)*	*102.87 (12.54)*	*2.0*
BSID-II and Bayley-III[4] (ages 0–3.5)	13	93.90 (12.74)	102.07 (13.41)	−6.3

[1]Score change is calculated using the score obtained on the older version minus the score obtained on the newer version; the decade change is calculated by dividing the score change by the publication gap then times 10.
[2]FSIQ was compared.
[3]GCA was compared.
[4]Mental Index of the BSID-II was compared to the Converted Coginitive Score on the Bayley-III.

Analysis on the Wechsler FSIQ

Analyses were first conducted to investigate differences in the FSIQ change across ability levels and among demographic groups. The verbal composite score obtained on the newer editions of the tests was used to categorize the ability levels of the examinee (i.e., VIQ was used in WPPSI-III and VCI was used in the other three comparisons). Five verbal ability levels were used: 120 or higher, 110–119, 90–109, 80–89, and 79 or less.

A preliminary ANOVA was conducted to investigate whether statistical difference exists in the FSIQ change across the ability levels among the four samples. The results showed neither significant main effect of test batteries (F $(3,832) = 2.18$, $P = 0.09$, partial $\eta^2 = 0.008$) nor significant interaction between ability level and test ($F(12,832) = 1.20, P = 0.28$, partial $\eta^2 = 0.018$). Significant main effects of ability level (F $(4,832) = 3.55$, $P < 0.01$, partial $\eta^2 = 0.018$) and testing order (F $(1,832) = 64.00, P < 0.01$, partial $\eta^2 = 0.075$) were found. These results suggest a consistent relation between ability level and FSIQ changes across the four datasets. Therefore, the four samples were combined for further analysis in order to increase statistical power. In this combined sample, the effects of ability level and demographics on FSIQ change were investigated using general linear models as well as a t-test. Specifically, for the analysis on ability levels, the actual and the demographic-adjusted decade FSIQ change rates for each ability group were plotted and compared; *post hoc* analysis and t-test were used to study the differences across demographics such as gender, education level, and age.

Because the verbal index used for ability grouping is composed of half of the subtests in the FSIQ, the result of general linear modeling could be exaggerated, to some degree, by the regression-to-the-mean effect. In a recent study (Zhou *et al.*, 2010) a similar analysis strategy was applied with the PRI, which has no overlapping subtest elements with verbal index, as the dependent variable and verbal index as the independent variable. After comparing the results on the FSIQ in the current study with those on the PRI, no elevated difference was evident. Therefore, we have reason to believe that the differences in decade FSIQ change across ability groups reported in this chapter are, at least in part, the results of the variability in performance at various ability levels. In their analysis on the PRI, Zhou and colleagues also used an equal-percentile equating method. However, the authors acknowledge that the limitations in equating restricted the contribution of this method to the explanation of the patterns in PRI change. Thus, in the current analysis, the equating method is not used.

Analysis on the Wechsler CPI

To further explore the variation in the change of intelligence across domains, the CPI in the WAIS-III and WAIS-IV and the WISC-III and WISC-IV was studied. In this analysis, the General Ability Index (GAI) obtained in the newer version of the test was used for ability grouping. The CPI is composed of Working Memory and Processing Speed subtests – the domains of intelligence that have been increasingly viewed as more pertinent elements in fluid intelligence. Because this index has only recently been made narrowly available for the WISC-IV as an experimental score (Weiss & Gabel, 2008) and for the WAIS-IV (in this book), little is known about how the change in this score across time complies with the Flynn effect. In order to compare the CPI change, this index for the WISC-III and the WAIS-III was developed. Because the GAI has no over-lapping component with the CPI, the pattern of CPI change across the GAI group should be little influenced by the regression effect. The decade CPI change was also compared by demographic categories.

Analysis on the DAS and the Bayley

Similar analyses were then applied to the DAS and the Bayley samples. Linear conversion was applied to the Bayley-III cognitive score so that it is on the same scale as the mental composite on the BSID-II, which is on a scale with mean of 100 and standard deviation of 15. The verbal ability composite (Verb) obtained on the DAS-II was used for ability grouping in the DAS; the motor index (Mot) obtained on the Bayley-III was used for the ability grouping in the Bayley. Because both Verb and Mot are normed on the same metric as the verbal composite in the Wechsler scales (i.e., N (100, 15)), the ability groups were formed using the same score ranges described for the Wechsler scales. However, due to the small sample size in the Bayley, the two lower ability groups were further combined. Separately on each sample, ANOVA was used to investigate effects of ability and demographics on score change.

RESULTS

The average decade score change for each sample is shown in Table 5.2. The FSIQ increases per decade are 0.9, 2.5, 1.7, and 2.7 on the WPPSI, WISC, WAIS-R, and WAIS-III, respectively. On the DAS, the average decade change in GCA is 1.6, with the early-years sample having a decade increase of 1.2 points and the school-age sample having a 2.0-point gain. In contrast to the Wechsler scales and the DAS, the average change in the Bayley is a decrease of 6.3 points. (Readers should refer to Yang *et al.* (2006) for an in-depth discussion on the negative score change from the BSID-II to the Bayley-III; in this chapter we focus on the relative score change among ability and demographics groups, and thus the reasons for the reversed Flynn effect on the Bayley-III and BSID-II are not discussed.) Overall, the preschool-age samples seem to have relatively smaller score gains than the samples including older examinees.

FSIQ change by ability

The descriptive statistics of the FSIQ change at each ability level are presented in Table 5.3. With the exception of the WISC, the two highest ability groups in the WPPSI and WAIS have lower FSIQ gains than the three lower ability groups. Among the middle three ability groups (i.e., 80–89, 90–109, 110–119), where the sample sizes are decent on all scales, it can be seen that the higher the ability level, the lower the average score gain. Overall, on the combined sample, an inverse relation between ability level and decade FSIQ change is evident.

The ANOVA was conducted on the combined sample. Ability level, testing group categories (i.e., test battery and testing order), and demographics (i.e., age, gender, ethnicity, education level) were entered in the model for FSIQ change. Significant main effects of ability level $(F(4,832) = 3.10, P = 0.02$, partial $\eta^2 = 0.02)$, testing order $(F(1,832) = 77.95, P < 0.01$, partial $\eta^2 = 0.09)$, gender $(F(1,832) = 9.41, P < 0.01$, partial $\eta^2 = 0.01)$, and age $(F(1,832) = 9.40, P < 0.01$, partial $\eta^2 = 0.01)$ were found.

TABLE 5.3 Descriptive statistics of FSIQ change per decade[1] by verbal ability

Scales		≤79	80–89	90–109	110–119	120
				VCI/VIQ[2] levels		
WPPSI	N	13	35	84	35	7
	Mean	2.72	3.21	1.23	−2.66	0.22
	SD	6.76	5.66	6.69	5.71	3.89
	Median	4.62	3.85	2.31	−4.62	−1.54
WISC	N	6	26	126	51	21
	Mean	−2.78	3.37	3.06	1.39	2.50
	SD	5.37	5.15	7.00	8.09	6.74
	Median	−4.58	4.17	3.75	0.83	2.50
WAIS-R	N	15	24	93	33	26
	Mean	3.58	2.37	1.76	0.78	1.25
	SD	3.27	3.65	4.15	4.62	4.59
	Median	3.75	2.81	1.88	0.63	0.63
WAIS-III	N	20	43	113	37	25
	Mean	3.27	3.47	2.82	1.18	2.33
	SD	2.46	5.04	5.06	4.46	6.58
	Median	3.18	4.55	2.73	0.91	3.64
Overall	N	54	128	416	156	79
	Mean	2.55	3.17	2.34	0.30	1.82
	SD	4.67	4.98	5.92	6.32	5.78
	Median	3.13	3.85	2.50	0.00	0.91

[1]FSIQ change is calculated using the score obtained on the older version minus score obtained on the newer version; the decade change is calculated by dividing the score change by the publication gap then times 10.
[2]VIQ is used on WPPSI.

The least-square adjusted FSIQ change for each ability level was calculated with other factors controlled as covariates. This adjusted FSIQ change partials out the effect of the other factors in the models, thus giving a purer representation of the ability effect alone. Figure 5.1 shows the observed and the adjusted FSIQ change per decade at each ability level. The adjusted FSIQ changes are plotted with the solid line. This figure shows that, consistent with the pattern observed in descriptive analysis, the adjusted FSIQ change is higher at low ability levels than at high ability levels – the FSIQ changes at the two below-average ability levels are 2.61 and 3.54, and at the two above-average ability levels are 1.20 and 2.16.

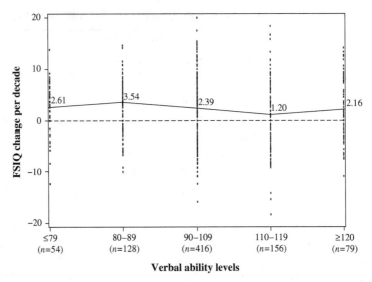

FIGURE 5.1 Actual and demographically adjusted average FSIQ change per decade by ability level (combined Wechsler sample). Average FSIQ changes at each ability level adjusted by demographics are plotted by the solid line.

FSIQ change by gender, education, and age

Figure 5.2 shows the decade FSIQ change by gender for each sample. The WISC and the WAIS (but not the WPPSI) samples show a larger gain in FSIQ in males. Independent sample t-tests were conducted to compare the gender difference in each sample. A significant difference was found on the WISC ($P < 0.01$, $d = 0.47$), and a marginally significant difference was found on the WAIS-III ($P = 0.07$, $d = 0.22$). Small effect sizes, which do not have significant t-values (i.e., 0.06 and 0.11, respectively), were also found on the WPPSI and the WAIS-R. The largest gender difference was observed in the WISC sample, with males gaining 2.2 more IQ points every 10 years than females.

Figure 5.3 shows the decade FSIQ change by education level for each sample. The largest difference in FSIQ change across education groups exceeds 2 points in all samples. However, large variance within the groups warrants no statistically significant finding.

To further investigate the significant age effect, the combined sample was divided into 11 age groups. The average FSIQ gain is shown in Figure 5.4. In the preschool groups (i.e., ages 3–4 and 5–6), the FSIQ change is the smallest. In the next three age groups (i.e., 7–9, 10–12, and 13–15 years), which are predominantly the WISC ages, the 7–9 age group has a much larger FSIQ gain (3.9 points) than do the two older groups (2.3 and 1.3 points, respectively). Within the adult age group (16 and above), the

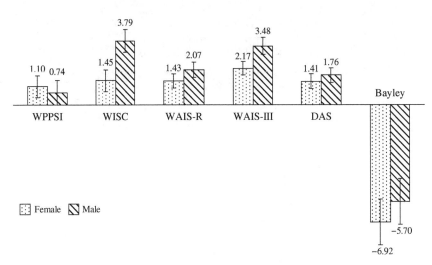

FIGURE 5.2   Score change per decade by gender.

older adults (age 55 and above) have a larger FSIQ gain than do the younger adults. In a *post hoc* analysis using Bonferroni adjustment, the FSIQ gain in the 7–9 age group was found to be significantly higher than that in the preschool and 16–24 age groups. The FSIQ gain in the 70–74 age group was also found to be significantly higher than that in the preschoolers.

In summary, the above analyses on the FSIQ suggest that the magnitude of the FSIQ change could vary among different ability groups (e.g., lower ability groups tend to have larger increase in FSIQ than do higher ability groups), between males and females (e.g., males tend to have a larger increase in FSIQ than do females), and across age ranges. In the next set of analyses, a similar analytical approach was applied to the CPI and two non-Wechsler scales – the DAS and the Bayley – to investigate whether or not any of the patterns identified with the FSIQ would hold on other general intellectual ability measures that have different construct.

CPI change by ability and demographics

Owing to missing data, the number of observations available in the WISC and WAIS-III for the analysis on CPI was reduced to 119 and 151, respectively. The overall decade CPI change is 2.22 in the WISC and 0.48 in the WAIS-III. Table 5.4 shows the descriptive statistics regarding CPI change at each GAI ability level. In both samples, the decade CPI change shows a decrease at below-average ability levels and an increase at average and above-average levels. This trend is totally reversed compared to the patterns observed on both the FSIQ (above) and the PRI (Zhou *et al.*, 2010).

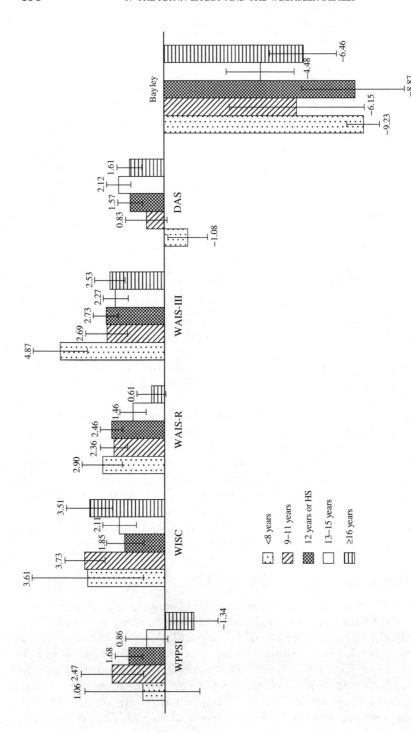

FIGURE 5.3   Score change per decade by education level.

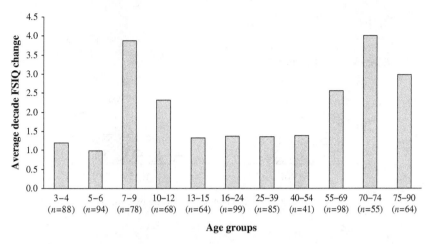

FIGURE 5.4 Decade FSIQ change in the combined sample by age group.

Figure 5.5 shows the average CPI change by gender. Consistent with the trend in the FSIQ, the male samples in both tests tend to have a higher CPI gain than do females, although no statistical significance is evident. Figure 5.6 shows the average CPI change by education. The sample size in the lowest education group in both samples was only five; thus, these values are not interpretable. For the other groups, similar to the patterns observed in the FSIQ, the discrepancy between the highest CPI gain and the lowest CPI gain is notable, but does not reach statistical significance.

TABLE 5.4 Descriptive statistics of CPI change per decade[1] by general ability

Scales		GAI Levels				
		≤79	80–89	90–109	110–119	≥120
WISC	N	5	11	66	22	15
	Mean	−1.29	−0.41	0.27	1.10	2.64
	SD	5.21	6.83	6.47	9.33	6.63
	Median	−2.27	2.72	0.00	2.72	0.46
WAIS-III	N	12	20	80	19	20
	Mean	−4.67	−0.83	3.56	1.47	1.94
	SD	6.03	6.74	9.71	7.93	8.98
	Median	−5.00	−1.67	4.17	1.67	1.67

[1]CPI change is calculated using the score obtained on the older version minus score obtained on the newer version; the decade change is calculated by dividing the score change by the publication gap then times 10.

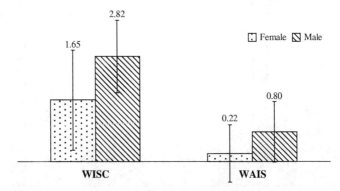

FIGURE 5.5   CPI change per decade by gender.

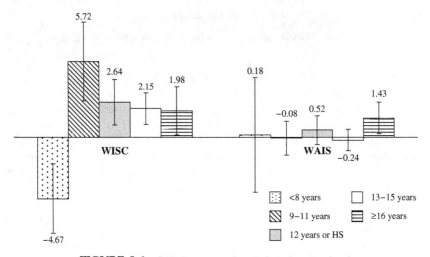

FIGURE 5.6   CPI change per decade by education level.

Overall, the results on the CPI in the WISC and WAIS-III samples suggest that:

1. The CPI change is rather stable across time in the adult sample (less than 1 point decade gain on average) compared to children aged 6–16 years, who have an average decade CPI gain of 2 points
2. The higher ability groups may have a higher CPI gain than the lower ability groups
3. Males may have a higher CPI gain than do females.

Score change in the DAS and the Bayley

Table 5.5 shows the descriptive statistics of score change at each ability level for the DAS and the Bayley. In the DAS, the average GCA change does not show a clear pattern with respect to the level of verbal ability.

TABLE 5.5   Descriptive statistics of score change per decade[1] by ability: DAS and Bayley

Scales (score)		≤ 79	80–89	90–109	110–119	≥ 120
				Ability levels[2]		
DAS (GCA)	N	13	36	182	49	30
	Mean	2.49	0.34	1.55	2.50	1.39
	SD	4.54	3.98	5.09	6.15	6.26
	Median	0.59	−0.29	1.18	1.76	2.35
Bayley (Cog/Mental)	N	11[3]		49	26	8
	Mean	−2.80		−6.33	−6.42	−10.38
	SD	8.16		9.30	9.48	8.83
	Median	−3.08		−6.15	−8.46	−12.31

[1]Score change is calculated using the score obtained on the older version minus score obtained on the newer version; the decade change is calculated by dividing the score change by the publication gap then times 10.
[2]Ability levels are defined by Verbal Ability Composite for the DAS, by Motor Composite for the Bayley.
[3]Motor Composite below 89.

An ANOVA was conducted, using ability level, testing order, and demographics (i.e., gender, education, ethnicity, and age) as factors on GCA change. No significant main effect of verbal ability (F (4,309) = 1.83, $P = 0.12$, partial $\eta^2 = 0.02$), gender (F (1,309) = 0.84, $P = 0.36$, partial $\eta^2 < 0.01$), education (F (4,309) = 1.42, $P = 0.23$, partial $\eta^2 = 0.02$), or age (F (1,309) = 2.05, $P = 0.15$, partial $\eta^2 < 0.01$) was found. The only significant main effect is seen in testing order (F (1,309) = 65.87, $P < 0.01$, partial $\eta^2 = 0.18$). The least-square adjusted GCA changes for the five ability levels, from low ability to high ability, are 2.35, −0.11, 1.15, 2.61, and 1.55, which, similar to the observed change by ability shown in Table 5.5, do not show any consistent association with ability levels.

The gender and education comparisons on the GCA change are presented in Figures 5.2 and 5.3. Similar to the majority of the Wechsler samples, males show a slightly higher GCA gain than do females, although the difference does not reach statistical significance. On the education comparison, the GCA shows a decrease at the lowest education level (decade decrease of −1.08 points). The highest GCA increase is observed in the group that has some college education (decade increase of 2.12 points).

Similarly, an ANOVA was conducted regarding the effects of ability and demographics on the change between the BSID-II mental composite and the Bayley-III cognitive score. No significant main effect of motor ability (F (3,93) = 1.81, $P = 0.15$, partial $\eta^2 = 0.06$), gender (F (1,93) = 0.02, $P = 0.89$, partial $\eta^2 < 0.01$), education (F (4,93) = 0.81, $P = 0.52$, partial $\eta^2 = 0.04$), age

(F (1,93) = 1.10, P = 0.30, partial η^2 = 0.01), or testing order (F (1,93) = 1.27, P = 0.26, partial η^2 = 0.02) was found. The least-square adjusted decade score changes for the four ability groups are −1.52, −6.92, −6.74, and −12.14. Thus, both the observed and the adjusted score changes show the pattern of relatively higher score decrease in higher ability groups than in lower ability groups, which is consistent with the FSIQ change pattern demonstrated earlier. However, owing to either the small sample size or the large variance within the sample, no conclusion could be drawn statistically.

The gender and education comparisons on the Bayley score change are also presented in Figures 5.2 and 5.3. On the gender comparison, females show a slightly larger score decrease than do males (6.92 vs 5.70). On the education comparison, ignoring the lowest education group for its tiny sample size (n = 2), the largest score decrease is observed in the group that has high school education (decade decrease of 8.87 points). The smallest score decrease is in the group that has some college education (decade decrease of 4.48 points).

Overall, the above results on the DAS and the Bayley samples had little resemblance to the patterns found on the FSIQ. Neither of these two samples showed significant differences in decade score change across ability groups. Further, no reliable gender, age, or education effect was found. Yang and colleagues (2006) have stated that the Flynn effect may not be applicable to the Bayley scales, in part due to the different test construct from intelligence measures. The results from the current study further support that the Flynn effect could either be sensible to the test construct or be more variable at particular (e.g., younger) age ranges.

DISCUSSION

This is a classic unit of analysis problem which is well known in many academic disciplines. For example, economists point out that increases in gross national product (GNP) are not shared equally by all citizens. Similarly, we show that mean IQ score increases at the country level (i.e., total sample) are not shared equally by all members (i.e., by different ability and demographic groups) of the population. As a moral philosopher in the political science faculty, Flynn's work is eminently useful in the study of population trends in ability within and across nations and cultures. Psychology is unique among the academic disciplines, however, in that it is the study of individual differences. As Zhu and Tulsky (1999) cautioned, there is always a danger when applying group level data to individual practice. The present exploration of the relation between FSIQ change and ability and demographics elucidates those dangers with data.

The Flynn effect and test construct

As Flynn observes, his effect is not consistent across all subtests. Under the same concept of the FSIQ, different subtest components were selected for particular target age groups in different instruments. A quick comparison of the average decade changes in Table 5.2 across the four Wechsler samples supports more the variation of the FSIQ change across scales than the consistency among them. Furthermore, our analyses on the CPI in the WAIS and the WISC, and on the DAS and the Bayley, suggest potentially different patterns in the variability of the Flynn effect in intelligence measures other than the FSIQ.

As test developers add or delete subtests when revising existing intelligence test batteries based on newer theories of cognition and brain functioning, the pattern of IQ change across time may deviate from expectations based on Flynn's original data. In the more recent development in the construct of intelligence scales, more subtests measuring working memory and processing speed were used to supplement traditional measures of crystallized knowledge and visual spatial skills. For example, in the WAIS-III FSIQ, 3 out of 11 subtests, or 27 percent, are Working Memory and Processing Speed subtests; in the WAIS-IV FSIQ, 4 out of 10 subtests, or 40 percent, measure these two domains. Although such construct changes are necessary to advance the field of intellectual assessment, the new subtests may not show the same rate of change over time as the replaced ones. Thus, these changes in test construct make it difficult to study changes in intelligence across test editions (Zhu and Tulsky, 1999; Kaufman, 2010). In addition, the modification in test construct at revisions also introduces more random or unknown variance, making generalization of the aggregated effect obtained from previous tests less applicable to the new test.

The debate over adjusting IQ scores based on the Flynn effect is further complicated by applied issues in clinical practice. When the Full Scale IQ cannot be obtained for a particular examinee, the clinician sometimes must use the VIQ, PIQ, GAI, or an abbreviated IQ as the best estimate of intellectual ability. In such instances, applying an adjustment derived based on Full Scale IQ could yield an erroneous interpretation of the person's ability, because different domains of intelligence may have different patterns of change over time. A quick example can be drawn from comparing the current research to the studies by Zhou *et al.* (2010). Although similar methodologies were used in both studies, not only was the magnitude of the average score change different between the PIQ and the FSIQ, but the impact of the ability and demographics factors on the score change was also different. Thus, without adequate definition of restrictions, forcing an IQ adjustment using a fixed rate, such as moving the cutoff point for intellectual and developmental disability classification

(Kanaya, Sullin, & Ceci, 2003), could cause misleading results and potentially misclassify a proportion of examinees.

As noted earlier, data from several independent research groups suggest a recent slowing of the magnitude of the effect such that the 0.3 points per year expectation is in question. The WAIS-IV data, however, do not support this trend. WAIS-III to WAIS-IV difference in FSIQ is 0.27 points per year (Table 5.2), which is higher than the 0.17 points per year in the WAIS-R to WAIS-III FSIQ change.

Ultimately, however, the Flynn effect is a theory rather than a scientific law. The orderly progress of science demands that theories be revised to reflect new data, and not the other way around. We call upon the field to cease treating the Flynn effect as if it were an immutable law of nature. At the same time, clinical practice must continue even as research is progressing that may impact practice. Although the evidence for differential adjustments based on ability level is still nascent, early indications appear to favor slightly larger adjustments in the lower range of scores where high stakes legal evaluations are most likely to occur.

Is IQ change due to population change?

Based on current findings, we suggest that the phenomenon of IQ change could be the result of the change in population characteristics. Our hypothesis is from the perspective of the historical development of the human intelligence. There are two key elements. First, for the entire human specie, we hypothesize that the range of population intelligence has stayed relatively stable in recent history – that is, the intelligence of the smartest and the slowest people today is similar to that of the smartest and the slowest people 50–100 years ago. Second, the population intelligence change took place as continuous shifting in the skewness of the score distribution. We hypothesize that at early historical points, due to the limited learning opportunities and resources, the population intelligence might have been slightly positively skewed (Figure 5.7a) – a higher percentage of people were towards the lower side of intelligence than towards the higher side of intelligence. With improvements in overall

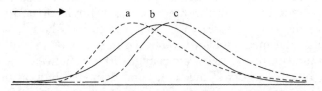

FIGURE 5.7 Hypothetical historical development of distribution of population intelligence. The distribution of the population intelligence changes from a slightly positive skewed curve (a), to a normal bell-curve (b), to a slightly negatively skewed curve (c).

socio-economic conditions, and increasing opportunities for education, more and more people were provided with the chances to discover their potential. The intelligence curve then progressed from positively skewed to a normal bell-shaped curve (Figure 5.7b). The development of society is continuing to push people in the middle ability range to move towards a higher level, causing the population intelligence distribution to become slightly negatively skewed (Figure 5.7c).

Evidence of such population change could be derived from a quick comparison of education levels using census data. For example, according to the 1988 US census, 18 percent of the sample had parental education levels lower than high school graduate. The majority of the sample, 37 percent, had parental education levels of high school or equivalent, and 45 percent had parental education levels of some college-level or higher education. In the 2000 US census, the below high school proportion dropped to 15 percent; and the high school and equivalent proportion dropped to 28 percent. A much higher proportion of the population (i.e., 57 percent) had received some college-level or higher education. Thus, the distribution of population education levels – a strong predictor of IQ – has become more negatively skewed. In addition, recent research has demonstrated the possibility of improving the skills and ability required to perform on the IQ tests through training in certain types of tasks (Jaeggi, Buschkuehl, Jonides, & Perrig, 2008). The effects of such learning and training also seem to be long lasting and transferable to performance on various domains of intelligence. Therefore, with the improvement in education opportunities, the distribution of the population IQ will change correspondingly.

Because of this population change, during the development of newer versions of tests, the norm at the lower end needs to become a little more difficult, and the norm at the higher end needs to become a little easier. This change may contribute, in part, to the finding, reported in this chapter, that the Flynn effect on the FSIQ is larger at lower ability levels and smaller at higher ability levels.

CONCLUSION

The research presented in this chapter demonstrates the differences in FSIQ change in various subgroups of the population and the variations in score change across time in different test domains and under different test constructs. Our results, together with previous research, strongly suggest the highly variable nature of the Flynn effect when seen as beyond an aggregated phenomenon. Based on current results, we offer one explanation for the cause of the Flynn effect: that it is the consequence of the change in the distribution of the population intelligence.

References

Barber, N. (2005). Educational and ecological correlates of IQ: A cross-national investigation. *Intelligence, 33*(3), 273–284.

Bayley, N. (1993). *Bayley Scales of Infant Development* (2nd ed.). San Antonio, TX: Psychological Corporation.

Bayley, N. (2006). *Bayley Scales of Infant and Toddler Development* (3rd ed.). San Antonio, TX: Harcourt Assessment.

Bronfenbrenner, U., & Ceci, S. J. (1994). Nature–nurture reconceptualized in developmental perspective: A bioecological model. *Psychological Review, 101*, 568–586.

Ceci, S. J., & Williams, W. M. (1997). Schooling, intelligence, and income. *American Psychologist, 52*, 1051–1058.

Colom, R., Lluis-Font, J. M., & Andres-Pueyo, A. (2005). The generational intelligence gains are caused by decreasing variance in the lower half of the distribution: Supporting evidence for the nutrition hypothesis. *Intelligence, 33*, 83–91.

Daley, T. C., Whaley, S. E., Sigman, M. D., Espinosa, M. P., & Neumann, C. (2003). IQ on rise. The Flynn effect in rural Kenyan children. *Psychological Science, 14*, 215–219.

Dickens, W. T., & Flynn, J. R. (2001). Heritability estimates versus large environmental effects: The IQ paradox resolved. *Psychological Review, 108*, 346–369.

Elliott, C. (1990). *Differential Abilities Scales*. San Antonio, TX: Psychological Corporation.

Elliott, C. (2007). *Differential Abilities Scales* (2nd ed.). San Antonio, TX: Harcourt Assessment.

Espy, K. A., Molfese, V. J., & DiLalla, L. F. (2001). Effects of environmental measures on intelligence of young children: Growth curve modeling of longitudinal data. *Merrill-Palmer Quarterly, 47*, 42–73.

Fernandez-Ballesteros, R., & Juan-Espinosa, M. (2001). Sociohistorical changes and intelligence gains. In R. J. Sternberg, & E. L. Grigorenko (Eds.), *Environmental Effects on Cognitive Abilities*. Mahwah, NJ: Lawrence Erlbaum.

Flynn, J. R. (1984). The mean IQ of Americans: massive gains 1932 to 1978. *Psychological Bulletin, 95*, 29–51.

Flynn, J. R. (1987). Massive IQ gains in 14 nations: what IQ tests really measure. *Psychological Bulletin, 101*, 171–191.

Flynn, J. R. (1998a). IQ gains over time: Toward finding the causes. In U. Neisser (Ed.), *The Rising Curve: Long-term Gains in IQ and Related Measures*. Washington, DC: American Psychological Association.

Flynn, J. R. (1998b). WAIS-III and WISC-III gains in the United States from 1972 to 1995: How to compensate for obsolete norms. *Perceptual and Motor Skills, 86*, 1231–1239.

Flynn, J. R. (1998c). Israeli military IQ tests: Gender differences small; IQ gains large. *Journal of Biosocial Science, 30*, 541–553.

Flynn, J. R. (2009). Requiem for nutrition as the cause of IQ gains: Raven's gains. *Economics and Human Biology, 7*, 18–27.

Jaeggi, S.M., Buschkuehl, M., Jonides, J., & Perrig, W. J. (2008). Improving fluid intelligence with training on working memory. *Proceedings of the National Academy of Sciences of the United States of America*, 0801268105v1-0.

Kanaya, T., Scullin, M. H., & Ceci, S. J. (2003). The Flynn effect and US policies: The impact of rising IQ scores on American society via mental retardation diagnoses. *American Psychologist, 58*(10), 778–790.

Kaufman, A.S. (2010). "In what way are apples and oranges alike?": A critique of Flynn's interpretation of the Flynn effect. Unpublished paper.

Kaufman, A. S., & Lichtenberger, E. O. (2006). *Assessing Adolescent and Adult Intelligence* (3rd ed.). New York, NY: Wiley.

Lynn, R. (2009). Fluid intelligence but not vocabulary increased in Britain, 1979–2008. *Intelligence, 37,* 249–255.

Must, O., Must, A., & Raudik, V. (2003). The secular rise in IQs: In Estonia, the Flynn effect is not a Jensen effect. *Intelligence, 31,* 461–471.

Nettelbeck, T., & Wilson, C. (2003). The Flynn effect: Smarter not faster. *Intelligence, 32*(1), 85–93.

Pollitt, E. (2000). Developmental sequel from early nutritional deficiencies: conclusion and probability judgments. *Journal of Nutrition, 130,* 350–353.

Rodgers, J. L., & Wanstrom, L. (2007). Identification of a Flynn effect in the NLSY: Moving from the center to the boundaries. *Intelligence, 35,* 187–196.

Rönnlund, M., & Nilsson, L. G. (2009). Flynn effects on sub-factors of episodic and semantic memory: Parallel gains aver time and the same set of determining factors. *Neurologia, 47,* 2474–2180.

Schmidt, I. M., Jorgensen, H. M., & Michaelsen, K. F. (1995). Height of conscripts in Europe: Is post neonatal mortality a predictor? *Annals of Human Biology, 22,* 57–67.

Spitz, H. H. (1989). Variations in Wechsler interscale IQ disparities at different levels of IQ. *Intelligence, 13,* 157–167.

Sundet, J. M., Barlaug, D. F., & Torjussen, T. M. (2004). The end of the Flynn effect? A study of secular trends in mean intelligence test scores of Norwegian conscripts during half a century. *Intelligence, 32,* 349–362.

Teasdale, T. W., & Owen, D. R. (1989). Continuing secular increases in intelligence and a stable prevalence of high intelligence levels. *Intelligence, 13,* 255–262.

Teasdale, T. W., & Owen, D. R. (2008). Secular declines in cognitive tests scores: A reversal of the Flynn effect. *Intelligence, 36,* 121–126.

Truscott, S. D., & Frank, A. J. (2001). Does the Flynn effect affect IQ scores of students classified as LD? *Journal of School Psychology, 39*(4), 319–334.

Tuddenham, R. D. (1948). Soldiers' intelligence in World Wars I and II. *American Psychologist, 3,* 54–56.

Tuvemo, T., Jonsson, B., & Persson, I. (1999). Intellectual and physical performance and morbidity in relation to height in a cohort of 18-year-old Swedish conscripts. *Hormone Research, 52,* 186–191.

US Bureau of the Census. (2006). *Current Population Survey, October 2006: School Enrollment Supplement File [Data file].* Washington, DC: Author: Retrieved from DataFerret.

Wechsler, D. (1981). *Wechsler Adult Intelligence Scale* (Revised). San Antonio, TX: Psychological Corporation.

Wechsler, D. (1989). *Wechsler Preschool and Primary Scale of Intelligence* (Revised). San Antonio, TX: Psychological Corporation.

Wechsler, D. (1991). *Wechsler Intelligence Scale for Children* (3rd ed.). San Antonio, TX: Psychological Corporation.

Wechsler, D. (1997). *Wechsler Adult Intelligence Scale* (3rd ed.). San Antonio, TX: Psychological Corporation.

Wechsler, D. (2002). *Wechsler Preschool and Primary Scale of Intelligence* (3rd ed.). San Antonio, TX: Psychological Corporation.

Wechsler, D. (2003). *Wechsler Intelligence Scale for Children* (4th ed.). San Antonio, TX: Psychological Corporation.

Wechsler, D. (2008a). *Wechsler Intelligence Scale for Children* (4th ed.). China: King May Psychological Assessment Technology Limited.

Wechsler, D. (2008b). *Wechsler Adult Intelligence Scale* (4th ed.). San Antonio, TX: Pearson.

Wechsler, D. (2010). *Wechsler Intelligence Scale for Children* (4th ed.). Hong Kong: King May Psychological Assessment Technology Limited, in press.

Weiss, L.G., & Gabel, A.D. (2008). WISC-IV technical report #6: Using the cognitive proficiency index in psychoeducational assessment. Retrieved December 26, 2009 from http://www.pearsonassessments.com/NR/rdonlyres/E15367FE-D287-46B4-989A-609160D94DA8/0/WISCIVTechReport6.pdf.

Wicherts, J. M., Dolan, C. V., Hessen, D. J., Oosterveld, P., Caroline, G., van Baal, M., Boomsma, D. I., & Span, M. M. (2004). Are intelligence tests measurement invariant over time? Investigating the nature of the Flynn effect. *Intelligence, 32,* 509–537.

Yang, Z., Zhu, J., Pinon, M., & Wilkins, C. (2006). *Comparison of the Bayley-III and the Bayley-II.* New Orleans, LA: Paper presented at the annual meeting of the American Psychological Association.

Zhou, X., Zhu, J., & Weiss, L. (2010). Peaking into the "blackbox" of the Flynn effect. Unpublished paper.

Zhu, J., & Tulsky, D. (1999). Can IQ gain be accurately quantified by a simple difference formula? *Perceptual and Motor Skill, 88,* 1255–1260.

WAIS-IV Use in Neuropsychological Assessment

C. Munro Cullum [1] and Glenn J. Larrabee [2]

[1] University of Texas Southwestern Medical Center at Dallas, Dallas, Texas, USA

[2] Independent Practice, Sarasota, Florida, USA

INTRODUCTION

The Wechsler scales have played an important role in the history of neuropsychological assessment and cognitive neuroscience, not to mention their importance to clinical, counseling, school, and forensic psychologists. Just as the original goals of intellectual assessment included the characterization and delineation of individual differences in mental abilities, neuropsychological assessment has at its core the goal of identifying individual cognitive strengths and weaknesses. The study of innate cognitive abilities, as well as the understanding of the effects of neuropathological processes on human cognitive performance, is the touchstone of modern clinical neuropsychology. Assessment and careful characterization of patterns of cognitive strength and weakness form neurocognitive profiles which not only characterize individuals, but also are useful in the identification and differential diagnosis of various cognitive disorders and tracking changes over time (see, for example, Naugle, Cullum, & Bigler, 1998).

For decades, neuropsychological evaluations and test batteries have incorporated the Wechsler scales fully or in part, often in order to provide an index of global intellectual function by which to compare other neuropsychological test results and also to provide an evaluation of component cognitive functions that are tapped by the various Wechsler tasks. Since the early days of the field, neuropsychologists were aware that the Wechsler tests could form useful parts of the armamentarium of human cognitive assessment measures, and Wechsler subtests continue to commonly be used as a "core" component of modern neuropsychological evaluations. Reasons for this include the following:

1. Many of the tests were clearly affected by brain damage of different types
2. The tests were well-standardized in terms of administration and scoring and showed good psychometric properties
3. Standard scores were based on large normative and stratified populations.

The role of the Wechsler intelligence scales in neuropsychological assessment dates back to the Wechsler-Bellevue I (Reitan, 1955). A plethora of studies have since investigated the effects of left, right, and diffuse brain injury or illness, and specific neurobehavioral disorders such as traumatic brain injury and Alzheimer-type dementia, on subsequent iterations of the Wechsler intelligence scales, including the WAIS, WAIS-R, and WAIS-III (see, for example, Matarazzo, 1972; Tulsky, Saklofske, & Zhu, 2003; Kaufmann & Lichtenberger, 2006). Furthermore, various interpretive algorithms for neuropsychological test batteries include Wechsler profiles as part of the criteria for inferring lateralized neuropsychological deficits. Kaufmann and Lichtenberger (2006) concluded, following a review of the literature on WAIS/WAIS-R and WAIS-III investigations, that Verbal IQ greater than Performance IQ was a more consistent finding in right-hemisphere damaged individuals than was the converse pattern of PIQ higher than VIQ in left-hemisphere damaged persons. This may well be due to the effects of language impairment on so-called "non-verbal" tasks (see Larrabee, 1986, who found substantial correlations of aphasia severity with Performance IQ subtests of the WAIS, including a correlation of −0.44 with Block Design, and equivalent correlations of aphasia severity with VIQ, −0.77, and PIQ, −0.74).

Composite scores from the Wechsler scales such as VIQ, PIQ, and FSIQ have compared favorably to global neuropsychological summary scores in the discrimination of brain impaired vs non-impaired samples (Loring & Larrabee, 2006). In fact, in one early report, Cohen's d (i.e., the *effect size*) was essentially identical for WAIS PIQ ($d = 1.19$) and other global neuropsychological summary scores such as the Halstead Impairment Index ($d = 1.07$) (Vega & Parsons, 1967) in discriminating brain impaired from non-impaired subjects. In subsequent investigations, the effect size for WAIS IQ scores was larger than the effect size for global neuropsychological composite scores (e.g., FSIQ $d = 0.92$ *vs* Halstead Impairment Index $d = 0.43$, Sherer, Scott, Parsons, & Adams, 1994; VIQ $d = 2.40$, *vs* Average Impairment Rating $d = 1.88$, Loring & Larrabee, 2008). The sensitivity of the Wechsler composite scores and their component subtests to the presence of brain dysfunction is directly related to subtests sharing common factors with other neuropsychological measures of similar cognitive domains such as perceptual organization, attention/concentration, processing speed, language function, etc. (Leonberger, Nicks, Larrabee, & Goldfader, 1992; see also Larrabee, 2000).

The move towards greater specification of domains of cognitive function, starting with the WAIS-III, has identified components of the Wechsler scales that are particularly sensitive to acquired brain impairment. For example, Donders, Tulsky, & Zhu (2001) reported that Letter–Number Sequencing and Symbol Search yielded significant differences between patients with moderate–severe TBI and those with mild TBI and demographically matched controls. Inspection of the data reported in the *WAIS-III WMS-III Technical Manual* (Wechsler, 1997) for patients with various neurological disorders including Alzheimer's disease, Huntington's disease, Parkinson's disease, traumatic brain injury, and multiple sclerosis, reveals that the Processing Speed Index was most affected by these different disorders. In fact, in some conditions such as TBI the WAIS-III Processing Speed Index yields lower scores than the various Wechsler Memory Scale III Indexes, which is similar to preliminary findings with the WAIS-IV as outlined later in this chapter.

Although the present chapter focuses on the WAIS-IV, the WMS-IV was co-standardized with the WAIS-IV, and the two instruments together provide a much more comprehensive evaluation of an individual's neurocognitive status. Specifically, measures of learning, memory, and processing speed are the neuropsychological domains that are most sensitive to acquired brain impairment in general (Powell, Cripe, & Dodrill, 1991; Dikmen, Machamer, Winn, & Temkin, 1995; Lezak, Howieson, & Loring, 2004). Moreover, the WMS-IV in comparison to the WAIS-IV can demonstrate patterns specific for amnestic disorders (i.e., impaired memory with preserved intellectual, working memory, and processing speed), or patterns consistent with a dementing disorder (e.g., impaired memory accompanied by declines in intellectual skills and processing speed). These data and the material reviewed in this section illustrate why the Wechsler intelligence and memory scales were found to be the Number 1 and Number 2 ranked neuropsychological instruments in a recent survey by Rabin, Barr, and Burton (2005).

FROM WAIS-III TO WAIS-IV

The decision of any test publisher or author to develop a revised version of a popular measure is a daunting task fraught with challenges and inherent risks. Neuropsychological test users tend to like familiarity, yet wish to be on the cutting edge of neurocognitive assessment, which requires periodic review and updating of stimuli, constructs, and norms.

A careful approach to this process also allows an opportunity for procedural modifications, and incorporation of practical changes that may enhance user-friendliness and/or clarify instructions or procedures for those administering, scoring, interpreting, and taking the test. Each update of the WAIS has incorporated more modern theory and test items, along with input from test users as well as the literature on brain–behavior relationships in various populations. Some of the specific goals that were established for the WAIS-IV included the following:

- Update norms ($n = 2200$, reflecting 2005 US Census $\times$ age, education, gender, ethnicity, region)
- Incorporate and update theoretical foundations
- Maintain or improve psychometric properties
- Provide data from additional clinical populations
- Increase developmental appropriateness (e.g., developed for age 16–91)
- Enhance clinical utility by improving user-friendliness and decreasing administration time
- Emphasize more specific cognitive processes
- Do all of the above while not disrupting the overall style, content, and structure of the previous version.

Chapter 1 of this book provides an overview of changes in the WAIS-IV incorporated from the WAIS-III, and Chapter 2 discusses the cognitive constructs tapped by the WAIS-IV. There was interest not only in updating items for the WAIS-IV but also in incorporating more cognitive neuroscience constructs, given the important contributions advances in this area have made to our understanding and characterization of the processes that comprise some of the primary elements of our current notions of human intelligence. The WAIS-IV was notably influenced to a greater degree than its predecessors by cognitive neuroscience and neuropsychology concepts and, as such, may have even more promise as a neuropsychological tool.

CHANGES TO THE WAIS-IV

A number of changes were made in the transition to the WAIS-IV, as reviewed in previous chapters of this edition. For example, the long-familiar Verbal IQ and Performance IQ score concepts were eliminated from the WAIS-IV, although Full Scale IQ was retained, in keeping with WISC-IV procedures. The move away from the traditional "IQ" labels not only reflects more contemporary nomenclature and practice, but also better reflects the psychometric properties of the test. For neuropsychological applications, the emphasis on more robust and specific underlying cognitive factors helps bring the WAIS-IV more in line with modern neuropsychology as we have moved away from the VIQ–PIQ concept of functional hemispheric implications and become more focused on cognitive processes. The four-factor structure of the WAIS-IV, representing a conceptually cleaner and analytically more cohesive depiction of WAIS-IV scores, is presented in Table 6.1, along with the common abbreviations of the subtests. A discussion of these component factors and their underlying cognitive constructs is presented in Chapters 1 and 3.

Correlations between each of the factor scores and Full Scale IQ range from 0.68 for Processing Speed, 0.82 for Verbal Comprehension, 0.92 for Working Memory, and 0.87 for Perceptual Reasoning, for subjects ages 16–69 years. This also reflects a relative emphasis of the WAIS-IV on working memory and reasoning, with slightly less weight placed on overlearned verbal material and crystallized cognitive abilities. Such

TABLE 6.1   Primary factors of the WAIS-IV and their component subtests

Factor and subtests	Subtest abbreviation
Verbal Comprehension	
Similarities	SI
Vocabulary	VC
Information	IN
Comprehension[a]	CO
Perceptual Reasoning	
Block Design	BD
Matrix Reasoning	MR
Visual Puzzles	VP
Figure Weights[b]	FW
Picture Completion[a]	PC
Working Memory	
Digit Span	DS
Arithmetic	AR
Letter–Number Sequencing[b]	LN
Processing Speed	
Symbol Search	SS
Coding	CD
Cancellation[b]	CA

[a]Supplemental subtest for ages 16–90
[b]Supplemental subtest for ages 16–69.

emphasis is consistent with current neuroscience models of cognitive processing that place greater weight on these core cognitive abilities. Regardless of moniker, the concept of global intellectual functioning or "g" thus continues to be well-represented by the WAIS-IV Full Scale IQ summary score, and, consistent with previous editions, FSIQ continues to be the most reliable of the Wechsler scores.

COMPARABILITY OF WAIS-IV AND WAIS-III

With the revision of any clinical test, questions arise as to how the new version compares with the old. To clinicians who have been using the WAIS-III since its release in 1997, concerns may arise in terms of changes in administration rules (for example, added items, altered discontinue rules) that must be adapted to, as well as alterations in subtest content that might impact the interpretation of otherwise familiar tasks. For example, about 40 percent of the item content of the VCI subtests is new. Fortunately, preliminary data comparing the WAIS-IV and WAIS-III yield uniformly high correlations between the two test versions, very similar to the correlations between the WAIS-III and its predecessor, the WAIS-R. For example, FSIQ scores were highly correlated ($r = 0.94$) in a sample of 240 adults ages 16–88 tested twice in counterbalanced fashion over an average of 5 weeks (Wechsler, 2008). Similarly high correlations were found for the Verbal Comprehension ($r = 0.91$), Perceptual Organization ($r = 0.84$), Working Memory ($r = 0.87$), and Processing Speed Index scores ($r = 0.86$). In terms of mean differences between the different test versions, the *Technical Manual for the WAIS-IV* (Wechsler, 2008) reports that an FSIQ score from the WAIS-IV will be on average 2.9 points lower than a WAIS-III FSIQ score. This is identical to the 2.9 point difference in FSIQ scores seen between the WAIS-R and the WAIS-III. This is also consistent with changes over time as per the so-called Flynn effect, which suggests that, on average, Americans have improved their performance on intellectual tests by approximately 3 points each decade (Flynn, 1987; also see Chapter 5 of this volume for a more detailed discussion of this phenomenon). In terms of changes in individual subtests, it will comfort users to know that split-half and test–retest reliabilities of the 15 subtests of the WAIS-IV were high, with split-half reliabilities ranging from 0.78 on Cancellation to 0.94 on Vocabulary. Similarly, test–retest reliabilities ranged from 0.74 on Visual Puzzles and Matrix Reasoning to 0.90 on Information. Furthermore, 96 percent of examinees with borderline intellectual capacity obtained FSIQ values less than 85 on both the WAIS-III and WAIS-IV. Thus, it appears that despite the various changes in subtests and item content, users can feel comfortable knowing that no changes in interpretation of the familiar subtests and scores should be needed when moving from WAIS-III to WAIS-IV.

IMPLICATIONS OF CHANGES IN WAIS-IV FOR NEUROPSYCHOLOGICAL APPLICATIONS

Decreased administration time was one of the goals of the WAIS-IV development, including reduced discontinuation rules on BD, SI, MR, AR, CO, VC, IN, and PC.

Longest digit span forward and backward is now included as a routine score, whereas many clinicians have recorded this information independently and found it useful for years. Importantly, norms are now provided for each of these scores, reflecting more "pure" measures of simple attention (longest Digit Span Forward) and working memory (longest Digit Span Backward). Digit Span now also includes a digit sequencing trial (Digit Span Sequencing), which enhances the assessment of working memory on the WAIS-IV. Other changes in the WAIS-IV that have particular relevance to neuropsychological applications include the following:

- Increased explicitness of examinee instructions
- Decreased emphasis on time bonuses
- Decreased auditory discrimination demands
- Decreased visual acuity demands
- Decreased motor demands
- Shortened discontinue rules (resulting in decreased testing time and less frustration for impaired examinees).

NEUROPSYCHOLOGICAL INTERPRETATION OF THE WAIS-IV

The WAIS-IV and its predecessors have long been used as a core component of neuropsychological evaluations for several purposes:

1. To obtain an overall measure of general intellectual ability (or "g") by which to compare specific cognitive functions. That is, given the general intercorrelations among many neurocognitive measures (which often tend to hover around 0.4–0.6), having a global estimate of "g" is useful so that other test scores can be interpreted within the context of the individual's other mental abilities. Knowing, for example, that a person has a Full Scale IQ (the most robust score from the WAIS-IV) of 100 or of 75 informs the examiner about what level of functioning to expect in other cognitive domains

(depending, of course, upon the degree to which any particular neuropsychological test correlates with FSIQ; see Larrabee, 2000), and in fact may help guide subsequent test selection.

2. As an indicator of specific cognitive abilities. The various subtests of the Wechsler scales have proven useful in the detection and characterization of various types of cognitive impairment, including assessment of lateralized dysfunction. Specific subtests are also good reflections of some underlying cognitive constructs, such as the ability of the Wechsler tests to assess attention/concentration, working memory, visuospatial functioning, and aspects of language and crystallized cognitive abilities.

When used in conjunction with other standard neuropsychological tests, the WAIS-IV can help provide a detailed examination of various global and specific component cognitive abilities, and often forms a "core" component of many neuropsychological test batteries used in clinical and research settings. The rich normative database on which the WAIS-IV was developed provides standard scores with strong psychometric properties that allow a direct comparison across tasks and domains which aids in clinical interpretation and augments the research utility of the scales. With the advent of some of the new subtests that look promising comes the opportunity for further exploration and enhancement of the WAIS-IV as a neuropsychological tool.

CLINICAL ANALYSIS OF WAIS-IV SCORES

Interpretation of scores from the WAIS-IV or any neuropsychological measure involves the analysis of levels of performance, patterns of performance, and response/item analysis. Individual test performances are compared across neuropsychological measures within an individual's cognitive record, as well as compared to (1) normative reference values (standard scores), and (2) relevant clinical groups. Typically, when a full WAIS-IV is administered, the overall measure of "g," or FSIQ, is examined, which represents a sum of scaled scores that make up the four primary Index scores:

1. Verbal Comprehension Index (VCI). While similar to the VIQ score from previous versions of the WAIS-IV, VCI does not include Arithmetic or Comprehension. As such, VCI represents a more "pure" measure of verbal reasoning and concept formation.
2. Perceptual Reasoning Index (PRI). Similar conceptually to the PIQ score from the WAIS-III, PRI is comprised of Block Design and Matrix Reasoning, along with a new core subtest, Visual Puzzles (Figure Weights is supplemental for age < 70, and Picture

Completion is also supplemental). Whereas PIQ was influenced by motor performance and processing speed, PRI was designed to reflect a more "pure" measure of "fluid reasoning, spatial processing, and visual–motor integration" (*Technical Manual for the WAIS-IV*, Wechsler, 2008: 128).

3. Working Memory Index (WMI). This Index is made up of Digit Span and Arithmetic, similar to the WAIS-III, although some changes were made to the Digit Span subtest and its components. Separate scores are now available for Digit Span Forward and Digit Span Backward due to the different factor loadings of these tasks, as Digits Forward is more of a measure of simple attention, while Digits Backward relies more upon working memory. Digit Sequencing also relies heavily upon working memory, as subjects must listen to digit strings and reply with the numbers in order. Thus, because Digit Sequencing was added to the Digit Span subtest, and in view of the overlap between Digit Sequencing and Letter–Number Sequencing, the latter was retained only as a supplemental test for subjects under age 70.

4. Processing Speed Index (PSI). General mental efficiency has long been associated with processing speed, as more efficient brains tend to process information more rapidly. The subtests that make up this Index include Symbol Search and Coding, which were retained from the WAIS-III. As such, the PSI requires a variety of cognitive skills, including visual scanning, attention, and psychomotor speed. Cancellation, a measure of visual scanning and sustained concentration, was added as a supplementary subtest for those under age 70.

The next level of analysis typically encompasses examination and comparison of the four index scores to look for overall strengths and weaknesses in these domains. This should include careful analysis of the component subtest scores such that other potential deficits (e.g., motor impairment) are ruled out before interpretation of a specific cognitive domain is made. Furthermore, consistency within cognitive domains should be considered – for example, someone said to show evidence of attentional impairment should show consistent problems with attention that may affect other higher-level abilities as well.

Atypical "scatter" among index or subtest scores, as often commented on in clinical reports, should be carefully considered relative to normative data, base rates, and information from clinical groups, as well as the individual case at hand. With this information in mind, users should familiarize themselves with the base rates of index score discrepancies that are presented in the WAIS-IV Administration and Scoring Manual, as this is a complex issue in terms of how often "significant" score discrepancies are seen and what they mean. For example, index score discrepancies of up to 10 points occurred in 22–26 percent of the overall standardization sample, indicating that such differences are not rare in the general population. In contrast, 15-point discrepancies were seen in 12–18 percent of the sample, and discrepancies of up to 20 points were seen in only 6–11 percent of the standardization group. Thus, clinical interpretation of score differences is needed that factors in performance on the individual subtests and items and considers measurement error of the test as well as individual performance variability. Along these lines, it should also be noted that some index and scaled scores, like the constructs they tap, are more closely associated than others, and that this association may be highlighted or attenuated depending upon the underlying deficit.

TEST–RETEST RELIABILITY

Stability of any neuropsychological test is important, as is knowledge of how different clinical populations tend to perform over time. Retesting individuals with the same neuropsychological measure often results in an increase in scores on subsequent administrations, and the Wechsler scales are no exception. This so-called "practice effect" is evident in the WAIS-IV standardization sample, as represented in the mean score differences for composite scores presented in Table 6.2.

As seen in Table 6.2, the smallest mean test–retest improvement was seen on VCI, which is not surprising, given its representation of crystallized verbal tasks, and the WMI showed impressive consistency as well, with only a 3.1-point difference. Scores on FSIQ, PRI, and PSI all showed around a 4-point increase with the second administration in this normative sample. Of course, these numbers reflect group tendencies, and variability across scores and individuals differs. Also, when considering test–retest changes over time, an important factor to consider is the base rate of change for a test in the normal population, as nicely demonstrated for the WAIS-R in the classic paper by Matarazzo and Herman (1984). In that seminal report, the authors point out how common it is to see test–retest IQ

TABLE 6.2 Mean WAIS-IV test–retest differences for composite scores

Score	Time 1	Time 2	Difference
FSIQ	99.7	104.0	+4.3
VCI	99.3	101.8	+2.5
PRI	100.4	104.3	+3.9
WMI	99.5	102.6	+3.1
PSI	100.2	104.6	+4.4

TABLE 6.3 Percentages of WAIS-IV standardization sample obtaining specified test–retest composite score differences between

	≥ −10	−7 to −9	−4 to −6	−1 to −3	0	+1 to +3	+4 to +6	+7 to +9	≥ +10
FSIQ	>1	1	4	8	5	25	27	16	14
VCI	1	2	8	10	14	24	23	11	8
PRI	5	5	8	8	10	14	17	12	22
WMI	4	6	6	8	13	18	16	13	16
PSI	4	3	5	9	14	16	15	10	25

discrepancies in the general population, which is critical to consider in clinical and research situations. Table 6.3 presents the percent of the WAIS-IV standardization sample that showed test–retest changes of various magnitudes on FSIQ and index scores.

With these base rates and test–retest parameters from the standardization sample in mind, test–retest data on clinical groups along these lines will be an important area of examination in the future. Test–retest comparisons incorporating other more advanced approaches to data analysis, such as reliable change indexes, will also prove useful (see Lineweaver & Chelune, 2003). Two such methods are reliable change adjusted for practice effects (Chelune, 2003) and regression methods (Crawford & Garthwaite, 2007). Tables estimating reliable change scores adjusted for practice effects on both the WAIS-IV and WMS-IV have been published by Brooks, Strauss, Sherman, Iverson, and Slick (2009). However, the Brooks *et al.* tables are based on a statistical estimation technique. Reliable change tables derived from the actual base rate data observed in the WAIS-IV and WMS-IV standardization samples are preferable due to the increased accuracy afforded, and such tables have been made available (Wechsler, 2009).

INITIAL VALIDITY STUDIES OF WAIS-IV

The WAIS-IV included a variety of special populations for its initial clinical studies, in addition to extending the normative age range up to 90 years. A list of the special clinical groups for which data are provided in the Technical Manual is presented in Table 6.4.

Whereas these groups were not added to represent definitive studies or clinical profiles, their inclusion allows for a preliminary examination of the

TABLE 6.4   WAIS-IV clinical group studies

Alzheimer's Disease

Mild Cognitive Impairment

Traumatic Brain Injury

Depression

Gifted Intellectual Functioning

Intellectual Disability (including borderline, mild & moderate severity levels)

Learning Disability (including Reading and Math disabilities)

Attention Deficit Hyperactivity Disorder (ADHD)

Autistic Disorder

Asperger's Disorder

new and amended scales, and gives users an initial sense as to how the various subtest and index scores may tend to behave in some of the more commonly encountered clinical populations. These data also serve to set the stage for additional larger-scale investigations exploring the use of the WAIS-IV as an important neuropsychological tool in the neurobehavioral characterization of cognitive function and dysfunction.

SUPPLEMENTAL ANALYSES OF CLINICAL SCALES

Preliminary data for the new clinical groups are presented in the *Technical Manual for the WAIS-IV* (Wechsler, 2008: 98–122). Each table includes mean scaled and index scores for a particular clinical group, along with comparison data from a matched sample of controls. It should be stressed that these tables are not "norms;" rather, these data allow for initial examination of these populations in relation to healthy controls, and provide for preliminary analysis of patterns across the various subtests and scores. The following section provides a graphical depiction of mean index and subtest scaled scores for some of the special clinical groups included in the WAIS-IV development (adapted from Technical Manual Tables 5.20–5.32).

Intellectual giftedness and disability

Figure 6.1 presents FSIQ and index score data from the WAIS-IV Technical Manual in graphical form for four groups with varying levels of intellectual functioning, ranging from intellectually gifted to moderately impaired. The gifted group ($n = 34$) had scores on a standard measure of cognitive ability that were at least 2 SDs above the mean, or had to have

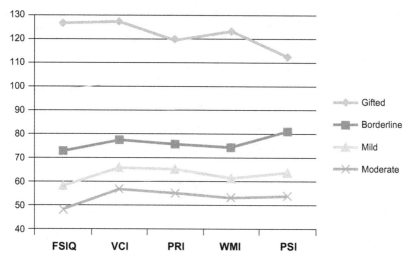

FIGURE 6.1   WAIS-IV results for Gifted, Borderline, mild, and moderate Intellectual Disability groups.

received special services from an intellectually gifted program in school. The intellectual disability groups (previously referred to as having varying degrees of mental retardation) had to meet DSM-IV-TR criteria that included subnormal scores on a standard cognitive ability measure in addition to showing evidence of impairment in adaptive functioning. The sample included 27 individuals with borderline intellectual functioning, 73 subjects with mild disability, and 31 with moderate disability.

The groups demonstrated clear separation of mean scores consistent with the diagnostic labels, with average FSIQ scores ranging from just below 50 in the moderate disability sample to over 125 in the gifted group. Among the index scores, the gifted group's lowest relative score was on PSI, with higher scores on VCI. Interestingly, PSI tended to be among the higher index scores across the borderline, mild, and moderate disability groups, although most index scores were similar. Subtest scaled scores for these groups are presented in Figure 6.2.

As seen in Figure 6.2, the intellectual disability groups show similar patterns of performance across most WAIS-IV subtests, with the lowest mean scores in the lower functioning groups on Letter–Number Sequencing, Digit Span, and Coding. The intellectually gifted group showed the highest scores on Vocabulary, Digit Span, and Information, with relatively lower scores (though, notably, still around the 75th percentile) on Symbol Search and Cancellation. The overall pattern of subtest scores furthermore shows the expected differences across groups, and all differed significantly from their respective control samples.

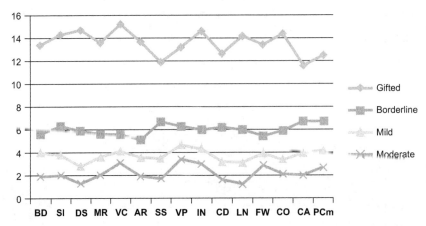

FIGURE 6.2 WAIS-IV subtest scores for Gifted, Borderline, Mild, and Moderate Intellectual Disability groups.

Traumatic brain injury

Because traumatic brain injury is one of the more common causes of cognitive disability, the WAIS-IV was administered to a preliminary sample of 22 subjects ages 20–44 with a history of moderate to severe traumatic brain injury sustained within 6 to 18 months of testing. FSIQ and index scores are presented in Figure 6.3.

As would be predicted based upon the nature of common cognitive impairment following TBI, the largest effect size among the index scores was seen for PSI, with VCI being relatively much more intact.

The TBI sample showed the greatest impairments on Symbol Search and Coding, both falling below a scaled score of 7, or 1 SD beneath the mean, followed by scores around 7 on Cancellation and Matrix Reasoning (Figure 6.4). In terms of effect sizes, the largest differences between the TBI

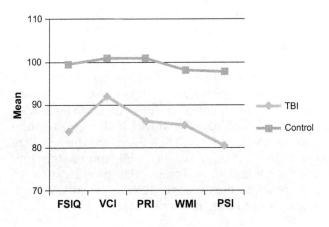

FIGURE 6.3 FSIQ and Index scores for the TBI sample versus controls.

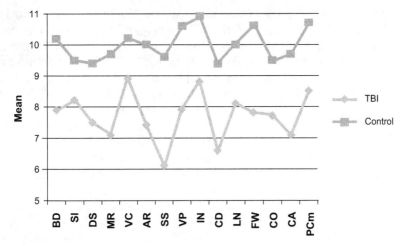

FIGURE 6.4   WAIS-IV subtest scaled scores for TBI and control samples.

sample and matched controls were on Symbol Search, Figure Weights, Visual Puzzles, Arithmetic, and Matrix Reasoning. Coding has historically been the most sensitive WAIS subtest to cerebral dysfunction overall, and Symbol Search appears to be similarly sensitive among patients with TBI.

Mild cognitive impairment and Alzheimer's disease

Data from individuals with mild cognitive impairment (MCI) and early-stage or mild Alzheimer's disease (AD) are presented in Figures 6.5 and 6.6. The MCI sample was comprised of 53 subjects ranging in age from 53 to 90 (mean = 73.7). The diagnosis of MCI was made using standard clinical

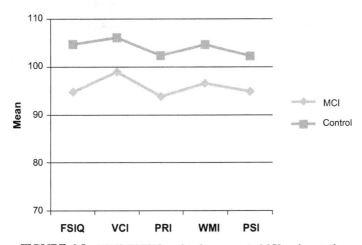

FIGURE 6.5   WAIS-IV FSIQ and index scores in MCI and controls.

criteria (Petersen, Stevens, Ganguli, Tangalos, Cummings, & DeKosky, 2001), although such groups tend to be inherently heterogeneous. Only 13 percent of the sample had less than a high school education, and as a result, the controls were selected to be higher in education than most of the other control groups. Subjects with early AD ($n = 44$, age range $= 58–90$) were also diagnosed using standard clinical criteria (McKhann, Drachman, Folstein, Katzman, Price, & Stadlan, 1984).

MCI subjects scored significantly lower across all index scores than the matched control group, showing the lowest performances on FSIQ and PSI. It is worth noting, however, that all scores for both groups are well within normal limits, which is not unexpected, given the diagnostic criteria of MCI as being a primary memory disorder without gross cognitive impairment or deficits in everyday functioning. Similar results from FSIQ and index scores from the mild AD sample are presented in Figure 6.6.

The AD sample demonstrated significantly lower scores across all WAIS-IV measures, reflecting expectedly large effect sizes, with a particularly large deficit on PSI in the AD group.

The MCI group demonstrated the highest mean scores (scaled scores around 10) on Vocabulary, Similarities, and Information, consistent with findings from previous WAIS versions which indicate that these latter subtests tapping more "crystallized" verbal abilities tend to be less sensitive to acquired cognitive dysfunction. Picture Completion, Visual Puzzles and Block Design were the lowest scores, followed by Symbol Search and Coding, although all scores were within normal range and around a scaled score of 9 (Figure 6.7). The mild AD group demonstrated the greatest impairments on Symbol Search, Coding, Information, and Picture Completion, with the highest scores on Vocabulary, followed by Comprehension and Block Design. Of note is that differences between

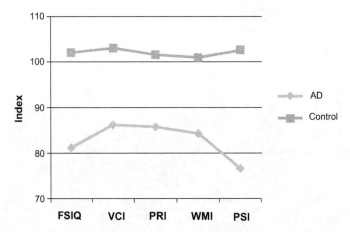

FIGURE 6.6 WAIS-IV subtest scaled scores in Mild AD and controls.

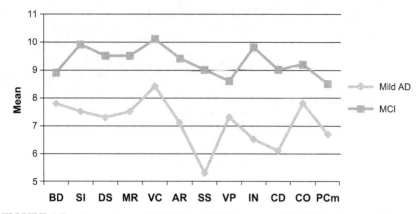

FIGURE 6.7 Comparison of Mild AD and MCI groups on WAIS-IV subtest scaled scores.

groups were greater than 1 SD on Symbol Search (hence driving the much lower PSI score as seen above) and Information, and approached 1 SD on Coding. These findings are largely consistent with previous literature on earlier versions of the WAIS-IV, and also illustrate some general similarities and differences in patterns across subtests.

Major depression

Some patients with depression can occasionally demonstrate cognitive inefficiency which may or may not be reflected in neuropsychological test performance, although debate remains regarding this topic, and a recent review of the literature revealed minimal effects of even severe depression on cognitive test performance (McClintock, Husain, Greer, & Cullum, 2010). WAIS-IV findings from 41 subjects age 50–86 with DSM-IV-TR Major Depressive Disorder are depicted in Figure 6.8.

There was a small effect size observed on the PSI (mean PSI Depression group = 95.8 *vs* 99.4 in controls), but other index scores were almost identical between groups, lending support to the notion that uncomplicated major depression should generally have minimal effects on the WAIS-IV index scores. Mean scaled scores for major depression and control groups are presented in Figure 6.9.

As seen in Figure 6.9, the depressed sample and matched controls performed similarly across most subtests, and all were well within normal limits in the scaled score range of 9–11. Interestingly, the lowest mean scores among the depressed group were on Coding, followed by Visual Puzzles and Figure Weights. These reflect *relatively* lower functioning on measures of non-verbal processing speed and fluid reasoning, albeit still well within normal limits and not suggestive of clinical impairment.

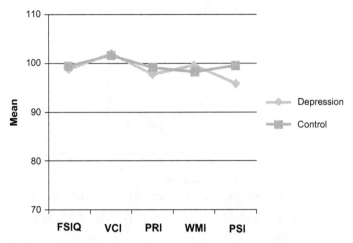

FIGURE 6.8   WAIS-IV FSIQ and index scores from patients with major depression.

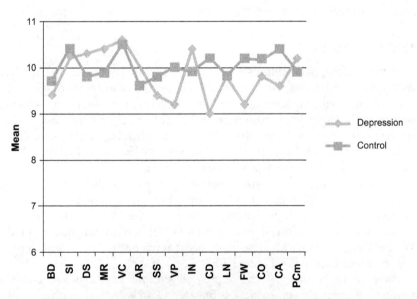

FIGURE 6.9   WAIS-IV scaled scores in Major Depression and controls.

SUMMARY

Taken together, these initial results of the WAIS-IV index and subtest scores across intellectual disability, neurologic, and psychiatric groups are promising from several perspectives:

1. The intellectual disability groups demonstrated robust and predictable differences across all scores and showed similar patterns
2. The neurologic groups showed significant differences from respective matched control samples and demonstrated different patterns of impairment
3. The depressed group showed a relatively normal pattern across scores
4. The pattern of findings in different clinical conditions is generally consistent with expected findings based upon existing literature and clinical presentation of disorders.

These comparisons furthermore suggest that the revisions made in the WAIS-IV have been successful in maintaining most of the familiar measures and scores, while adding new subtests and indexes that support the WAIS-IV's ability to characterize neurocognitive patterns and distinguish clinical disorders. As such, the WAIS-IV indeed shows promise as a more highly evolved tool for neuropsychological use that will usher in a new generation of clinical studies. Data from these preliminary clinical samples provide useful comparison benchmarks for clinical and research purposes so as to allow test users a means of comparing various scores with clinical samples ahead of the many research studies that will be forthcoming as the WAIS-IV enters wide-spread clinical application.

FUTURE RESEARCH

The release of any new version of a widely used and well-standardized assessment tool such as the WAIS-IV invites a new wave of clinical studies in order to explore the performance of the revised test, new subscales, and scores (including contrast scores) in various clinical populations. The WAIS-IV includes more initial clinical samples than previous versions of the WAIS, which will be helpful to clinicians and researchers as a starting point for comparisons and further validation studies. Additional investigations with larger samples and various comparison groups will be needed, however, and specialized comparisons of performance on the revised and new subtests with other neuropsychological measures, including the WMS-IV, will be of particular interest. Determining which subtests or combinations of subtests best distinguish or identify specific clinical groups will be important, as will developing an understanding of which disorders tend to be associated with what patterns of index and scaled scores from the WAIS-IV. Two- and four-subtest short forms of the new test will no doubt be forthcoming, as clinicians and researchers sometimes need brief estimates of FSIQ for gross subject characterization (see, for example, Ringe, Saine, Lacritz, Hynan, & Cullum, 2002). As was the hope of the WAIS-IV development team and the advisory panel, the changes incorporated into the WAIS-IV appear promising in terms of further augmenting its use in neuropsychological applications.

References

Brooks, B. L., Strauss, E., Sherman, E. M. S., Iverson, G. L., & Slick, D. J. (2009). Developments in neuropsychological assessment: Refining psychometric and clinical interpretive methods. *Canadian Psychology, 50*, 196–209.

Chelune, G. J. (2003). Assessing reliable neuropsychological change. In R. D. Franklin (Ed.), *Prediction in Forensic and Neuropsychology: Sound Statistical Practices* (pp. 65–88). Mahwah, NJ: Erlbaum.

Crawford, J. R., & Garthwaite, P. H. (2007). Using regression equations built from summary data in neuropsychological assessment of the individual case. *Neuropsychology, 21*, 611–620.

Dikmen, S. S., Machamer, J. E., Winn, H. R., & Temkin, N. R. (1995). Neuropsychological outcome at 1-year post head injury. *Neuropsychology, 9*, 80–90.

Donders, J., Tulsky, D. S., & Zhu, J. (2001). Criterion validity of new WAIS-III subtest scores after traumatic brain injury. *Journal of the International Neuropsychological Society, 7*, 892–898.

Flynn, J. R. (1987). Massive IQ gains in 14 nations: what IQ tests really measure. *Psychological Bulletin, 101*, 171–191.

Kaufman, A. S., & Lichtenberger, E. O. (2006). *Assessing Adolescent and Adult Intelligence* (3rd ed.). Hoboken, NJ: John Wiley & Sons.

Larrabee, G. J. (1986). Another look at VIQ–PIQ scores and unilateral brain damage. *International Journal of Neuroscience, 29*, 141–148.

Larrabee, G. J. (2000). Association between IQ and neuropsychological test performance: Commentary on Tremont, Hoffman, Scott, and Adams (1998). *The Clinical Neuropsychologist, 14*, 139–145.

Leonberger, F. T., Nicks, S. D., Larrabee, G. J., & Goldfader, P. R. (1992). Factor structure of the Wechsler Memory Scale – Revised within a comprehensive neuropsychological battery. *Neuropsychology, 6*, 239–249.

Lezak, M. D., Howieson, D. B., & Loring, D. W. (2004). *Neuropsychological Assessment* (4th ed.). New York, NY: Oxford University Press.

Lineweaver, T. T., & Chelune, G. J. (2003). Use of the WAIS-III and WMS-III in the context of serial assessments: interpreting reliable and meaningful change. In D. S. Tulsky, D. H. Saklofske, & G. J. Chelune et al. (Eds.), *Clinical Interpretation of the WAIS-III and WMS-III* (pp. 304–334). New York, NY: Academic Press.

Loring, D. W., & Larrabee, G. J. (2006). Sensitivity of the Halstead and Wechsler test batteries to brain damage: evidence from Reitan's original validation sample. *The Clinical Neuropsychologist, 20*, 221–229.

Loring, D. W., & Larrabee, G. J. (2008). "Psychometric intelligence" is not equivalent to "crystallized intelligence," nor is it insensitive to brain damage: A reply to Russell. *The Clinical Neuropsychologist, 22*, 524–528.

Matarazzo, J. D. (1972). *Wechsler's Measurement and Appraisal of Adult Intelligence* (5th and enlarged ed.). Baltimore, MD: Williams & Wilkins.

Matarazzo, J. D., & Herman, D. O. (1984). Base rate data for the WAIS-R: test–retest stability and VIQ–PIQ differences. *Journal of Clinical Neuropsychology, 6*(4), 351–366.

McClintock, S. M., Husain, M. M., Greer, T. L., & Cullum, C. M. (2010). Association between depression severity and neurocognitive function in major depressive disorder: a review and synthesis. *Neuropsychology, 24*, 9–34.

McKhann, G., Drachman, D., Folstein, M., Katzman, R., Price, D., & Stadlan, E. M. (1984). Clinical diagnosis of Alzheimer's disease: report of the NINCDS-ADRDA work group under the auspices of Department of Health and Human Services Task Force on Alzheimer's disease. *Neurology, 34*, 939–944.

Naugle, R. I., Cullum, C. M., & Bigler, E. D. (1998). *Introduction to Clinical Neuropsychology.* Austin, TX: Pro-Ed.

Petersen, R. C., Stevens, J. C., Ganguli, M., Tangalos, E. G., Cummings, J. L., & DeKosky, S. T. (2001). Practice parameter: early detection of dementia: Mild cognitive impairment (an evidence-based review). *Neurology, 56*, 1133–1142.

Powell, J. B., Cripe, L. I., & Dodrill, C. B. (1991). Assessment of brain impairment with the Rey Auditory Verbal Learning Test: A comparison with other neuropsychological measures. *Archives of Clinical Neuropsychology, 6*, 241–249.

Rabin, L. A., Barr, W. B., & Burton, L. A. (2005). Assessment practices of clinical neuropsychologists in the United States and Canada: A survey of INS, NAN, and APA Division 40 members. *Archives of Clinical Neuropsychology, 20*, 33–65.

Reitan, R. M. (1955). Certain differential effects of left and right cerebral lesions in human adults. *Journal of Comparative and Physiological Psychology, 48*, 474–477.

Ringe, W. K., Saine, K. C., Lacritz, L. H., Hynan, L. S., & Cullum, C. M. (2002). Dyadic short forms of the Wechsler Adult Intelligence Scale-III. *Assessment, 9*, 254–260.

Russell, E. W., Neuringer, C., & Goldstein, G. (1970). *Assessment of Brain Damage: A Neuropsychological Key Approach.* New York, NY: Wiley Interscience.

Sherer, M., Scott, J. G., Parsons, O. A., & Adams, R. L. (1994). Relative sensitivity of the WAIS-R subtests and selected HRNB measures to the effects of brain damage. *Archives of Clinical Neuropsychology, 9*, 427–436.

Tulsky, D. S., Saklofske, D. H., & Zhu, J. (2003). Revising a standard: an evaluation of the origin and development of the WAIS-III. In D. S. Tulsky, D. H. Saklofske, & G. J. Chelune et al. (Eds.), *Clinical Interpretation of the WAIS-III and WMS-III* (pp. 43–92). New York, NY: Academic Press.

Vega, J. A., & Parsons, O. A. (1967). Cross-validation of the Halstead-Reitan tests for brain damage. *Journal of Consulting Psychology, 31*, 619–623.

Wechsler, D. (1997). *WAIS-III WMS-III Technical Manual.* San Antonio, TX: Psychological Corporation, Harcourt Brace and Co.

Wechsler, D. (2008). *Technical Manual for the WAIS-IV.* Minneapolis, MN: Pearson.

Wechsler, D. (2009). *Advanced Clinical Solutions for WAIS®-IV and WMS®-IV.* San Antonio, TX: Pearson.

7

The Wechsler Intelligence Scales in the Assessment of Psychopathology

Gerald Goldstein [1] *and Donald H. Saklofske* [2]

[1] Mental Illness Research, Educational and Clinical Center (MIRECC) and Research Service, VA Pittsburgh Healthcare Center, Pittsburgh, Pennsylvania, USA

[2] Division of Applied Psychology, University of Calgary, Calgary, Alberta, Canada

HISTORICAL INTRODUCTION

The Wechsler intelligence scales were first developed at the Bellevue Hospital, a psychiatric facility in New York City. In his book *Measurement of Adult Intelligence*, David Wechsler (1941) wrote a brief section on schizophrenia, stating that patients with this disorder produce a profile characterized by relatively good performance on verbal tests that do not require much verbalization, but poor performance on tests involving attention to details, such as Picture Completion. Since that time an extensive literature has grown involving identification of test profiles that characterize various disorders ranging from schizophrenia and depression to Attention Deficit Hyperactivity Disorder (ADHD) and learning disabilities. For some time, the Wechsler scales have been commonly administered in psychiatric clinics and hospitals, often as part of a comprehensive psychological assessment, and are used along with other tests in diagnosis formulation and treatment planning. David Rapaport, a pioneer in application of the Wechsler scales to psychopathology, said:

> Diagnostic testing of intelligence and concept formation scrutinizes the extent and quality of a subject's achievements. From the relationships between different achievements, and from the types of falling-short of or deviation from expected

achievements, we infer the maturity and strength, as well as the degrees and kinds of impairments, of the functions underlying the achievements and the personality structure or maladjustment type in which these would be likely to occur. **(Rapaport, 1946)**

This statement still characterizes the nature of the clinical application of intelligence testing to psychopathology. In essence, the Wechsler scales are viewed within this theoretical framework as a personality test to be used in conjunction with a broader personality assessment. In these applications, an intelligence test is rarely administered in isolation from other procedures. In the evaluation of psychopathology, an intelligence test was typically used in conjunction with interviewing and personality tests that may have included projective techniques such as the Rorschach or Thematic Apperception Test, or objective procedures such as the MMPI. However, clinical psychology has come through an era in which intelligence tests were used as part of a battery of other cognitive tests and projective techniques for the purpose of doing comprehensive personality evaluations. This practice was at its height during the time of David Rapaport and his colleagues at the Menninger Foundation, and is presented in the two-volume *Diagnostic Psychological Testing* (Rapaport, 1946). Evidence for the presence and characteristics of psychopathology was elicited by comparing one test with the other, such as noting anxiety indicators on the Rorschach with intact intellectual function. The use of these test batteries has apparently diminished in clinical psychology and has been replaced by a number of other forms of assessment (i.e., multimethod), including structured interviews, systematic observation, objective tests and scales, behavioral assessment methods, and neuropsychological testing. In part because of changing views and models of psychopathology and psychological disorders, and also because of limited diagnostic and prescriptive utility, projective techniques are not used as widely as they were in the past, and have been replaced by a number of objective tests and structured interviewing.

Research in psychopathology with the Wechsler scales may be divided into three components. The earliest, described by Wechsler himself, involves the search for clinical pathognomonic signs or profiles that uniquely characterize specific disorders; is there a "schizophrenia profile" or an "autism profile" with which one can diagnose the disorder? The second set of studies involves exploratory or confirmatory factor analysis asking the question of whether intelligence has different latent structures in different clinical groups. For example, do individuals with schizophrenia have the traditional Verbal Comprehension, Perceptual Organization, Working Memory, and Processing Speed structure found in normal individuals? The third area has centered on the problem of heterogeneity within clinical entities, focusing on the identification of subtypes of a disorder using such techniques as cluster analysis. One aspect of heterogeneity focuses on the matter of recovery, involving research evaluating change in intellectual function following treatment, or in conjunction with clinical trials.

It may be stated in advance that the search for single pathognomonic profiles has essentially been abandoned. While subtest profiles continue to be reported in research studies they are typically not done so with the implication that they are specifically diagnostic of a particular disorder. The observation of intellectual heterogeneity in essentially all psychiatric disorders has discouraged talking of a "schizophrenia profile" or a "traumatic brain injury profile." These three components pertain to studies of the Wechsler intelligence scales themselves, but there is also an enormous literature in which the Wechsler scales were used in conjunction with other procedures, for various purposes. Thus, the Wechsler scales may be used in combination with various neuropsychological tests (Reitan & Wolfson, 1993), neuroimaging procedures (see, for example, Kraemer, Rosenberg, & Thompson-Schill, 2009), measures of social functioning, and other behavioral assessments. In the case of autism, the Wechsler IQ is used to classify the disorder into "high functioning" and "low functioning" subtypes (Rutter & Schopler, 1987). In some cases, it is used with other tests to derive indexes such as the Thought Disorder Index (Solovay et al., 1986), where it is used in combination with the Rorschach Test to document disordered thinking such as confabulation or peculiar verbalizations. There is an extensive literature on use of the Wechsler scales in conjunction with the Halstead-Reitan Neuropsychological Battery (Goldstein & Beers, 2004). The Wechsler scales are in fact now considered as being a part of that Battery (Reitan & Wolfson, 1993). The linking and co-norming studies conducted with new versions of the Wechsler tests, such as the Wechsler Adult Intelligence Scale – Fourth Edition (WAIS-IV; Wechlser, 2008a), with other measures, such as the Wechsler Memory Scales (WMS-IV; Wechlser, 2008a) and Wechsler Individual Achievement Tests (WIAT-II; Wechsler, 2001) and the Wechsler Fundamentals: Academic Skills (WF:AS; Wechsler, 2008b), are intended to extend the description of cognitive functioning to related areas such as memory and achievement. Thus, rather than employing such measures in search of consistent and reliable diagnostic profiles, the intent is to describe the cognitive and related functioning of the individual client. At the same time, it should be pointed out that there are some more or less characteristic performances of particular clinical groups, but again these are not marker variables for classification or diagnosis (see WAIS-IV Technical Manual).

FACTOR ANALYTIC STUDIES

In recent years, factor analytic studies of the Wechsler scales have taken note of the distinction now made between exploratory and confirmatory factor analysis (CFA). More recent applications of factor analysis have employed confirmatory approaches, made possible by advances in structural equation modeling (Jöreskog & Sörbom, 1993). Confirmatory factor analysis (CFA) is designed to evaluate specific hypotheses about the number of factors that make up a particular test battery and the pattern of factor loadings. CFA studies of the Wechsler scales in normal and clinical samples have typically confirmed a three-factor model for the WAIS-R. More recently, the addition of several subtests to the WAIS-III has allowed for testing of four- and five-factor models. The addition of these subtests made a four-factor solution more optimal than the previously reported three-factor model. The CFA results presented in the WAIS-IV manual indicate that the best-fitting models involve four first-order factors with or without a second-order factor. The factors are now called Verbal Comprehension, Perceptual Reasoning, Working Memory, and Processing Speed. The second-order factor is "g"; general intelligence. In this chapter, we are largely concerned with whether or not this factor structure replicates in various clinical groups. There are preliminary data available for the WAIS-IV, some of which are contained in the manual.

Aside from analyses supporting these structures appearing in the test manuals, several other studies have presented CFA results supporting a four-factor structure for the WAIS III in normal (Saklofske, Hildebrand, & Gorsuch, 2000; Taub, McGrew, & Witta, 2004) and clinical (Allen, Huegel, Seaton, Goldstein, Gurkils, & van Kammen, 1998; Dickinson, Iannone, & Gold, 2002; van der Heijden & Donders, 2003) samples, with somewhat different solutions reported by another group of investigators who supported either a two- (Ward, Ryan, & Azelrod, 2000) or six- (Burton, Ryan, Axelrod, & Schellenberger, 2002) factor solution. However, a three-factor model for the WAIS-R and a four-factor model for the WAIS-III appear to be the most commonly found solutions. This material is discussed in some detail in Tulsky, Zhu, and Prifitera (2000) and Tulsky, Ivnik, Price, and Wilkins (2003). For these earlier Wechsler tests, in addition to or instead of Verbal and Performance IQ scores, clinicians would commonly use three summary scores called factor-based index scores. The first of them, called Verbal Comprehension, is based on most of the Verbal subtests. The second is called Perceptual Organization, and is based on most of the Performance subtests. However, when a three-factor solution was employed, Arithmetic, Digit Span, and Digit Symbol (Coding) partialled out as a separate factor, initially called Freedom from Distractibility (Cohen, 1952). It was essentially an attention factor. When the WAIS-III appeared, containing several new tests, a four-factor solution became more appropriate, based on splitting Freedom from Distractibility into Working Memory (Arithmetic, Digit Span, and the new Letter–Number Sequencing test) and Processing Speed (Digit Symbol and the new Symbol Search Test). Since most clinicians to date have used the WAIS-III, the four-factor system is now the most widely accepted one and has been replicated in both American and Canadian studies (Bowden, Lange, Weiss, & Saklofske, 2008). The WAIS-IV has adopted a four-factor structure, producing Verbal Comprehension, Perceptual Reasoning, Working Memory, and Processing Speed Index scales. The Perceptual Reasoning factor was so named because there was a higher loading of "fluid" subtest. The second-order factor was replicated, and continues to be termed Full Scale IQ. This finding has been replicated in a comparative study of the US and Canadian standardization studies (Bowden, Saklofske, & Weiss, 2010). The WAIS-IV also produces a General Ability Index (GAI) consisting of scaled scores only from the three Verbal Comprehension and three Perceptual Reasoning tests. Its purpose is that of reducing the influence of working memory and processing speed on ability. Also, a Cognitive Proficiency Index comprised of the Working Memory and Processing Speed subtests has been found intermediate between the four index scores and FSIQ. This factor reflects the efficiency of cognitive processing.

Of course, the critical question is whether the established factor structure observed with various standardization samples is replicated for clinical samples. We have selected three groups for study; schizophrenia, autism, and traumatic brain injury (TBI).

SCHIZOPHRENIA

There has been particular interest in use of the Wechsler scales in studies of cognitive function in schizophrenia. Studies of the Wechsler scales in schizophrenia are very numerous, dating back to research done with the original Wechsler-Bellevue. As indicated above, we will not review studies here in which the Wechsler scales were used as a measure of intelligence along with other cognitive, neuropsychological, or neurobiological procedures, but will only describe studies in which the Wechsler scales themselves were the focus of attention. Earlier interest concentrated on the identification of a "Schizophrenic Profile," or pattern of subtest scores that had high levels of sensitivity and specificity for identification of schizophrenia. However, numerous studies have shown that patients with schizophrenia may demonstrate a wide range of Wechsler scale scores and profiles. There is no support for a single prototypic profile. An empirical demonstration of this view was provided by Crockett (1993), who cross-validated a categorization into nine "core profiles" for the WAIS-R

(McDermott, Jones, Glutting, & Noonan, 1989) using patients with schizophrenia as a portion of his sample. He found that there were some schizophrenia patients in all but the highest intellectual level core profile, with the largest number falling into a "Slightly Below Average" profile. In the McDermott *et al.* study, this core profile had a mean Full Scale IQ of 89 with a relatively flat profile containing mean subtest scores ranging between 6 and 8.

Efforts have been made to discover the basis for the heterogeneity. There are contradictory findings concerning gender difference, with some studies reporting a superiority of males (Weiser *et al.*, 2000) or of females (Voglmaier, Seidman, Niznikeiwicz, Dickey, Shenton, & McCarley, 2005), and some reporting no difference (Andia *et al.*, 1995). Other studies have focused on premorbid cognitive performance, type of schizophrenia, particularly with regard to deficit and non-deficit or positive and negative subtypes, and family history (Seckinger *et al.*, 2004; Wolitzky *et al.*, 2006). There have been several studies of intellectual heterogeneity in patients with schizophrenia with an emphasis on the status of individuals with average or above intelligence who have been characterized as having "Neuropsychologically Normal Schizophrenia." This controversial area of research was apparently initiated by a paper by Palmer *et al.* (1997), entitled "Is it possible to be schizophrenic yet neuropsychologically normal?" This paper showed that a portion of the schizophrenia patients studied produced performance levels indistinguishable from normal on the Halstead-Reitan Battery, including subtests of the Wechsler intelligence scales.

This phenomenon was also reported by Goldstein (1990) in the context of a cluster analytic study of a set of tests of abstraction and problem-solving ability. A cluster containing about 20 percent of the sample produced a cognitive profile with all of the tests within the normal range. This cluster had a mean Full Scale IQ of 108.6 (SD = 11.0) and 13.5 (SD = 2.2) years of education. The Wechsler scales (WAIS) were considered in more detail in a subsequent study of neuropsychologically normal schizophrenia, which was defined as having well-diagnosed schizophrenia and an Average Impairment rating on the Halstead-Reitan Battery of 1.55 or less (normal range), again found in about 20 percent of the total sample (Allen, Goldstein, & Warnick, 2003). This group had a mean Full Scale IQ of 103.64 (SD = 10.75) with 13.23 (SD = 1.66) years of education. The subtest scores ranged from 8.14 (SD = 1.98) for Digit Symbol to 11.36 (SD = 3.26) for Comprehension. In a subsequent study, the spectrum of schizophrenia subtypes was considered. The highest mean subtest scores tended to occur in the patients with Schizoaffective disorder or in the Paranoid subtype. When Schizoaffective disorder and Undifferentiated, Paranoid and Residual subtypes were compared, significant univariate differences were found for Vocabulary, Arithmetic, and Comprehension.

The Schizoaffective group had particularly high Comprehension, Vocabulary, and Arithmetic scores, all of which approached or exceeded 10. Heinrichs *et al.* (2008) compared a group of verbally superior schizophrenia patients, defined as having a WAIS-III Vocabulary score of 14 or higher, with comparison patients, verbally superior healthy participants, and comparison healthy participants. Comparison subjects were those with scores less than 14. The verbally superior patients had better life skills than the other patients, but poorer skills than the controls. Severity of symptoms was equivalent in all patient groups.

The concept of neuropsychologically normal schizophrenia has been contested in the literature, particularly in a paper by Wilk, Gold, McMahon, Humber, Iannone, & Buchanan (2005) entitled "No, it is not possible to be schizophrenic yet neurospychologically normal." These authors advocate the view that neuropsychological impairment is a core feature of schizophrenia. They attempted to demonstrate their point by comparing IQ-matched schizophrenia patients with normal controls, showing that the schizophrenia group nevertheless did substantially more poorly than controls on tests of memory and processing speed, but did well on tests of verbal comprehension and perceptual organization. They argue that obtaining some cognitive test scores in the normal range does not preclude neuropsychological impairment. Palmer *et al.* (1997) reported that visual memory appears to be particularly discrepant in the poorer performance direction relative to other cognitive abilities. This controversy continues, but there is little question that there is a small subgroup of patients with well-diagnosed schizophrenia with average or above general intelligence and performance on numerous cognitive tests at levels that make them indistinguishable from individuals without schizophrenia. It is understood that on close and detailed observation, these individuals may demonstrate selective cognitive deficits.

Aside from the distinction between neuropsychologically normal and abnormal schizophrenia, efforts to establish other empirically based subtypes, accomplished largely with cluster analysis, have not been entirely successful (Seaton, Goldstein, & Allen, 2001). Some efforts include distinctions that have been made among subtypes with different forms of memory deficit using differences between cortical, subcortical, and normal memory (Paulsen *et al.*, 1995). Heinrichs and Awad (1993) cluster analyzed their schizophrenia sample into what they called "Executive," "Normal," "Executive-Motor," "Dementia," and "Motor" clusters. Goldstein (1990) also identified five clusters, including a "neuropsychologically normal" subgroup and other clusters with varying levels of impairment. The 1990 study did not utilize the Wechsler scales, but several subsequent studies did (Allen *et al.*, 2003; Goldstein, Shemansky, & Allen, 2005), showing that both the Wechsler scales and a series of cognitive tests produced normal and abnormal subgroups. In their study of neuropsychologically normal schizophrenia, this group had a Full Scale IQ of 103.64 (SD = 10.75) with scaled subtest scores all close to 10 with the exception of Digit Symbol, which was 8.14 (SD = 1.98). The authors suggested that "neuropsychologically normal schizophrenia" may be a misleading term, and it might be more productive to use the term "high functioning schizophrenia", as is done in the case of autism.

In summary, the Wechsler scales, along with other cognitive tests, have produced a picture of substantial heterogeneity in the pattern and level of performance among patients with schizophrenia, and efforts have been made to characterize meaningful cognitive subtypes. This concept of heterogeneity appears to have replaced the idea of there being a single prototype "schizophrenia profile." A major difficulty in developing subtypes has to do with the distinction between pattern and level of performance. Thus, while preliminary efforts have been made to characterize the subtypes in the form of differing cognitive profiles, it is nevertheless the case that much of the variation among individuals is attributable to global level of performance regarding general intellectual functioning. Future research is needed to provide greater specificity in identifying subtypes of this complex disorder.

Factor analytic studies

The question of whether patients with schizophrenia produce a different factor structure from normal individuals was asked within 10 years of the initial publication of the Wechsler-Bellevue (Wechsler, 1941), although a factor analysis using normal individuals was performed earlier (Balinsky, 1941). The analysis of patients with schizophrenia was performed by Cohen (1952), who compared the factor structures of patients with psychoneurosis, schizophrenia, and brain damage. He identified the same three factors in all of these groups, which he called "Verbal" (Vocabulary, Information, Comprehension, Similarities), "Nonverbal Organization" (Object Assembly, Block Design, Picture Arrangement, Picture Completion), and "Freedom from Distractibility" (Digits Forward, Digits Backward, Digit Symbol, and Arithmetic). Regarding schizophrenia, he made the following conclusion:

> Although there are minor differences in factor loadings among the groups, from a factorial viewpoint, the same three functional unities, named Verbal, Nonverbal Organization, and Freedom from Distractibility, underlie Wechsler-Bellevue functioning in psychoneurotic, schizophrenic, and brain damaged groups.

This conclusion was confirmed many years later with the WAIS-III (Dickinson *et al.*, 2002), using exploratory and confirmatory methods. The confirmatory analysis demonstrated that the best-fitting model contained four factors: Verbal Comprehension, Perceptual Organization, Working

Memory, and Processing Speed. This model also characterized the test performance of the general population, as described in the WAIS-III manual. A similar finding based on exploratory and confirmatory factor analyses was reported by Allen *et al.* (1998) for the WAIS-R. Here, a three-factor model similar to Cohen's and to the one provided in the WAIS-R manual provided the best fit. In summary, while patients with schizophrenia perform more poorly than normal individuals, their ability structure is roughly the same, with minor variations in factor loadings. One variation of potential significance involves the possibility of a Social Cognition factor in schizophrenia. Allen, Strauss, Donohue, and van Kammen (2007), using confirmatory factor analysis of the WAIS-R, reported good fit for a four-factor model, with Picture Arrangement and Picture Completion forming a factor. They characterized this newly reported factor as a "Social Cognition" factor, and found small but significant correlations between it and measures of symptoms and social functioning.

Data obtained in connection with development of the WAIS-IV provided the opportunity to do a limited factor analysis based on 41 diagnosed schizophrenic cases. A principal components extraction was used with Varimax rotation (Table 7.1). A three-factor solution was generated, but not all of the subtests were included. There is a clear Verbal Comprehension and a Perceptual Reasoning factor. The first factor is mainly the Freedom from Distractibility factor, but there is a high loading from Matrix Reasoning. The framework presented in the WAIS-IV manual places Matrix Reasoning in the Perceptual Reasoning factor. Other than

TABLE 7.1 Schizophrenia sample – Varimax rotated factor loadings

Ar	0.839	0.323	−0.021
Ds	0.784	0.215	0.160
Ss	0.739	−0.014	0.324
Ln	0.706	0.130	0.262
Mr	0.609	0.364	0.384
Vc	0.184	0.853	0.105
Si	0.084	0.842	0.253
Co	0.311	0.782	0.217
Vp	0.061	0.419	0.818
Bd	0.277	0.060	0.794
Fw	0.246	0.405	0.700
Cd	0.382	0.045	0.444

Extraction method: Principal Component Analysis.
Rotation method: Varimax with Kaiser normalization.
Rotation converged in six iterations.

that difference, there is good agreement between solutions. If a four-factor solution is forced, the Freedom from Distractibility factor splits into the expected Working Memory and Processing Speed factors. With regard to the new tests, Visual Puzzles and Figure Weights load on the Perceptual Reasoning Factor, as occurred for the standardization sample. Cancellation data were not available. With regard to Matrix Reasoning, it is noted that there was a 0.64 correlation between it and Digit Span, and a 0.63 correlation with Arithmetic.

In summary, individuals with schizophrenia tend to have lower levels of intellectual function than normal individuals, but the structural organization of their intelligence, as evaluated with factor analysis, is the same as is typically found in normal people. An exception to the lower intellectual level in schizophrenia is a small subgroup, comprising about 20 percent of the schizophrenia population that has been characterized as neuropsychologically normal. These individuals are of average or above intelligence, and do well on a variety of cognitive tests. The presence of the same factor structure has been demonstrated across versions of the Wechsler intelligence scales, and appears to be the case for the WAIS-IV.

The schizophrenia spectrum

Another way of attempting to understand schizophrenia is as a trait. Individuals with this trait do not meet DSM criteria for schizophrenia, and, behaviorally, they are not psychotic. However, they have personality features that characterize, in an extreme form, individuals with schizophrenia. Some years ago, these traits were described by Meehl as "schizotypy" and "schizotaxia" (Meehl, 1962, 1989, 1990). They may appear in individuals as precursors of actual schizophrenia, and sometimes they remain stable throughout life. These traits can be measured with personality scales; the most commonly used being the MMPI. Since its first appearance, the MMPI has included Paranoia (6) and Schizophrenia (8) scales. However, elevated scores that exceed significant levels (e.g., > 70) on either scale do not necessarily mean that diagnosable paranoia, schizophrenia, or paranoid schizophrenia is present. That may be the case, but in the absence of additional data the most reasonable interpretation is that a clinically significant score indicates a relatively high level of a schizophrenia-type personality trait, such as social withdrawal. There has also been the establishment of a number of additional scales derived from the MMPI that evaluate different aspects of schizophrenia, such as aberrant thinking or magical ideation. The underlying view is that psychosis lies on a continuum ranging from infrequent symptoms in the general population, through schizotypy to full psychosis (Esterberg & Compton, 2009).

A widely accepted set of MMPI-2 subscales is the Personality Psychopathology Five (PSY-5), which provides a descriptive system for personality and personality disorders (Harkness & McNulty, 1994; Harkness, McNulty, & Ben-Porath, 1995). The traits described are Aggressiveness, Psychoticism, Constraint, Negative Emotionality/Neuroticism and Positive Emotionality/Extraversion.

In the course of development of the WAIS-IV, the MMPI-2 was administered to groups of 53 people with depression, 42 with anxiety disorders, and 28 with personality disorders. None of these individuals had a diagnosis of schizophrenia. Scores for the major Schizophrenia (8) scale and the PSY-5 scales were obtained for these individuals, providing the opportunity to evaluate the relationship between schizotypy and cognitive function. The literature in this area indicates that individuals with schizotypy but without schizophrenia have impairments of social intelligence (Aquirre, Sergi, & Levy, 2008), sustained attention deficits (Gooding, Matts, & Rollman, 2006), and span of apprehension (Asarnow, Nuechterlein, & Marder, 1983), and in Verbal IQ and subtests in the VC factor.

Based on this literature, it became a matter of interest to determine the extent to which individuals without schizophrenia but who had other psychiatric diagnoses or were psychiatrically normal showed an association between degree of schizotypy and cognitive function as assessed with the WAIS-IV. We therefore computed correlations between the full MMPI-2 Sc (8) Scale, the PSY-5 Psychoticism scale, and the FSIQ and index scores from the WAIS-IV. We also computed correlations with the other PSY-5 scales to evaluate whether if a strong relationship was found, it was specific to schizotypy. The results are presented in Table 7.2. While there are statistically significant correlations with several of the PSY-5 scales, all of the correlations with the Psychoticism scale are significant beyond the 0.01 level, and, with the exception of the Working Memory Index score, are substantially higher than is the case for the other PSY-5 scales. It would

TABLE 7.2 Correlations between MMPI scales and WAIS-IV indexes

	WMI	PSI	VCI	CPI	GAI	FSIQ
MMPI Sc scale	−0.21*	−0.31**	−0.29**	−0.29**	−0.31**	−0.31**
PSY-5 scales						
Aggressiveness	−0.23**	−0.24**	−0.21*	−0.30**	−0.21*	−0.24*
Psychoticism	−0.24**	−0.44**	−0.42**	−0.38**	−0.39**	−0.40**
Constraint	−0.10	−0.18	−0.07	−0.16	−0.12	−0.17
Neuroticism	−0.15	−0.29**	−0.21*	−0.25**	−0.22*	−0.24*
Extraversion	−0.02	−0.03	−0.02	−0.02	−0.04	−0.05

$*P < 0.05$;
$**P < 0.01$

therefore appear that schizotypy is more highly associated with cognitive function as assessed with the WAIS-IV than is the case for other major traits.

AUTISM

Autism is currently divided into low- and high-functioning types, operationally defined as an IQ ≤ 70 or > 70, respectively (Rutter & Schopler, 1987). Low-functioning individuals with autism are often severely mentally retarded, sometimes mute, and frequently not amenable to formal intelligence testing. Children and adults with high-functioning autism are typically testable, and may obtain IQ scores ranging from 70 to the superior level. They typically have a pattern characterized by a higher score on Block Design and a low point on Comprehension. While this profile is certainly not diagnostic as has been argued above, it is one of the more specific patterns existent for a neuropsychiatric disorder. A review study done by Siegel, Minshew, and Goldstein (1996) showed that, while there were exceptions, the great majority of individuals with high-functioning autism manifested this score pattern. From a review of 16 studies reporting Wechsler scale data in autism samples with Verbal or Performance IQs > 70 they reported that, with some exceptions, Verbal IQ was lower than Performance IQ, and there was a reasonably consistent subtest profile characterized by low Comprehension and high Digit Span on the Verbal scale, and high Block Design on the Performance scale relative to other tests. This prototypic profile is presented in Figure 7.1.

As can be seen, children and adults with high-functioning autism have similar subtest profiles, marked by high scores on Digit Span and Block Design and low scores on Comprehension, Picture Completion, and Coding/Digit Symbol. Caution was encouraged in interpreting this profile as prototypic, because it is also found among normal individuals, and not always or exclusively in individuals with high-functioning autism. A major exception was the identification of a subgroup of individuals with high-functioning autism that produced the profile that is said to be prototypic for non-verbal learning disability (NLD) (Williams, Goldstein, Kojkowski, & Minshew, 2008). NLD is a developmental disorder charac-terized by problems with social functioning, aspects of receptive language, poor arithmetic, and deficient visuospatial abilities. With regard to the Wechsler scales, rules have been developed for NLD, including an Arith-metic score ≥ 3 points $<$ Vocabulary; Block Design ≥ 3 points $<$ Vocabu-lary; and Performance IQ ≥ 15 points $<$ Verbal IQ. Williams *et al.* (2008) found that at least one of these rules was observed in 21–33 percent of their adults with autism, with 5 percent of them meeting criteria for all three rules. The percentages were substantially lower in their normal controls,

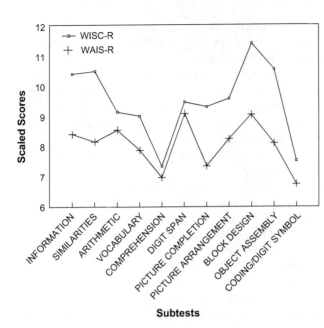

FIGURE 7.1 Sub-
test profile for the
WISC-R and WAIS-R.

with none of them meeting the criteria for all three rules. Thus, a substantial exception to the prototypic profile for autism is a subgroup that meets some or all of the Wechsler scale rules for identification of NLD.

With regard to verbal learning disabilities, there have been studies showing substantial differences between adults with LD and high-functioning autism. However, LD is not a unitary disorder, and there are well established subtypes. An empirically based subtyping system developed by Rourke (1998) distinguishes among individuals with uniform deficiency in reading and arithmetic (Global), poor reading with relatively good arithmetic (A > R), and at least average reading but poor arithmetic (R > A). The study by Goldstein, Beers, Siegel, & Minshew (2001) compared the WAIS-R profiles of individuals with high-functioning autism and individuals with adult learning disability, who were classified into the three Rourke subtypes. Overall, the subtest profile of the high-functioning autism group was most like that obtained by adults with LD who are not impaired in reading but who have difficulties with arithmetic. This finding is consistent with the observation that individuals with high-functioning autism may have excellent mechanical reading abilities, sometimes rightfully characterized as "hyperlexia" (Frith & Snowling, 1983).

Lincoln, Courchesne, Kilman, Elmasian, and Allen (1988) proposed that the prototype profile reflects a pattern involving preserved verbal abilities, particularly involving short-term sequential auditory memory, and good visual analysis and visual–motor integration. They made a distinction between relatively intact short-term sequential memory, perceptual organization, and visual–motor integrative ability, and relatively less intact representational capacity, hypothesis building, inferential ability, concept recognition, and verbal reasoning. Also noted was that relatively poor abilities involved comprehension of verbal, context, or social information. Thus, we see in the prototype profile a relatively high score on Digit Span and a low score on Comprehension. On the Performance scale, Block Design is done better than Picture Arrangement and Picture Completion, both of which have social content.

While autism is now viewed as a separate disorder from schizophrenia, with this distinction codified in DSM-III, the question of their resemblances has been raised. Eisenberg and Kanner (1958), developers of the concept of autism, believed it was a separate disorder from childhood schizophrenia, but indicated that the two disorders were "generically" related. They are both neurodevelopmental disorders with consequences for cognitive functioning, with one appearing early and the other later in life. This issue was raised with regard to cognitive functions by Goldstein, Minshew, Allen, and Seaton (2002), who did a comparison between high-functioning autism and schizophrenia patients using a battery of cognitive tests, including the WAIS-R. The schizophrenia sample was divided into four subgroups based upon cluster analysis, as described above (Goldstein, 1990). The question was, did a sample of individuals with high-functioning autism have a cognitive profile that resembled one or more of the schizophrenia clusters? It was found that the WAIS-R subtest profile of the autism sample was essentially identical to that of the cluster that has been described as "neuropsychologically normal," and both of these profiles were quite different, in the direction of superior performance, from those produced by the other schizophrenia clusters. This finding was of some importance, because it suggests the possibility that there is a subtype of schizophrenia with a pathophysiology similar to that which has been observed to occur in autism. Members of this subgroup may have a developmental background similar to the history of poor social relationships and social skill development that characterizes autism. In any event, the intellectual functioning of high-functioning autism does not resemble that of most of schizophrenia, but does resemble a small schizophrenia subtype. Thus, there appears to be evidence for both a high-functioning autism and a high-functioning schizophrenia obtained in part from the identification of almost identical profiles on the Wechsler scales.

Factor analytic studies

The factor structure of the Wechsler scales in samples with diagnosed autism has been reported on in two studies, one by Lincoln *et al.* (1988) and the other by Goldstein *et al.* (2008). Lincoln and colleagues did an exploratory analysis, while Goldstein *et al.* did a confirmatory analysis. The Lincoln *et al.* study of the WAIS-R used a principal components analysis with a Varimax rotation. They arrived at a three-factor solution, but the loading pattern was different from that which has been reported for the general population. There was a verbal factor, but the subtests typically loading on the Freedom from Distractibility factor also loaded on it so that a separate Freedom from Distractibility factor was not found. The second factor received its highest loading from the Perceptual Reasoning subtests, but only from Block Design and Object Assembly. Picture Completion and Picture Arrangement obtained high loadings on a separate, third factor. They described the first factor as relating to verbal intelligence, the second as reflecting visual analysis and visual–motor integration ability, and the third as representing non-verbal, social, and context-relevant information. This finding stimulated interest in the possibility of there being a social cognition or context factor in certain clinical groups.

Goldstein and colleagues (2008) pursued this idea in their CFA study, in which they evaluated seven models divided into three-factor and four-factor models. The best-fitting model was found to be a four-factor model that they described as Verbal Comprehension, Perceptual Organization, Freedom from Distractibility, and Social Cognition factors. As in the Lincoln *et al.* study, Picture Completion and Picture Arrangement loaded on a separate, fourth factor. Thus, both exploratory and confirmatory analyses have demonstrated a different structural organization in autism, marked by a separating out of an ability that can be called social cognition or context.

The WAIS-IV manual contains data for 19 adults with autism in the high-functioning range. While this sample is much too small to draw any firm views, a principal components analysis with Varimax rotation was performed. The rotated factor loadings are contained in Table 7.3. Factor 1 appears to be a version of the FFD factor, with high loadings from Letter–Number Sequencing, Digit Span, Coding, and Arithmetic. There do not appear to be separate Processing Speed and Working Memory factors. The second factor is a Perceptual Reasoning factor with high loadings from Block Design and Visual Puzzles. The third factor is clearly the Verbal Comprehension Factor. The fourth factor receives a high loading only from Picture Completion (0.91), and seems to represent a social context or cognition factor in the absence of Picture Arrangement, which is not included in the Fourth revision. These preliminary results from the WAIS IV appear to be supportive of the Lincoln *et al.* and Goldstein *et al.* studies, particularly with regard to the existence of a social intelligence factor. The new tests, notably Visual Puzzles and Figure Weights, load as anticipated on a Perceptual Reasoning Factor.

TABLE 7.3 Autism

Rotated component matrix[a]

	Component			
	1	2	3	4
Ln	0.924	0.120	0.139	0.131
Ds	0.847	0.016	0.226	−0.240
Cd	0.784	0.360	−0.209	−0.061
Ar	0.639	0.288	0.516	0.128
Ss	0.490	0.433	0.107	0.490
Bd	0.006	0.849	0.084	−0.005
Vp	0.065	0.799	0.426	0.295
Mr	0.471	0.655	0.244	−0.068
Ca	0.481	0.648	−0.225	0.112
Fw	0.473	0.622	0.139	0.291
Vc	−0.027	0.141	0.903	−0.061
Co	0.050	0.034	0.852	0.192
In	0.430	−0.007	0.665	0.272
Si	0.116	0.421	0.656	−0.378
Pc	−0.085	0.123	0.090	0.907

Extraction method: Principal Component Analysis.
Rotation method: Varimax with Kaiser normalization.
[a]Rotation converged in seven iterations.

TRAUMATIC BRAIN INJURY

The Wechsler scales have been used clinically for various purposes relating to traumatic brain injury (TBI). Their use in diagnostic neuropsychological assessment, generally as part of a battery of neuropsychological tests, is common. There are extensive literatures concerning specific subtest and test indexes, such as the relationship between Block Design and the right parietal lobe, or between Similarities and the left temporal lobe (Reitan & Wolfson, 1993). The significance of differences between Verbal and Performance IQs has been extensively studied with regard to differences in functioning of the left and right cerebral hemispheres. Broadly speaking, the Verbal scale tests assess left (dominant) hemisphere function, while the Performance scale assesses right hemisphere function.

There is also the matter of sensitivity and specificity of indexes from the Wechsler scales for correct identification of TBI. Intelligence tests are used to estimate severity of injury. Aside from these diagnostic applications, the Wechsler scales have been used in longitudinal studies to track the outcome of TBI, to aid in estimating pre-injury level of cognitive functioning, to test for malingering, as an assessment instrument in clinical trials evaluating cognition-enhancing drugs, and for prediction of vocational or educational success following head injury. There is a growing interest in the remote effects of mild TBI or concussion creating the potential for expanded use of intelligence tests in this area. For example, comparisons of scores before and after exposure to possible injury, often associated with military combat, may be of great value.

As in the case of schizophrenia, TBI is a heterogeneous disorder producing a wide range of variation in level and pattern of cognitive performance. At the extremes, a focal penetrating wound may produce a single symptom in the context of otherwise reasonably intact function, while a massive blunt injury could produce global dementia with generalized and severe cognitive impairment. However, it has been productive to study TBI as an entity in a search for general consequences seen in most patients. Somewhere between these extremes, there have been efforts to empirically derive subtypes of TBI on the basis of test scores obtained from heterogeneous populations, utilizing classification techniques such as cluster analysis. There has also been interest in cognitive factor structure in TBI, generally using the Wechsler scales. Thus, while the complexity of TBI is acknowledged, meaningful information can be derived from studies of heterogeneous samples of individuals who sustained TBI that can help answer important questions.

One important question concerns how much an individual has been impaired, not on an absolute basis but relative to his or her pre-injury level. As the use of intelligence tests in schools increases, it may become possible to obtain test scores achieved before injury for purposes of comparison. In the absence of the availability of such scores, methods have been devised to estimate pre-injury level from contemporary, post-injury data. Some of these methods are variants of the distinction made by David Wechsler between "Hold" and "Don't Hold" tests. Wechsler originally applied the distinction to aging, but it could be applied to many kinds of mental deterioration. Thus, for example, Information is a "Hold" test, while Block Design is a "Don't Hold" test. Thus, if Information is not sensitive to deterioration (in this case produced by brain trauma) while Block Design is, the Information score might provide a reasonable estimate of pre-injury ability. Since that time, more sophisticated methods have been developed involving the use of regression models, demographic variables, and scores obtained from other tests.

The matter of malingering has taken on increasing importance as psychological testing has become a standard part of assessment in forensic matters and determinations of disability. Several separate tests have been developed specifically to evaluate a client's motivation or effort, such as the Victoria Symptom Validity Test (Slick, Hopp, Strauss, & Thompson, 1997), but often it is possible to evaluate malingering from the cognitive or neuropsychological tests themselves (Forrest, Allen, & Goldstein, 2004; Allen, Caron, & Goldstein, 2006).There is a substantial literature concerning malingering on the Wechsler scales themselves, both the Intelligence and Memory scales, as well as a literature on malingering and head injury. Particular emphasis has been placed on the Digit Span subtest. Malingerers may generally suppress performance on this procedure or obtain a substantially lower score on it than on Vocabulary (Iverson & Tulsky, 2003). An unusually large discrepancy between observed IQ and the IQ estimate derived from one of the formulas used to predict pre-morbid IQ, such as the Barona estimate, may also suggest malingering (Greve, Lotz, & Bianchini, 2008).

There have been several efforts made to predict vocational outcome in TBI with assessments accomplished shortly after injury. In general, cognitive status has been found to be predictive of productivity outcome after TBI (Sherer, Sander, Nick, High, Malec, & Rosenthal, 2002) and of stability of employment (Machamer, Temkin, Fraser, Doctor, & Dikmen, 2005). Specifically, however, Ip, Dornan, and Schentag (1995) reported that the Performance IQ of the WAIS-R was the best predictor, of several indexes used, of return to work or school.

The Wechsler scales may be used on more than one occasion in people who have sustained head injury, as part of an effort to evaluate recovery and the success of rehabilitation. In these applications, the Wechsler scales are used as a part of a more extensive cognitive and functional assessment. A difficulty with repeated assessments has been the occurrence of practice effects that may substantially influence performance on the second testing. However, Iverson and Green (2001) and others (see, for example, Lineweaver & Chelune, 2003; Brooks, Strauss, Sherman, Iverson, & Slick, 2009) have produced confidence bands for determining measurement error as well as estimating average practice effects, surrounding test–retest difference scores, that can aid in accounting for the impact of practice effects. Using their calculations, the Wechsler scales have improved potential for use in longitudinal studies. In an early study, Mandleberg and Brooks (1975), in an investigation of 40 severely head-injured individuals, found that verbal subtests recovered more rapidly than performance subtests, and that verbal IQ approached that of a healthy comparison group within 1 year of injury. Lansdell and Smith (1975) used the method of correlating length of time since injury with Verbal and Performance scale factor scores. The correlation between time since injury was statistically significant ($r = 0.31$), but was zero for the Performance score. It was concluded that there is resiliency of verbal abilities following TBI, and perhaps some permanent impairment of performance abilities. In a study of language skills in children, using the WISC-III Vocabulary subtest, there was substantial recovery by 24 months post-TBI (Catroppa & Anderson, 2004). Drudge, Williams, Kessler, and Gomer (1984) did repeated testings, using the Halstead-Reitan Battery, of 15 adults with coma-producing closed head injury, showing improvement on essentially all of the measures used, but evidence of residual impairment relative to performance of a demographically matched healthy control group.

Cluster and factor analytic studies

Since TBI is such a heterogeneous disorder, there is particular interest in the possibility of subtypes that may be evidence based. Crosson, Greene, Roth, Farr, and Adams (1990) studied this matter using WAIS-R subtest data obtained from 93 patients with blunt head injury, and used average linkage cluster analysis to identify 6 clusters with varying WAIS-R profiles. Some of the clusters demonstrated substantial variability among subtests, but others were relatively flat, with minimal inter-subtest differences. Length of coma demonstrated a significant association with cluster membership. Using the WAIS-III, van der Heijden and Donders (2003) used the index scores in their cluster analysis, producing three clusters, varying in level of performance – an above-average, an average, and a below-average cluster. Using WAIS-R unpublished data, Goldstein performed a Ward's method cluster analysis of 87 head-injured individuals, and identified three clusters that varied mainly in level of performance (Goldstein, Allen and Caponigro, 2010). All of the cluster subtest profiles were relatively flat, but all had a substantially lower score on Digit Symbol than on the other subtests. One of the clusters, however, produced close to average scores on the Verbal scale subtests, but relatively substantially impaired scores on the Performance scale subtests. It may be described as a "Visual Reasoning" cluster.

Probably the major factor analytic study of the Wechsler scales was carried out, using the WAIS-III, by van der Heijden and Donders (2003). Using confirmatory analysis, they indicated that the model with the best fit of four models considered involved four factors. They were identified as Verbal Comprehension, Perceptual Organization, Working Memory, and Processing Speed – the same model proposed in the WAIS-III manual for the standardization sample. Preliminary efforts to replicate this finding, at least with exploratory analysis, were accomplished for the WAIS-IV utilizing data obtained from 31 individuals with TBI tested as part of the development of the WAIS-IV. Two principal components analyses with Varimax rotation were performed. The first analysis applied Kaiser's Rule, requiring stopping extracting factors when the eigenvalue falls below 1, and the second with a specific request for four factors. The rotated factor loadings are presented in Table 7.4. When Kaiser's Rule was

TABLE 7.4 Psychological Corporation TBI: two-factor solution

Traumatic brain injury rotated component matrix[a]		
	Component	
	1	2
Mr	0.821	0.062
Fw	0.819	0.203
Vc	0.813	0.340
Ds	0.807	0.275
In	0.792	0.426
Ar	0.788	0.288
Si	0.784	0.184
Pc	0.776	0.322
Co	0.762	0.270
Vp	0.738	0.280
Ln	0.733	0.282
Bd	0.676	0.564
Ca	0.136	0.943
Cd	0.237	0.867
Ss	0.423	0.759

Extraction method: Principal Component Analysis.
Rotation method: Varimax with Kaiser normalization.
[a]Rotation converged in three iterations.

applied, a two-factor solution was obtained that essentially separated out the Processing Speed subtests from the others. When four clusters were requested, a solution very similar to the one proposed for the general population was found, with fairly clear Verbal Comprehension, Perceptual Reasoning, Processing Speed, and Working Memory factors (see Table 7.5).

The same analyses were performed for Goldstein's 98 TBI patients. Again a two-factor solution was obtained when Kaiser's Rule was used, but with a somewhat different structure (see Table 7.6). There was a rather clear Verbal–Performance split, corresponding almost completely to the Verbal and Performance scales of the WAIS-R itself. When four factors were requested, the solution was somewhat more difficult to interpret, as shown in Table 7.7. There was a clear Verbal Comprehension factor, except that Similarities was split between this factor and a third factor. The second factor resembled the Perceptual Reasoning factor somewhat, except that it had a high loading from Digit Symbol. The third factor is difficult to interpret, with the highest loadings coming from Picture Completion and

TABLE 7.5 Psychological Corporation TBI: four-factor solution

Rotated component matrix[a]

	Component			
	1	2	3	4
Si	0.851	0.140	0.134	0.357
Vc	0.773	0.360	0.274	0.286
Co	0.751	0.396	0.199	0.172
In	0.675	0.420	0.361	0.305
Vp	0.241	0.836	0.202	0.238
Pc	0.361	0.783	0.241	0.234
Fw	0.339	0.748	0.130	0.358
Bd	0.219	0.623	0.512	0.407
Ca	0.189	0.178	0.921	−0.030
Cd	0.139	0.058	0.868	0.326
Ss	0.295	0.367	0.719	0.155
Mr	0.223	0.492	0.027	0.739
Ds	0.446	0.315	0.243	0.678
Ln	0.425	0.247	0.256	0.639
Ar	0.533	0.278	0.251	0.587

[a]Rotation converged in six iterations.

Similarities. The fourth factor received a single, very high (0.93), loading from Digit Span.

This difficulty in interpretation was somewhat relieved by requesting a three-factor solution, which is presented in Table 7.8. Here, there is a clear Verbal Comprehension factor, a Perceptual Reasoning factor, and a somewhat attenuated FFD factor with a very high loading from Digit Span, and high but lesser loadings from Arithmetic and Digit Symbol.

Wechsler scale studies of TBI indicate that it is a heterogeneous disorder that can be classified into subtypes primarily on the basis of level of performance. However, a wide variety of levels and patterns of performance may be found. It is sensitive to recovery, and pre-injury level can be predicted with reasonable accuracy, allowing for assessment of degree of impairment resulting from the injury. Most of the somewhat limited evidence indicates that individuals with TBI have the same factor structure as the general population, but there is substantial evidence for particularly severe impairment of processing speed. Preliminary evaluation of the WAIS-IV suggests that a four-factor solution similar to the one found in the general population may be the best-fitting model.

TABLE 7.6   Goldstein TBI factor analysis: two-factor solution

Rotated component matrix[a]		
	Component	
	1	2
Vc	0.855	0.207
In	0.837	0.223
Si	0.788	0.242
Co	0.738	0.265
Ar	0.677	0.330
Ds	0.540	0.052
Oa	0.090	0.879
Bd	0.155	0.869
Pa	0.334	0.779
Dsy	0.242	0.720
Pc	0.482	0.654

Extraction method: Principal Component Analysis.
Rotation method: Varimax with Kaiser normalization.
[a]Rotation converged in three iterations.

TABLE 7.7   Goldstein TBI factor analysis: four-factor solution

Rotated component matrix[a]				
	Component			
	1	2	3	4
In	0.841	0.159	0.285	0.064
Vc	0.839	0.152	0.252	0.147
Co	0.813	0.242	0.089	0.047
Ar	0.648	0.345	−0.044	0.414
Bd	0.235	0.875	0.037	−0.005
Oa	0.101	0.852	0.210	−0.016
Ds	0.183	0.734	0.025	0.345
Pa	0.296	0.704	0.430	−0.034
Pc	0.254	0.534	0.671	0.225
Si	0.589	0.110	0.657	0.195
Dsy	0.169	0.036	0.173	0.934

Extraction method: Principal Component Analysis.
Rotation method: Varimax with Kaiser normalization.
[a]Rotation converged in five iterations.

TABLE 7.8   Goldstein TBI factor analysis: three-factor solution

Rotated component matrix[a]		
Component		
1	2	3
In	0.880	0.193	0.070
Vo	0.867	0.179	0.150
Co	0.788	0.238	0.037
Si	0.761	0.218	0.236
Ar	0.581	0.313	0.394
Oa	0.126	0.875	−0.005
Bd	0.197	0.862	−0.010
Pa	0.387	0.766	−0.008
Ds	0.147	0.718	0.339
Pc	0.430	0.642	0.273
Dsy	0.207	0.054	0.941

Extraction method: Principal Component Analysis.
Rotation method: Varimax with Kaiser normalization.
[a]Rotation converged in four iterations.

SUMMARY

We have selected three disorders that have received extensive study with the Wechsler scales and in which cognitive function is an important consideration. There have also been studies of mood and anxiety disorders, not reviewed here but certainly deserving of clinical consideration as related to intellectual function. We are just beginning to understand cognitive function in ADHD, which has only recently been studied in adults (Katz, Goldstein, & Beers, 2001), in contrast to children, where a considerable body of literature extends back to the WISC-III (see, for example, Schwean, Saklofske, Yackulic, & Quinn, 1993). There is a voluminous literature concerning cognitive changes related to substance use disorders, notably alcoholism, but that topic is deserving of separate treatment.

The Wechsler scales show varying descriptions in schizophrenia, autism, and TBI, with differences in characteristic profiles and structures of ability. Each of these disorders has its own cognitive signature, and cognitive tests have been shown to be helpful in identifying them. As early as 1952, Jacob Cohen said, "The past decade has witnessed the increasing utilization of the Wechsler-Bellevue Intelligence Scale in the psychological diagnosis of neuropsychiatric conditions" (Cohen, 1952: 359). In this paper, he proposed that the rationales for the test developed by David Wechsler himself and David Rapaport (1945) could be tested experimentally with factor analysis. It is clear that Cohen's proposal has been acted upon with a resulting enormous scientific literature.

ACKNOWLEDGMENT

The Medical Research Service, Department of Veterans Affairs is acknowledged for support of this work. The Pearson Corporation is acknowledged for provision of data used in this chapter.

References

Allen, D. N., Huegel, S. G., Seaton, B. E., Goldstein, G., Gurkils, J. A., Jr., & van Kammen, D. P. (1998). Confirmatory factor analysis of the WAIS-R in patients with schizophrenia. *Schizophrenia Research, 34*, 87–94.

Allen, D. N., Goldstein, G., & Warnick, E. (2003). A consideration of neuropsychologically normal schizophrenia. *Journal of the International Neuropsychological Society, 9*, 56–63.

Allen, D. N., Caron, J. E., & Goldstein, G. (2006). Process index scores for the Halstead Category Test. In A. Poreh (Ed.), *The Quantified Process Approach to Neuropsychological Assessment*. Lisse: Swets and Zeitlinger.

Allen, D. N., Strauss, G. P., Donohue, B., & van Kammen, D. P. (2007). Factor analytic support for social cognition as a separable cognitive domain in schizophrenia. *Schizophrenia Research, 93*, 325–333.

Andia, A. M., Zisook, S., Heaton, R. K., Hesselink, J., Jernigan, T., Kuck, J., et al. (1995). Gender differences in schizophrenia. *Journal of Nervous and Mental Disease, 183*, 522–528.

Aquirre, F., Sergi, M. J., & Levy, C. A. (2008). Emotional intelligence and social functioning in persons with schizotypy. *Schizophrenia Research, 104*, 255–264.

Asarnow, R. F., Nuechterlein, K. H., & Marder, S. R. (1983). Span of apprehension performance, neuropsychological functioning, and indices of psychosis-proneness. *Journal of Nervous and Mental Disease, 171*, 662–669.

Balinsky, B. (1941). An analysis of the mental factors in various age groups from nine to sixty. *Genetic Psychology Monographs, 23*, 191–234.

Bowden, S. C., Lange, R. T., Weiss, L. G., & Saklofske, D. H. (2008). Invariance of the measurement model underlying the Wechsler Adult Intelligence Scale-III in the United States and Canada. *Educational and Psychological Measurement, 68*, 1024–1040.

Bowden, S.C., Saklofske, D.H., & Weiss, L.G. (2010). Invariance of the measurement model underlying the Wechsler Adult Intelligence Scale IV in the United States and Canada. Unpublished paper.

Brooks, B. L., Strauss, E., Sherman, E. M. S., Iverson, G. L., & Slick, D. J. (2009). Developments in neuropsychological assessment: refining psychometric and clinical interpretive methods. *Canadian Psychology, 50*, 196–209.

Burton, D. B., Ryan, J. J., Axelrod, B. N., & Schellenberger, T. (2002). A confirmatory factor analysis of the WAIS-III in a clinical sample with crossvalidation in the standardization sample. *Archives of Clinical Neuropsychology, 17*, 371–387.

Catroppa, C., & Anderson, V. (2004). Recovery and predictors of language skills two years following pediatric traumatic brain injury. *Brain and Language, 88*, 68–78.

Cohen, J. (1952). A factor-analytically based rationale for the Wechsler-Bellevue. *Journal of Consulting Psychology, 16*, 272–277.

Crockett, D. J. (1993). Cross-validation of WAIS-R prototypical patterns of intellectual functioning using neuropsychological test scores. *Journal of Clinical and Experimental Neuropsychology, 15*, 903–920.

Crosson, B., Greene, R. L., Roth, D. L., Farr, S. P., & Adams, R. L. (1990). WAIS-R pattern clusters after blunt-head injury. *The Clinical Neuropsychologist, 4*, 253–262.

Dickinson, D., Iannone, V. N., & Gold, J. M. (2002). Factor structure of the Wechsler Adult Intelligence Scale-III in schizophrenia. *Assessment, 9*, 171–180.

Drudge, O. W., Williams, J. M., Kessler, M., & Gomer, F. B. (1984). Recovery from severe closed head injuries: Repeat testings with the Halstead-Reitan Neuropsychological Battery. *Journal of Clinical Psychology, 40*, 259–265.

Eisenberg, L., & Kanner, L. (1958). Early infantile autism, 1943–1955. In C. F. Reed, I. E. Alexander, & S. S. Tomkins (Eds.), *Psychopathology: A Source Book* (pp. 209–233). Cambridge, MA: Harvard University Press.

Esterberg, M. L., & Compton, M. T. (2009). The psychosis continuum and categorical versus dimensional diagnostic approaches. *Current Psychiatry Reports, 11*, 179–184.

Forrest, T. J., Allen, D. N., & Goldstein, G. (2004). Malingering indexes for the Halstead Category Test. *The Clinical Neuropsychologist, 18*, 334–347.

Frith, U., & Snowling, M. (1983). Reading for meaning and reading for sound in autistic and dyslexic children. *British Journal of Developmental Psychology, 1*, 329–342.

Goldstein, G. (1990). Neuropsychological heterogeneity in schizophrenia: a consideration of abstraction and problem solving abilities. *Archives of Clinical Neuropsychology, 5*, 251–264.

Goldstein, G., & Beers, S. R. (Eds.), (2004). *Comprehensive Handbook of Psychological Assessment: Intellectual and Neuropsychological Assessment*. New York, NY: Wiley.

Goldstein, G., Beers, S. R., Siegel, D. J., & Minshew, N. J. (2001). A comparison of WAIS-R profiles in adults with high-functioning autism or differing subtypes of learning disability. *Applied Neuropsychology, 8*, 148–154.

Goldstein, G., Minshew, N. J., Allen, D. N., & Seaton, B. E. (2002). High-functioning autism and schizophrenia: a comparison of an early and late onset neurodevelopmental disorder. *Archives of Clinical Neuropsychology, 17*, 461–475.

Goldstein, G., Shemansky, W. J., & Allen, D. N. (2005). Cognitive function in schizoaffective disorder and clinical subtypes of schizophrenia. *Archives of Clinical Neuropsychology, 20*, 153–159.

Goldstein, G., Allen, D. N., Minshew, N. J., Williams, D. L., Volkmar, F., Klin, A., & Schultz, R. T. (2008). The structure of intelligence in children and adults with high functioning autism. *Neuropsychology, 22*, 301–312.

Goldstein, G., Allen, D. N., & Caponigro, J. M. (2010). A retrospective study of heterogeneity in neurocognitive profiles associated with traumatic brain injury. *Brain Injury, under review*.

Gooding, D. C., Matts, C. W., & Rollman, E. A. (2006). Sustained attention deficits in relation to psychometrically identified schizotypy: Evaluating a potential endophenotypic marker. *Schizophrenia Research, 82*, 27–37.

Greve, K. W., Lotz, K. L., & Bianchini, K. J. (2008). Observed versus estimated IQ as an index of malingering in traumatic brain injury: Classification accuracy in known groups. *Applied Neuropsychology, 15*, 161–169.

Harkness, A. R., & McNulty, J. L. (1994). The personality psychopathology five (PSY-5): issue from the pages of a diagnostic manual instead of a dictionary. In S. Strack, & M. Lorr (Eds.), *Differentiating Normal and Abnormal Personality*. New York, NY: Springer.

Harkness, A. R., McNulty, J. L., & Ben-Porath, Y. S. (1995). The personality psychopathology (PSY-5): constructs and MMPI-2 scales. *Psychological Assessment, 7*, 104–114.

Heinrichs, R. W., & Awad, A. G. (1993). Neurocognitive subtypes of chronic schizophrenia. *Schizophrenia Research, 9*, 49–58.

Heinrichs, R. W., Miles, A. A., Smith, D., Zargarian, T., Vaz, S. M., Goldberg, J. O., & Amman, N. (2008). Cognitive, clinical, and functional characteristics of verbally superior schizophrenia patients. *Neuropsychology, 22*, 321–328.

Ip, R. Y., Dornan, J., & Schentag, C. (1995). Traumatic brain injury: factors predicting return to work or school. *Brain Injury, 9*, 517–532.

Iverson, G. L., & Green, P. (2001). Measuring improvement or decline on the WAIS-R in inpatient psychiatry. *Psychological Reports, 89*, 457–462.

Iverson, G. L., & Tulsky, D. S. (2003). Detecting malingering on the WAIS-III. Unusual Digit Span performance patterns in the normal population and in clinical groups. *Archives of Clinical Neuropsychology, 18*, 1–9.

Jöreskog, K. G., & Sörbom, D. (1993). *LISREL 8 User's Reference Guide*. Chicago, IL: Scientific Software International.

Katz, L. J., Goldstein, G., & Beers, S. R. (2001). *Learning Disabilities in Older Adolescents and Adults*. New York, NY: Kluwer Academic.

Kraemer, D. J., Rosenberg, L. M., & Thompson-Schill, S. L. (2009). The neural correlates of visual and verbal cognitive styles. *Journal of Neuroscience, 29*, 3792–3798.

Lansdell, H., & Smith, F. J. (1975). Asymmetrical cerebral function for two WAIS factors and their recovery after brain injury. *Journal of Consulting and Clinical Psychology, 43*, 923.

Lincoln, A. J., Courchesne, E., Kilman, B. A., Elmasian, R., & Allen, M. (1988). A study of intellectual abilities in high-functioning people with autism. *Journal of Autism and Developmental Disorders, 18*, 505–524.

Lineweaver, T. T., & Chelune, G. J. (2003). Use of the WAIS-III and WMS-II in the context of serial assessments: Interpreting reliable and meaningful change. In D. S. Tulsky, D. H. Saklofske, & G. J. Chelune et al. (Eds.), *Clinical Interpretation of the WAIS-III and WMS-III*. San Diego, CA: Academic Press.

Machamer, J., Temkin, N., Fraser, R., Doctor, J. N., & Dikmen, S. (2005). Stability of employment after traumatic brain injury. *Journal of the International Neuropsychological Society, 11*, 807–816.

Mandleberg, I. A., & Brooks, D. N. (1975). Cognitive recovery after severe head injury. 1. Serial testing on the Wechsler Adult Intelligence Scale. *Journal of Neurology, Neurosurgery and Psychiatry, 38*, 1121–1126.

McDermott, P. A., Jones, J. N., Glutting, J. J., & Noonan, J. V. (1989). Typology and prevailing composition of core profiles in the WAIS-R standardization sample. *Psychological Assessment, 1*, 118–125.

Meehl, P. E. (1962). Schizotaxia, schizotypy, schizophrenia. *American Psychologist, 17*, 827–838.

Meehl, P. E. (1989). Schizotaxia revisited. *Archives of General Psychiatry, 46*, 935–944.

Meehl, P. E. (1990). Schizotaxia as an open concept. In A. I. Rabin, R. Zucker, R. Emmons, & S. Frank (Eds.), *Studying Persons and Lives* (pp. 248–303). New York, NY: Springer.

Palmer, B. W., Heaton, R. K., Paulsen, J. S., Kuck, J., Braff, D., Harris, M. J., et al. (1997). Is it possible to be schizophrenic yet neuropsychologically normal? *Neuropsychology, 11*, 437–446.

Paulsen, J. S., Heaton, R. K., Sadek, J. R., Perry, W., Delis, D. C., Braff, D., Kuck, J., Zisook, S., & Jeste, D. V. (1995). The nature of learning and memory impairments in schizophrenia. *Journal of the International Neuropsychological Society, 1*, 88–99.

Rapaport, D. (1945). *Diagnostic Psychological Testing*. Chicago, IL: Year Book.

Reitan, R. M., & Wolfson, D. (1993). *The Halstead-Reitan Neuropsychological Test Battery*. Tucson, AZ: Neuropsychology Press.

Rourke, B. (1998). Significance of verbal–performance discrepancies for subtypes of children with learning disabilities: opportunities of WISC-III. In A. Prifitera, & D. H. Saklofske (Eds.), *WISC-III Clinical Use and Interpretation: Scientist–Practitioner Perspectives* (pp. 139–156). San Diego, CA: Academic Press.

Rutter, M., & Schopler, E. (1987). Autism and pervasive developmental disorders: concepts and diagnostic issues. *Journal of Autism and Developmental Disorders, 2*, 159–186.

Saklofske, D. H., Hildebrand, D. K., & Gorsuch, R. L. (2000). Replication of the factor structure of the Wechsler Adult Intelligence Scale (3rd ed.) with a Canadian sample. *Psychological Assessment, 12*, 436–439.

Schwean, V. L., Saklofske, D. H., Yackulic, R. A., & Quinn, D. (1993). WISC-III performance on ADHD children. *Journal of Psychoeducational Assessment, WISC-III Monograph 56–70.*

Seaton, B. E., Goldstein, G., & Allen, D. N. (2001). Sources of heterogeneity in schizophrenia: The role of neuropsychological functioning. *Neuropsychology Review, 11*, 45–67.

Seckinger, R. A., Goudsmit, N., Coleman, E., Harkavy-Friedman, J., Yale, S., Rosenfield, P. J., et al. (2004). Olfactory identification and WAIS-R performance in deficit and nondeficit schizophrenia. *Schizophrenia Research, 69*, 55–65.

Sherer, M., Sander, A. M., Nick, T. G., High, W. M., Malec, J. F., & Rosenthal, M. (2002). Early cognitive status and productivity outcome after traumatic brain injury: Findings from the TBI model systems. *Archives of Physical Medicine and Rehabilitation, 83*, 183–192.

Siegel, D. J., Minshew, N. J., & Goldstein, G. (1996). Wechsler IQ profiles in diagnosis of high-functioning autism. *Journal of Autism and Developmental Disorders, 26*(4), 389–406.

Slick, D. J., Hopp, G., Strauss, E., & Thompson, G. B. (1997). *Victoria Symptom Validity Test.* Odessa FL: Psychological Assessment Resources.

Solovay, M. R., Shenton, M. E., Gasperetti, C., Coleman, M., Kestenbaum, E., Carpenter, J. T., & Holzman, P. S. (1986). Scoring manual for the Thought Disorder Index. *Schizophrenia Bulletin, 12*, 483–496.

Taub, G. E., McGrew, K. S., & Witta, E. L. (2004). A confirmatory analysis of the factor structure and cross-age invariance of the Wechsler Adult Intelligence Scale (3rd ed.). *Psychological Assessment, 16*, 85–89.

Tulsky, D. S., Zhu, J., & Prifitera, A. (2000). Assessment of adult intelligence with the WAIS-III. In G. Goldstein, & M. Hersen (Eds.), *Handbook of Psychological Assessment* (3rd ed.) (pp. 97–129). Amsterdam: Pergamon.

Tulsky, D. S., Saklofske, H., Chelune, G. J., Heaton, R. K., Ivnik, R. J., Bornstein, R., Prifitera, A., & Ledbetter, M. F. (Eds.), (2003). *Clinical Interpretation of the WAIS-III and WMS-III.* San Diego, CA: Academic Press.

Tulksy, D. S., Ivnik, R. J., Price, L. R., & Wilkins, C. (2003). Assessment of cognitive functioning with the WAIS-III and WMS-III: Development of a six-factor model. In D. S. Tulsky, D. H. Saklofske, G. J. Chelune, R. K. Heaton, & R. J. Ivnik (Eds.), *Clinical interpretation of the WAIS-III and WMS-III* (pp. 147–179). San Diego, CA: Academic Press.

van der Heijden, P., & Donders, J. (2003). A confirmatory factor analysis of the WAIS-III in patients with traumatic brain injury. *Journal of Clinical and Experimental Psychology, 25*, 59–65.

Voglmaier, M. M., Seidman, L. J., Niznikeiwicz, M. A., Dickey, C. C., Shenton, M. E., & McCarley, R. W. (2005). A comparative profile analysis of neuropsychological function in men and women with schizotypal personality disorder. *Schizophrenia Research, 74*(1), 43–49.

Ward, L. C., Ryan, J. J., & Axelrod, B. N. (2000). Confirmatory factor analyses of the WAIS-III standardization data. *Psychological Assessment, 12*, 341–345.

Wechsler, D. (1941). *The Measurement of Adult Intelligence* (2nd ed.). Baltimore, MD: Williams & Wilkins.

Wechsler, D. (1955). *Wechsler Adult Intelligence Scale (WAIS).* New York, NY: Psychological Corporation.

Wechsler, D. (1981). *Wechsler Adult Intelligence Scale (WAIS-R)*. San Antonio, TX: Psychological Corporation.

Wechsler, D. (1997). *Wechsler Adult Intelligence Scale (3rd ed.). (WAIS-III)*. San Antonio, TX: Psychological Corporation.

Wechsler, D. (2001). *Wechsler Individual Achievement Tests (WIAT-II)*. San Antonio, TX: Psychological Corporation.

Wechsler, D. (2008a). *Wechsler Adult Intelligence Scale (4th ed.). (WAIS-IV)*. San Antonio, TX: Pearson.

Wechsler, D. (2008b). *Wechsler Fundamentals: Academic Skills*. San Antonio, TX: Psychological Corporation.

Wechsler, D. (2009). *Wechsler Memory Scale (4th ed.). (WMS-IV)*. San Antonio, TX: Pearson.

Weiser, M., Reichenberg, A., Rabinowitz, J., Kaplan, Z., Mark, M., Nahon, D., et al. (2000). Gender differences in premorbid cognitive performance in a national cohort of schizophrenic patients. *Schizophrenia Research, 45*, 185–190.

Wilk, C. M., Gold, J. M., McMahon, R. P., Humber, K., Iannone, V. N., & Buchanan, R. W. (2005). No, it is not possible to be schizophrenic yet neuropsychologically normal. *Neuropsychology, 19*, 778–786.

Williams, D. L., Goldstein, G., Kojkowski, N., & Minshew, N. J. (2008). Do individuals with high functioning autism have the IQ profile associated with nonverbal learning disability? *Research in Autism Spectrum Disorders, 2*, 353–361.

Wolitzky, R., Goudsmit, N., Goetz, R. R., Printz, D., Gil, R., Harkavy-Friedman, J., et al. (2006). Etiological heterogeneity and intelligence scores in patients with schizophrenia. *Journal of Clinical and Experimental Psychology, 28*, 167–177.

Do the WAIS-IV Tests Measure the Same Aspects of Cognitive Functioning in Adults Under and Over 65?

Timothy A. Salthouse[1] *and Donald H. Saklofske*[2]

[1] University of Virginia, Gilmer Hall, Charlottesville, Virginia, USA
[2] Division of Applied Psychology, University of Calgary, Calgary, Alberta, Canada

INTRODUCTION

One of the important questions that needs to be considered when evaluating cognitive functioning in older adults is whether the scores on the tests have the same meaning as they do in young and middle-aged adults. While it is generally agreed that crystallized intelligence (*Gc*) measures such as those derived from vocabulary subtests tend to "hold" well with age, barring neurological complications arising from, for example, Alzheimer's disease, traumatic brain injury (TBI), or stroke, other areas commonly tapped by intelligence tests such as abstract reasoning, working memory, and processing speed tend to show decline with normal aging. Thus two questions come to the fore when evaluating the results of a test such as the fourth edition of the Wechsler Adult Intelligence Scale (WAIS-IV; Wechsler, 2008); specifically, do the cognitive abilities of adults change quantitatively or qualitatively with age, and do the scores obtained from them reflect the same constructs in people of different ages? These questions are relevant to the clinical evaluation of older adults because the test scores may not have the same interpretation at different ages if the meanings are different for adults under and over 65 years of age. The major purpose of the current chapter is to address this issue using the normative data from the WAIS-IV standardization study.

It is sometimes suggested that adult age differences in the performance on cognitive tests might reflect qualitative differences as much as, or more than, quantitative differences, because people of different ages vary considerably in their backgrounds and life situations. For example, adults over the age of 65 may have less recent testing experience, and therefore it is possible that their performance on cognitive tests could be more limited than in younger adults by unfamiliarity with testing situations. In addition, the amount of education and differential exposure to educational opportunities by younger versus older adults may very well influence how assessment and evaluation is viewed as part of everyday life. Older adults might be less concerned with how others evaluate them, and hence could have lower levels of motivation in the test situation. It is also possible that adults of different ages could have different perceptions of the face validity of certain tests, such as the Block Design test, which some older adults might view as similar to activities performed by their grandchildren and thus may not take very seriously. Finally, as postulated by Socio-Emotional Selectivity Theory (Carstensen, Fung, & Charles, 2003), adults of different ages might have different goals, with young adults more focused on information acquisition and older adults more focused on emotion regulation and positive emotion as well as addressing every day practical needs, and these different goals could affect how adults of different ages approach and perform cognitive tests.

There are clearly a large number of potential reasons why cognitive assessments might have different meanings at different ages. However, little empirical evidence relevant to these speculations is currently available, and a major goal of this chapter is to examine data from the standardization sample to evaluate whether the WAIS-IV cognitive tests measure the same areas and factors of intelligence among adults under and over 65 years of age. To anticipate, although a definitive conclusion is not yet possible, the available evidence strongly suggests that the tests in this battery have similar meaning at different ages, although measured ability levels may change on some factors.

A number of analyses using data from the USA standardization of the WAIS-IV will be reported in this chapter. Because the primary interest is in evaluating measurement properties in older adults, the normative sample was divided into two broad age bands. While other age sampling categories could be applied, we elected to define two groups for this analysis. Adults between 16 and 64 years of age ($n = 1600$) were designated as younger adults, and adults between 65 and 90 years of age ($n = 600$) were considered older adults. Because the sample sizes are moderately large, there is considerable power to detect even small differences as statistically significant, and therefore effect sizes are reported rather than significance levels. By convention (see, for example, Cohen, 1988), effect sizes in d units (i.e., the difference between the means divided by the pooled standard deviation) less than about 0.3 are considered small, while those greater than 0.8 are considered large, and intermediate values are considered to represent medium-sized effects.

COMPARISONS OF LEVEL OF PERFORMANCE

The first analysis simply examined mean raw score levels of performance on each subtest in the two age groups. The means for each WAIS-IV variable are reported in Table 8.1, where it can be seen that the values for most of the variables were higher in the younger (under-65) age group. Entries in the right column of the table indicate that the effect sizes were small for the Verbal Comprehension variables, moderate for the Working Memory variables, and very large for the Perceptual Reasoning and Processing Speed variables. The bottom portion of the table reports the same type of information for composite scores and index scores. Composite scores are created by averaging the z-scores across all ages for the subtests in each of the four domains of ability. Index scores are based on age-corrected scaled scores, and are transformed to have means of 100 and standard deviations of 15 in the total sample. The patterns for the subtests and composite scores are similar to those in many previous studies of adult age differences in cognition (see, for example, Craik & Salthouse, 2008; Salthouse, 2010). As might be expected, the age trends are much smaller for the index scores because these scores are based on scaled scores that are equated across age groups.

A popular interpretation of the cross-sectional age differences in cognitive functioning attributes them to cohort effects, which are often interpreted as generational differences in quantity or quality of schooling, cultural stimulation, health practices, etc. Although the idea of cohort influences has been widely accepted, it has been difficult to identify measures reflecting cohort status to allow this interpretation to be directly investigated. That is, if the cross-sectional differences in cognitive functioning are attributable to cohort differences, then successive age groups should differ in the values of the cohort-defining measures, and statistical control of the variation in those measures should result in a reduction of the cross-sectional age-cognition differences.

One variable that can be investigated in this manner is amount of formal education. The rationale is that if some of the cross-sectional age differences in cognitive test performance are attributable to progressively lower or higher amounts of education with increased age, then statistical control of amount of education should be associated with a reduction in the magnitude of the age differences in cognitive test performance. A statistical

TABLE 8.1   Means and standard deviations in the two groups and effect sizes for the group differences

Variable	Mean (SD)		d	$d(Ed)$
	16–64	65–90		
Verbal Comprehension (VC)				
Vocabulary	34.5 (10.9)	34.8 (11.6)	−0.02	−0.29
Information	13.6 (5.1)	13.4 (5.7)	0.03	−0.20
Similarities	24.5 (5.5)	22.4 (6.4)	0.33	0.18
Comprehension	23.2 (6.0)	22.0 (6.4)	0.20	−0.02
Working Memory (WM)				
Arithmetic	14.0 (3.7)	12.6 (3.5)	0.38	0.20
Letter–Number Sequencing	19.7 (3.7)	18.1 (3.9)	0.43	0.35
Digit Span Forward	10.5 (2.4)	9.5 (2.3)	0.41	0.30
Digit Span Backwards	8.8 (2.5)	7.6 (2.2)	0.49	0.16
Digit Span Sequencing	8.7 (2.3)	6.9 (2.7)	0.70	0.57
Perceptual Reasoning (PR)				
Block Design	42.3 (13.0)	29.5 (10.9)	1.07	0.96
Matrix Reasoning	17.6 (4.8)	11.6 (5.0)	1.20	1.09
Visual Puzzles	14.9 (4.8)	10.1 (3.9)	1.10	0.98
Picture Completion	13.1 (4.0)	9.4 (4.1)	0.92	0.81
Figure Weights	14.9 (4.9)	9.4 (4.2)	0.74	0.71
Processing Speed (Speed)				
Symbol Search	32.5 (8.4)	21.6 (7.9)	1.34	1.21
Coding	69.1 (16.9)	46.0 (16.6)	1.37	1.25
Cancellation	40.2 (9.6)	35.0 (9.1)	0.55	0.52
Composite Scores				
Verbal Comprehension	0.05 (0.83)	−0.14 (0.90)	0.22	−0.03
Working Memory	0.13 (0.78)	−0.35 (0.77)	0.63	0.47
Perceptual Reasoning	0.26 (0.75)	−0.69 (0.71)	1.31	1.19
Processing Speed	0.31 (0.79)	−0.84 (0.78)	1.47	1.34
Index Scores				
Verbal Comprehension	100.7 (15.0)	98.1 (14.7)	0.18	0.17
Working Memory	100.5 (14.9)	98.6 (15.1)	0.13	0.12
Perceptual Reasoning	100.4 (15.1)	98.7 (14.8)	0.11	0.12
Processing Speed	100.6 (14.9)	98.5 (15.3)	0.14	0.13

Note: d is effect size, and $d(Ed)$ is effect size after partialling educational level from the variable.

adjustment of this type essentially allows adults of different ages to be compared at the same average level of education. The d values in the right-most column of Table 8.1 are the effect size estimates for each subtest score after statistically controlling level of education. Although many of the values are smaller after amount of education was controlled, the effect sizes were still in the very large range for the Perceptual Reasoning and Processing Speed variables. Research with other data sets has also found relatively small attenuation of the cross-sectional age differences in cognitive functioning after adjusting for amount of education (see, for example, Salthouse, 2009a). These results suggest that although educational differences can distort age comparisons in cognitive functioning, they are unlikely to be responsible for large proportions of the observed differences in the WAIS-IV or other similar data sets.

There are at least two other reasons to question the cohort interpretation of cross-sectional age differences in cognition. One is that although the absolute level of test performance has increased in several generations, as documented in the Flynn Effect (see, for example, Flynn, 2007), if people of all ages experience these increases, then the influence would likely be greater for longitudinal comparisons than on cross-sectional comparisons (*cf.* Salthouse, 2010). That is, because longitudinal observations are obtained at different points in time they may be distorted by time-related inflationary effects on the test scores, whereas cross-sectional comparisons are unlikely to be distorted by time-related changes since all of the observations are obtained at the same point in time.

A second reason to be cautious about cohort interpretations of cross-sectional age differences is the results of a clever set of analyses by Kaufman (Kaufman, 2001; Lichtenberger & Kaufman, 2009). He compared similar scales in different versions of the Wechsler tests for people in the same birth cohort after adjusting for time-of-measurement or period effects. These contrasts do not involve the same people and thus are not true longitudinal studies, but they do involve people from the same birth cohorts, and thus are relevant to the question of whether cross-sectional age differences primarily reflect cohort differences. Lichtenberger and Kaufman (2009: 276) concluded that these "cohort-substitution studies provide results that agree remarkably well with the cross-sectional data." It is premature to conclude on the basis of the results just described that cohort factors do not contribute to cross-sectional age differences in cognitive functioning, but, by the same token, it is also too early to conclude that all of the cross-sectional age differences are artifacts of cohort differences.

Because it is sometimes postulated that a presumed lifetime of differential experiences results in people becoming more different from one another as they grow older, the magnitude of the individual differences in test performance was also examined in the two age groups. Group differences in between-person variability (i.e., the square of the standard deviation) in the level of performance were investigated for all variables with F-tests. The individual differences in test scores were significantly greater in the older group on only four variables (i.e., Digit Span Sequencing, Vocabulary, Information, and Similarities). It is noteworthy that three of these variables represent the Verbal Comprehension factor, which tends to have relatively small mean age differences. The individual differences were significantly larger for adults under 65 years of age for Block Design and Visual Puzzles, which are both tests that load on the Perceptual Reasoning factor. Even though many of the mean subtest raw scores were lower in the older group, these results indicate that there was no consistent pattern of age differences in the magnitude of between-person variability. In other words, for most of the subtests of the WAIS-IV, the performance differences among people under age 65 were approximately the same as the performance differences among people 65 and older.

Another potentially informative comparison involving level of performance consists of contrasts of the age differences across different percentiles of the score distribution within each age group. That is, rather than simply focusing on average differences in the middle of the distribution, the two groups can be contrasted at different regions of the distribution. Comparisons such as these allow determination of whether the differences are more pronounced among the highest- or lowest-performing individuals within each group, or are nearly constant across all ability levels.

The procedure used to make these comparisons involved first dividing the distribution of scores within each age group into percentiles (i.e., 0–10 percent, 11–20 percent, etc.), and then computing regression equations relating performance of the older group at each percentile to the performance of the younger group at the corresponding percentile. If there is no difference between the groups, then these functions will have intercepts close to 0 and slopes close to 1, and if the difference is constant across all regions of the distribution then the intercept will differ from 0 but the slope will be 1. However, if there are larger age differences at lower ability levels then the slope of the regression equation will be greater than 1, and if age differences are larger at higher ability levels then the slope will be less than 1.

The intercepts, slopes, and R^2 values (which indicate how accurately the equations described the data) for each variable common to the two age groups are presented in Table 8.2. Because the Figure Weights, Letter–Number Sequencing, and Cancellation tests were not administered to adults over 69 years of age, these variables are not included in the analyses. The pattern of age differences reflected in the intercepts resembles that for the means in Table 8.1, and in fact the correlation between the d values in

TABLE 8.2 Regression coefficients relating successive percentiles in the under-65 and over-64 groups for individual variables

Variable	Intercept	Slope	R^2
Verbal Comprehension (VC)			
Vocabulary	0.04	1.06	0.98
Information	−0.04	1.22	0.99
Similarities	−0.37*	1.14*	0.99
Comprehension	−0.28*	1.18	0.99
Working Memory (WM)			
Arithmetic	−0.42*	0.94	0.97
Digit Span Forward	−0.33*	0.96	0.96
Digit Span Backwards	−0.44*	0.93	0.90
Digit Span Sequencing	−0.68*	1.35	0.96
Perceptual Reasoning (PR)			
Block Design	−0.94*	0.75	0.95
Matrix Reasoning	−1.11*	0.98	0.86
Visual Puzzles	−0.91*	0.68	0.91
Picture Completion	−0.86*	1.01	0.97
Processing Speed (Speed)			
Symbol Search	−1.14*	0.94	0.99
Coding	−1.19*	1.00	0.99

*$P < 0.01$ for intercept compared to 0, and for slope compared to 1.

Table 8.1 and the intercepts in Table 8.2 was −0.99. The pattern with the slopes differed across variables, with the slope values ranging from 0.68 to 1.35.

Figure 8.1 portrays the percentile comparisons for composite scores of the four abilities created by averaging the relevant z-scores. It can be seen that the Verbal Comprehension composite score had an intercept close to 0 but a slope greater than 1, indicating that the age differences were greater among the lowest-performing individuals in the two groups. A different pattern is evident with the Perceptual Reasoning composite score, as the intercept was negative and the slope was slightly less than 1, indicating that age differences were evident at all ability levels but were somewhat more pronounced among the highest-performing individuals. The slopes were very close to 1 with the Working Memory and Processing Speed composites, indicating that the age differences in these variables were nearly constant at all ability levels.

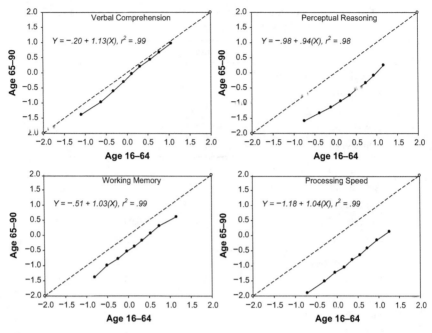

FIGURE 8.1   Plot of percentiles from the distribution from adults 65–90 as a function of percentiles of the distribution from adults 16–64.

The results summarized in Table 8.2 and Figure 8.1 raise the possibility that age differences might not be uniform across all ability levels, but rather may be larger at lower ability levels for Verbal Comprehension, and larger at higher ability levels for Perceptual Reasoning. However, there are at least two reasons why this conclusion should be considered cautiously. One reason is that the patterns do not hold for all subtests within each factor. In particular, the Vocabulary subtest within Verbal Comprehension, and the Matrix Reasoning and Picture Completion subtests within the Perceptual Reasoning factor, each had slopes very close to 1. These discrepancies raise the possibility that the phenomenon of differential aging according to region of the score distribution may be specific to particular variables and not necessarily to broader abilities. The second reason why the patterns in Table 8.2 and Figure 8.1 need to be interpreted cautiously is that they could be attributable to differential selection at different ages, such that the entire distribution may not have been represented to the same degree at all ages. The sampling procedures in the WAIS-IV project were designed to obtain a sample that was stratified with respect to major demographic characteristics, but it is very difficult to ensure complete representation of all relevant characteristics, such as ability levels within specific tests, in each demographic category.

The next set of analyses examined relations of age to the level of performance within each of the two age groups. These analyses differ from the earlier ones in that instead of comparing the mean levels of performance for the entire group, or group differences at different percentiles within the groups, the relation between age and performance (i.e., the slopes of performance as a function of age) is examined in each age group defined for this analysis. Age slopes in total sample standard deviation units per year are presented in Table 8.3 for all variables except those in which the maximum age in the sample was 69 years of age (i.e., Figure Weights, Letter–Number Sequencing, and Cancellation). Inspection of the values in the table reveals that the relation with age was more negative in the older group for every variable, and most of the effect sizes were in the small to moderate range. These results indicate that not only is the average level of performance in many cognitive variables lower in the

TABLE 8.3 Relations between age and performance in z-score units in the two groups and effect sizes (d units) for the group difference

	Age slope		
Variable	18–64	65–90	d
Verbal Comprehension (VC)			
Vocabulary	0.02	−0.03	−0.44
Information	0.01	−0.03	−0.40
Similarities	0.01	−0.04	−0.49
Comprehension	0.01	−0.04	−0.52
Working Memory (WM)			
Arithmetic	0.01	−0.03	−0.45
Digit Span Forward	−0.00	−0.02	−0.13
Digit Span Backwards	−0.00	−0.02	−0.18
Digit Span Sequencing	−0.01	−0.04	−0.36
Perceptual Reasoning (PR)			
Block Design	−0.02	−0.04	−0.25
Matrix Reasoning	−0.02	−0.04	−0.33
Visual Puzzles	−0.02	−0.04	−0.31
Picture Completion	−0.01	−0.04	−0.36
Processing Speed (Speed)			
Symbol Search	−0.01	−0.05	−0.50
Coding	−0.01	−0.05	−0.47

older group, but the relation of the variable to age is also more negative than among adults at younger ages. Other studies have reported similar acceleration of the cross-sectional age-related declines on cognitive variables (see, for example, McArdle, Ferrer-Caja, Hamagami, & Woodcock, 2002; Salthouse, 2004, 2009b; Lee, Gorsuch, Saklofske, & Patterson, 2008).

Results such as those just described are the kinds of findings that have led to speculations that there might be qualitative differences in what cognitive tests are assessing among adults of different ages. The remaining sections of this chapter describe analyses designed to examine the plausibility of these sorts of speculations.

RELIABILITY

One type of evidence relevant to the issue of measurement equivalence in different age groups is whether the scores on the tests are equally consistent, or systematic, among adults of different ages. Reliabilities (internal consistency and test–retest) obtained from the WAIS-IV Manual are reported in Table 8.4 for the two age groups. It can be seen that the retest reliability for the composite Digit Span variable was slightly higher in the older group, although it was slightly higher in the younger group for the Visual Puzzles variable. Most of the remaining values were very similar in the two groups, and only two were not within 0.1 units of each other. Based on this reliability information, it appears that whatever is being measured in the tests is assessed as consistently in adults over and under age 65.

CORRELATIONS AMONG VARIABLES

The magnitudes of the interrelations among the variables in the two groups are also relevant to the issue of measurement equivalence. One method of examining interrelations among variables is with a factor analytic model. Confirmatory factor analyses based on the model described in Chapter 4 of the WAIS-IV: Technical and Interpretive Manual (Wechsler, Coalson, & Raiford, 2008) were therefore conducted in the two age groups. The model specified four factors, with only the Arithmetic variable loading on more than one factor.

Standardized factor loadings and correlations between factors for the variables common to both groups are reported in Table 8.5. As in some earlier analyses, the Figure Weights, Letter–Number Sequencing, and Cancellation tests were excluded because they were only administered to adults up to 69 years of age. Because for many variables there were strong age relations within each group, the influence of age within each group

TABLE 8.4 Estimates of internal consistency and test–retest reliability in the two groups

Variable	Internal consistency		Retest	
	16–64	65–90	16–64	65–90
Verbal Comprehension (VC)				
Vocabulary	0.94	0.95	0.90	0.91
Information	0.91	0.94	0.88	0.93
Similarities	0.86	0.90	0.83	0.84
Comprehension	0.87	0.87	0.87	0.85
Working Memory (WM)				
Arithmetic	0.89	0.89	0.80	0.80
Letter–Number Sequencing	0.88	0.88*	0.78	NA
Digit Span Forward				
Digit Span Backwards	0.94	0.93	0.74	0.84
Digit Span Sequencing				
Perceptual Reasoning (PR)				
Block Design	0.88	0.83	0.80	0.79
Matrix Reasoning	0.90	0.91	0.78	0.73
Visual Puzzles	0.90	0.89	0.72	0.57
Picture Completion	0.84	0.84	0.71	0.77
Figure Weights	0.90	0.90*	0.76	NA
Processing Speed (Speed)				
Symbol Search	0.81	0.86	0.80	0.80
Coding	0.85	0.86	0.83	0.81
Cancellation	0.81	0.80*	0.74	NA

Note: Internal consistency reliability based on median of correlations across age groups in Table 4.1 of Wechsler (2008). Test–retest reliability based on average correlation of ages 16–29 and 30–54 for the younger group, and ages 70–90 for the older group (from Table 4.5 of Wechsler, 2008). Only a single combined estimate is available from the three digit-span variables.
*indicates that data were only from ages 65 to 69; NA means that the estimate was not available.

was partialled from each variable in these analyses in order to minimize misleading relations attributable to the common relations of the variables with age.

Inspection of the entries in Table 8.5 indicates that the standardized factor loadings in the factor analyses were generally similar in the two groups, and the effect-size estimates computed from the raw coefficients

TABLE 8.5   Standardized coefficients for a four-factor confirmatory factor analysis in the two groups with effect sizes for the group differences

Variable	Standardized factor loading		
	16–64	**65–90**	*d*
Verbal Comprehension (VC)			
Vocabulary	0.87	0.86	−0.05
Information	0.77	0.80	−0.15
Similarities	0.84	0.82	−0.14
Comprehension	0.85	0.81	−0.00
Arithmetic	0.32	0.39	−0.04
Working Memory (WM)			
Arithmetic	0.51	0.41	0.09
Digit Span Forward	0.65	0.61	0.06
Digit Span Backwards	0.74	0.72	0.09
Digit Span Sequencing	0.74	0.69	−0.05
Perceptual Reasoning (PR)			
Block Design	0.77	0.72	0.22
Matrix Reasoning	0.70	0.68	−0.00
Visual Puzzles	0.77	0.66	0.28
Picture Completion	0.62	0.65	−0.05
Processing Speed (Speed)			
Symbol Search	0.77	0.69	0.14
Coding	0.80	0.77	0.05
Factor Correlations			
VC – WM	0.66	0.70	−0.06
VC – PR	0.72	0.77	−0.07
VC – Speed	0.52	0.61	−0.10
WM – PR	0.70	0.77	−0.09
WM – Speed	0.63	0.69	−0.07
PR – Speed	0.63	0.75	−0.15
Factor Variances			
VC	91.44	99.96	−0.05
WM	3.01	3.40	−0.05
PR	101.55	61.57	0.22
Speed	182.59	163.93	0.05

Note: The effect size estimates (*d*) were based on comparisons of the unstandardized coefficients.

were very small. The only trends were for slightly smaller loadings for two Perceptual Reasoning subtests in the older group, and consequently slightly smaller variance for the Perceptual Reasoning factor in that group. For the most part, however, the relations among variables under and over age 65 were quite similar, which is consistent with the assumption that the variables have the same meaning in the two groups.

Because the factors were moderately correlated with one another, they can be organized into a hierarchical structure in which a higher-order factor is assumed to be responsible for the relations among the factors. The standardized coefficients for this model are portrayed in Figure 8.2 for the under-65 and 65-and-older groups. The values in parentheses are the effect sizes in d units for the group differences in the loadings. It can be seen that the loadings were slightly higher in the older group for all factors, particularly for the Perceptual Reasoning and Speed Processing factors, but that all of the effect sizes were quite small. These results suggest that the composition of general cognitive ability is similar in the two groups.

First observed by Spearman (Spearman, 1927), and often referred to as Spearman's "Law of Diminishing Returns," a number of researchers have reported that correlations among cognitive variables tend to be highest among individuals with the lowest levels of ability (see, for example, Detterman & Daniel, 1989; Abad, Colom, Juan-Espinosa, & Garcia, 2003; Saklofske, Yang, Zhu, & Austin, 2008; Tucker-Drob, 2009). Saklofske and colleagues (2008) tested this ability differentiation effect using WAIS-III standardization samples from Australia, Canada, the Netherlands, and the United States, and did not find support for either the ability or age aspects of the law of diminishing returns. However, the ability groups employed in

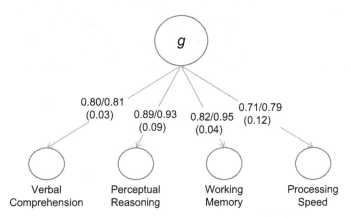

FIGURE 8.2   Standardized loadings of first-order cognitive abilities on a "g" factor. The first number is the coefficient for adults between 16 and 64 years of age, and the second number is the coefficient for adults between 65 and 90 years of age. The numbers in parentheses are the d values for the difference between the unstandardized coefficients.

the Saklofske *et al.* (2008) study were split at 45 years of age. Because it is possible that the "ability de-differentiation" phenomenon differs as a function of how the age groups are comprised, this effect was again examined in the two age groups with the current WAIS-IV data. Selection of a measure to stratify groups into different ability levels is somewhat arbitrary, since any measure could be used as a stratification measure. Because the Verbal Comprehension factor had similar mean values at different ages and nearly identical loadings on the higher-order factor in Figure 8.2, the Verbal Comprehension composite score was used as the ability stratification variable in the current analyses. However, it should be noted that a similar pattern was evident when other composite scores were used to create the different ability levels.

There are two contradictory goals in analyses examining relations at different ability levels, because a small number of groups is desirable to increase sample size and precision of the estimates, but a large number of groups is desirable to provide sensitive assessment of ability relations. A compromise was adopted in the current analyses by creating several overlapping groups which allowed each of several ability levels to be examined with moderately large samples. The overlapping subgroups were each composed of 20 percent of the sample, with the first group consisting of individuals up to the 20th percentile, the second group consisting of people with scores from the 10th to the 30th percentile, etc.

The correlations of the composite scores for each ability at different levels of Verbal Comprehension ability are portrayed in the four panels of Figure 8.3. The top left panel contains medians of the three correlations involving Verbal Comprehension ability, which is the composite score used to create the ability levels, and the remaining panels contain correlations between pairs of other composites. The patterns in each panel, and in each group, are generally similar, with the highest correlations at the lowest level of Verbal Comprehension ability, and most of the remaining correlations at nearly the same value. The ability de-differentiation phenomenon in these data therefore appears to be primarily attributable to very high correlations in the lowest ability groups. Of greatest interest in the current context is that although some of the correlations were higher in the 65-and-over age group, the pattern as a function of ability levels in adults under age 65 closely resembled that in adults 65 and over.

CORRELATIONS WITH OTHER VARIABLES

A final set of analyses consisted of examining correlations in the two age groups between the cognitive ability composite scores with two demographic variables, sex and education. The sex variable was coded as 1 for female and 0 for male, and the education variable was coded into five

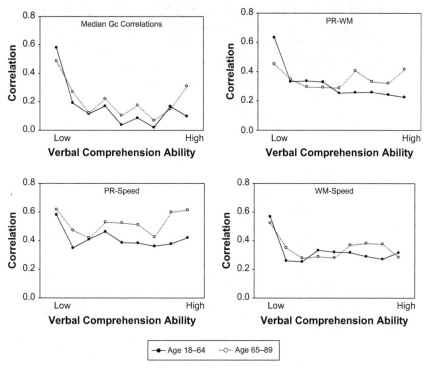

FIGURE 8.3 Correlations between composite cognitive ability scores at different levels of verbal comprehension ability for adults under and over 65.

categories, ranging from 1 for 0–8 years of education, 2 for 9–11 years of education, 3 for 12, 4 for 13–15, and 5 for 16 or more years of education. Results of these analyses are summarized in Table 8.6, where it can be seen that several of the correlations were significantly different from 0. At least in these data, males tended to have higher composite scores on the Verbal Comprehension, Perceptual Reasoning, and Working Memory domains, but females had higher scores in the Processing Speed domain. Whether these differences reflect genuine differences in the population, or are consequences of differential sampling of males and females, cannot be determined from the available data. However, the important point for the current purpose is that similar results were apparent in the two age groups, and the group differences in the correlations were fairly small, with none of the effect sizes exceeding 0.1.

All of the correlations between the educational level variable and the cognitive ability composite scores were moderately large, indicating that people with more years of education had higher scores on the four composite scores. Because causal direction is ambiguous with simple

TABLE 8.6   Correlations of the cognitive factors with sex and education level in the two age groups and effect sizes for the group difference

	Correlation		
Variable	16–64	65–90	d
Correlations with sex			
Verbal Comprehension (VC)	−0.09*	−0.07*	−0.02
Perceptual Reasoning (PR)	0.12*	−0.13*	−0.01
Working Memory (WM)	−0.07*	−0.03	−0.03
Processing Speed (Speed)	0.20*	0.10*	0.09
Correlations with education level			
Verbal Comprehension (VC)	0.54*	0.67*	−0.06
Perceptual Reasoning (PR)	0.35*	0.47*	0.02
Working Memory (WM)	0.41*	0.44*	−0.03
Processing Speed (Speed)	0.34*	0.41*	−0.02

Note: Sex was coded with 0 for males and 1 for females, and education level was coded with higher numbers for greater amounts of formal education (i.e., 1 for 0–8, 2 for 9–11, 3 for 12, 4 for 13–15, and 5 for 16 or more). The effect size estimates (d) were based on comparisons of the unstandardized (covariance) coefficients.
*$P < 0.01$.

correlations, these relations could reflect a positive influence of education on cognitive ability, an enabling effect of cognitive ability on access to more education, the operation of some other factor responsible for both education and cognitive ability, or various combinations of influences. Regardless of the causes, it is noteworthy that the association of cognitive ability and education is just as strong among adults 65 years and older as among adults at younger ages.

It is unfortunate that more variables were not available to allow additional comparisons of this type across the two groups. Nevertheless, the discovery of similar correlations with the demographic variables of sex and education in the two groups is consistent with the assumption that the cognitive ability factors have comparable meanings among adults under and over 65 years of age.

DISCUSSION

The analyses reported above should provide some relevant information to clinicians when using the WAIS-IV and trying to understand the effects that age might have on the measurement and interpretation of cognitive abilities. Average levels of performance are clearly lower in adults over 65 years of age compared to adults under age 65 on many cognitive tests. Furthermore, the relation of age to level of cognitive performance is often stronger among older adults, which indicates that age is a more salient predictor of level of cognitive functioning at older ages. However, it is noteworthy that the magnitude of individual differences (i.e., between-person variance) in level of performance was very similar in adults under and over age 65, which implies that factors other than age must have greater influences on the individual differences in performance among younger adults. The estimated reliabilities in Table 8.4 were similar in the two age groups, and thus the non-age variance in the younger group is not simply due to measurement error. Unfortunately there is no evidence in the available data regarding what these other age-independent influences might be, or why they would be greater in young adulthood and middle age than in old age.

The primary question of interest in the chapter was whether, despite the markedly different levels of performance in the two groups, the WAIS-IV tests measure the same aspect of functioning in adults under and over age 65. A tentative answer, based on the results described above, is "yes".

Among the evidence leading to this conclusion is the finding that the composite score reliabilities for adults under and over age 65 were very similar, indicating nearly equivalent consistency of measurement. The assessments in older adults were therefore no less systematic than those in younger adults.

One of the most informative methods of investigating the meaning of a variable consists of examining relations of that variable with other variables. The reasoning is that a variable can be inferred to be similar to variables with which it has strong correlations, and to be dissimilar from variables with which it has weak relations. The discovery of a close resemblance of the factor structures based on the patterns of correlations in the two age groups is therefore relevant to the issue of measurement equivalence. That is, variables can be organized into ability factors which are correlated with one another, and the results indicated that this organizational structure was quantitatively very similar in the two groups. Not only were the standardized coefficients in Table 8.5 close in magnitude, but also all of the effect sizes computed from the unstandardized coefficients in the two groups were quite small. Furthermore, the coefficients in Figure 8.2 were again very similar, which suggests nearly equivalent composition of the higher-order cognitive ability factor at different ages. Finally, although correlations among the constructs were greatest at lower ability levels, this was true to nearly the same extent for adults under and over 65 years of age. This combination of results is clearly consistent with the interpretation that the subtests and factors reflect the same constructs in the two age groups.

In addition to examining relations among other cognitive variables, relations with other types of variables can also be informative in investigating measurement equivalence. Only two other variables were available from the standardization program to allow examination of external relations: sex and educational level. However, both variables had very similar patterns of relations with the cognitive factors in the two groups, which is compatible with the interpretation that the cognitive variables have similar meaning in adults under and over 65 years of age.

Despite the evidence summarized above, it is still possible that there are qualitative differences in what the variables represent among adults of different ages. For example, when performing various cognitive tests young and old adults could use different strategies, or they could rely on different constellations of regional brain activation. However, until relevant empirical evidence is available, speculations of qualitative differences in cognitive performance at different ages should be viewed as hypotheses to be investigated, rather than as established conclusions. The methods reported above represent only a limited set of those that could be used to investigate measurement equivalence across different groups of people, but they provide no evidence of qualitative differences in the measures in adults under and over 65 years of age.

References

Abad, F. J., Colom, R., Juan-Espinosa, M., & Garcia, L. F. (2003). Intelligence differentiation in adult samples. *Intelligence, 31*, 157–166.

Carstensen, L. L., Fung, H. H., & Charles, S. T. (2003). Socioemotional selectivity theory and the regulation of emotion in the second half of life. *Motivation and Emotion, 27*, 103–123.

Cohen, J. (1988). *Statistical Power Analysis for the Behavioral Sciences* (2nd ed.). Hillsdale, NJ: Lawrence Erlbaum Associates.

Craik, F. I. M., & Salthouse, T. A. (Eds.), (2008). *Handbook of Aging and Cognition* (3rd ed.). New York, NY: Psychology Press.

Detterman, D. K., & Daniel, M. H. (1989). Correlations of mental tests with each other and with cognitive variables are highest for low-IQ groups. *Intelligence, 13*, 349–359.

Flynn, J. R. (2007). *What is Intelligence?* New York, NY: Cambridge University Press.

Kaufman, A. S. (2001). WAIS-III IQs, Horn's theory, and generational changes from young adulthood to old age. *Intelligence, 29*, 131–167.

Lee, F. L., Gorsuch, R. L., Saklofske, D. H., & Patterson, C. A. (2008). Cognitive differences for ages 16 to 89 years (Canadian WAIS-III): Curvilinear with Flynn and Processing Speed Corrections. *Journal of Psychoeducational Assessment, 26*, 382–394.

Lichtenberger, E. O., & Kaufman, A. S. (2009). *Essentials of WAIS-IV Assessment*. Hoboken, NJ: John Wiley & Sons.

McArdle, J. J., Ferrer-Caja, E., Hamagami, F., & Woodcock, R. W. (2002). Comparative longitudinal structural analyses of the growth and decline of multiple intellectual abilities over the life span. *Developmental Psychology, 38*, 113–142.

Saklofske, D. H., Yang, Z., Zhu, J., & Austin, E. J. (2008). Spearman's Law of Diminishing Returns in normative samples for the WISC-IV and WAIS-III. *Journal of Individual Differences, 29*, 57–69.

Salthouse, T. A. (2004). Localizing age-related individual differences in a hierarchical structure. *Intelligence, 32*, 541–561.

Salthouse, T. A. (2009a). When does age-related cognitive decline begin? *Neurobiology of Aging, 30*, 507–514.

Salthouse, T. A. (2009b). Decomposing age correlations on neuropsychological and cognitive variables. *Journal of the International Neuropsychological Society, 15*, 650–661.

Salthouse, T. A. (2010). *Major Issues in Cognitive Aging*. New York, NY: Oxford University Press.

Spearman, C. (1927). *The Abilities of Man*. London: Macmillan.

Tucker-Drob, E. M. (2009). Differentiation of cognitive abilities across the lifespan. *Developmental Psychology, 45*, 1097–1118.

Wechsler, D. (2008). *WAIS-IV: Administration and Scoring Manual*. San Antonio, TX: Pearson.

Wechsler, D., Coalson, D. L., & Raiford, S. E. (2008). *WAIS-IV: Technical and Interpretive Manual*. San Antonio, TX: Pearson.

CHAPTER

9

Using WAIS-IV with WMS-IV

James A. Holdnack[1] and Lisa W. Drozdick[2]

[1] Pearson Assessment, Bear, Delaware, USA
[2] Pearson Assessment, San Antonio, Texas, USA

INTRODUCTION

The Wechsler Memory Scale – Fourth Edition (WMS-IV; Wechsler, 2009) is the most recent revision to the Wechsler memory scale. This chapter provides an overview of the development of the WMS-IV, the structure and content of the scale, and interpretive guidelines. In addition, an overview of using the WMS-IV along with the Wechsler Adult Intelligence Scale – Fourth Edition (WAIS-IV; Wechsler, 2008) is provided with particular detail on the use of contrast scaled scores. Case studies illustrate the use of the two instruments in clinical assessment.

OVERVIEW OF WMS-IV

Brief history of the Wechsler memory scale

The Wechsler memory scales were introduced in 1945, and have provided detailed assessments of clinically relevant aspects of memory functioning for over half a century. Versions of the scale are commonly used in individuals with suspected memory deficits or diagnosed with a wide range of neurological, psychiatric, and developmental disorders. The initial version of the Wechsler memory scale (WMS; Wechsler, 1945) was a brief survey of immediate memory skills. The WMS included four memory subtests: Logical Memory, Associate Learning, Visual Reproduction, and Mental Control, a working memory task. The Wechsler memory scale has evolved along with memory research.

The first revision of the test, WMS-R (Wechsler, 1987), expanded the normative sample, added measures of delayed recall, and attempted to improve the assessment of visual memory by adding a new visual memory task, Visual Paired Associates. The assessment of attention and concentration was also expanded in the WMS-R with the inclusion of Spatial Span. Subsequent research demonstrated the utility of comparing memory ability to intellectual functioning. Memory functions are more susceptible to brain injury than other cognitive functions, and comparison of memory functioning to intellectual functioning improves the clinical utility of memory assessment. Comparison statistics between the WAIS and the WMS were introduced after the WMS-R was published.

The third revision of the WMS (WMS-III; Wechsler, 1997a) incorporated a number of changes recommended by researchers using the WMS-R. The norms were updated and expanded to include ages 16 to 89. Delayed recognition trials were added to assess for encoding versus retrieval deficits, the working memory tasks were updated to include multi-tasking, additional comparative scores were derived, and two new visual memory tasks (Face Memory and Family Pictures) were introduced. Visual Reproduction was revised to enable clinicians to rule out motor dysfunction as a cause of impaired performance. The most dramatic change introduced with WMS-III was the co-norming with Wechsler Adult Intelligence Scale – Third Edition (WAIS-III; Wechsler, 1997b). The co-norming enabled clinicians to have comparative statistics between performance on WAIS-III and WMS-III essential to identifying memory impairments beyond general intellectual deficits.

The WMS-IV continues many of the traditional aspects of the Wechsler memory scales. It is an individually administered assessment of memory functioning for adolescents and adults ages 16–90. The WMS-IV assesses various memory functions, including auditory memory, visual memory, and visual working memory. Immediate and delayed recall and recognition tasks are used to provide detailed information on an individual's memory processes. The WMS-IV also introduces a brief measure of cognitive status.

Two batteries are included in the WMS-IV: the Adult battery, designed for adolescents and adults ages 16–69; and the Older Adult battery, designed for use with adults ages 65–90. The Older Adult battery was developed to improve the assessment of older adults. It contains fewer subtests than the Adult battery, resulting in a decreased testing time. In general, subtests with manipulatives were not included in the Older Adult battery to increase portability and usability of the kit in a variety of settings, including medical and home settings. In addition to fewer subtests, many of the included subtests are modified for older adults to improve the psychometric functioning of the battery. The shorter administration time and subtest modifications reduce examinee fatigue and improve the usability of the WMS-IV in older adults. The two batteries overlap for ages 65–69, allowing examiners to choose the most appropriate battery for individuals at these ages.

WMS-IV structure

The subtest composition and content of the WMS-IV differ across the Adult and Older Adult batteries. The structure of the WMS-IV batteries is described in detail in this section.

Subtest content and description

The WMS-IV Adult battery contains seven subtests: three subtests retained from the WMS-III (Logical Memory, Verbal Paired Associates, and Visual Reproduction), and four new subtests (Brief Cognitive Status Exam, Designs, Spatial Addition, and Symbol Span). Logical Memory, Verbal Paired Associates, Designs, and Visual Reproduction are separated into immediate (I) and delayed (II) conditions, which are administered 20–30 minutes apart. In addition, several subtests include optional tasks (e.g., Logical Memory II Recognition, Visual Reproduction II Copy) used to derive process scores.

The WMS-IV Older Adult battery contains five subtests: Brief Cognitive Status Exam, Logical Memory, Verbal Paired Associates, Visual Reproduction, and Symbol Span. Logical Memory and Verbal Paired Associates are modified versions of the subtests found in the Adult battery. Logical Memory, Verbal Paired Associates, and Visual Reproduction have both immediate (I) and delayed (II) conditions administered 20–30 minutes apart. In addition, several subtests have optional tasks used to derive process scores. The Older Adult battery does not include Designs or Spatial Addition. The WMS-IV subtests are listed in Table 9.1 along with a brief description of each.

Six of the seven WMS-IV subtests are considered primary subtests, and are used to derive the five index scores. The Brief Cognitive Status Exam (BCSE) is optional, and is not used to derive any index score. Although it is not mandatory to administer the BCSE, it provides information on the examinee's overall cognitive functioning ability, which may be helpful during administration of the remainder of the WMS-IV battery.

Index composition and description

Many of the WMS-IV subtests contain multiple scores; however, only a few of the scores contribute to the index scores. Each index is comprised of at least two subtest scores, although subtest scores may contribute to more than one index. For example, the Verbal Paired Associates I scaled score is used to derive both the Auditory Memory Index and the

TABLE 9.1 Descriptions of subtests contained in the WMS-IV

Subtest	Description
Brief Cognitive Status Exam	The BCSE is an assessment of current cognitive functioning. It contains items assessing orientation, time estimation, mental control, clock drawing, incidental recall, inhibition, and verbal production. Raw scores are used to obtain a classification level that describes the examinee's overall cognitive functioning.
Logical Memory	Logical Memory measures memory for narrative stories. The examinee is read two stories and asked to recall them immediately and after a 20- to 30-minute delay. A recognition task is also available for the delayed condition. In the Older Adult battery, one story is repeated during immediate recall. Scaled scores are available for immediate and delayed recall, and a cumulative percentage is provided for recognition.
Verbal Paired Associates	Verbal Paired Associates measures memory for word pairs. The examinee is read 10 or 14 word pairs and then given the first word of the pair and asked to recall the second. Only a few of the word pairs are semantically related. There are immediate and delayed cued recall conditions, a delayed recognition condition, and a free recall condition in which the examinee is asked to state all the words from the pairs without requiring the pairing. Scaled scores are provided for the immediate and delayed cued recall and free recall conditions. A cumulative percentage is provided for the recognition condition.
Designs	Designs measures spatial and content memory for visual stimuli. The examinee is shown a series of grids with abstract visual designs in cells of the grid. After each stimulus is removed, the examinee is asked to recreate the grid with cards that contain both actual and distracter designs before being shown the next grid. Each response is scored on both correct content and correct location. There are immediate and delayed conditions and a delayed recognition condition. In addition, separate content and spatial location scores are calculated for both the immediate and delayed conditions. Scaled scores are provided for the immediate and delayed conditions, as well as for the content and spatial scores for the immediate and delayed conditions. A cumulative percentage is provided for the recognition condition.
Visual Reproduction	Visual Reproduction measures visual memory for abstract designs. The examinee is shown a series of figures. After each stimulus is removed the examinee is asked to draw the design from memory before being presented the next design. Each design is scored for the presence of key components of the design. There are immediate and delayed conditions, a delayed recognition condition, and a copy condition. Scaled scores are provided for the immediate and delayed conditions. A cumulative percentage is provided for the recognition and copy conditions.
Spatial Addition	Spatial Addition measures working memory for spatial content. It requires mental manipulation of spatial information across two stimuli. The examinee is shown two grids with red or blue dots. The examinee is then asked to create a grid with blue and white dots based on a series of rules. A scaled score is provided for the total score.

TABLE 9.1   Descriptions of subtests contained in the WMS-IV—Cont'd

Subtest	Description
Symbol Span	Symbol Span measures working memory for abstract designs. The examinee is shown an array of symbols. After the array is removed, the examinee is shown an array of symbols that contains the original symbols as well as distracters and asked to identify the previously shown symbols in the order they were shown on the original array. Partial credit is awarded for the correct symbols in the incorrect order. A scaled score is provided for the total score.

Immediate Memory Index. The indexes represent more general abilities than the subtest scores, and are the initial interpretive focus. Like the FSIQ and index scores from the WAIS-IV, the WMS-IV index scores are scaled on a metric of a mean of 100 and a standard deviation of 15. The primary subtests are used to derive the WMS-IV index scores: Auditory Memory, Visual Memory, Visual Working Memory, Immediate Memory, and Delayed Memory. The WMS-IV Older Adult battery contains fewer subtests than the Adult battery, and only four of the five index scores can be derived for the Older Adult battery; the Visual Working Memory Index is not available in this battery.

The WMS-IV introduces cross-battery substitution with the ability to substitute California Verbal Learning Test – Second Edition (CVLT-II; Delis, Kramer, Kaplan, & Ober, 2000) scores for Verbal Paired Associates scores when calculating the Auditory Memory, Immediate Memory, and Delayed Memory Indexes. Users of the CVLT-II may convert the Trials 1–5 Free Recall T score and Long-Delay Free Recall z-score to equated scaled scores, and substitute the equated scores for Verbal Paired Associates I and II scaled scores. This substitution can help shorten the overall assessment session time across instruments without affecting the comprehensiveness of the WMS-IV.

Table 9.2 lists the five indexes of the WMS-IV along with a brief description of each index.

Interpretation

Score types

The WMS-IV utilizes three types of standardized scores: standard scores, scaled scores, and cumulative percentages. The purpose of the scores is to describe the examinee's rank order of performance relative to the normative sample, same-age peers, or ability-level peers. The Brief Cognitive Status Examination (BCSE) does not utilize a standard score transformation paradigm, but uses a classification system based on specified age bands and education levels.

TABLE 9.2   Descriptions of indexes contained in the WMS-IV

Index	Description
Auditory Memory	The Auditory Memory Index (AMI) measures memory for orally presented information, including cued and free recall tasks in immediate and delayed conditions. For both batteries, both the immediate and delayed conditions of Logical Memory and Verbal Paired Associates are used to derive the AMI. CVLT-II equated scores may be substituted for the Verbal Paired Associates subtest scores.
Visual Memory	The Visual Memory Index (VMI) measures memory for visually presented information, including spatial and content memory in immediate and delayed conditions. For the Adult battery, both the immediate and delayed conditions of Designs and Visual Reproduction are used to derive the VMI. For the Older Adult battery, both the immediate and delayed conditions of Visual Reproduction are used to derive the VMI.
Visual Working Memory	The Visual Working Memory Index (VWMI) measures the ability to manipulate and recall visually presented information, including spatial and content stimuli. For the Adult battery, Spatial Addition and Symbol Span are used to derive the VWMI. The VWMI is not available in the Older Adult battery.
Immediate Memory	The Immediate Memory Index (IMI) measures memory for both orally and visually presented information immediately after it is presented. For the Adult battery, the immediate recall conditions of Logical Memory, Verbal Paired Associates, Designs, and Visual Reproduction are used to derive the IMI. For the Older Adult battery, the immediate recall conditions of Logical Memory, Verbal Paired Associates, and Visual Reproduction are used to derive the IMI. CVLT-II equated scores may be substituted for the Verbal Paired Associates subtest scores.
Delayed Memory	The Delayed Memory Index (DMI) measures memory for both orally and visually presented information 20–30 minutes after it is presented. For the Adult battery, the delayed recall conditions of Logical Memory, Verbal Paired Associates, Designs, and Visual Reproduction are used to derive the DMI. For the Older Adult battery, the delayed recall conditions of Logical Memory, Verbal Paired Associates, and Visual Reproduction are used to derive the DMI. CVLT-II equated scores may be substituted for the Verbal Paired Associates subtest scores.

Subtest scores   The subtest scaled scores are derived from the total raw score for the subtest and condition (i.e., immediate or delayed), if appropriate. The scaled scores are derived from the 100 normative cases within a specific age band. The resulting score represents the rank order of the examinee's performance compared to same-age peers. The scores are represented on a scale with a mean of 10 and a standard deviation of 3.

The available score range is 1–19, which is 3 standard deviations below and above the mean.

Index scores   Standard scores are provided for the five indexes: Auditory Memory, Visual Memory, Visual Working Memory, Immediate Memory, and Delayed Memory. These scores are derived from summing the appropriate age-adjusted scaled scores into a single total score. This total score is normed on the entire normative sample, as the contributing scores are already age corrected. Compared to subtest level norms, index norms have more cases on which to rank order the scores and more data points to differentiate individual examinees. Subsequently, the index scores provide a greater range of values above and below the mean than do scaled scores. The index scores use a mean of 100 and a standard deviation of 15 points. The available score range is 40–160, which is 4 standard deviations below and above the mean.

Process scores   Process scores are available for some subtests. These scores provide information regarding specific aspects of an examinee's performance that may be masked in the total score provided for the subtest. For example, the Designs subtest has additional scores for Spatial and Content recall. These optional scores indicate different component cognitive processes that may not be evident in the total score. The process scaled scores are derived using the same procedure as the primary subtest scaled scores.

Process scores that have highly skewed, non-normal frequency distributions are normed using cumulative percentages. There are seven broad percentage groups into which the normative sample is divided; ≤ 2, 3–9, 10–16, 17–25, 26–50, 51–75, and > 75. Cumulative percentages differ from percentiles. Percentiles are based on a z transformation to determine where the scores fall relative to a normal distribution. Cumulative percentages indicate the percentage of examinees who obtain specific scores, and are minimally smoothed for reversals across age groups. A cumulative percentage of 9 percent is interpreted to mean that 9 percent of the examinees in the age group had the same or a lower score. Cumulative percentages are usually looked at in terms of rareness of the finding, rather than how the performance compares to a normalized distribution (e.g., distance from average performance on the task). The cumulative percentages are derived using the 100 cases in each normed age band. The scores that represent the percentages in the broad bands are identified.

Contrast scaled scores   Most WMS-IV subtests offer contrast scaled scores, particularly those with immediate and delayed conditions or recall and recognition tasks. The contrast scaled scores are designed to allow the examiner to compare higher- to lower-level cognitive functions (e.g., recall versus recognition) or to differentiate statistically between modalities of presentation (e.g., oral versus visual).

Contrast scaled scores apply a scaled score metric (e.g., mean of 10 and a standard deviation of 3) to score comparisons within or between subtests or indexes, providing information on the performance of a higher-level skill or ability while controlling for a lower-level or more basic skill. For example, one WMS-IV contrast scaled score reflects an examinee's ability to recall a set of newly-learned designs after a delay, dependent upon his or her ability to learn the information when first exposed to it (e.g., delayed Designs recall adjusted for immediate Designs recall). Additionally, the examiner may wish to compare a similar cognitive construct across different presentation modalities.

Contrast scaled scores test hypotheses about the degree to which common variance may account for performance of one score on a related score. It adjusts one score (i.e., the dependent score) based on the examinee's performance on another variable (i.e., the control variable). The control variable is the context by which the dependent measure is adjusted. For example, a common clinical question asks if the obtained delayed memory score is good or bad in light of the examinee's immediate memory. In this case, the context is the examinee's immediate memory ability, and the dependent measure is delayed memory. The contrast scaled score adjusts the delayed memory score for the examinee's level of immediate memory.

The contrast scaled scores are derived by classifying examinees based on the control variable (e.g., standard score, scaled score, or cumulative percentage). In each ability level of the control variable, the frequency distribution, mean, and standard deviation of the age-adjusted standard score or scaled score is evaluated. In the same way that age-adjusted scaled scores are derived, a new scaled score for the dependent measure is computed. This score represents the examinee's rank order on the dependent measure relative to ability-level peers. It may be useful to think of contrast scaled scores as "adjusted" scores rather than difference scores. The resulting contrast scaled score is interpreted in the same manner at all ability levels on the control variable (e.g., if the delayed memory score controlling for immediate memory is a scaled score of 6, then the examinee is at the 9th percentile on delayed memory when compared to individuals of similar immediate memory ability). Contrast scaled scores are provided for both subtest- and index-level comparisons.

The delayed memory age-adjusted scaled score informs the practitioner of the individual's recall after 20 minutes compared to same-age peers. However, the contrast score has a different meaning than the age-adjusted scaled score. The contrast score reflects the examinee's ability on delayed recall when you take into account how much information he or she recalled in the immediate condition. It reflects the degree to which the examinee forgot the material learned during the immediate condition.

Brief Cognitive Status Exam classification level   The BCSE is an optional procedure assessing global cognitive functioning. It is designed to yield a performance classification primarily focused on impaired rather than normal or superior performance. Each score contributing to the BCSE total raw score is weighted relative to the percentage of normative cases achieving a specific score. The highest weighted raw score typically represents the score attained by at least 25 percent of the normative sample. The lowest weighted raw score represents the score attained by less than 2 percent of the normative sample. The weighted raw scores between the highest and lowest classification typically represent 10–24 percent and 3–9 percent of the sample. The overall classification is based on four broad age categories and five education levels. The classification labels – Average, Low Average, Borderline, Low, and Very Low – represent the following percentages of cases within the specified age and education bands: 25–100 percent, 10–24 percent, 5–9 percent, 2–4 percent, and < 2 percent, respectively.

Descriptive classifications and level of performance   It is often difficult for practitioners to agree at what level a score, be it a standard score, scaled score, or cumulative percentage, indicates impairment or a cognitive weakness. There are some important statistical and clinical considerations to keep in mind when interpreting results. Scaled scores are not linear scores. The difference between scores of 7 and 8 is larger (in terms of percentile rank) than between scores of 6 and 7. The difference between scaled scores of 7 and 8 is 9 percent of the population; however, the difference between scaled scores of 6 and 7 is 7 percent of the population. While 34 percent of the population obtains scaled scores between 7 and 10, only 14 percent falls between the scaled scores of 4 and 7. The differences in percentile ranks between scaled scores get smaller as you reach the extremes of the distribution.

Individuals identified with mild intellectual disability (ID) do not score, on average, a scaled score of 1 on memory tests, cognitive ability tests, or measures of neuropsychological functioning (see the WISC-IV Integrated Manual; Kaplan, Fein, Kramer, Delis, Morris, & Maerlender, 2004). Rather, individuals with mild ID have mean scaled scores between 3 and 6.

Similarly, the Probable dementia of the Alzheimer's type – mild severity group performs in the deficient to borderline range at the subtest level. Because these groups represent the most globally impaired, relative to most disorders excluding moderate and severe levels of ID, it would be anticipated that adults suffering from mild to moderate developmental disorders or acquired neurological conditions not resulting in ID would score higher on average than adults with mild ID, in terms of overall cognitive impairment and adaptive behavior. Therefore, mean scores in the range of 5–8 on average for clinical populations with mild to moderate impairments would be expected. Based on these assumptions, scores in the range of 5–7 and, in some cases, 8, may indicate a cognitive weakness that affects the individual's functioning in a specific domain.

Additionally, inclusion in the normative sample does not indicate the absence of all cognitive weaknesses, behavioral problems, or academic difficulties. Adults in the normative sample may have difficulty with employment or schooling. Within the general population, there are adults who have difficulty maintaining employment, work at jobs that have few cognitive demands, or have failed courses in school. These individuals may not have ever been diagnosed with a specific clinical condition, but are low-functioning, healthy individuals. Employment difficulties may be attributed to other factors, such as environmental issues (e.g., lack of opportunity) or effort. Some of these individuals may have poor memory skills that contribute to employment or academic difficulties without having experienced a specific brain injury or having a diagnosed clinical condition.

Normative data based primarily on non-clinical subjects, as in the WMS-IV, stratify all cases on the 1–19 scaled score range. That is, some adults in the normative sample have to be assigned a scaled score of 1, even though they have never been identified as having a developmental or neurological condition. While a scaled score of 1 suggests very poor performance and adults with this score may exhibit difficulties in daily functioning, they have never been identified by their school, employer, parent, or physician as having a disorder. Interpreting a single score as being diagnostic of a specific condition will likely result in a high false-positive rate; likewise, using a single low score to indicate impaired daily functioning will likely result in a high rate of false-positive errors. By the same token, only interpreting very low scores, such as 5 or less, as impaired will result in many false negatives, because most clinical groups perform in the range of 5–8 scaled score points, depending upon the severity of cognitive deficits.

Ultimately, requiring multiple measures to show impairment and using a relatively higher (e.g., scaled score = 7–8) than lower threshold will optimize sensitivity and specificity. Index scores represent multiple subtest indicators such that a single index score that is unexpectedly low may be considered an indication of memory problems in the absence of other explanations for low performance.

Interpreting WMS-IV index scores

General information The WMS-IV is designed to answer questions about an examinee's memory functioning. At the index level, the following questions can be addressed:

- Are there auditory memory deficits or strengths?
- Are there visual memory deficits or strengths?
- Are there visual working memory deficits or strengths?

- Are there immediate memory deficits or strengths?
- Are there delayed memory deficits or strengths?

The scores required to answer these questions are the Auditory Memory Index, Visual Memory Index, Auditory Memory Index vs Visual Memory Index contrast scaled score, Visual Working Memory Index, Visual Working Memory Index vs Visual Memory Index contrast scaled score, Immediate Memory Index, Delayed Memory Index, and Immediate Memory Index vs Delayed Memory Index contrast scaled score. Index level scores represent multiple indicators of memory functioning, and provide a statistically robust assessment of general memory functioning.

All index scores are age-adjusted. Therefore, the score represents the examinee's recall abilities relative to same-age peers and to the normative sample as a whole. This is important because the actual amount of information represented by the raw score will be dramatically lower in the older age groups compared to younger adults. In other words, the same standard score does not reflect retention of the same amount of information across the age groups. A low score in the oldest age groups is indicative of very poor memory functioning in general, with very little information being retained.

Auditory Memory   The Auditory Memory Index (AMI) is composed of the Logical Memory I, Logical Memory II, Verbal Paired Associates I, and Verbal Paired Associates II scaled scores. The AMI measures the ability to listen to oral information and repeat it immediately, and then recall it again after a 20- to 30-minute delay. The index combines measures of single-trial learning and multi-trial learning for verbally presented information. An index score of 70 or less represents very significant auditory memory dysfunction, while scores of 70–85 represent moderate difficulties with memory functioning.

If there is significant subtest variability (e.g., the subtests that compose the index significantly differ from one another), the AMI may be influenced by a more specific form of auditory memory difficulty. Variability does not invalidate the AMI; however, interpretation of the score must account for inconsistency in auditory memory functioning across measures.

Secondary factors influencing performance on the Auditory Memory Index   While a low score on the Auditory Memory Index indicates difficulties with auditory memory functioning, other cognitive problems may influence performance and need to be considered when interpreting results. These problems include:

- auditory acuity deficits
- language impairment
- severe attention problems

- impaired executive functioning
- poor working memory
- global intellectual impairment.

Visual Memory   The Visual Memory Index (VMI) for the Adult battery is composed of the Visual Reproduction I, Visual Reproduction II, Designs I, and Designs II scores. For the Older Adult battery, the VMI is composed only of the Visual Reproduction I and II scores. The VMI measures the ability to recall designs from memory, and draw them or replicate their placement in a grid. Visual memory on WMS-IV assesses memory both for visual details and for spatial location. An index score of 70 or less represents very significant visual memory dysfunction, while scores of 70–85 represent moderate difficulties with memory functioning.

If there is significant subtest variability (e.g., the subtests that compose the index significantly differ from one another), the VMI may be influenced by a more specific form of visual memory difficulty. Variability does not invalidate the VMI; however, interpretation of the score must account for inconsistency in visual memory functioning across measures.

Secondary factors influencing performance on the Visual Memory Index   While a low score on the VMI indicates difficulties with visual memory functioning, other cognitive problems may influence performance and need to be considered when interpreting results. These problems include:

- visual acuity deficits
- visual–spatial processing impairment
- severe attention problems
- impaired executive functioning
- poor working memory
- global intellectual impairment.

Auditory Memory Index vs Visual Memory Index contrast scaled score   This contrast scaled score helps to determine if visual memory is a strength or weakness compared to auditory memory. This score tests the hypothesis that there might be a material specific memory deficit, and represents how good the visual memory score is when compared to individuals with a similar level of auditory memory. Low scores indicate that visual memory is low compared to an examinee's auditory memory performance; high scores indicate better visual than auditory memory. A contrast scaled score of 7 would be interpreted to mean that the examinee's visual memory is at the 16th percentile in comparison to individuals of similar auditory memory ability, or that the examinee's visual memory is in the low average range when compared to individuals of similar auditory memory ability. Likewise, a contrast scaled score of 13 indicates that the examinee is at the 84th percentile of individuals with similar auditory memory abilities.

Visual Working Memory   The Visual Working Memory Index (VWMI) is composed of the Spatial Addition and Symbol Span subtests. The VWMI measures the ability to temporarily hold and manipulate spatial locations and visual details. Poor working memory for spatial locations or visual details may result in a lower score on the VWMI. An index score of 70 or less represents very significant visual working memory dysfunction while scores of 70–85 represent moderate difficulties with memory functioning.

If there is significant subtest variability (e.g., Spatial Addition and Symbol Span significantly differ from each other), then the VWMI may be influenced by a more specific form of working memory difficulty. Variability does not invalidate the VWMI; however, interpretation of the score must account for inconsistency in visual working memory functioning across measures.

Secondary factors influencing performance on the Visual Working Memory Indexes   While a low score on the VWMI indicates difficulties with visual working memory functioning, other cognitive problems may influence performance and need to be considered when interpreting results. These problems include:

- visual acuity deficits
- visual–spatial processing impairment
- severe attention problems
- impaired executive functioning
- global intellectual impairment.

Visual Working Memory Index vs Visual Memory Index contrast scaled score   This contrast scaled score helps to determine if low visual memory scores are due to deficits in visual working memory. It tests the hypothesis that there might be a visual memory deficit beyond a working memory deficit. The contrast scaled score represents how good the visual memory score is when compared to individuals with a similar level of visual working memory. Low scores indicate that an examinee's visual memory performance is low compared to his or her visual working memory performance; high scores indicate better than expected visual memory. A contrast scaled score of 7 would be interpreted to mean that the examinee's visual memory is at the 16th percentile compared to individuals of similar visual working memory ability, or that the examinee's visual memory ability is in the low average range when compared to individuals with similar visual working memory ability. Likewise, a contrast scaled score of 13 indicates that the examinee is at the 84th percentile of individuals with similar visual working memory abilities.

Immediate Memory Index   The Immediate Memory Index (IMI) is composed of the immediate recall conditions for each of the primary subtests. The IMI measures an examinee's ability to recall verbal and visual information immediately after the presentation of the stimuli. An index score of 70 or less represents significant immediate memory dysfunction, while scores of 70–85 represent moderate difficulties with memory functioning.

If there is significant subtest variability (e.g., the subtests that compose the index significantly differ from one another), the IMI may be influenced by a more specific form of memory difficulty. Variability does not invalidate the IMI; however, interpretation of the score must account for inconsistency in immediate memory functioning across measures.

Secondary factors influencing performance on Immediate and Delayed Memory Indexes   While a low score on the Immediate Memory Index indicates difficulties with memory functioning, other cognitive problems may influence performance and need to be considered when interpreting results. These problems include:

- auditory acuity deficits
- language impairment
- visual acuity deficits
- visual–spatial processing impairment
- severe attention problems
- impaired executive functioning
- poor working memory
- global intellectual impairment.

Delayed Memory Index   The Delayed Memory Index (DMI) is composed of the delayed recall conditions for each of the primary subtests. The DMI measures an examinee's ability to recall information after a 20- to 30-minute delay. An index score of 70 or less represents significant delayed memory dysfunction, while scores of 70–85 represent moderate difficulties with memory functioning.

If there is significant subtest variability (e.g., the subtests that compose the index significantly differ from one another), the DMI may be influenced by a more specific form of memory difficulty. Variability does not invalidate the DMI; however, interpretation of the score must account for inconsistency in delayed memory functioning across measures.

Secondary factors influencing performance on Immediate and Delayed Memory Indexes   While a low score on the Delayed Memory Index indicates difficulties with memory functioning, other cognitive problems may influence performance and need to be considered when interpreting results. These problems include:

- auditory acuity deficits
- language impairment
- visual acuity deficits
- visual–spatial processing impairment
- severe attention problems
- impaired executive functioning
- poor working memory
- global intellectual impairment.

Immediate Memory Index vs Delayed Memory Index contrast scaled score   This contrast scaled score helps to determine if the DMI score is higher or lower than expected given the examinee's IMI score. An individual's delayed memory will, in part, be limited by the amount of information that is initially encoded. The contrast scaled score represents how good the delayed memory score is when compared to individuals with a similar level of immediate memory or initial encoding. Low scores indicate that an examinee's delayed memory performance is low compared to his or her immediate memory performance; high scores indicate better than expected delayed memory. A contrast scaled score of 7 would be interpreted to mean that the examinee's delayed memory is at the 16th percentile in comparison to individuals of similar immediate memory ability or that the examinee's delayed memory ability is in the low average range when compared to examinees of similar immediate memory ability. Likewise, a contrast scaled score of 13 indicates that the examinee is at the 84th percentile of examinees with similar immediate memory abilities.

This contrast scaled score is an overall indicator of forgetting and consolidation. Some individuals lose information between immediate and delayed recall, while others actually improve their memory performance over time. This score replaces the Auditory Retention Index of the WMS-III. The methodology applied in WMS-IV is designed to take into account regression to the mean effects observed in healthy controls between immediate and delayed memory recall. This means that, in controls, delayed memory scores will be slightly higher than immediate memory scores the further below the mean the immediate score is, and slightly lower for immediate memory scores above the mean. Therefore, a delayed score of 70, when the score for immediate is 75, represents poorer delayed memory functioning than if the examinee had a delayed score of 110 and an immediate score of 115.

Interpreting WMS-IV subtest scores

Within each modality (e.g., auditory and visual memory) the WMS-IV subtests measure similar memory functions; however, each subtest differs in a manner that may be related to specific memory problems. When interpreting the WMS-IV at the subtest level, the practitioner should be cautious not to over-interpret subtest differences, as both variability in cognitive functioning and low scores on one or two subtests occur frequently in the general population (Matarrazo & Prifitera, 1989; Brooks, Iverson, Holdnack, & Feldman, 2008). Interpreting subtest differences between modalities does not necessarily add more information than the index level comparison. For example, a difference between Logical Memory and Visual Reproduction would generally be understood in terms of auditory versus visual memory, rather than story detail recall versus visual construction memory. The latter interpretation focuses on cognitive aspects of the subtest that are not necessarily related specifically to memory functioning, but represent differences in secondary aspects of the subtest.

Auditory Memory subtests

Logical Memory I and II   The Logical Memory (LM) subtests vary slightly in the Adult battery compared to the Older Adult battery. In the Adult battery, the examinee hears two stories of similar length and complexity. LM I and II represent single-trial learning ability. In the Older Adult battery, one of the stories is repeated once. The repeated story is significantly shorter and has less linguistic complexity to ensure adequate floor in this age range.

Low scores on the LM subtest indicate difficulty recalling verbal information that is conceptually organized and semantically related. In the Adult battery, low scores may also indicate that the examinee does not recall information after only a single exposure. Logical Memory does not measure the ability to retell a story; it measures the ability to recall story elements. The story elements may be important or relatively minor. The examinee is not assessed on the global quality of the story that is recalled but on individual details recalled, and most of the elements do not have to be recalled in proper sequence or context to receive credit. The semantic relatedness of the story elements and the presentation in an organized, meaningful way may promote ease of recall; however, it does not necessarily create a dependency in recalling specific details (e.g., recalling "Anna" does not necessarily mean an examinee will also recall "Thompson").When interpreting results of the LM subtest, it is important to report whether or not the examinee is able to recall specific details of information presented in a story or conversational format, and to avoid interpreting the subtest as the ability to retell a story.

Logical Memory II Recognition versus Delayed Recall. Logical Memory II is a free recall task with minimal prompting allowed. LM II Recognition represents the examinee's ability to answer specific questions about details from the story. This contrast scaled score indicates the degree to which examinees' free recall is relatively better or worse than their recognition memory. The LM II Recognition process score is highly skewed because most neurologically healthy examinees achieve a perfect or near-perfect score; therefore, this score is presented in cumulative percentage bands. Examinees performing at or below a cumulative percentage of 25 percent have below average recognition memory. The comparison between an examinee's recognition performance and his or her delayed free recall performance measures the degree to which the examinee benefits from story details being presented in a recognition format instead of a free recall format.

A low LM II Recognition vs Delayed Recall contrast scaled score of 7 or less indicates that the examinee's free recall performance is below average compared to individuals with a similar level of recognition memory. The contrast scaled score has the same meaning regardless of the examinee's level of recognition memory. Low scores suggest the examinee may have difficulties retrieving information from memory. High scores of 13 or more are atypical. These examinees may have better free recall than recognition, suggesting that asking specific questions to help them remember results in poorer performance.

Logical Memory Immediate Recall versus Delayed Recall. In the Adult and Older Adult batteries, Logical Memory I represents an examinee's ability to recall details from a story immediately after hearing it. Logical Memory II measures the examinee's ability to recall story details after a 20- to 30-minute delay. Delayed recall is not a direct measure of forgetting. Performance on delayed recall is related to the level of information acquired at the initial presentation. Forgetting is the amount of information lost from immediate recall to delayed recall. On WMS-IV, forgetting is measured using the Logical Memory Immediate Recall vs Delayed Recall contrast scaled score. This score is a representation of the examinee's delayed memory ability controlling for the initial level of recall. Low scores of 7 or less on this contrast scaled score indicate that the examinee has relatively poor delayed recall when controlling for the initial level of recall of story details. For example, an examinee who has a contrast scaled score of 6 is performing at the 9th percentile compared to examinees that had similar levels of immediate encoding. It does not matter if the examinee's Logical Memory I score is 5 or 15, the contrast scaled score has the same meaning. The low score suggests a higher than expected rate of forgetting. High scores of 13 or more mean that the examinee has relatively good delayed recall controlling for the initial level of recall. A contrast scaled score of 15 indicates that the examinee is at the 95th percentile compared to an examinee with similar immediate recall abilities. Examinees with high contrast scaled scores appear to benefit from the time between immediate and delayed recall by consolidating story details in long-term memory.

Verbal Paired Associates I and II   The Verbal Paired Associates (VPA) subtest measures the examinee's ability to recall novel and semantically related word associations. The WMS-IV version uses both easy and hard items: easy items are defined as words that are semantically related, and hard items are defined as associations between two words with no known semantic relationship. Hard items represent a more pure association memory task and they are more difficult to recall, particularly for older adults and those with low education levels. Combining easy and hard items resulted in better floors in the older age groups. The Older Adult battery differs from the Adult battery in that there are four fewer hard items, which was done to obtain acceptable floors.

Both the Older Adult and Adult versions of VPA are multi-trial learning measures. The examinee has multiple exposures to the stimuli, and should improve recall after each exposure to the list of word pairs. Verbal Paired Associates uses a cued-recall paradigm – that is, the examinee is provided with one of the words from the pair and must recall the correct word with which it is associated. The VPA I scaled score measures immediate learning of verbal associations. Low scores may indicate difficulties learning new associations and/or a failure to improve memory performance after multiple learning trials. The VPA II score measures delayed cued recall for word associations. Low scores on VPA II indicate difficulties retrieving word associations from long-term memory.

Verbal Paired Associates II Recognition versus Delayed Recall. Verbal Paired Associates II indicates the examinee's ability to recall information with a salient prompt. VPA II Recognition represents an examinee's ability to identify specific learned word associations. Recognition indicates the degree to which the examinee is able to recognize information he or she has previously learned regardless of the ability to access it with cuing. The VPA II Recognition process score is highly skewed because most neurologically healthy examinees achieve a perfect or near-perfect score; therefore, this score is presented in cumulative percentage bands. Examinees performing at or below a cumulative percentage of

25 percent have below average recognition memory. The comparison between an examinee's recognition performance and his or her delayed cued-recall performance measures the degree to which he or she benefits from the word associations in recognition versus cued-recall format.

A low VPA II Recognition vs Delayed Recall contrast scaled score of 7 or less indicates that the examinee's delayed cued-recall performance is below average compared to individuals with a similar level of recognition memory. Low scores suggest the examinee may have difficulties retrieving information from memory. High scores of 13 or more are atypical. These examinees may have better cued recall than recognition, which suggests that the recognition format interferes with memory retrieval.

Verbal Paired Associates Immediate Recall versus Delayed Recall. VPA I measures immediate cued recall for word associations, and VPA II measures the examinee's ability to recall verbal associations after a 20- to 30-minute delay. The Verbal Paired Associates Immediate Recall vs Delayed Recall contrast scaled score measures forgetting on this subtest. Low scores of 7 or less on this contrast scaled score indicate a greater rate of forgetting than is expected. High scores of 13 or more suggest the examinee's performance improves from the immediate to delayed condition. The 20- to 30-minute time delay may enable better memory consolidation for the verbal associations in examinees with high contrast scaled scores.

Verbal Paired Associates Delayed Word Recall. This delayed free-recall task requires an examinee to recall as many of the words from the list of word pairs as he or she can remember. This task does not require the words to be correctly associated, just recalled. Performance on this task is not considered a measure of associative memory; rather, it is a word list recall task. Also, the juxtaposition of the recognition trial prior to the administration of the free recall condition provides the examinee with another exposure to the correct information, as well as competing incorrect information. Performance on this task is not a true delayed recall condition due to the re-exposure of the stimuli just prior to recall. This is best interpreted as a measure of immediate word recall for previously learned material. Low scores suggest that the examinee did not encode many of the words required to perform the association task and did not benefit from re-exposure to the word pairs. The examinee may have a more basic word list learning problem that may have limited the amount of verbal associations encoded. Also, the task is a free-recall measure compared to the Verbal Paired Associates I and II tasks, which are cued recall. Problems with retrieving information from memory may also contribute to low scores on this measure.

Auditory Memory subtest variability It is important to examine performance across the auditory memory subtests to determine if there are any specific auditory memory deficits. The difference between an auditory memory subtest score and the AMI mean is an indicator of variability in auditory memory functioning. While both auditory memory subtests measure aspects of semantic and auditory memory, they differ in respect to how the information is organized and presented. Profile variability does not invalidate the AMI as a general measure of auditory memory functioning. It does, however, indicate that there is variability in that cognitive domain that should be described.

It is recommended to compare similar scores, as doing multiple comparisons across or within domains without a specific hypothesis or rationale may result in finding statistically significant differences that may not be clinically meaningful. Specifically, the comparison between Verbal Paired Associates I and Logical Memory I and between Verbal Paired Associates II and Logical Memory II may yield useful information. In the Adult battery, this difference represents the impact of multi-trial learning compared to single-trial learning. In the Adult and Older Adult batteries, the difference represents the impact of the presentation of the information (e.g., organized/meaningful presentation in Logical Memory versus unorganized presentation in Verbal Paired Associates). If differences are observed, the practitioner can discuss the variability in auditory memory as related to qualities of the stimulus presentation.

In addition to differences in stimulus presentation, the two subtests vary in the responses required by the examinee. While Verbal Paired Associates requires only single word responses, Logical Memory is designed to elicit a longer, more cohesive response. An examinee with better expressive language skills might find the response process of Logical Memory easier in that it facilitates his or her ability to express knowledge or recall, while examinees with lower expressive abilities may find Verbal Paired Associates easier. Any hypothesis about why differences exist between the two subtests should be verified using other clinical, observational, or test data.

CVLT-II substitution for Verbal Paired Associates as a measure of Auditory Memory Some practitioners may prefer to use the CVLT-II to measure auditory learning instead of the Verbal Paired Associates (VPA) subtest. In some cases, an examinee may have difficulty understanding the concept of Verbal Paired Associates and respond with a comment such as "but *wish* and *feet* don't go together." In such situations, the CVLT-II may be easier for the examinee to understand. The CVLT-II is a word list learning task. The examinee is told 16 words that he or she must remember. There are five learning trials: an interference trial, two short-delay recalls, two long-delay recalls, and a delayed recognition trial. Subsets of the 16 words are semantically related in such a manner that the examinee can organize the stimuli to facilitate storage and retrieval. The CVLT-II is not an association memory test, so it differs slightly in function from the VPA. The WMS-IV does not provide any materials or scoring for the CVLT-II.

Practitioners using the CVLT-II substitution should be familiar with administering and interpreting the CVLT-II and have a kit available.

The CVLT-II substitution affects the AMI, IMI, and DMI. The CVLT-II has a different normative base and uses a different score metric from the WMS-IV; therefore, scores from the CVLT-II cannot be directly entered into the sum of scaled scores for the affected indexes. The first step requires the practitioner to convert CVLT-II scores into Verbal Paired Associates equivalent scaled scores. The CVLT-II Trials 1–5 Free Recall T Score is converted into a VPA I scaled score equivalent. This equivalent VPA I score is then used in each index where VPA I would typically be applied. The CVLT-II Long-Delay Free Recall z-score is converted into the VPA II scaled score equivalent. This equivalent VPA II score is then used in each index where VPA II would typically be applied. Prior to applying the VPA II equivalents, it is important for the practitioner to review the possible scaled score ranges of VPA II scores for that age range. If the VPA II score range for a specific age stops at a scaled score of 15, however, a VPA II equivalent score of 17 is obtained from the CVLT-II conversion; the practitioner should use 15 not 17. This also applies to the lower end of the distribution. If the lowest possible VPA II score is 2 for a specific age, then the practitioner should not use a VPA equivalent scaled score that is less than 2. The resulting index scores when using CVLT-II substitution are very similar to those obtained with the standard VPA scaled scores. While the scores are similar, the practitioner should note the differences between the tasks and the meaning for the index scores when interpreting results.

Visual Memory subtests

Designs I and II   The Designs (DE) subtest was created to measure both spatial recall and memory for visual details. The visual designs were made to be very difficult to verbally encode. Consequently, some examinees will initially respond to this task with concern about the ability to complete the task, and may say something like "How am I supposed to remember these?" or "I can't do this, it's impossible." Despite these concerns, most examinees are able to do quite well on the task. The scoring for Designs differentiates between spatial memory and memory for content. Bonus points are given for perfect recall of the correct content in the correct location. For each condition, immediate and delayed, three scores are calculated. The *spatial score* is the number of cards placed in the correct locations on the grid, regardless of ability to recall details. The *content score* is the number of correctly identified visual details, regardless of spatial location recall. The *total score* is the sum of the spatial and content scores plus bonus points for perfect recall. The total score has the best psychometric properties and score distribution, and is considered the primary measure. The spatial and content scores are calculated to test specific hypotheses about the nature of the visual memory problems (i.e., spatial or detail).

Designs Spatial versus Content. The comparison between spatial memory and content memory indicates if an examinee has a specific strength or weakness with a particular component of visual memory. The comparison is made at both immediate recall and delayed recall. The Designs I Spatial vs Content contrast scaled score assesses the examinee's recall of visual details controlling for the level of spatial memory during the immediate recall condition. The Designs II Spatial vs Content contrast scaled score assesses the examinee's recall of visual details controlling for the level of spatial memory during the delayed recall condition. On either contrast scaled score, low scores of 7 or less indicate that the examinee's memory for details is below average, controlling for spatial memory abilities. A high score of 13 or more indicates that the examinee's memory for details is above average, controlling for spatial abilities.

Designs II Recognition versus Delayed Recall. Designs II is a delayed memory task for visual details and spatial locations. The Designs subtest has elements of free recall and recognition memory. Examinees must place cards in proper locations and recognize which designs are correct. The Designs II Recognition condition requires the examinee to recognize the correct design and the correct location for that design. The Designs II Recognition process score is highly skewed because most neurologically healthy examinees achieve a perfect or near-perfect score. The comparison between an examinee's recognition performance and delayed free-recall performance measures the level of free-recall performance relative to recognition memory.

A low DE II Recognition vs Delayed Recall contrast scaled score of 7 or less indicates that the examinee's free-recall performance is below average compared to examinees with a similar level of recognition memory. Low scores suggest the examinee may have difficulties retrieving information from memory. High scores of 13 or more are atypical. These examinees may have better free recall than recognition, which suggests that the recognition format may interfere with memory retrieval.

Designs Immediate Recall versus Delayed Recall. Designs I measures the examinee's visual memory ability after immediately seeing the designs and spatial locations. The DE II subtest measures delayed memory for spatial location, visual details, and the total of those plus bonus points for perfect recall after a 20- to 30-minute delay. Comparing immediate and delayed memory performance provides an indication of how much visual information is forgotten. The Designs Immediate Recall vs Delayed Recall contrast scaled score provides an indication of delayed memory performance controlling for initial level of recall.

Low scores of 7 or less indicate that the examinee's delayed recall performance is below average compared to individuals with a similar level of immediate recall; that is, he or she lost more information than others with the same initial level of encoding. By comparison, a high score of 13 or more indicates that the examinee's delayed recall is above average compared to examinees with a similar level of recall. Examinees with high scores may have benefited from the additional time.

Visual Reproduction I and II   The Visual Reproduction (VR) subtest requires the examinee to view a design and then to draw it from memory, both immediately and after a 20- to 30-minute delay. Elements of the stimuli can be named (e.g., "triangle," "square," "dots") such that verbalization of elements may facilitate encoding. However, to draw the design the examinee is required to recall the size and relative spatial relationship among elements, so a purely verbalized strategy would be inadequate to perform this subtest. The drawing requirement of the task introduces some visuo-constructional abilities; however, the scoring rules focus primarily on precision of recall rather than drawing accuracy. This subtest is administered and scored the same way in both the Adult and Older Adult batteries.

Visual Reproduction II Recognition versus Delayed Recall. Visual Reproduction II indicates an examinee's ability to freely recall information without prompting. VR II Recognition represents an examinee's ability to discriminate the design he or she saw previously from other similar designs that were not shown. It indicates the degree to which the examinee is able to accurately recognize previously learned information regardless of the ability to freely access it. The Visual Reproduction II Recognition process score is highly skewed because most neurologically healthy examinees achieve a perfect or near-perfect score; therefore, this score is presented in cumulative percentage bands. The comparison between an examinee's recognition performance and the delayed free-recall performance measures the degree to which he or she benefits from the designs being presented in a recognition versus a free-recall format.

A low VR II Recognition vs Delayed Recall contrast scaled score of 7 or less indicates that the examinee's free-recall performance is below average compared to individuals with a similar level of recognition memory. Low scores suggest the examinee may have difficulties retrieving information from memory. High scores of 13 or more are atypical. These examinees may have better free recall than recognition, which suggests that the recognition format interferes with memory retrieval.

Visual Reproduction Copy versus Immediate Recall. Visual Reproduction I is an immediate memory task that requires drawing to express the amount of information retained immediately after presentation. The

Visual Reproduction Copy condition is an optional procedure that has the examinee copy the designs as he or she looks at them. This is a rough estimate of the examinee's ability to simply draw the designs. The designs are scored using the same criteria as the memory portions of the test. If the examinee loses a substantial amount of points while the drawing is within view, then performance on the memory portion will be confounded by the examinee's poor copying ability. It is important to note that copying ability is influenced by multiple factors including motor control, visuo-constructional ability, and attention to detail. The Visual Reproduction Copy process score is highly skewed because most neurologically healthy examinees achieve a perfect or near-perfect score. The comparison between an examinee's copy performance and immediate free-recall performance measures the degree to which his or her memory scores are better, equivalent, or worse than the copy score.

A low VR Copy vs Immediate Recall contrast scaled score of 7 or less indicates that the examinee's memory performance is below average compared to examinees with a similar level of copying ability. The contrast scaled score has the same meaning regardless of the examinee's level of copying ability. Low scores suggest the examinee may have difficulties retrieving information from memory. High scores of 13 or more indicate very good memory regarding copying ability.

Visual Reproduction Immediate Recall versus Delayed Recall. In the Adult and Older Adult batteries, VR I measures an examinee's ability to recall and draw designs immediately after seeing the design. VR II measures an examinee's ability to recall and draw the designs after a 20- to 30-minute delay. On WMS-IV, forgetting rate for drawn designs is measured using the Visual Reproduction Immediate Recall vs Delayed Recall contrast scaled score. This score is a representation of examinees' delayed memory ability controlling for their initial level of recall. Low scores of 7 or less on this contrast scaled score indicate that an examinee has relatively poor delayed recall when controlling for his or her initial level of recall of visual designs. Examinees with high contrast scaled scores appear to benefit from the time between immediate and delayed recall to consolidate their ability to recall and draw the designs.

Visual Memory subtest variability It is important to examine performance across the visual memory subtests to determine if there are any specific visual memory deficits. The difference between a visual memory subtest score and the VMI mean is an indicator of variability in visual memory functioning. While both visual memory subtests measure aspects of visual details and spatial memory, they differ in respect to response processes and the degree to which spatial memory is assessed. Profile variability (i.e., as indicated by one or more significant differences between a subtest score and the mean) does not make the VMI invalid as a general measure of visual memory functioning; it does, however, indicate that there is some variability in the domain that should be described.

Another method of examining subtest variability is comparing subtest scores within an index to each other. Table F.5 in the Administration and Scoring Manual provides statistically significant values for comparing WMS-IV subtest scores. Moreover, immediate versus delayed recall conditions may be compared using the specific contrast scores for these subtests. Also, it is prudent to compare similar scores, as doing multiple comparisons across or within domains without a specific hypothesis or rationale may result in finding statistically significant differences that might not be clinically meaningful. Specifically, the comparison between Designs I and Visual Reproduction I and between Designs II and Visual Reproduction II may yield useful information. Differences may be due to response processes, such as the requirement of Visual Reproduction to draw the designs, which has more visuo-construction and fine motor demands than the Designs subtest. Differences may also be related to Designs having a greater recognition memory component to it than the free-recall response format of the Visual Reproduction subtest. The Designs subtest also explicitly evaluates spatial memory, while in Visual Reproduction spatial memory is not explicitly measured. Further, the stimuli for Visual Reproduction are easier to name, which may facilitate memory by using verbal cues; however, that would be very difficult to do on the Designs subtest.

There are many hypotheses about why differences may be observed between these two subtests. The practitioner should identify corroborating information from other test scores or observations when selecting one hypothesis as the explanation of test results over other possible hypotheses. In the Older Adult battery, only VR I and II contribute to the Visual Memory Index. A difference between these scores indicates variability in performance on the Visual Memory Index. The index may still be reported, but the variability between these two scores should be described.

Visual Working Memory subtests

Spatial Addition and Symbol Span   The Spatial Addition (SA) and Symbol Span (SSP) subtests are new to the Wechsler memory scale. These two subtests are combined to derive the Visual Working Memory Index in the Adult battery. For Spatial Addition, the examinee sees a pattern of blue and red circles on a grid. While the examinee holds that image in working memory, he or she is shown a second grid with blue and red circles. After seeing the second grid, the examinee must add the two images together. Where there is only one blue circle across the two images, the examinee puts in a blue circle (i.e., addition), where two blue images spatially overlap, the examinee places a white circle (i.e., subtraction). The red circles must be ignored. The test is a visual analog to the WAIS-IV Arithmetic subtest. It measures spatial working memory, and requires storage (i.e., visual sketch pad), manipulation (i.e., central executive), and ability to ignore competing stimuli (i.e., central executive).

Symbol Span is a visual analog to the WAIS-IV Digit Span subtest. The examinee sees a series of symbols that are difficult to verbalize. Subsequently, he or she must identify the symbols seen and identify the correct order of the symbols from left to right. The subtest measures the capacity to keep a mental image of a design in mind and the relative spatial position on the page. In the Baddeley (2000) model, this would represent the visual sketch pad with support from the central executive (e.g., help maintain sequence and ignore competing stimuli).

Visual Working Memory subtest variability   It is important to examine the performance across the visual working memory subtests to determine if there are any specific visual working memory deficits. A difference between these two subtests does not invalidate the VWMI as a global indicator of current visual working memory functioning. However, if differences are observed, the practitioner should describe these differences and note the variability within visual working memory skills.

Spatial Addition and Symbol Span both measure aspects of visual working memory; however, the tasks require very different cognitive skills in other respects. Spatial Addition taps spatial location memory as well as the ability to compare spatial images. By comparison, Symbol Span is highly focused on recall of visual details, and the sequence of the images must also be maintained in memory. Differences in these tests may reflect issues related to the nature of the stimuli (i.e., spatial versus visual detail) or be due to response process differences. Spatial Addition uses a free-recall format, and the Symbol Span task uses a recognition memory format. These differences in response demands may also result in performance discrepancies. The practitioner should explore these hypotheses by reviewing the examinee's performance on other subtests.

Immediate and Delayed Memory subtests   The Immediate and Delayed Memory Indexes are composed of the immediate or delayed score from each of the subtests.

Immediate and Delayed Memory subtest variability   The clinician should determine if there is significant variability among the scores that contribute to the indexes. Variability among the subtest scores does not invalidate the indexes; however, the source of the variability should be reported. In some cases, there may be an obvious advantage for visual or verbal memory tasks (i.e., supported by the index level contrast score). In other cases, there may be one score or a score in each modality that is low.

These differences may be difficult to explain. Any hypotheses should consider that the base rate for a single low score is relatively common in healthy controls. Also, how the stimuli and tasks differ on cognitive dimensions other than pure immediate or delayed recall should be reported. Evidence to account for observed differences between scores may be found on other tests or supported through observation.

Brief Cognitive Status Exam   The Brief Cognitive Status Exam (BCSE) is an optional subtest that was developed to identify examinees with significant cognitive dysfunction. To identify atypically low performance the BCSE uses a variety of tasks, including orientation to time, mental control, planning and visual–perceptual processing, incidental recall, inhibitory control, and verbal productivity. The raw scores for each set of tasks are converted into weighted raw scores. The weighting was developed to maximize the differences between healthy controls and examinees diagnosed with dementia. The weighted raw scores are summed to obtain the BCSE total raw score. Each set of tasks must be administered and scored to obtain the total raw score. The total raw score is adjusted based on four wide age bands (i.e., 16–29, 30–44, 45–69, and 70–90) and five levels of education (i.e., 8 or less years, 9–11, 12, 13–15, and 16 years or more).

The BCSE classification levels are based on base rates of performance in the control sample: Very Low, Low, Borderline, Low Average, and Average. The classifications are not diagnostic in themselves, as a number of factors contribute to performance on the subtest. If examinees fall in the Very Low classification, they have less than a 2 percent chance that their score is consistent with healthy controls. Scores in the Very Low range are often obtained by examinees diagnosed with dementia or mild to moderate mental retardation. Scores in the Low range are obtained by healthy controls approximately 2–4 percent of the time, such that 5 percent of the controls will obtain scores in the Low to Very Low range. Scores in the Low range are often obtained by examinees diagnosed with dementia or mild mental retardation. A few examinees in other clinical groups will obtain scores in the Low to Very Low range, but these are not typical of most clinical groups. Approximately 9 percent of healthy controls will obtain a score in the Borderline to Very Low range. More clinical group subjects will fall into this range as well, but the diagnostic implications are less certain.

Scores in the Very Low range have a high probability of being considered abnormal, though not specifically diagnostic. Scores in the Low range have a moderately high probability of being abnormal, though not necessarily diagnostic. At the Borderline range and higher there is less evidence that these scores are associated with significant cognitive impairment, and the interpretation may focus on specific aspects of poor performance (e.g., poor inhibitory and mental control). The BCSE score needs to be considered in light of the clinical question and overall clinical presentation. The classification level can help practitioners provide evidence for or against significant cognitive impairment when that is an important clinical question.

Interpreting WAIS-IV/WMS-IV profiles

The co-norming of the WAIS-IV and the WMS-IV enables the practitioner to directly compare performance between the two instruments. Effort was directed toward reducing the impact of general cognitive *ability* on the WMS-IV normative data. In each age band of the WMS-IV, the average WAIS-IV General Ability Index score is 100, indicating that the WMS-IV normative sample is not biased toward examinees of either higher or lower ability.

Comparing the two measures allows testing of specific hypotheses about an examinee's strengths and weaknesses in cognitive functioning. Often, a practitioner will have a general question, such as "Is the examinee's memory functioning consistent with his general cognitive functioning, or is it atypical?" To answer this type of question and identify specific memory impairments, the practitioner needs to interpret the memory scores within the context of general intellectual capacity. Ultimately, the goal of comparing the tests is to aid in differential diagnosis.

Comparison between tests should be done to answer specific hypotheses about an examinee's performance. Reviewing all possible combinations of scores will likely result in the identification of a large discrepancy even among neurologically normal individuals, potentially resulting in over-pathologizing test performance (Matarazzo & Prifitera, 1989; Brooks *et al.*, 2008).

A memory test is not simply a measure of memory ability, but also an assessment of other cognitive processes. For example, it measures oral comprehension when information is presented orally. The degree to which language factors play a role on memory performance can be reduced but not eliminated. In the case of an examinee with aphasia, verbal memory functions will likely be a secondary deficit to the language deficits. While this is an obvious case, more subtle influences related to the relationship between prior knowledge and memory facilitation are likely to be observed in individuals with low educational attainment or in ethnic minorities, in that standard American English may be less well learned than other languages or dialectic variations. Language skills are not the only processes that influence scores on memory tests. Aptitude for visual–spatial information or overall high general ability may also facilitate aspects of memory performance that are not memory functions.

COMBINING WAIS-IV/WMS-IV SCORES

The WAIS-IV/WMS-IV comparisons are computed using three methods: simple-difference, predicted-difference, and contrast scaled scores. Only those comparisons related to specific hypotheses are provided.

The following WAIS-IV/WMS-IV comparisons are included:

- WAIS-IV General Ability Index vs WMS-IV Auditory Memory Index
- WAIS-IV General Ability Index vs WMS-IV Visual Memory Index
- WAIS-IV General Ability Index vs WMS-IV Visual Working Memory Index
- WAIS-IV General Ability Index vs WMS-IV Immediate Memory Index
- WAIS-IV General Ability Index vs WMS-IV Delayed Memory Index
- WAIS-IV Verbal Comprehension Index vs WMS-IV Auditory Memory Index
- WAIS-IV Perceptual Reasoning Index vs WMS-IV Visual Memory Index
- WAIS-IV Perceptual Reasoning Index vs WMS-IV Visual Working Memory Index
- WAIS-IV Working Memory Index vs WMS-IV Auditory Memory Index
- WAIS-IV Working Memory Index vs WMS-IV Visual Working Memory Index.

Methods for comparing scores

Simple-difference method

With the simple-difference method, a WMS-IV index score is subtracted from the WAIS-IV composite score. This method is easy to explain to an examinee, his or her family, or other health professionals. The simple-difference method requires the practitioner to determine if the difference is statistically significant and, if it is, to determine how frequently a difference of its size occurred in the normative sample (Berk, 1984). The statistical significance of the difference between two scores accounts for measurement error and allows the practitioner to conclude if the difference is a "real" or a "chance" occurrence. That is, the difference must be of sufficient size to minimize the probability that it has occurred because of unreliability in the measures.

Another consideration when interpreting the difference between two scores should be the frequency of that difference within the general population. The difference should be of a magnitude that is relatively rare in the sample that links the two measures (i.e., the co-normative sample of the WAIS-IV and the WMS-IV). Even though a difference is statistically significant, it may occur frequently in normally developing and aging individuals and thus not clinically meaningful.

Predicted-difference method

Shepard (1980) was one of the first to advocate a predicted-difference method based on the correlation between two variables. For discrepancies between ability and memory, the ability score is used in a regression equation to calculate a predicted memory score. As with the simple-difference method, in order for differences to be meaningful, the difference score should be statistically significant and rare. The predicted-difference method is superior to the simple-difference model, which does not account for regression to the mean effects and may under- or overestimate the atypicality of differences in scores if they are below or above the mean.

Contrast scores method

The contrast score methodology provides another way to evaluate whether a score is unexpectedly high or low versus a marker variable (e.g., General Ability). The contrast score methodology applies standard norming procedures to adjust a dependent measure by a control variable. These scores answer specific clinical questions, such as, "Is the Delayed Memory Index score considered average or low given the examinee's intellectual level?" The independent variable is grouped into ability bands, and the age-adjusted dependent measures are normed comparing individuals of similar ability level on the control variable. For WAIS-IV/ WMS-IV contrast scores, the WAIS-IV composite will always serve as the control variable and the WMS-IV index score will be the dependent measure that is adjusted. The contrast score has the advantage of identifying the infrequency of the score relative to the level of the control variable.

The score obtained from the contrast comparison is a contrast scaled score, and is interpreted in the same manner as all scaled scores. For example, a scaled score of 6 indicates that an examinee's performance on the dependent variable is at the 9th percentile relative to examinees who have a similar level of ability on the control variable. For example, if a 53-year-old examinee has a GAI score of 87 and a Delayed Memory Index score of 76, the contrast scaled score for this combination of scores is 6 (9th percentile). The contrast scaled score has the same meaning regardless of where the examinee starts on the independent measure. For example, if the GAI in the example above is 120 and the DMI is 92, the contrast scaled score is still 6 (9th percentile). The interpretation of the two scores is the same – the examinee is at the 9th percentile of delayed memory ability compared to examinees with similar general cognitive ability. When the contrast score and regression methods return very similar results, the estimated regression line (e.g., linear or non-linear) is a good fit for the data and the variances are reasonably equal. When these conditions are not met, the regression line may systematically under- or over-predict performance at certain points along the regression line.

WAIS-IV versus WMS-IV comparisons

GAI versus Auditory Memory Index

The comparison between GAI and AMI enables the practitioner to test the hypothesis that the AMI is unexpectedly low or high for an examinee's level of general cognitive functioning. AMI is a global measure of an examinee's ability to recall verbal information. The correlation between GAI and AMI is 0.54, which is in the moderate range.

GAI versus Visual Memory Index

The comparison between GAI and VMI enables the practitioner to test the hypothesis that the VMI is unexpectedly low or high for an examinee's level of general cognitive functioning. VMI is a global measure of an examinee's ability to recall spatial location and visual details. The correlation between GAI and VMI is 0.58, which is in the moderate range.

GAI versus Visual Working Memory Index

The comparison between GAI and VWMI enables the practitioner to test the hypothesis that the VWMI is unexpectedly low or high for an examinee's level of general cognitive functioning. VWMI is a global measure of an examinee's ability to mentally hold and manipulate spatial locations and visual details. The correlation between GAI and VWMI is 0.66, which is in the moderate range.

GAI versus Immediate Memory Index

The comparison between GAI and IMI enables the practitioner to test the hypothesis that the IMI is unexpectedly low or high for an examinee's level of general cognitive functioning. IMI is a global measure of an examinee's ability to recall information shortly after having seen or heard it. The correlation between GAI and IMI is 0.66, which is in the moderate range.

GAI versus Delayed Memory Index

The comparison between GAI and DMI enables the practitioner to test the hypothesis that the DMI is unexpectedly low or high for an examinee's level of general cognitive functioning. DMI is a global measure of an examinee's ability to recall information after having seen or heard it 20 to 30 minutes earlier. The correlation between GAI and DMI is 0.58, which is in the moderate range.

VCI versus Auditory Memory Index

The comparison between VCI and AMI enables the practitioner to determine if low scores on the AMI are consistent with general language problems or if auditory memory deficits exist beyond the impact of language impairment. The correlation between VCI and AMI is 0.53, which is in the moderate range.

PRI versus Visual Memory Index

The comparison between PRI and WMI enables the practitioner to determine if low scores on the VMI are consistent with general visual–perceptual problems, or if visual memory deficits exist beyond the impact of visual–perceptual problems. The correlation between PRI and VMI is 0.62, which is in the moderate range.

PRI versus Visual Working Memory Index

The comparison between PRI and VWMI enables the practitioner to determine if low scores on the VWMI are consistent with general visual–perceptual problems, or if visual working memory deficits exist beyond the impact of visual–perceptual problems. The correlation between PRI and VWMI is 0.66, which is in the moderate range.

WMI versus Auditory Memory Index

The comparison between WMI and AMI enables the practitioner to determine if low scores on the AMI are consistent with auditory working memory deficits, or if auditory memory deficits exist beyond the impact of auditory working memory deficits. The correlation between WMI and AMI is 0.50, which is in the moderate range.

WMI versus Visual Working Memory Index

The comparison between WMI and VWMI enables the practitioner to determine if there is a modality-specific (i.e., auditory versus visual) deficit in working memory. The correlation between WMI and VWMI is 0.62, which is in the moderate range.

CASE STUDIES

Probable dementia of the Alzheimer's type – mild severity

Mrs D is an 83-year-old White female with 14 years of education who was referred by her family for evaluation subsequent to complaints of increasing memory loss and concerns over her living situation. Her family reports problems with word retrieval, sequencing complex information, and memory. In addition, Mrs D is easily overwhelmed with completing her complex daily activities, such as managing her finances and shopping. Other family members note that although Mrs D was very intelligent, she seems to have declined over the past several years, requiring greater amounts of assistance to remain living independently. Medically, Mrs D is relatively physically healthy. She is diagnosed with atrial fibrillation and osteoporosis, for which she takes medication. In addition, she is currently taking Namenda, prescribed by her family physician, to treat her apparent cognitive decline. Neurological evaluation and brain imaging were inconclusive, so Mrs D was referred for neuropsychological testing.

Figure 9.1 presents Mrs D's scores on the WAIS-IV and WMS-IV. She demonstrated average verbal skills, and visual–perceptual and working memory abilities. Processing speed was in the borderline range, and was a relative weakness compared to her overall abilities. Her FSIQ was in the low average range but her general problem-solving abilities were in the average range when processing speed and working memory were removed. WAIS-IV subtest scores indicated generally average abilities. The processing speed subtests were in the low average and borderline range, with the lowest score obtained on Coding. The Processing Speed Index was the only composite score less than 1 standard deviation below the mean. The Block Design, Symbol Search, and Coding subtests were also at least 1 standard deviation below the mean.

On the WMS-IV, Mrs D demonstrated average memory for orally presented material and extremely low visual memory. Auditory memory was extremely low, given her visual memory ability. Her immediate memory was in the low average range, and delayed memory was in the borderline range in comparison to her peers. At the subtest level, she scored in the high average range on Logical Memory immediate recall and obtained average to low average scores on Verbal Paired Associates. All her remaining scores were in the low average, borderline, and extremely low ranges in comparison to her peers. Memory functioning is relatively weaker than general intellectual functioning, with the exception of auditory memory. Of the memory indexes, all but the AMI were at or below 1 standard deviation below the mean. In addition, six subtest scores were at or below 1 standard deviation below the mean.

Score		Percentile	Confidence Interval (95%)
WAIS-IV Indexes			
General Ability Index	95	37	90–100
FSIQ	89	23	86–93
Verbal Comprehension Index	98	45	92–104
Perceptual Reasoning Index	92	30	86–99
Working Memory Index	97	42	90–104
Processing Speed Index	74	4	68–85
WAIS-IV Subtests			
Similarities	8		
Vocabulary	10		
Information	11		
Block Design	7		
Matrix Reasoning	10		
Visual Puzzles	9		
Digit Span	9		
Arithmetic	10		
Symbol Search	6		
Coding	4		
WMS-IV Indexes			
Auditory Memory Index	90	25	84–97
Visual Memory Index	66	1	67–72
Immediate Memory Index	85	16	80–92
Delayed Memory Index	71	3	66–81
AMI vs VMI Contrast Scaled Score	3		
IMI vs DMI Contrast Scaled Score	3		
WMS-IV Subtests			
BCSE Classification Level	Low		
LM I Scaled Score	13		
LM II Scaled Score	2		
LM Immediate Recall vs Delayed Recall Contrast Scaled Score	1		
LM II Recognition Percentage	17–25%		
LM II Recognition vs Delayed Recall Contrast Scaled Score	1		
VPA I Scaled Score	7		
VPA II Scaled Score	9		
VPA Immediate Recall vs Delayed Recall Contrast Scaled Score	13		
VPA II Word Recall Scaled Score	7		
VPA II Recognition Percentage	10–16%		

FIGURE 9.1   WAIS-IV and WMS-IV Scores for Mrs D.

VPA Recognition vs Delayed Recall Contrast Scaled Score	12		
VR I Scaled Score	3		
VR II Scaled Score	5		
VR Immediate Recall vs Delayed Recall Contrast Scaled Score	8		
VR II Recognition Percentage	17–25%		
VR Recognition vs Delayed Recall Contrast Scaled Score	6		
VR Copy Percentage	>75%		
VR Copy vs Immediate Recall Contrast Scaled Score	2		
Symbol Span Scaled Score	6		
Ability–Memory Contrast Scores			
GAI vs AMI Contrast Scaled Score	8		
GAI vs VMI Contrast Scaled Score	2		
GAI vs IMI Contrast Scaled Score	6		
GAI vs DMI Contrast Scaled Score	4		
VCI vs AMI Contrast Scaled Score	8		
PRI vs VMI Contrast Scaled Score	2		
WMI vs AMI Contrast Scaled Score	8		

FIGURE 9.1—Cont'd

The WMS-IV contrast scaled scores provide additional insight into Mrs D's memory functioning. Her delayed memory was unexpectedly low given her immediate memory ability. This is mostly due to her performance on Logical Memory II, which was well below what was expected given her above average performance on Logical Memory I. Although her delayed memory was also low on Visual Recognition, it was at the expected level given her poor performance on Visual Reproduction I. Her poor performance on Visual Reproduction I cannot be attributed to motor difficulties, as her performance on VR I was worse than expected given her copy ability.

Ability–memory contrast scores demonstrate that with the exception of auditory memory, Mrs D's memory skills were lower than expected given her general cognitive ability. Her visual memory is particularly low, given her general cognitive and perceptual reasoning skills. The profile of scores suggests weaknesses in processing speed, visual memory, and delayed memory. Most of Mrs D's WAIS-IV scores are average, with very few below average. Compared to her age peers she is functioning within normal limits on most measures, with the exception of processing speed. However, her performance on the memory measures suggests impairment in several memory abilities. Since the examinee was noted to have been fairly well functioning in the past, the current cognitive performance likely represents a decline in her abilities. The scores on WAIS-IV and WMS-IV confirm the family's impression that Mrs D is not functioning well. Overall, she demonstrated weaknesses in processing speed and memory. Given the number of areas in which low scores were obtained, and family reports of decline, a diagnosis of dementia was given with a recommendation of further testing to evaluate her ability to remain independent; continued monitoring; and retesting in 6 months.

Mild cognitive impairment

Mr J is a 63-year-old White male, with 16 years of education. He is a regional manager for a large grocery chain. Mr J recently visited his family physician for symptoms of chest pains and shortness of breath which have intensified over the past month. During the evaluation, he reported significant problems at work in which he has been forgetting to complete work or follow up on conversations. He reported that while his memory was not as good as it used to be, he thought that it was just part of getting older. Mr J was referred for a complete cardiac work-up and neurological evaluation.

Cardiac evaluation was normal for EKG and stress test, although he did have elevated cholesterol levels. The cardiologist recommended regular exercise, dietary changes, and stress reduction. Neurological evaluation was normal, with MRI findings consistent with normal aging. At the advice of his family physician, Mr J started psychological intervention for stress and anxiety.

The treating psychologists initial evaluation reported anxiety disorder, NOS and dysthymia. Mr J's depressed mood was characterized as slowed cognitive processing, physical symptoms, and low mood. After 6 weeks of therapeutic intervention, the psychologist noted significant problems with memory, as Mr J had difficulty recalling important information from one session to the next. Concerned about his cognitive functioning, the psychologist referred Mr J for neuropsychological evaluation.

Figure 9.2 presents WAIS-IV/WMS-IV scores for Mr J. His overall level of intellectual functioning is in the high average range. Verbal, perceptual reasoning, and auditory working memory skills are within the high average range. Processing speed, which is in the low average range, is a significant weakness compared to general intellectual functioning. Most subtest scores were in the average to high average range, with the exception of Symbol Search, which was in the low average range. Compared to age peers, Mr J shows above average intellectual abilities, in general. Of the obtained scores, only PSI and Symbol Search were at or below 1 standard deviation below the mean.

Score		Percentile	Confidence Interval (95%)
WAIS-IV Indexes			
General Ability Index	117	87	112–121
FSIQ	110	66	100–110
Verbal Comprehension Index	116	86	110–121
Perceptual Reasoning Index	113	81	106–119
Working Memory Index	117	87	109–123
Processing Speed Index	84	14	77–94
WAIS-IV Subtests			
Similarities	12		
Vocabulary	14		
Information	13		
Block Design	13		
Matrix Reasoning	13		
Visual Puzzles	11		
Digit Span	14		
Arithmetic	12		
Symbol Search	6		
Coding	8		
WMS-IV Indexes			
Auditory Memory Index	97	34	88–101
Visual Memory Index	95	25	85–96
Visual Working Memory Index	92	16	79–93
Immediate Memory Index	102	34	88–101
Delayed Memory Index	90	21	82–95
AMI vs VMI Contrast Scaled Score	9		
VWMI vs VMI Contrast Scaled Score	10		
IMI vs DMI Contrast Scaled Score	6		
WMS-IV Subtests			
BCSE Classification Level	Average		
LM I Scaled Score	10		
LM II Scaled Score	8		
LM Immediate Recall vs Delayed Recall Contrast Scaled Score	7		
LM II Recognition Percentage	51–75		
LM II Recognition vs Delayed Recall Contrast Scaled Score	7		
VPA I Scaled Score	11		
VPA II Scaled Score	9		
VPA Immediate Recall vs Delayed Recall Contrast Scaled Score	6		

FIGURE 9.2 WAIS-IV and WMS-IV scores for Mr J.

VPA II Word Recall Scaled Score	10		
VPA II Recognition Percentage	51–75		
VPA Recognition vs Delayed Recall Contrast Scaled Score	7		
DE I Scaled Score	9		
DE II Scaled Score	8		
DE I vs DE II Contrast Scaled Score	8		
DE I Content Scaled Score	9		
DE I Spatial Scaled Score	9		
DE I Spatial vs Content Contrast Scaled Score	10		
DE II Content Scaled Score	8		
DE II Spatial Scaled Score	8		
DE II Spatial vs Content Contrast Scaled Score	9		
DE II Recognition Percentage	51–75		
DE II Recognition vs Delayed Recall	7		
VR I Scaled Score	11		
VR II Scaled Score	9		
VR Immediate Recall vs Delayed Recall Contrast Scaled Score	7		
VR II Recognition Percentage	51–75		
VR Recognition vs Delayed Recall Contrast Scaled Score	8		
VR Copy Percentage	>75		
VR Copy vs Immediate Recall Contrast Scaled Score	8		
Spatial Addition Scaled Score	8		
Symbol Span Scaled Score	9		
Ability–Memory Contrast Scaled Scores			
GAI vs AMI Contrast Scaled Score	8		
GAI vs VMI Contrast Scaled Score	6		
GAI vs VWMI Contrast Scaled Score	5		
GAI vs IMI Contrast Scaled Score	8		
GAI vs DMI Contrast Scaled Score	6		
VCI vs AMI Contrast Scaled Score	8		
PRI vs VMI Contrast Scaled Score	7		
PRI vs VWMI Contrast Scaled Score	6		
WMI vs AMI Contrast Scaled Score	7		
WMI vs VWMI Contrast Scaled Score	6		

FIGURE 9.2—Cont'd

On the WMS-IV, Mr J performed in the average range on measures of auditory, visual, visual–working, immediate and delayed memory. Memory scores were consistent with each other with the exception of the Immediate versus Delayed Memory Index, which yielded a contrast score of 6 (9th percentile). This indicates that, compared to individuals with similar levels of initial encoding into memory, Mr J shows low average ability to recall that information after a long delay. Mr J performed in the average range on the BCSE, showing no specific deficits in mental status.

At the subtest level, Mr J performed in the average range on each of the core measures, indicating no specific strengths or weaknesses in memory functioning. Recognition trials were consistently in the upper end of the average range. His delayed free recall was in the low average range, compared to his ability to recognize the information, on all subtests except Visual Reproduction. Similarly, delayed recall is in the low average range when compared to his initial recall level for all the subtests except Designs. Compared to his age peers, Mr J shows average delayed memory functions; however, compared to his immediate encoding abilities and delayed recognition; his delayed memory is low average. This profile suggests that he has difficulty retrieving information from long-term memory stores after a long delay.

While Mr J shows average memory functioning compared to his age peers, compared to individuals with similar intellectual functioning his memory functions are in the borderline to average range. Specifically, auditory memory and immediate memory are in the average range compared to general ability level. Visual and delayed memory are low average compared to general ability, while visual working memory is in the borderline range. Visual and visual working memory problems are not low due to general difficulties with visual–perceptual reasoning abilities. While auditory memory is consistent with verbal abilities, it is low average considering auditory working memory skills. Visual working memory functioning is in the low average range compared to auditory working memory. Compared to his intellectual functioning, his memory skills are low average.

The profile of scores indicates that Mr J does not have obvious, severe memory problems. However, his memory functioning, particularly his retrieval problem for delayed memory, is a concern in light of his concurrent problems at work. Additionally, his processing speed is considerably lower than expected for his general intellectual functioning. The neuropsychologist made a provisional diagnosis of mild cognitive impairment, with recommendations for follow-up evaluation in 6–9 months. Mr J worked with the neuropsychologist and his treating psychologist to develop strategies to help him compensate for his memory difficulties.

Traumatic brain injury

Mr B is a 23-year-old Hispanic male with a Bachelor's degree in Business, who is employed as an assistant store manager. He reports being a good student, and graduated from college magna cum laude. He sustained a moderate head injury in a motor vehicle accident in February 2007. He obtained a Glasgow Coma Scale score of 7 on admission to the hospital. CT scans showed hemorrhagic contusions with depressed skull fracture in the right frontal area, and blood was noted in the anterior temporal tip. At 4 months post-injury, a psychological evaluation demonstrated average intelligence with above average verbal skills accompanied by low average non-verbal abilities. He reports difficulties with attention, concentration, and memory. In addition, he has difficulty organizing his daily schedule and is frequently overwhelmed with completing his more complex work activities, such as managing employee schedules and dealing with frustrated customers. Mr B is relatively healthy, and was taking no medications at the time of evaluation. He was referred by his family physician for a 1-year follow-up evaluation subsequent to complaints of continued difficulties.

Figure 9.3 presents Mr B's scores on the WAIS-IV and WMS-IV. In general, his scores fell into the average range. His verbal abilities were high average and his processing speed, visual working memory, and delayed memory were in the low average range. Processing speed was a relative weakness for Mr B compared to his overall verbal abilities. WAIS-IV subtest scores indicated generally average abilities. The processing speed subtests and Block Design were in the low average and borderline range, with the lowest scores obtained on Block Design and Coding. Of the subtest scores, only Block Design and Coding were at least 1 standard deviation below the mean.

On the WMS-IV, Mr B demonstrated average memory for orally presented material and recall for visual details and spatial information. His immediate memory was in the average range and delayed memory was in the low average range in comparison to his peers. At the subtest level, he scored in the average range on most subtests. His lowest scores were obtained on the Spatial Addition and Designs subtest, with both in the low average range. The Designs score was impacted by poorer recall for visual details than in his peers and compared to individuals with similar memory for spatial information. His delayed recall memory was unexpectedly low, given his recognition memory ability on both Logical Memory and Verbal Paired Associates. He also performed poorly on the copy task of Visual Reproduction. He did much better than expected on immediate recall, given his performance on copy. Of the memory indexes, only the Visual Working Memory Index was 1 standard deviation below the mean. The WMS-IV contrast scaled scores provide additional insight into Mr B's memory functioning.

Score		Percentile	Confidence Interval (95%)
WAIS-IV Indexes			
General Ability Index	106	66	101–111
FSIQ	101	53	97–105
Verbal Comprehension Index	114	82	108–119
Perceptual Reasoning Index	98	45	92–104
Working Memory Index	100	50	93–107
Processing Speed Index	86	18	79–96
WAIS-IV Subtests			
Similarities	11		
Vocabulary	15		
Information	12		
Block Design	7		
Matrix Reasoning	11		
Visual Puzzles	11		
Digit Span	10		
Arithmetic	10		
Symbol Search	8		
Coding	7		
WMS-IV Indexes			
Auditory Memory Index	94	34	88–101
Visual Memory Index	90	25	85–96
Visual Working Memory Index	85	16	79–93
Immediate Memory Index	94	34	88–101
Delayed Memory Index	88	21	82–95
AMI vs VMI Contrast Scaled Score	8		
VWMI vs VMI Contrast Scaled Score	10		
IMI vs DMI Contrast Scaled Score	8		
WMS-IV Subtests			
BCSE Classification Level	Average		
LM I Scaled Score	10		
LM II Scaled Score	9		
LM Immediate Recall vs Delayed Recall Contrast Scaled Score	9		
LM II Recognition Percentage	>75		
LM II Recognition vs Delayed Recall Contrast Scaled Score	7		
VPA I Scaled Score	9		
VPA II Scaled Score	8		

FIGURE 9.3 WAIS-IV and WMS-IV scores for Mr B.

VPA Immediate Recall vs Delayed Recall Contrast Scaled Score	8		
VPA II Word Recall Scaled Score	12		
VPA II Recognition Percentage	>75		
VPA Recognition vs Delayed Recall Contrast Scaled Score	6		
DE I Scaled Score	8		
DE II Scaled Score	7		
DE I vs DE II Contrast Scaled Score	7		
DE I Content Scaled Score	7		
DE I Spatial Scaled Score	9		
DE I Spatial vs Content Contrast Scaled Score	8		
DE II Content Scaled Score	6		
DE II Spatial Scaled Score	9		
DE II Spatial vs Content Contrast Scaled Score	6		
DE II Recognition Percentage	10–16		
DE II Recognition vs Delayed Recall	9		
VR I Scaled Score	10		
VR II Scaled Score	9		
VR Immediate Recall vs Delayed Recall Contrast Scaled Score	8		
VR II Recognition Percentage	10–16		
VR Recognition vs Delayed Recall Contrast Scaled Score	11		
VR Copy Percentage	0–2		
VR Copy vs Immediate Recall Contrast Scaled Score	15		
Spatial Addition Scaled Score	7		
Symbol Span Scaled Score	8		
Ability-Memory Contrast Scaled Scores			
GAI vs AMI Contrast Scaled Score	8		
GAI vs VMI Contrast Scaled Score	6		
GAI vs VWMI Contrast Scaled Score	5		
GAI vs IMI Contrast Scaled Score	7		
GAI vs DMI Contrast Scaled Score	5		
VCI vs AMI Contrast Scaled Score	7		
PRI vs VMI Contrast Scaled Score	8		
PRI vs VWMI Contrast Scaled Score	7		
WMI vs AMI Contrast Scaled Score	8		
WMI vs VWMI Contrast Scaled Score	7		

FIGURE 9.3—Cont'd

Ability–memory contrast scaled scores demonstrate that Mr B's memory skills were lower than expected given his general cognitive ability. Compared to individuals with similar General Ability index scores, Mr B's visual and immediate memory were in the low average range, while his visual working memory and delayed recall were in the borderline range. Relative to his high average verbal abilities, his verbal memory is low average. His visual working memory skills are low average compared to both his visual perceptual abilities and auditory working memory.

The profile of scores suggests weaknesses in processing speed, visual memory, visual working memory, and delayed memory. Most of Mr B's WAIS-IV scores are average, with very few below average. Compared to his age peers, he is functioning within normal limits on most measures, with the exception of processing speed, visual working memory, and delayed memory. Relative to Mr B's general cognitive ability and his above average verbal skills, these cognitive weaknesses will be more pronounced, and likely reflect a loss of functioning in these domains.

Mr B exhibited some difficulty with motor control and visuo-construction abilities which did not appear to inhibit his ability to recall designs but may have an impact in his ability to perform tasks requiring fine motor control. Additionally, his ability to rapidly identify and recall visual details appears more affected than his overall visual spatial recall; subsequently, he may experience difficulty in situations requiring the ability to quickly identify and remember visual details. While his auditory memory functions are within the average range compared to the general population, his verbal memory is below expected for his verbal intellectual abilities and ability to recognize verbal information. This reflects a subtle problem in his ability to access recently acquired verbal knowledge, which may be more noticeable to Mr B than to outside observers. He may need to use memory aids, such as writing down important information in a memory book, to help him recall this information.

Since Mr B was fairly well functioning in the past, the current evaluation likely represents a decline in his abilities. Overall, he demonstrated weaknesses in processing speed and memory. Further evaluation of his executive functioning would shed light on his organizational and emotional concerns.

Left temporal epilepsy

Ms K is a 34-year-old White female, with 12 years of education. She has a part-time job working in a clothing store. Ms K has suffered from temporal lobe epilepsy since the age of 9. She has been treated with anti-convulsants with a moderate degree of success. Until recently, she was experiencing seizures approximately once or twice a month. Within the past 6 weeks she has been experiencing daily seizures, which have significantly interfered with her ability to work. Ms K's neurologist has made several changes to her medication without any improvement in her seizure rate. Her neurologist recommended hospitalization for further diagnostic evaluation with EEG monitoring, imaging studies, and neuropsychological testing.

Figure 9.4 presents Ms K's scores on the WAIS-IV and WMS-IV. In general, her intellectual functioning was in the low average range. Among WAIS-IV indexes, Ms K shows relatively better visual–perceptual skills than verbal, auditory working memory, and processing speed skills. WAIS-IV subtest scores ranged from borderline to high average. Performance within cognitive domains was generally consistent; however, in the visual–perceptual domain Ms K displays better visuo-construction abilities compared to visual reasoning abilities. Most of her WAIS-IV indexes and subtests are well below 1 standard deviation from the mean, indicating moderate difficulties with aspects of intellectual functioning.

On the WMS-IV, Ms K performed in the borderline to average range on memory measures. Visual and visual working memory were in the average range, while immediate and delayed recall were in the low average range. Auditory memory is in the borderline range. There is significant variability among the measures contributing to each of these indexes, indicating that immediate and delayed memory functions will be inconsistent depending on the type of information to be recalled. Comparisons between memory functions do not indicate any specific area of weakness. Her BCSE score is in the average range, indicating adequate current mental status and general cognitive functioning.

On WMS-IV subtests, there is some variability in auditory memory abilities. Her lowest score is on immediate Logical Memory, which is significantly lower than her immediate Verbal Paired Associates recall score. This profile suggests that immediate memory may be enhanced through repetition of information to be recalled; however, that advantage would not result in significantly better long-term recall. Visual memory scores are in the average range, and consistent with each other across subtests. On recognition measures, Ms K performs in the low average to average range. Delayed recall scores are low average compared to recognition on verbal but not visual memory measures, indicating retrieval difficulties in the auditory memory domain.

Overall, Ms K shows borderline auditory memory skills and borderline immediate and delayed functioning compared to age-peers. The cognitive skills may be a reflection of generally low average cognitive abilities. Compared to her general ability index, she displays borderline auditory memory and low average immediate and delayed memory. Visual working memory is above average compared to her overall cognitive functioning. Her auditory memory problems are not due simply to overall weak verbal abilities or low auditory working memory, as her auditory

Score		Percentile	Confidence Interval (95%)
WAIS-IV Indexes			
General Ability Index	89	23	84–94
FSIQ	84	14	80–88
Verbal Comprehension Index	80	9	75–86
Perceptual Reasoning Index	102	55	96–108
Working Memory Index	80	9	74–88
Processing Speed Index	84	14	77–94
WAIS-IV Subtests			
Similarities	5		
Vocabulary	7		
Information	7		
Block Design	11		
Matrix Reasoning	8		
Visual Puzzles	12		
Digit Span	6		
Arithmetic	7		
Symbol Search	8		
Coding	6		
WMS-IV Indexes			
Auditory Memory Index	74	34	88–101
Visual Memory Index	93	25	85–96
Visual Working Memory Index	103	16	79–93
Immediate Memory Index	81	34	88–101
Delayed Memory Index	81	21	82–95
AMI vs VMI Contrast Scaled Score	11		
VWMI vs VMI Contrast Scaled Score	8		
IMI vs DMI Contrast Scaled Score	8		
WMS-IV Subtests			
BCSE Classification Level	Average		
LM I Scaled Score	4		
LM II Scaled Score	5		
LM Immediate Recall vs Delayed Recall Contrast Scaled Score	10		
LM II Recognition Percentage	17–25		
LM II Recognition vs Delayed Recall Contrast Scaled Score	6		
VPA I Scaled Score	7		
VPA II Scaled Score	6		
VPA Immediate Recall vs Delayed Recall Contrast Scaled Score	8		

FIGURE 9.4 WAIS-IV and WMS-IV scores for Ms K.

VPA II Word Recall Scaled Score	6		
VPA II Recognition Percentage	26–50		
VPA Recognition vs Delayed Recall Contrast Scaled Score	6		
DE I Scaled Score	9		
DE II Scaled Score	8		
DE I vs DE II Contrast Scaled Score	8		
DE I Content Scaled Score	8		
DE I Spatial Scaled Score	10		
DE I Spatial vs Content Contrast Scaled Score	11		
DE II Content Scaled Score	8		
DE II Spatial Scaled Score	9		
DE II Spatial vs Content Contrast Scaled Score	10		
DE II Recognition Percentage	26–50		
DE II Recognition vs Delayed Recall	8		
VR I Scaled Score	9		
VR II Scaled Score	10		
VR Immediate Recall vs Delayed Recall Contrast Scaled Score	11		
VR II Recognition Percentage	51–75		
VR Recognition vs Delayed Recall Contrast Scaled Score	10		
VR Copy Percentage	26–50		
VR Copy vs Immediate Recall Contrast Scaled Score	9		
Spatial Addition Scaled Score	10		
Symbol Span Scaled Score	11		
Ability–Memory Contrast Scaled Scores			
GAI vs AMI Contrast Scaled Score	5		
GAI vs VMI Contrast Scaled Score	10		
GAI vs VWMI Contrast Scaled Score	13		
GAI vs IMI Contrast Scaled Score	7		
GAI vs DMI Contrast Scaled Score	7		
VCI vs AMI Contrast Scaled Score	6		
PRI vs VMI Contrast Scaled Score	8		
PRI vs VWMI Contrast Scaled Score	10		
WMI vs AMI Contrast Scaled Score	6		
WMI vs VWMI Contrast Scaled Score	13		

FIGURE 9.4—Cont'd

memory is low average relative to her functioning in these domains. Visual memory and visual working memory are consistent with her overall strength in visual–perceptual processing.

The overall results of her evaluation showed increased abnormality in the mesial temporal cortex compared to previous EEG data. Increased regions of scarring were noted in the left temporal region. These results appear consistent with neuropsychological findings that indicate long-term verbal/auditory processing deficits in conjunction with relatively weak auditory memory functions. Ms K's seizures are occurring less frequently after multiple medication trials identified the best combination for her. She is able to work again, albeit on a much reduced schedule.

References

Baddeley, A. (2000). The episodic buffer: a new component of working memory? *Trends in Cognitive Sciences, 4*, 417–423.

Berk, R. A. (1984). *Screening and Diagnosis of Children with Learning Disabilities*. Springfield, IL: Charles C. Thomas.

Brooks, B. L., Iverson, G. L., Holdnack, J. A., & Feldman, H. H. (2008). The potential for misclassification of mild cognitive impairment: A study of memory scores on the Wechsler Memory Scale – III in healthy older adults. *Journal of the International Neuropsychological Society, 14*, 463–478.

Delis, D. C., Kramer, J. H., Kaplan, E., & Ober, B. A. (2000). *California Verbal Learning Test* (2nd ed.). San Antonio, TX: Psychological Corporation.

Kaplan, E., Fein, D., Kramer, J., Delis, D., Morris, R., & Maerlender, A. (2004). *Wechsler Intelligence Scale for Children – Fourth Edition Integrated*. San Antonio, TX: Pearson, Inc.

Matarazzo, J. D., & Prifitera, A. (1989). Subtest scatter and pre-morbid intelligence: Lessons from the WAIS-R standardization sample. *Psychological Assessment: A Journal of Consulting and Clinical Psychology, 1*, 186–191.

Shepard, L. (1980). An evaluation of the regression discrepancy method for identifying children with learning disabilities. *Journal of Special Education, 14*, 79–91.

Wechsler, D. (1945). *Wechsler Memory Scale*. San Antonio, TX: Psychological Corporation.

Wechsler, D. (1987). *Wechsler Memory Scale – Revised*. San Antonio, TX: Psychological Corporation.

Wechsler, D. (1997a). *Wechsler Memory Scale (3rd ed.)*. San Antonio, TX: Psychological Corporation.

Wechsler, D. (1997b). *Wechsler Adult Intelligence Scale (3rd ed.)*. San Antonio, TX: Psychological Corporation.

Wechsler, D. (2008). *Wechsler Adult Intelligence Scale (4th ed.)*. San Antonio, TX: Pearson, Inc.

Wechsler, D. (2009). *Wechsler Memory Scale (4th ed.)*. San Antonio, TX: Pearson, Inc.

Index

CPSIA information can be obtained
at www.ICGtesting.com
Printed in the USA
BVHW040831020919
557341BV00009B/87/P